With regards

Action and Interactive Research

Action and Interactive Research

Beyond Theory and Practice

Edited by

Lennart Svensson and Kurt Aagaard Nielsen

Printed in The Netherlands.

ISBN 10: 90-423-0289-5
ISBN 13: 978-90-423-0289-1

Shaker Publishing BV
St. Maartenslaan 26
6221 AX Maastricht
Tel.: 043-3500424
Fax: 043-3255090
http:// www.shaker.nl

Preface

This book is part of a long-term co-operation between the University of Roskilde in Denmark and the University of Linköping in Sweden in which a lot of researchers and doctoral students have been involved.

In 2004 a doctoral course was organised in Action Research with more than 20 participants from the Nordic countries. Some of the contributions in this book are based on the papers presented there.

Different organisations have supported the editorial work with this book – the University of Roskilde, the National Institute for Working Life, the University of Linköping (the Helix programme), and APeL (a R&D centre; see www.apel.nu).

We want to thank the authors for their co-operation in the editorial process. We also want to thank Andrew Crabtree (Roskilde University) for a patient cooperation bringing our texts into a proper English language, and Torbjörn Santérus for the editorial and lay-out work.

Kurt Aagaard Nielsen and *Lennart Svensson*

Contents

List of illustrations · viii
Contributors · ix

PART I

1. LENNART SVENSSON AND KURT AAGAARD NIELSEN
   Introduction and Background · 1

2. LENNART SVENSSON AND KURT AAGAARD NIELSEN
   Action Research and Interactive Research · 13

3. GUNNELA WESTLANDER
   Researcher Roles in Action Research · 45

4. KURT AAGAARD NIELSEN AND BIRGER STEEN NIELSEN
   Methodologies in Action Research · 63

5. LISE DREWES NIELSEN
   The Methods and Implication of Action Research · 89

6. EWA GUNNARSSON
   The Snake and the Apple in the Common Paradise · 117

7. THOMAS TYDÉN (ED.)
   The Organisation of Action Research in Nordic countries · 143
   – Denmark: Steen Elsborg · 145
   – Finland: Touimo Alasoini and Elise Ramstad · 158
   – Norway: Morten Levin · 170
   – Sweden: Thomas Tydèn · 179

8. OLAV EIKELAND
   Validity *of* Action Research and Validity *in* Action Research · 193

vi

PART II

9. ANN-CHRISTINE LARSSON
   Interactive Research • 241

10. MIA HUSTED AND DITTE TOFTENG
    The Common Third • 259

11. EVA AMUNDSDOTTER
    Interactive Research for Gender Equality in Workplaces • 277

12. CHRISTOPHER KJAER
    On-line Courses Supporting Local Project Work• 297

13. MARJA VEHVILÄINEN
    Situated Agency in Interactive Research • 317

14. RONNY SANNERUD
    Methods for Developing the Construction Site as a
    Learning Space• 333

15. JENS CHRISTIAN ELLE
    Other Futures are Possible • 353

16. EVA SCHWENCKE *
    Free Space in Action Research
    and in Project Oriented Traineeship • 371

17. KURT AAGAARD NIELSEN AND LENNART SVENSSON
    How to Learn Action Research • 389

INDEX • 399

Illustrations

TABLES

2.1   Mode I and Mode II:
      two different models for undertaking research • 20
12.1 A Developmental and Production Rationale
      – some characteristics • 300

FIGURES

3.1   Researcher role in Action Research • 57
5.1   Comparing Action Research Methodologies • 111
9.1   An illustration of an Interactive Research process with different
      roles and interests • 245
9.2   Some phases in the research process with the results and partici-
      pants involved. • 247
12.1 Learning Arenas for Course Participants Combining formal and
      informal learning • 311
14.1 Phases and perspectives in the project. • 336
14.3 LAV-concept • 346

Contributors

KURT AAGAARD NIELSEN is a professor in social science at Roskilde University and one of the initiators of the Danish Action Researcher Network. He has been responsible for PhD-courses in Action Research for several years. His field of research has for many years been "Sustainability and democracy in working life" and in recent years he has also published books and articles in the field of "environmental planning and citizens' participation."

TUOMO ALASOINI is Project Manager of the Finnish Workplace Development Programme at the Ministry of Labour. He also works as Docent of Sociology at the University of Helsinki. His main areas of interest are work place development, human resource management, industrial relations and innovation policy.

EVA AMUNDSDOTTER is a doctoral student in Human Work Sciences at Luleå University of Technology in Sweden. Her research project focuses on gender and change processes in work organisations, combining feminist and interactive approaches. Eva is an expert in gender studies and has been working for several years with different development-projects for gender equality.

OLAV EIKELAND is a Norwegian philosopher who has worked practically and theoretically with Action Research over the last 20 years at the Work Research Institute in Oslo. He holds a PhD in classical Greek philosophy and has as one of his special interests the relevance of ancient dialogical/dialectical philosophy for modern Action Research and social research in general.

JENS CHRISTIAN ELLE is educated at Roskilde University within the field of Geography and Educational studies. His main interests and thesis focused on the creation of Alternative Food Networks through participation of producers and consumers. The Future Creating Workshop has been an import inspiration and tool both within and outside academia. His PhD is concerning the conditions and possibilities for democratic and sustainable transformation of public sector catering.

STEEN ELSBORG is a work place sociologist and PhD student in the development of organizations and competencies at LLD (Learning Lab Denmark), DPU (The Danish University of Education). His research is focused on exploring the opportunities for working simultaneously as an external consultant supporting learning at the work place and as an Action Researcher. In this way he contributes to a research based development and creation of critical science at the same time.

EWA GUNNARSSON is a professor in work sciences at Luleå University of Technology and leader of the programme Working Lives in Urban Areas at The National Institute of Working Life. She is partner in WORKS (Work Organisation and Restructuring in the Knowledge Society, in EUs 6th framework programme). Her main research focus is on gender, technology and organisation, formation of skills and qualifications.

MIA HUSTED is an assistant professor at the Department of Environment, Technology and Social studies at Roskilde University, Denmark. Her field of research is within the area of sustainable working life, with a special interest in inclusion and exclusion of people from labour market. She has recently finished her PhD-thesis, which examined challenges for the labour market development, when including experiences from people excluded from labour market.

CHRISTOPHER KJÆR holds a Master of Arts in Psychology and Educational studies and PhD-candidate at Institute of Business Communication and Information Science, University of Southern

Denmark. Until recently his main field has been the use of web-based technology in adult education. However, with his PhD-project his main field of interest now involves global organizations where applied web-based technology in work place learning has been the main focus.

ANN-CHRISTINE LARSSON is PhD student in Sociology at the University of Linköping, Sweden. She is also an employee at the R & D centre APeL in Lindesberg, Sweden since 2002. Her research focuses on empowerment, gender relations, and change processes. Ann-Christine has a long experience in working with discriminated and marginalised groups.

MORTEN LEVIN is a Professor at the Department of Industrial Economics and Technology Management, The Faculty of Social Sciences and Technology Management at the Norwegian University of Science and Technology in Trondheim, Norway. He holds graduate degrees in engineering and in sociology. Throughout his professional life, he has worked as an Action Researcher with particular focus on processes and structures of social change in the relationships between technology and organization. He has developed and been in charge of a number of PhD programs in Action Research. He is author of a number of books and articles, including *Introduction to Action Research: Social Research for Social Change*.

BIRGER STEEN NIELSEN is an associate professor at the Department of Educational Studies, Roskilde University, Denmark. His field of research is Action Research, Critical Theory, psychoanalytical social psychology and in-dept hermeneutics. He works with the development of Future Creating Workshops in relation to Action Research.

LISE DREWES NIELSEN is a professor in social science at Roskilde University and research leader of the Transport Research Group. Her field of research has been studies of mobility patterns and behaviour. Her research has focused several projects designed as Action Research projects in fields as sustainable production and fields as distribution systems and planning, democracy and politics. She has been responsible for several courses at PhD and master level with action oriented methods.

ELISE RAMSTAD is a PhD-student in the Department of Industrial Engineering and Management at the Helsinki University of Technology. She also works as a Project Coordinator in the Finnish Workplace Development Programme at the Ministry of Labour. Her interest areas are human resource development, organizational change and innovation systems.

RONNY SANNERUD is an associate professor in Programme for Research on Education and Work at Akershus University College. He has been responsible for guidance of students and master-courses in "Vocational Education and Training" for several years. His field of research has for the last years been work-based learning/work-place learning.

EVA SCHWENCKE is PhD-student at Roskilde University and Senior Lecturer at Norwegian School of Information Technology (NITH) in Oslo. Her field of interest is project organized learning and generally social implications of technology. She has made several experiments on project-organised learning and works with development of pedagogical culture.

LENNART SVENSSON is a professor in sociology at the University of Linköping and a co-leader of the Helix programme there. He is also a research leader at the National Institute of Working Life and APeL, an R & D centre for work place learning (www.apel.nu). His research focuses on organisational change, adult learning, project work, union work and health.

DITTE TOFTENG is an assistant professor at the department of Environment, Technology and Social studies at Roskilde University, Denmark. Her field of research is within the area of sustainable working life. She has carried out Action Research since 1998. She has recently defended her PhD-thesis within the field of marginalisation studies and working life. Ditte Tofteng has been working with democratic innovations in working life, with a special interest in the field of "creativity".

THOMAS TYDÉN is professor in pedagogic at Örebro University and also director of Dalarna Research Institute. His main research areas are science and practice interplay and knowledge creation and dissemination.

MARJA VEHVILÄINEN is an assistant professor in women's studies at the University of Tampere and a docent in gender and information technology at the University of Jyväskylä, Finland. Her research topics include: gendered agency in technically mediated society; cultural interpretations of technology; gender, expertise and technology; gendering of global ICT production.

GUNNELA WESTLANDER is Professor emeritus since 1995 and holds from 1995 and on expert appointments at the University of Linköping, and at The Royal Institute of Technology, Stockholm. She has held faculty positions at Stockholm University since 1974 and was 1986–1995 Director and Professor of the National Institute of Occupational Health, Division of Social and Organizational Psychology. Research areas: quality of work life, technological change; organizational change and development; human aspects of intervention strategies.

PART I

LENNART SVENSSON

AND KURT AAGAARD NIELSEN

1. Introduction and Background

1.1 A renewed interest in Action Research

For many years, intellectuals have dominated Action Research with a critical attitude towards the traditional academic curricula. In the Nordic countries, researchers involved in research institutions outside the sphere of universities initiated some of the most famous Action Research projects.

The large number of books on Action Research which have been published since the early nineties contain only a small number of volumes that are relevant for the systematic academic training of students at universities and business schools. Hilary Bradbury and Peter Reason's *Handbook of Action Research* (2000) and Morten Levin's *Introduction to Action Research* (1998) are two of the few examples of texts which successfully present Action Research in an overall perspective, however, neither of these books are written for students who need a pluralistic introduction to different traditions that they are not familiar with. Nor are these books written as a presentation of Action Research as part of competence development in which Action Research co-exists on equal terms with other forms of research. This book tries to make up for these gaps.

International discussion concerning the theory of science and theory of knowledge comes close to the position of Action Research. The so-called "New production of Knowledge", introduced by Gibbons and Nowotny (in 1994), has opened up the possibility for discussing new types of connections between research and contextual problem solving. In Sweden, Göran Brulin's book *Den tredje uppgiften*[1] made a strong argument for putting Action Research on the universities' agenda. In the book *Interaktiv forskning: för utveckling av teori och praktik* (2002) Svensson, Brulin, Ellström and Widegren tried to stress the importance of making Action Research a co-operative part of the academic world by introducing the concept of *Interactive Research*. The shift from Action Research to Interactive Research signals that Action Research is not just to be considered an alternative to empirical, analytical (social) science, but that it should be understood as a complementary research activity.

This book represents a new discussion in the tradition of Action Research – a discussion we do not want to close in this book. But we insist that contemporary Action Research or Interactive Research is an organic part of academic community, and that it should no longer be seen as a sect or an exclusive belief system among some isolated researchers.

This book is about Action Research. It is written with the same readers in mind as many other recent books in the field. Nevertheless, we try to be systematic in a way that makes the book especially useful for *students who want to learn about Action Research*. We think that one cannot be a good Action Researcher unless one gets involved in practical training. Today, many students do not have the possibility to undertake Action Research because they do not know enough about the conditions under which it can be undertaken and the tools they need to undertake it: they do not know enough about epistemology, the methods used, the working conditions, time pressures, ethical considerations, career prospects, the prestige attributed to this research in the academic community, and so forth.

1.2   A pluralistic approach

In this book we present a pluralistic approach to action or Interactive Research. It is pluralistic in the following two ways:

---

1   Brulin wrote an article presenting the same analysis in English (Brulin 1998)

a) It is pluralistic in that we will not present one single school of Action Research. Instead, we will present different branches of Action Research based on a dialogue among the authors of the various Chapters;

b) It is also pluralistic in that we will present confrontations between academic research and Action Research – both in the theoretical and methodological senses. We will also present examples of co-operation between Action Research and other research traditions. We think that the students in the academic world will benefit from some of the epistemological discussions which Action Research has catalysed during its 50 years of existence. At the same time, Action Researchers can learn a lot from the progress made in theoretical and methodological matters by the academic community.

However, our pluralism has some restrictions. We will neither avoid epistemological conflicts, nor transform the divergent traditions of science into "anything goes" or "everything is of equal value". On the contrary! We believe that the tension between different forms of Action Research and different conceptions of academic research is important. Because of the conflicting perspectives, a dialogue between them about theories of science, different methods, and about practical, social and political issues could be fruitful. With a dialogue, which is based on these divergent perspectives, we can clarify the normative impact of different research traditions. We can also see when the different epistemological approaches can become complementary, and when they should compete with each other.

1.3 What do we mean by Action Research and Interactive Research?

Academic research is defined here as research in which the researcher understands himself to be in a privileged position together with other scientists in the construction of their theories and methods. They might be positivists, hermeneutic phenomenologists or even constructivist relativists. But, unlike Action Researchers, they understand themselves as having an important role in the development of knowledge, which is seen as of quite a different kind compared to the ordinary, practical oriented everyday experience. Action Researchers see themselves as co-producers in the creation of new knowledge, but they do not see themselves as being in a privileged position in this joint learning process. On the contrary, Action Researchers can only create knowledge in co-operation with social actors based on trust and a free agreement to participate. But at the same time, the researchers must possess and be respected for her/his professional competence in handling data, in constructing theories, in organising a learning process, in relating the results to existing research, in ethical matters, and so on.

The rapid development of Action Research has contributed to creating a dialogical atmosphere between researchers and practitioners in different fields of research. Still, most of the academic researchers have not left "their ivory tower". For many academic colleagues, the ivory tower represents a kind of retreat – for criticism, reflection, theoretical development, systematic thinking, open dialogue with colleagues etc. Two hundred years ago Humboldt argued for the necessity of an independent academic community. We think his argument is needed once again in order to protect science from a submission to the interests of the business or other powerful groups in society. Today, we face a situation where Action Research could be linked to critical thinking in the universities – a co-operation that would benefit both.[2] In order to stress this "bridging" role of Action Research, a group of researchers in Sweden has introduced the concept of *Interactive Research* (see Chapter 2). Interactive Research is based on joint learning between the participants and the researcher during the whole research process. The participants in a study have an important role in the analytic work. The ambition is to carry out research together with – not *on* – the participants (Svensson et al. 2002).

Both of us want to underline the necessity of an academic independence for action and Interactive Research, something, which is becoming more urgent because of the strong economic interests related to "the new production of knowledge."

---

2 Compare J. From Lauridsen and Kurt Aagaard Nielsen (2002): "Regional Universities". In Svensson et al. *Interaktiv forskning: för utveckling av teori och praktik.* (Work life in Transition No. 7). (The article is written in English).

Not all contributions to this book will follow the above-mentioned approach; nor will they agree to our perspective on Action Research. We have tried to choose authors expressing a diversity of understandings of Action Research.

In Sweden and Denmark, attempts have been made to create networks for such a pluralistic discussion of action and Interactive Research. We see these networks as an expression of a pluralistic spirit and an interest in learning more about Action Research and its potential for the future. These networks will be a way to create connections to a lot of people who are interested in Action Research, but who, as a minority group in the scientific community, are scattered without knowledge of each other (see www.aktionsforskning.net and www.arbetslivsinstitutet.se).

1.4   The content of the book

We will make a short presentation of the chapters in the book.

Chapter 2 (written by the editors) provides the background to and a framework for the following Chapters. The discussion of Mode I and Mode II (Gibbons et al. 1994) is used for an interpretation of the development of the Action Research tradition in the Nordic countries. The following tendencies in the Nordic context are concentrated on:

1.   The move from an experimental to a learning design;
2.   The move from a consensus, to a conflict and back to a consensus perspective;
3.   The move from employer and employee based values to broader values;
4.   The move from a grand theory to a pragmatic approach;
5.   The move from a single method to broad variations in the use of methods.

The *second* part of the book, which includes seven chapters, discusses important issues that are implicit in Action Research, namely the theory of knowledge, different methods, values and norms, the role of the researcher, problems of gender and power structure, the organisation of the R & D work and its relationship to the universities, questions of validity and the possibilities of generalising results. This part of the book offers a plurality of conceptions that sometimes contrast with the Action Research perspective that we presented in Chapter one.

Chapter 3 (written by *Gunnela Westlander*) is a presentation of different researcher roles in the history of Action Research. In the original Action Research experimental tradition, designed by Kurt Lewin, the researcher had a strong and organising role. The participants run the risk of being objectified in the change process. In the later versions of Action Research, the need for collaborations with the participants on more equal terms was stressed. New qualifications were needed in terms of communication, feedback, trustworthiness, integrity, and flexibility. The help-seeking client is replaced and a new relationship sought. This is based on a partnership in which co-operation, co-learning and reflection are essential elements.

Chapter 4 (written by *Kurt Aagaard Nielsen* and *Birger Steen Nielsen*) is a philosophical discussion of Action Research methodologies. The authors present controversies about Action Research in the light of ontological and epistemological assumptions. Special attention is given to the role of hermeneutics and Critical Theory in relation to Action Research. The authors argue that Action Research can become a kind of solution to the problem of academic isolation in the tradition of Critical Theory. They also argue that you can practice Action Research and be consistent with and loyal to the concept of societal critique in Critical Theory. To do so you need to develop and strengthen a utopian dimension in Action Research practice.

In Chapter 5, *Lise Drewes Nielsen* presents three methods, which are widely used in Action Research: The Search Conference (mainly used in Norway), the Dialogue Conference (in Sweden and Norway), and the Future Creating and Scenario Workshop (mainly in Denmark). These methods were all reactions to the failure of the traditional, controlled, exclusionary, hierarchical, and expert driven methodologies in including participants in Action Research. Instead, face-to-face interaction, participation, collaboration, networking and joint learning about goals and visions are foregrounded in these four methods. In the Dialogue Conferences, the focus of the research is changed from changes of organisations, which are oriented towards critical action to market driven business innovation in networks and regions. Action Research increasingly became a practical tool used in large programmes and the researcher's main role was to facilitate these changes. The Search Conference and the Future Workshops have a clear theoretical foundation in Critical Theory with a focus on emancipation.

Ewa Gunnarsson (in Chapter 6) discusses how feminist research can be used as a critical potential for qualifying contemporary Action Research and vice versa. She points to similarities in both traditions, but also to a lack of co-operation and learning between these traditions. One part of the discussion is about finding a common epistemological and methodological ground. Gunnarsson's ambition is to increase the validity – the scientific *robustness* – of both traditions. The exchange of experience would include a better grounding and contextualisation, a more democratic and equal relationship between the researcher and the participants, and an interactive reflexive research process, which includes a consciousness of gender.

Chapter 7 is a summary in four sections, which analyses the development of Action Research in the four Nordic countries. *Thomas Tydén* introduces and summarises these sections. He points to a growing interest in Action Research but that this interest is somewhat unclear as Action Research goes under different names. The most important mechanism behind the renewed interest is the usefulness of Action Research – both for companies and the public sector. To summarise, Mode II is growing in popularity. New forms of organisations are being developed, mainly outside of the universities.

In Chapter 8 *Olav Eikeland* discusses the validity *of* Action Research and the validity *in* Action Research. It is a more extensive chapter and has a more theoretical character. We think it is important to introduce a deeper discussion about methodology and epistemology. An Action Researcher should be able to defend her-/himself against the traditional claims made by the academic community. Eikeland stresses that mainstream validity challenges cannot be ignored by Action Research, but could be used to mainstream Action Research itself. But Action Research can also, when developed and justified properly, make an important contribution to solving some inherent contradictions, impasses, and validity-problems bothering mainstream social research. The approaches towards the participants are all in the "othering-business" of studying what *they* – the others – do, based on a distinct separation between the researcher and the researched. Action Research should instead be characterised by another relationship that is making research together with – not *on* – the participants. Eikeland presents different varieties of Action Research with various validity problems. The most important rule for securing validity is making the research process visible, exposed and understood, bringing it into a dialogue with the participants and for inspections of other researchers. The missionary task for Action Research is to enable people to – without danger – observe, tell, understand, and change what is actually done by power, neighbours, colleagues, themselves, or anyone – that is the details of actual practices and events. In this, a critical-counter public sphere is created with possibilities to learn individually and collectively.

The *third* part of the book presents some examples of methods used in Action Research. There is a special focus on the learning and socialisation of the doctoral students. How do they learn to be competent Action Researchers today, and what changes will be needed in the future? Most of the contributions to this part in the book come from conference papers and those presented on a doctoral course in Sweden and Denmark.

Ann-Christine Larsson (in Chapter 9) presents an Interactive Research method. She is working on a EU project with a group of women on long-term sick leave. Her theoretical focus is on empowerment processes in relation to structural changes in the involved authorities. The ambition is to make research together with, not *on*, the participants. She has tried to include the participants in the whole research process – from the definition of the research problem to the dissemination of the results. Larsson illustrates the usefulness of involving the participants in the analytical work in terms of new perspectives and a deeper understanding. The conditions for Interactive Research are discussed. A team, which includes both project leaders and researchers, is seen as being an important factor for success. With a division of developmental and research tasks between the team members there will be enough time for the theoretical work. The outsider role of the researcher is acknowledged, but, from time to time, the insider perspective can be used in a careful way based on an agreement with the participants.

Ditte Tofteng and *Mia Husted* (in Chapter 10) present an Action Research process in cooperation with socially marginalised people in

Denmark. The research process was initiated as an open space in which researchers and a small group of people, who defined themselves as marginalised or excluded from the normal labour market, worked together to write and publish a leaflet about "being on the edge of labour market". The cooperation also became an Action Research project as the group – including the two researchers – decided to begin a long term and systematic production of knowledge and practical solutions to overcome the degradation of people living marginalised lives. The two researchers reflect, in dialogue with the other participants, on the quality of social relations in the Action Research process. They argue that a researcher in the particular context of working with socially marginalised people has to be especially aware of the so called "common third" – for example the task of writing a leaflet – in order to overcome therapeutic biased dialogues. During the Action Research process they realised how important it is to stress the common third in order to improve respectful cooperation and expose the experience of the participants.

In Chapter 11 *Eva Amundsdotter* presents an Interactive Research approach to gender equality at work. The research project is presented with a short outline of the main methods and activities that have been used. The chapter is structured around three themes. The first theme concerns the way in which gender is constituted at the individual, group and organisational levels. The second theme concerns resistance and the discovery of gender specific experiences involved in taking a visible role in an organisation. The third theme concerns the acquisition of new knowledge about change processes in work organisations on the basis of action or lack of actions. In the concluding section, the author illustrates how the interactive method has been used both too promote development and the research process.

In Chapter 12 *Christopher Kjaer* presents his experience with a *Cogenerative Action Research* method in a global organisation. This is a difficult task because you have to adapt your method to the situation in the company – especially the balance between the *production* and *developmental rationale*. As a researcher, you have to be able to perform different research roles in different phases of the research process. Kjaer's ambition with the research is to contribute to the development of a democratic theory for work-based blended learning based on the pedagogical principles of project work. Central for such an approach to workplace learning is the integration of formal and informal learning supported by web-based technology. A virtual learning environment – made by combining synchronous on-line courses with local project – work seems to support the participants learning.

Marja Vehviläinen (Chapter 13) reflects on empirical research on agency and citizenship in a highly technically mediated society and its remote region, namely Finland and the North Karelia region. The research focused on the agency and expertise of people, the citizens, on the wrong sides of the Digital Divides in relation to gender and region. The research project made an alliance with the regional developers who emphasized the local, situated and communal activity of inhabitants in the eighties and aimed to support people's everyday expertise – as an alternative to heroic technical expertise of well educated male engineers of big cities. Vehviläinen used an interactive approach, but despite the favourable conditions conflicts appeared between the developers and the researcher. But the research was able continue as a parallel process with the development work. Some proposals are put forward by the author based on the experiences of the difficulties with Interactive Research: to make the research process transparent; the usefulness of being two researchers; the necessity for "an outsider" to co-operate with local researchers; the importance of defending the autonomy of the research; to be aware that Interactive Research is time-consuming; the dilemmas and difficulties for a doctoral student to carry out Interactive Research.

Jens Christian Elle (in Chapter 14) presents an Action Research process related to the catering sector in Copenhagen. The research process was based on a widespread desire to involve different group of professionals working in nursing homes in the development of ideas about how to implement and firmly anchor the continuing process of converting public sector catering to the use of organic foods. The Future Creating Workshops was chosen as a method in order to organise a change process "from below". Elle describes the severe problems with this approach to create utopian ideas because of the restricted horizons among the employees. A new "we" was created, which included a diverse group of professionals organised as a *discourse coalition*. In an idea laboratory, a cross-disciplinary understanding of *a good smelling nursing* home could be developed. It is a development from a *life world* perspective in order to overcome the functionally differentiated and neo-liberal rationality, which creates fear and anxiety among employees, professionals and administrators.

In Chapter 15 *Ronny Sannerud* presents an Action Research project taking place on a construction site in Norway. The research project was organised as a form of organisational learning defined as a transformation of the site to a systematic learning place. In the initial phase, the project was organised in an instrumentalist fashion. The ambition was to implement a learning arena based on practical learning. During the project process, the researcher became aware of the necessity of making values or orientations more explicit in relation to the methodology. He turned to the methodology used in a Future Creating Workshop. The ambition was to guarantee that the workers' experiences from both work practice and their personal lives were used in the development process. The normative orientations in the projects methodology can be characterised by words like democracy, dialogue, equity and freedom in learning. Bringing such normative methodologies into the learning organisation leaves you with interesting problematic questions in relation a further development of the theory of practice learning. It introduces a new focus on the meaning of individual life story in learning organisation.

In Chapter 16 *Eva Schwenke* discusses the concept of *free space* in Action Research and its contribution to project pedagogy as an element in creating professional competence. Personal experiences gained from an Action Research project developing project culture for third year students at a school of information technology in Norway, are presented. The main conclusion of the experiment is that the students were encouraged to gain new perspectives on their real life projects. They questioned the traditional student role and wanted to have more control over the initial phase of establishing the project. They challenged the IT school's project culture obtain extended free space in project learning, and for the students to benefit from the existing opportunities of free space. The other main conclusion involved questioning the tutor's role as a representative of the institution. The challenge was to depart from the role of tutoring based on the position of institutional power, and in enabling the students to benefit from the possibilities of free space in their projects. The experiment also revealed many similarities between critical Action Research and the project pedagogy, and the

11

project pedagogy benefiting from the utopian-based free space.

The final part (Chapter 17) is a summary of the book. Some conclusions are drawn based on the analysis made. There is also a discussion of how Action Research can be developed in the future.

The subtitle of the book *(Beyond practice and theory)* has a specific meaning, which is more or less reflected by all authors. The ambition, or rather the vision, of the book is to transcend a deep-rooted division in academic research between theory and practice. Instead, we promote a holistic paradigm, which is contrary to all dualistic thinking. In a holistic paradigm, practice and theory are seen as aspects of a totality or two sides of the same coin. Practical and theoretical knowledge are seen as complementary in a joint learning process between participants and researchers. This joint learning and critical knowledge production is the essence of action and interactive research. Learning will be promoted when it is part of a change process. According to Kurt Lewin: The best way to understand a thing is to change it!

References

Aagaard Nielsen, K. and From Lauridsen, J. (2002) "Regional Universities" in *Interaktiv forskning: för utveckling av teori och praktik,* Svensson, L. et al. (eds.) (Work Life in Transition No. 7). Stockholm: Arbetslivsinstitutet.

Bradbury, H. and Reason, P. (2001) (eds.) *Handbook of Action Research.* London: Sage.

Brulin, G. (1998) *Den tredje uppgiften: Högskola och samhälle i samverkan.* Stockholm: SNS.

– (1998b): "The new task of Swedish universities: Knowledge formation in interactive cooperation with practitioners" in *Concepts and Transformation,* 3 (1–2).

Gibbons, M. et al. (1994) *The New Production of Knowledge.* London: Sage.

Levin, M. (1998): *Introduction to Action Research.* London: Sage.

Svensson, L. et al. (2002): *Interaktiv forskning: för utveckling av teori och praktik.* (Work Life in Transition No. 7.) Stockholm: Arbetslivsinstitutet.

LENNART SVENSSON AND
KURT AAGAARD NIELSEN

2. A Framework for the Book

2.1 Introduction, background and objective

Action Research has a long tradition in the Nordic countries. It was introduced in the beginning of the sixties in Norway and has become established as part of the growing R&D work in all the Nordic countries, both inside and outside the universities.

In this book, we want to describe this development, discuss some important issues, and give some examples of the different methods used. It is an anthology, and in order to provide an overview over a divided field, we have tried to give priority to comprehensiveness and the interrelationship between the different chapters. Our focus is on Action Research/Interactive Research in working life in a broad sense, this includes professional institutions, local and regional development and NGO activities.

The first question, which arises, concerns what we mean by Action Research and Interactive Research. Action Research is not seen as a collection of principles, with distinct theories and methods, but more as a perspective on how to conduct research. However, there must, of course, be an *action* component, that is, the research should support a normative *change* in one way or another (in problem solving, developmental work, restructuring etc.) while, at the same time, producing new knowledge. The Danish network for Action Research's home page provides the following introduction:

"Action Research is understood as a scientific method for making research. It underlines the connection between understanding and change, between theory and practice, and an active co-operation between researchers and the participants in the production of new knowledge." (www.aktionsforskning.net).

Interactive Research stresses the *joint learning* that goes on between the participants and the researchers throughout the entire research process – from the definition of the problems to the analysis and the dissemination of the results (Svensson et al. 2002). An association for Interactive Research (SIRA; the Swedish Association for Interactive Research) has been organised (see www.arbetslivsinstitutet.se) to support interactive, developmental-oriented, critical and multi-disciplinary research, focusing on the processes of change in working life. The organisation of the research should be characterised by relationships among equals and a high degree of participation. The knowledge produced should be of practical relevance and of a high scientific standard.

The normative orientation of Interactive/Action Research activities is a very open and much discussed issue. In some parts of the tradition, the normative element concerns equality, in others, for example the original experiments done by Kurt Lewin, they include a question of giving people more competence and responsibility. In research, which closely involves business management development of participation as such is the main normative orientation. Democratic processes are, however, a utopian aim for many Action Researchers.

We will use the terms Action and Interaction Research in this book without defining them further or clarifying the resemblance with other similar concepts.

This textbook is mainly directed at university students, but it could also be used by senior researchers and by those actively involved in Action Research. It could be used both in teaching at universities and among the practitioners who are interested in preparing for or taking part in Action Research. We want to offer graduate and doctoral students an insight into Action Research and help them choose with their eyes wide open whether they would like to engage in this research tradition or not. We have asked postgraduate students what they want to know about in order to be able to make a decision about their future.

They have stressed the following issues:

- whether this field of research will be growing or diminishing in the near future;
- what kind of prestige it will have amongst (social) scientists;
- what career opportunities there will be in the short and long term perspectives;
- how Action Research is organised, and where it will be carried out (e.g. at the universities, in companies or in different types of R&D centres);
- what the foundations for Action Research are in terms of the theory of knowledge and the theory of science;
- what kind of methods are used, and if these methods are accepted by the scientific community;
- if the ambition to carry out R&D work will be an extra burden for the researcher and the consequences for her/his academic career;
- to what extent Action Research has, so far, been productive and of a high quality (when measured by traditional academic standards);
- what kind of professional competencies will be needed to carry out Action Research, and how this competence can be acquired.
- whether Action Research can be relevant for activities in social movements.

We think that Action Research can be a way to improve the conditions for doctoral students by making the training more relevant, challenging, interesting and useful for their future. Students can take part in research that combines practical usefulness with theoretical insight – closeness with detachment (Hansson 2003). Their position in the labour market will be stronger and new options will be available when they have to compete on the labour market.

The existing situation for doctoral students, where they are isolated from the surrounding society, was strongly criticised in a recent survey, which was distributed to all doctoral students in Sweden (in total 200). Not a single one (!) of the 200 students who took part in the survey had any kind practical experience or meetings with companies, organisations or authorities during their university education (*Högskolevärlden*, No. 3–4, 2003).

An evaluation of an action-oriented research programme was made at the same time. The doctoral students in this programme were much more positive, especially concerning their contact with working life. About 85 percent were very or rather satisfied with the programme. Their personal development and learning more about carrying out research was most appreciated. The combination of theory with practice was also highly valued (KK-report 2003:64).

However, of course, Action Research has its own problems and the working conditions for the students could be much better. One problem is the extremely low productivity in academic terms – in terms of scientific articles. This was the main criticism of Action Research in an evaluation of (parts of) Norwegian Action Research carried out by Aage Bøttger Sørensen (1992). He made an effort to de-legitimise Action Research as such by using the argument that the researchers were almost outside the academic world defined in terms of international refereed journals. As pointed out by Olau Eikeland (1992), Sørensens arguments were formalistic and did not reflect the epistemological nature of Action Research. The problems pointed out by Sørensen can be explained as an effect of the time pressure that is a result of the double burden of producing change and theoretical knowledge at the same time. Action Research is a complex and time-consuming activity. The low productivity can also be an effect of negative attitudes against Action Research among editors of scientific journals. Even though things have changed much since Aage Bøttger Sørensen made his hostile attack on Action Research, the impression remains that Action Researchers have difficulties in measuring their productivity by conventional academic standards.

Other weaknesses, or may be they are part of the productivity "problem", are a lack of theoretical integration and an unawareness of the relevant research in the field (Gustavsen 1996:9). Action Researchers in different research programmes often have been dispersed through different universities without sufficient support and training in their research roles.

2.2 Some important issues

This book can be seen as a learning process in which the participants obtain a deeper understanding of complex research issues. The questions presented above, together with the authors' own interests, can be summarised in the following dilemmas and reflections concerning Action Research (compare Svensson et al. 2002):

1) How can theory and practice be integrated in Action Research? What do these concepts mean? What is the relationship between them? Will a focus on the practical usefulness of Action Research lead to a neglect of theoretical knowledge?

2) Should the production of generalised knowledge be an ambition of Action Research? How useful is the knowledge that is produced for local users? If the participants have a strong impact on the organisation of the research process, will that not jeopardise the striving for general knowledge? Or can the impact become a challenge to general theoretical constructions and conceptualizations of societal development.

3) Can Action Research, with its interactive and ambition and trustful relationships, be critical? Can the researcher take a critical stand against something she/he has been part of, and has sometimes, been paid for doing? Will a conflict paradigm, therefore, be ruled out in Action Research?

4) How should Action Research be organised, and where should it be carried out? Will the demand based Mode II research take over and dominate university based Mode I? (See Gibbons et al. 1994; Nowotny et al. 2001.) What consequences will the development of different R&D centres have for the organisation of Action Research? Will they be an alternative or a complement to university based research?

In this book we want to illustrate what Action Research *could* be like, not what it should be. The main ambition is to present a pluralistic approach and show the variations in this growing field of research. The idea is not to promote a best way of carrying out Action Research, but instead to reflect on and analyse the different approaches used.

Another ambition is to draw attention to at least two important questions of power in Action Research: the gender perspective and the question of financial domination.

Gender differences can be seen as power relationships in the research organisation, in the selection and conceptualization of research problems and the methods used, whether the career opportunities and working conditions will be the same for women and men, etc. Traditional academic research has been criticised for excluding alternative views and perspectives by making false generalisations, mystifying concepts and circular reasoning. The male dominated and hierarchical way of producing "objective" knowledge is seen as a closed system, which excludes different social groups (Minnich 1990). What can be said about Action Research from this exclusion perspective? Does it include new groups in the production of knowledge? Is Action Research more egalitarian and democratic in this sense, compared to traditional academic research?

The financial domination of research is even more even precarious in Action Research. When one is undertaking research in direct co-operation with actors, one easily reproduces the financial power structure in the research design and in generating interesting research questions. How can Action Researchers find ways to insist on projects and project designs, which are different from the partners investing money, time and economic risks in projects? Can Action Researchers benefit from protection in the traditional ideals of free research in universities, or is the solution that Action Researchers have to find financial resources from, for example, NGO:s (Non Governmental Organisations) to modify the economic power structure in the field of research?

We hope that this book will be useful in reflecting these dilemmas, and that it will help Action Researchers in their future work. Even if we do not give any definitive answers to these issues, we will hopefully get a deeper understanding of the dilemmas presented.

2.3   A new production of knowledge?

In this section we will introduce discussion about "the New Production of New Knowledge" (Nowotny and Gibbons 1994) and we relate the ideas of Mode II to Action Research and Interactive Research. We see that discussion as a framework for understanding the development of Action Research in the Nordic countries. We use the distinction between Mode I and II in trying to understand the development of Action Research in the Nordic countries?

A "new production of knowledge" is developing quickly in the Nordic countries and elsewhere, quite in line with the prediction made by Gibbons and Nowotny. This interest is demand based and comes from companies, governments, municipalities, regions, organisations, consultants, and journalists in the highly industrialised countries. What does "the new production of knowledge" mean, where and how is it organised? The growing interest in research is not primarily directed to universities. Something new is being requested – a problem based approach, a multi-disciplinary perspective with interactive methods, which give the participants the possibility to influence the research process. The orientation towards problem-based research is not a totally new thing. In the university reforms which took place in the sixties and seventies, the same pragmatic arguments were used – recommended by OECD – as the reasoning behind the university reforms. In Denmark, two new universities, Aalborg and Roskilde, and in Norway the University of Tromsøe more or less followed these ideas and took important steps towards introducing a problem-oriented organisation of research and didactics. The new reform universities played a role in spreading Action Research among academics in the Nordic countries. However, anxious academics and politicians who saw an uncontrolled radicalization when Action Research was connected to the student movement disturbed the initial reforms and for a while the process towards problem-oriented and participatory research methods stopped at universities. They continued, however, in R&D institutions in Norway and Sweden.

Gibbons et al. (1994) and Nowotny et al. (2001) talked about an expansion of a Mode II way of carrying out research (see Table 1). We will briefly compare some elements of Mode II, with more traditional academic research – Mode I.

Table 2.1. *Mode I and Mode II: two different models for undertaking research* (see Gibbons et al. 1994; Nowotny et al 2001; compare Svensson et al. 2002:5).

DIFFERENT RESEARCH MODELS	MODE I	MODE II
Steering mechanism	The academic discipline	Problem based, multi disciplinary
Authorisation	Professional rules	Scientific and societal rules
Objectives	New theories	Usefulness
Type of knowledge	General	Specific
Time perspective	Long term	Short term
Responsibility	The scientific community	A societal responsibility
Actors	Researchers	Participants and researchers
Relationships	Hierarchical	Equal
Work forms	Planned, predetermined	Flexible, interactive
Approach	Closed	Open
Physical proximity	Distant	Close
Actors	Universities	R&D centres, institutes, companies, regional universities
Relations	Object relations	Subject relations
Strategy	First discovery, then Application	Simultaneous discovery and application

2. *A Framework for the Book*

Mode II research focuses primarily on being useful for the participants. It is organised in an interactive way with equal, close, informal and open relations between the participants and the researchers. The work forms are flexible, dynamic and effective, and are often supported by the new information and computer technologies (ICT). The research is multi-disciplinary, focusing on contextual understanding, and using Interactive Research methods. The validation of the research results is broader, encompassing different actors. In this way, the quality control of the research process will be broader and more varied compared to a traditional academic research. A more *"robust* knowledge" is created. The traditional sequential distinction between discovery, application and evaluation will not function in a rapidly changing society. Because of the intensity of processes of change, Mode II is based on a simultaneous process of learning and change.

In Table 1, we have also illustrated the traditional way of organising research – Mode I. This research is often referred to as "High Science" and focuses on universal theories, which are stated in terms of abstract concepts (Toulmin 1996:19). This research is based on the scientific discipline with professional rules concerning how to undertake research. The relationships are hierarchical – both inside and outside the system. Academic research is to a large extent "closed" for people from "the outside". The researchers themselves decide about the content of the research and the methods used. The quality of the research produced is solely based on peer-evaluations. The objective is to search for general knowledge in a long-term perspective, which will add to the existing stock of knowledge.

What are the driving forces behind the expansion of Mode II? Nowotny et al. (2001) point to fundamental societal changes increasing the importance of knowledge in the economy. Research is an important productive force in the new knowledge based or in Castells' (1996) terms – network society.

The growing interest for Mode II is thus an effect of a new perspective on change and innovation. The transformation of the society is speeding up, and the changes are becoming more difficult to foresee because of an increasing complexity. A linear and mechanistic model of changes is being replaced by a learning and interactive strategy (Svensson and von Otter 2001). In such an unforeseeable process, research can be useful for handling insecurity and in assessing the risks of investments, but also helpful in organising for change and innovation.

The pressure for the new production of knowledge comes from external actors – companies, municipalities, counties, different intermediaries etc. The need for expertise and professional knowledge is growing in an increasing number of new fields – such as marketing, innovation, learning, technical development, work-organisation, etc. However, such knowledge cannot be "bought from a shelf". Instead, the users themselves must be co-producers if the new knowledge is to be useful in their situation. Enterprises state that they have to be pro active – to be "one step ahead" – in understanding market demands and in finding new possibilities for innovation. The situation is similar for municipalities, counties, the state and other organisations and institutions. What is really meant by the necessity of being pro active or in constant change is of course not easy to understand. Why does the market express itself in that language? At least you can criticise the new need of increasing dynamism for being fetishism or a reified global matter, which does not necessarily correspond with human needs (Olsén, Nielsen and Nielsen 2003). Nevertheless, the new demands work as an unavoidable imperative.

This new learning strategy required for dynamic change and innovation will have fundamental consequences for the way research is organised. It can no longer be planned by the research community, but must be improvised and made more interactive. The research organisation has to be decentralised and based on a high degree of participation, networking, innovation, and an open dialogue.

A new kind of knowledge production is needed – a Mode II. The investments in the universities have not paid off in terms of innovation, growth and entrepreneurship (Brulin 2002). Instead, new alliances have to be organised, these include researchers, the public sector and the companies – that is *a Triple Helix* for innovation and growth (Etzkowitz and Leydesdorff 1997). The new production of knowledge often takes place outside the formal university system.

Thus, external actors request a new kind of co-operation with researchers. With the rising level of education and with new investors in R&D, the "practitioners" will no longer accept being objectified in the research process. Instead, they prefer co-operation, which is based on equality, flexibility, closeness and joint learning. Because of dissatisfaction with the inflexible and hierarchical universities, the interest for development research is to a large extent canalised outside the universities (Gibbons et al 1994; Nowotny et al. 2001; Tydén 1997).

Can we find a similar development in the Nordic countries, an expansion of Mode II research inside or outside the universities? Some universities, the reform universities which were built during the sixties and seventies, the technical universities and the business schools, have over a long period of time developed a more problem oriented, interactive and intensive co-operation with different organisations and companies. In Sweden, there are 34 research parks, all but one is situated close to a university (Brulin 2002). However, in general, the universities have not prioritised this kind of research, but rather devalued attempts that have been made in this direction (Brulin 1998, 2002; Sörlin et al. 2001).[1] The belief in the universities as producers of useful knowledge has also been put into question. Researchers have traditionally been good at describing and analysing different problems, but have been less successful at offering solutions to concrete problems (von Otter 2001:198).

Some attempts have been made in the Nordic countries to make the universities more open and interactive. In Sweden, the University Law was changed in 1997, from then onwards universities were obliged to interact with the surrounding society. This was called "the third task", something that had to be dealt together with the first and second tasks (education and research). The new resources which were invested as an effect of the law, were mainly used for organising contact persons inside the universities, but these new functions run the risk of being isolated from the informal life of the university and their discipline-based structure (Talerud 2000, Tydén 2002)

In Norway and Finland, a process aiming to create a closer connection between public (regional) institutions and universities has started, this is in order to open up for the possibility for local or decentralised research activities. In addition, in Denmark a new university law that

---

1   Representatives for the academic community in Sweden have criticized the new research and educational landscape from an elitist perspective (*DN* Debatt den 7/9 2003). The quantitative explosion of university education and research – with very limited resources – has lead to a deterioration of the quality, according to the author (a former director of a big university).

came into being in 2003 forces the universities to have external managing boards – mainly consisting of members from private business and
public administration. The aim is to stimulate a much more demand
oriented research and educational profile.

Action Research can be a way for the universities to fulfil the third
task (Hansson 2003) and also to pay attention to the demand for local
problem solving as well as for critical and democratic reflexivity. The
founders of Action Research were also open to the understanding of the
local foundation of knowledge as the road for general structural reforms
of society (Skjervheim 1956 and Thorsrud 1960).

The dissatisfaction with the dominance of Mode I research at the
universities has lead to the establishment of a lot of new R& D organisations in the Nordic countries. The R&D activities are based on
closeness, flexibility, usefulness and a multi-disciplinary approach. The
development of research projects is demand based and the centres are
therefore seen as important actors in a regional strategy for growth
and innovation (Tydén 2002). In Sweden, there are about 80 in total,
often organised outside the universities (Tydén 2002). These centres
are funded in different ways, often locally or regionally. They are often
connected to regional universities and can be seen as "bridging organisations", rather than as competitors. Nowotny et al. (2001) talk in a
similar way about the need for *transaction spaces* or *trading zones* between
the universities and the surrounding society.

The R&D work at these centres, thus, has a great deal of similarity
with Mode II research. But we do not know much about the quality of
the research produced at these R&D centres. Some facts point to the
vulnerability and short-sightedness in the organisation of these, often
very small units. Another weakness with the new R&D centres is the
absence of training facilities for doctorial students. It is only the universities that have the right to train researchers. This unity of research
and education is fundamental in the classical Humboldt vision of an
integrated university, but is, even today, often difficult to accomplish.

How should we assess the development of Mode II research as presented above, and how is it related to Action Research? The description
made of Mode I and II models of research has a general character. It
focuses on the organisation of the research and the mechanisms in the
society behind the development of "a new production of knowledge".

This analysis does not answer the questions that we are interested in, namely how to unite a short-term practical interest with a long-term theoretical one. We think that most of the spokespersons for Mode II have not addressed the risks of demand-based research, which is driven by short-term economic motives and practical applicability. The short-term perspective and instrumental ambitions with Mode II research will be no guarantee for a positive outcome, not even in their own limited way of defining success. Innovation cannot be organised or planned in a linear or mechanistic way, because they are to a large extent based on coincidences, chances, accidents and so forth (Brulin 2002: 106).

Another criticism is the undemocratic character in Mode II. People define the objectives and conditions for the research with a privileged position in society. There are no ways to guarantee democratic and humanistic values in Mode II research, nor theories that are of a more general interest or based on critical thinking.

In the following sections, we shall see to what extent Mode II research has invaded Action Research in the Nordic countries. Of course, Action Research was not a well-defined "unspoiled child" before the Mode II agendas arrived. Action Research was, from the beginning, a field with many interpretations and theoretical ambitions. However, across the diverse orientations of Action Research we observe the societal dynamic of knowledge production (invasion of Mode II strategies) as something, which strongly influences different parts of the field. We will discuss the possibilities and risks in the observed development and we will discuss the dilemmas and hopes.

2.4 Action and Interactive Research – trends and developments in a Nordic context

In this part of the book we will provide an overview of the developments in Action Research, which have taken place in the Nordic countries. We cannot give a detailed picture or a longitudinal description. Nor do we illustrate the various different developments in the Nordic countries. Instead, we concentrate on some important general aspects. It is in other words a kind of mainstream presentation – but in terms of a critical reading and interpretation.

The presentation will be based on the following shifts in the research and strategies, which have taken place over the last fifty years:

- from an experimental to a learning design
- from a consensus, to a conflict, and back to a consensus paradigm
- from employee-based values to broader values
- from a vision of a grand theory to a more pragmatic approach
- from the use of single methods to broad variations.

2.4.1. *From an experimental to a learning design*

The introduction of Action Research in the Nordic countries should be seen in a European and worldwide context. Kurt Lewin's influence was strong from the beginning, especially the idea of performing experiments in real work place settings (Lewin 1946). Practical usefulness, the applicability, was an essential part of Action Research and did influence the methods used – experiments in natural settings (Jahoda et al 1951).

The theoretical source of inspiration in the introductory phase was the socio-technical school as it had emerged in particular at the Tavistock Institute in the UK (Trist and Bamsforth 1951; Gustavsen 2002). The objective with the R&D programmes was often to introduce autonomous groups in a restricted sense and only in parts of a few companies.

In the Norwegian experiments with industrial democracy (first part 1963–69) Thorsrud and Emery were successful in the making of a Scandinavian model of a socio-technical school. In contrast to the English experiments, they had a better co-operation with societal organisations (Thorsrud and Emery 1969). The idea was that Scandinavian experiments had a better chance to promote a new societal order than what was seen in the English experiments initiated by the Tavistock Institute. That is also why the Norwegian experiments were termed "Industrial democracy".

Similar experiments, which were supported by the parties on the labour markets, were made in Sweden and Denmark in the sixties and seventies.

The outcomes of the changes were often positive, at least in a short-term perspective, but the main problem was the diffusion of the changes

– both inside and outside the work places. It was as though "a fence" had been built around these small-scale projects (Gustavsen 1996:15). The strategy for diffusion was based on presenting good examples, which should be disseminated on a larger scale. However, this strategy for reform or change did not function as intended. The diffusion of the changes seemed to be sporadic and unforeseeable (Svensson 1994). Conflicting interpretations in labour organisations also contributed to the absence of visible results. The employers' organisations were not willing to give up dominance of the production design in a longer-term perspective. The interpretation of socio-technical theory or principles as a demand for workers ownership to work organisation (Sandberg in Hoel and Hvinden 1983: 210) was a too big challenge for the individual employers and in spite of good results (measured in terms of efficiency) the good examples did not spread.

The necessity to develop a more comprehensive strategy for reform or change was obvious in the seventies. It was clear that the individual field experiments were not enough, neither in creating a sustainable change nor in accomplishing large-scale effects. It was clear that a dualism between development and diffusion was part of the socio-technical dilemma.

The dualism resulted in a split in Action Researchers` society. One group tried to change the perspective in the direction of a one-sided resource development in co-operation with unions. Process oriented experiments were developed in which Action Researchers, unions and local groups of workers co-operated in establishing local experiments as "political lighthouses" for the labour movement. They kept the idea of the importance of workers' control in labour process development and gave it a political image in terms of emancipation or empowerment. (Pelle Ehn 1988, Vogelius and Aagaard Nielsen 1996:42). The experiments were important contributions to knowledge about workers' experience-based learning and technological innovations. However, in the wake of the general trend towards neo-liberalism and the weakening of labour unions such experiments were not successful in spreading either. However, in all Nordic countries you will still find small niches of Action Research aiming at resource building and empowerment. In those projects, the unions play a key role as partners for the Action Researchers. In Denmark, an Action Research project organised as a social experiment in democratic industry ran for eight years in a co-operation between researchers, unskilled workers in the fishing industry, and the unskilled workers union. The project was not a success in a narrow sense that is in terms of a social experiment. However, learning processes and forms of practical development of sustainable technology and products resulted in materials and inspirations for unions and workers' participation in developmental processes in many branches (Olsén, Nielsen and Nielsen 2003).

A more consensus and system oriented Action Research, which was based on creating integrated processes for learning and participation, was adapted successfully in the eighties. The objectives for a change oriented research programme were now to be decided locally, often in a dialogue between the employees and employers and in connection with many external partners who were relevant for the particular company.

A system perspective about organisational change replaced the earlier design. Instead of solving local problems, the ambition was to initiate self-development process in larger systems. The approach was pro active focusing on future possibilities, rather than on immediate obstacles to change. The system perspective, compared with the socio-technical system, was more open and focused on interorganisational change and co-operation with external actors and organisations. The changes were seen in a larger context with a more cohesive and comprehensive effort in creating a sustainable change. The participants should develop *action knowledge* – a competence for organising change (Argyris and Schön 1989).

In this system approach, *networking* (both inside and outside a company) was an important strategy – both to promote change and to diffuse the results. The idea was to create "a critical mass" in order to initiate changes on a larger scale and in a more comprehensive way (Gustavsen 1996:18). This *horizontal* approach to change was combined with *vertical* co-operation between work places, organisations and institutions (on local, regional and national levels). Horizontal networking was thus combined with vertical co-operation in *developmental coalitions* (Gustavsen et al. 2001). In the nineties the networking strategies developed into theories of *innovative systems* and the *Triple Helix* (Lundvall 1992; Edquist 1997; Etzkowitz and Lyedesdorff 1992).

The system based approach for change was used for the first time in the Nordic countries when the Work Environment Law was introduced in Norway in the beginning of the eighties. It was no longer a question of implementing a law, more a system of activities and changes on different levels that had to be organised. These included training, experiments, research projects, seminars and so forth. A lot of actors and organisations had to be involved in long-term developments and in an organisational/regional learning perspective (Gustavsen 1996).

A system approach was considered to be necessary for creating *sustainable change* processes. The conditions for change were found to be very complex and included different actors, organisations and institutions. In Norway, a large programme, the Norwegian Enterprise Developmental 2000 Programme, was implemented at the end of the nineties. It was organised as modules, (different groups of researchers in co-operation with regional institutions) and lasted for several years (Alasoini 2002:67).

The change *process* – not the outcome of the changes– was stressed in these new R&D strategies. Because of this new orientation, the research role was changed. The new role for the Action Researcher was to organise this learning and developmental process (Gustavsen 2002). The need for support and consultation in the change *process* was stressed, while systematic documentation, critical analysis, and the production of general theories were seen as less important. Socio-technical and Marxist theories of work and technology were to a large extent replaced by theories of communication, learning, innovation and regional change.

To give up the experimental dimension and replace it with an understanding of change in terms of dialogue and network based innovation has, of course, a pragmatic reason. We can interpret the development as a convergence between Action Research and the rise of Mode II dynamics in knowledge society. Instead of normative theories of work and the need to reorganise work and social structure, Action Researchers interpreted their role as facilitators of dialogical processes and networking as a kind of experts in organising Mode II knowledge. The experimental logic has totally vanished and so have the potentials for Action Research as a contribution to understanding and challenging the structural nature of current global capitalism.

2.4.2 From consensus to conflict, and onwards to a consensus paradigm

The changes in perspectives, values and political orientations are very visible and distinct in the Action Research tradition in the Nordic countries. However, we have to keep in mind that different paradigms coexist and compete with each other. We will focus on some of the main tendencies.

The consensus model dominated until the middle of the sixties both in the change strategies and in the research perspectives used. The focus was on productivity issues and on the wellbeing of the employees – often with a focus on health or work-satisfaction. The issue of power was absent, while the *coalition model* of the enterprise dominated the discourse. The researchers played an important role in improving co-operation between the labour market parties who were introducing the socio-technical experiments in Norway and elsewhere (Gustavsen 2002: 25).

The consensus model was later put in question, because of left wing political radicalization, which was related to the situation in working life. The negative outcomes of the Tayloristic work organisation had become obvious, it had resulted in a high absenteeism and a high turn-over rate among the blue-collar employees (Alasoini 2002: 57). The political radicalization of society put the humanisation and democra-tisation of working life in the centre of the debate in the late sixties and the seventies. In Sweden, a strike among the miners was a concrete manifestation of a more critical and collectivist approach in the refor-mation of working life.

In Denmark, the new co-operation between academics and workers (AAA: Aktionskomiteen Arbejdere og Akademikere) was an umbrella for Action Research projects with a conflict oriented target: to build up knowledge to strengthen the workers part in the struggle for better health and safety and for defence of workers' culture in relation to new technological innovations.

This new conflict-orientation and pressure for more radical changes led to a new strategy, which involved a shift from informal and consen-sus based agreements to negotiations and actions. This shift in strategy was based on new rights for the employees – manifested in a new legis-lation (about work environment, co-determination and new rights for union officials; Korpi 1978, Hans Jørgen Limborg 2002).

At this time there was also a paradigm shift in working life research. New questions were being asked and new ways of organising research were being established. Employee-oriented research was organised, this focused on work enrichment, democracy, co-determination, the work environment, health and gender issues from a more conflict-oriented perspective. Some researchers wanted, as mentioned in the discussion of experimental aspects of Action Research, to undertake Action Research solely based on employee values, and with the unions as the prime driving force in the change process. Questions of productivity, profits and competition were not articulated. Some of the unions tried to develop their own strategies for change, including training programmes – often together with Action Researchers. The emergence of *emancipatory* research was something new in working life in the Nordic countries. The intention was to strengthen weak groups in different ways such as increasing their knowledge, strengthening their self-esteem, constructing new alternatives, and developing new strategies for change (Westlander 1999; Sandberg et al. 1981, Vogelius and Nielsen 1996).

In Sweden, the Working Life Centre was established in 1977 and the Work Environment Fund meant new opportunities for making research rooted in employee-based values, which was very uncommon at that time. Moreover, in Norway, the researchers at Arbeidsforskningsinstitu tet had the same possibilities. The traditional employer-based perspectives, which had been totally dominant in the academic world, were now challenged, but only for a while. In Denmark, Finland and Norway, the same financing of research was not possible, but even here research projects were established by other means of support for example from unions backing alternative research and development. Danish projects were inspired by the German critical theorist Oskar Negt, who practised workers education as a kind of Action Research (Negt 1975).

During the eighties and eighties the consensus paradigm came to dominate once again. Economic values – in terms of competition, innovation, productivity etc. – were given priority in the change processes. New programmes were established in many of the Nordic countries (Alasoini 2002:57). Individual values and an idealistic view of change processes were becoming more widespread, while the interest in the material conditions of work, including power relations, was less well articulated (compare Liedman 1998). The strategy for change was based

on co-operation in partnerships, networks, clusters, developmental coalitions, innovative systems, etc.

To understand the return of the consensus paradigm it is important
to know how Action Research has been financed. Various actors have
played different roles in the development of Action Research in the
Nordic countries. In Finland, as in Germany and France, the government or governmental agencies have played a key role as initiators and
co-ordinators of development programmes. In Norway and Denmark,
the labour market organisations have been more active in organising
these programmes. In Sweden, as in the UK and Italy, the regional
actors have had a more central role (Alasoini 2002:58).

In all the Nordic countries, these new actors and investors can explain
the enormous expansion of participative innovations during the eighties
and eighties. This expansion of Action Research is quite in line with the
development of Mode II research. We can take Sweden as an example
of this development. Private companies are now financing the majority
of the research: research, which is about three to four times as large,
compared to the research financed by the state.[2] This research is mainly
carried out by private or semi-private R&D organisations. A similar
expansion of development research has also taken place in the public
sector during recent decades. In the public sector, the research has a
more societal and humanistic approach focusing on care, health, social
work, education and regional development (Tydén 2002). Different
EU-programmes have also funded a large part of Action Research.

However, these new sources of funds have a clear idea of what the
research should be about and how it should be organised. A co-operative "step-by-step" strategy was strongly supported by the EU and other
funding institutions and authorities. To get developmental support and
research money from different EU-programmes, it became necessary
that the developmental work be organised in partnership.

There were other reasons for the revival of the consensus paradigm

---

2   The growing influence over research from industry is manifested in an accessing numbers
    of adjunct professors in Sweden. In some regional universities one in four of the profes-
    sors is financed in this way. In some agreements, it is stated that the companies have
    the exclusive rights to the results of the research. When critical results are published the
    researchers run the risk of losing their jobs (*Dagens Nyheter* den 1/10 2002). In Denmark a
    growing number of PhD students are financed by private firms. In Norway PhD students
    are in a growing number integrated in Action Research programs.

in Action Research. Some important factors had to do with changes in the labour market, in the new political climate, and the limited outcome of the labour laws. The laws and the agreements introduced in the eighties were not effective and did not change the balance of power in the companies or the labour market in Sweden. The private companies were more offensive and gained a stronger position, while the state, as was the case with the unions, was on the defensive (1998; Karlsson and Svensson 1997: compare Liedman 1998). The situation differs between Sweden Denmark and Norway. At least in Denmark unions often play a "civilising and mediating" role in participatory development (Helge Hvid and Peter Hasle 2003). However, the union's perspective is expressed along the same consensus orientation as we see in Sweden.

The radicalization of the unions and the political parties was short-lived. The earlier, more conflict-oriented, strategy was seen to be a mistake but no deeper analysis was made concerning its failure. The proactive attitudes and earlier visions of a democratic working life among the unions were almost done away with in the eighties.

The change in situation on the labour market was of particular importance in explaining the changes in attitudes. There was a higher rate of unemployment and an increasing segmentation, segregation and exclusion of large groups of the population. These changes signalled a shift in the balance of power, which meant that the employers became stronger and the unions weaker. Ideas concerning job security were replaced by the widely used concept of *employability*, which meant that the individual had to take a greater responsibility for her/his position on the labour market by constantly investing in her/his competence development and adapting to the new flexible labour market (Jakobsson and Garsten 2004). Market mechanisms were more widely used and also practised in new fields. The strategy was to privatise a large part of the public sector.

The changes to more employer-oriented attitudes were manifested in different ways such as new management concepts (reengineering, downsizing, profit-centres, just-in-time production (Björkman 2001). Implicit in the consensus model for work place development, the values became those of the neo-liberals and were individualistic. There was a growing belief in the individual, rather than collective, solutions in housing, insurance, savings, care and health. The new political and economic climate was inspired by authors like Friedman, Porter, La Page, Hayek and others who received a lot of attention in the public debate (see Liedman 1998).

It is easy to understand why researchers adapted to this changing situation and the dominance of a consensus perspective concerning change. It is quite obvious that working life research – and especially Action Research – must be seen as an integrated part of the economic, political, and ideological changes in the society.

This is not surprising, because Action Researchers have to be funded for their work. Nevertheless, what should be thoroughly discussed are the ideological and legitimising functions of working life research. The researchers have not been passive during the ideological and political changes, but strong actors, and indeed organisers of these changes. The ethical implications of taking this role in decision-making are tremendous. Despite this, the absence of a critical debate in the scientific community is sensational.

2.4.3 From employee-based values to broader values.

> To put the point in an epigram: "A democratic (rather than elitist) methodology for science is the methodology for a democratic (rather than elitist) science." (Stephen Toulmin, 1996: 224)

Does the development towards co-operative values and a consensus perspective in Action Research mean a return to the situation of the early eighties? Was the radicalization during the eighties and (part of) the eighties only a parenthesis? Not necessarily.

New, critical, perspectives concerning working life have been put forward based on health, regional change, gender and ethnicity. Earlier Action Research often had a focus on the work place in a more circumscribed meaning. In the eighties, the work place was seen in a wider societal context focusing on more universal values. Experience at Roskilde University points to limitations of local and regional approaches to change (Aagaard Nielsen and From Lauridsen 2002). The earlier workers' oriented Action Research at Roskilde has now been replaced by a new and broader based regional approach. In theoretical terms one can express the new Action Research in Roskilde as being based on life-world development in which more universal values are propounded. This focus is in line with traditional humanitarian and democratic values. The values are, however, not universal in the sense of being eternally true. The combined practical and theoretical aim of the research is to create a connection between the life world in a local context and the development of "a common good" or sustainable development at society and global levels.

These changes at Roskilde University were due to reflections about the risks of consensus based, pragmatic, and partnership organised research. Such Action Research will often be instrumental, short-sighted and too locally or narrowly oriented to an organisational rationality. The new critical research at University of Roskilde tries to involve broader values, which concern environmental, health, cultural, security and gender issues, and also democracy in society. The intention is to develop a form of Action Research that provokes and questions established truths and partial solutions.

The new types of critical Action Research are not in opposition to Mode II strategies. However, they go further and try to mediate an unavoidable contradiction between common societal problems often expressed in generalised expert alarms (about, for example, biodiversity in nature) and contextual or local problem formulation. The mediation is not a compromise, but an opening up for societal structural change in the field of Action Research that also means for some kind of generalisations based on contextual knowledge (Olsén, Nielsen and Nielsen 2003).

Any researcher has to deal with values in her/his research. An Action Researcher is more involved in immediate changes and in situations of conflicting interests. There is no simple way to handle the dilemmas with values in Action Research. One way is to be open and discuss the value basis of one's research. Hidden values should be spelled out clearly (Toulmin 1996: 222). The impact of values on the content of the research and research methods should also be part of such a reflective attitude. Action Research in the Nordic countries has not been characterised by such an approach involving self-reflection. Another way of entering discussions about values is through the creation of public arenas for dialogues about general values and orientations; such arenas need to be constructed in a way that open up the possibility for "local knowledge" to be included. This procedure is analogous to Habermas' concept of the classical bourgeois public sphere in which instrumental local interests are lifted to general societal or common strategies and values (Habermas 1962).

2.4.4 *From a vision of a grand theory to a pragmatic approach*

The experimental design used in the eighties was based on one single, grand theory – the socio-technical school. This idea of a grand theory was later abandoned. There was a growing belief that the problems in working life could neither be solved by a single theory, or by distant armchair theorising. Experiments had to be made in real situations and different theories had to be used to explain divergent contexts and unexpected outcomes. Different case studies of local changes could be presented, but not as a "best practice" to be used everywhere.

A changed R&D design having a focus on participation and local solutions led to a theoretical re-orientation. The experimental sites were now identified as resources to be utilised, instead of models to be applied (Gustavsen 2002:26). Changes could not be developed "from above", but had to be organised "from below". Theories of learning, and communication were used for analysing such complicated change processes, which were based on participation.

In Sweden, in the beginning of the eighties, the LOM-programme led to a "communicative turn" in the R&D strategies used. A practical discourse was now seen as the main mechanism for change in working life. In this new strategy, the traditional use of grand theories to steer the change process became outdated. Instead, different theories could be used in a flexible way to guide and inform the changes – for inspiration and enlightenment in the construction of new practices. The theories needed to be linked to specific work place processes to be useful (Gustavsen 2002:29, 36).

The ambition to generalise the results was low, while the context for change was made explicit and seen as determinate for the outcome. Instead of generalisation, the argument for a societal effect of research was increasingly a question of size or amount of the population involved in programmes. If the population or number of enterprises were big enough, the impact of new practices, and methods, on society passed the critical mass.

The theoretical re-orientation in Action Research can be seen as a part of a relativistic trend in the theory of science. The search for structures – mechanisms, regularities, and patterns – became less important (see further Liedman 1998). Instead, the focus was on subjective aspects such as understanding, interpretation, constructions, reflections and communication. Qualitative methods have dominated Action Research for a long time. The limited number of case studies used made it difficult to generalise from the results (Toulmin and Gustavsen 1997). The priority of local and contextual perspectives in Action Research made it unclear how the theoretical ideas were related to the particular case studies (Toulmin 1996: 211).

2.4.5 *From use of single methods to broad variations*

Action Research in the Nordic countries has used a variety of methods – experimental design, stage setting (Johannisson 2003), participant observation, interviews, surveys, dialogue-conferences (Gustavsen et al. 2001), research circles (Holmstrand and Härnsten 1993) and so forth. The traditional distinction between an observing researcher and an object of study has been eliminated in participatory research (Toulmin 1996: 19). Qualitative methods became very dominant in the Nordic countries in working life research during the last decades. In the Roskilde tradition, Action Research methods are often based on Future Creating Workshops developed by Robert Jungk (1984). The researcher moderates, that means has a catalytic role in, a process aimed at a shared utopian horizon among subgroups in the workshop. In the shaping of a utopian horizon one gradually creates common values and understanding of problems, which go beyond pure local problems and needs. In the very nature of the methods, one should produce the elementary preconditions for joint reflection and learning. In many ways, the most visual results of Action Research development can be seen in the emergence of new methods, and the theories behind the methods.

The research role in Action Research was rather traditional from the beginning. The research should, according to Lewin, have an active and decisive role in the planning and organisation of a project. It was the role of an expert with its patronising and manipulative elements. The idea was to conduct laboratory like experiments in natural settings (Westlander 1999). It was a research *on*, not *with* the participants (Svensson et al. 2002: 10–11).

In recent decades, more co-operative research strategies have been developed in different countries. The practitioners are no longer seen as passive and seeking for help or clients, but as active partners with a potential for carrying out innovative development and learning (Westlander 1999). The vision is to organise a *collaborative inquiry*, which would give the participants some influence over the change and learning processes. They should be partners in the construction of a mutually accepted framework. The definition, analysis and diffusion of the results should be a joint effort.

In the socio-technical school, the practitioners' main role was to provide the researchers with data. In the Search Conferences, introduced in the eighties, their participation was based on facilitating joint learning and reflection more than giving substantial contributions to the research. Lewin's planned model for change had been replaced by a more open and interactive approach, which included the learning process.

The competence for undertaking Action Research will be different in a collaborative inquiry. Instead of planning and organising the change and learning process in advance, a more interactive approach is needed. The Action Researcher must be able to present alternatives, understand various situations and different perspectives, communicate with a lot of actors, support the participants' own learning, have communicative competence, and so forth (Westlander 1999).

An important question remains unanswered – to what extent *interactive* methods have been used in Action Research. Action Research has strongly criticised the reifying tendencies of academic research. This is illustrated in the following quotation (Toulmin 1996:222):

Still, participatory Action Research is untypical, just because it is participatory: in respect the fault in Mayo's work is that he was *not participatory enough*. His attitude to immigrant women who were the primary objects of the Hawthorne study was too patronising: it never has occurred to him that it was valuable to engage their interests as co-equal partners in the research.

However, this statement about the participatory character of Action Research has to be proved. Has actual Action Research treated the actors as co-equals in the research process? We have seen very few systematic descriptions of such Interactive Research methods. Despite all the rhetoric about involving the participants in the research process, Action Research seems to have similar objectifying tendencies. Participation in the research process has often been of a limited character – based on information, feedback, dialogue (in prearranged ways), etc. Action Research has seldom been organised as participation among individuals on equal ground based on free agreements or a genuine partnership. To do so one needs to develop forms of validation, which means methods, which are able, critically, to illuminate the processes in the research activities including the interaction between researchers and other participants in projects.

Some methods, based on co-action through the whole research process, have been tried in creating a co-equal partnership between the researcher and participants (Svensson et al. 2002). The methods used are similar to the joint learning that takes place in a collaborative inquiry (Schön 1983). The researcher and the participants are involved in an exploration of problematic situations. Both are engaged in the analysis. Together, they test different hypothesis and explanations in trying to understand connections and causes. In this joint process of inquiry, the learning and action are simultaneous. The outcome is both of practical and theoretical importance.

Similar interactive methods are often used in the development of information and computer technology (ICT). Different solutions are tested by simulation. This practice-orientation makes it easier for the participant to influence the R&D process. The curiosity and joint interest in exploring a new field is the driving force in this learning and developmental process. So primarily we follow the credo by using the Mode II strategy: that is to suggest the research question very openly and involve all relevant groups in specifying the problem. A critical method is to give space for social imagination and shared utopian ideas in the population. With a developed utopian horizon it becomes possible to radicalize a project's research question and to come closer to the dialogue on general values and problems of "common goods" mentioned before.

What is the role for the researcher in an interactive process of joint learning? The researchers' main role is not to solve problems, but to assist the participants in defining and analysing them – often by re-contextualising them or creating arenas where participants can play with ideas. This is a critical approach in which reflection, imagination, and analysis are necessary elements. Such a long-term learning approach differs form the way many consultants are working (Alasoini 2002:67).

To carry out Action Research or Interactive Research of this kind, new competencies are needed among the researchers. An organisational capacity is needed. The researcher must be able to organise the co-operation with the participants in a way that stimulates joint learning. A social competence and a democratic attitude are also needed. The researcher is often in a superior position when it comes to defining, explaining, and interpreting the research data. In Action Research and Interactive Research, it is necessary to establish a close, trusting and reciprocal relation with the participants. You have to be respectful, open and accepting. These capacities are important elements in feminist research (Davies 1999, Barret 2001, Ribbens and Edwards 1998).

2.5 Conclusion

It has not been our intention to compare Nordic Action Research to international developments in the field. Rather, it has been to present how global trends towards a knowledge society and the Mode II paradigm influence and interact with the Nordic actors in Action Research. However, in most of the story told above, the Nordic actors have been at the centre of global events. Action Research as a tradition in social science is fairly highly internationalised: networks have had close contacts with Australia, Dutch, German, English and American research teams (van Beinum, Hans 1996). We do not say that Nordic Action Research is a mirror of local trends elsewhere, but we can see that Action Researchers in the Nordic countries have more Action Researchers – defined as intellectuals expressing and discussing the basic principles – than any other part of the world. However, we are not sure that will be the state of affairs in future, because the coming Mode II production of knowledge will call for a more widespread discussion of the basic principles of Action Research.

References

Aagaard Nielsen, K. and From Lauridsen, J. (2002) "Regional Universities" in *Interaktiv forskning: för utveckling av teori och praktik,* Svensson, L. et al. (eds.) (Work Life in Transition No. 7). Stockholm: Arbetslivsinstitutet.

Alasoini, T. (2002) "Workplace Development Programmes in the Knowledge-Based Economy" in *Interaktiv forskning: för utveckling av teori och praktik,* Svensson, L. et al. (eds.) (Work Life in Transition No. 7). Stockholm: Arbetslivsinstitutet.

Argyris, C. & Schön, D. (1989) "Participatory Action Research and Action Science Compared". *American Behavioural Scientist,* Vol. 32, No. 5, pp. 612–623.

Barrett, P. (2001) "The Early Mothering Project: What Happened When the Worlds 'Action Research' Came to Life for a Group of Midwifes" in *Handbook of Action Research. Participative. Inquiry and Practices.* Reason, P. & Bradbury, H. (eds.) London: Sage.

Bashkar, R. (1978) *A Realist Theory of Science.* Sussex: The Harvester Press.

Björkman, T. (2002) "Den långlivade Taylorismen" in *Kompetens, utbildning och arbetsliv: från överutbildning till underlärande.* Abrahamsson, K. et al. (eds.) Lund: Studentlitteratur.

van Beinum, H. (1996) "Om aktionsforskningens udvikling i Europa, Et perspektiv." in *Aktionsforskning: medarbejderindflydelse på forskning og udvikling i arbejdsmiljøet.* Vogelius, P. and Aagaard Nielsen, K. (eds.), Copenhagen: Arbejdsmiljøfonden.

Brulin, G. (1998) *Den tredje uppgiften. Högskola och samhälle i samverkan.* Stockholm: SNS

– (2002) *Faktor X. Arbete och företagande i en globaliserad värld.* Stockholm: Atlas.

Castells, M. (1996) *The rise of the network society.* Malden, MA: Blackwell Publishers.

Danemark, B. et al. (1997). *Att förklara samhället.* Lund: Studentlitteratur.

Davies, K. (1999) "Närhet och gränsdragning – att nå andra sorters kunskaper genom deltagande observation" in *Mer än kalla fakta. Kvalitativ forskning i praktiken.* Sjöberg, K. (ed.) Lund: Studentlitteratur.

Edquist, C. (ed.) (1997) *Systems of Innovation. Technologies, Institutions and Organizations*. London: Pinter.

Ehn, P. (1988) *Work oriented Design Of Computer Artefacts*. Stockholm: Arbetslivscentrum

Gustavsen, B. (1996) "Development and the Social Sciences. An uneasy relationship" in *Beyond Theory: Changing Organization through Participation*. Toulmin, S. and Gustavsen, B. (eds.) Amsterdam: John Benjamin Publishing.

– (2002) "Research and the Challenges of Working Life". in *Interaktiv forskning: för utveckling av teori och praktik*, Svensson, L. et al. (eds.) (Work Life in Transition No. 7). Stockholm: Arbetslivsinstitutet.

Hansson, A. (2003) *Praktiskt taget. Aktionsforskning som teori och praktik i spåren efter LOM*. Doctoral Thesis, Halmstad: Halmstad högskola.

Holmstrand, L. & Härnsten, G. (1993) "Forskningscirkeln – ett pedagogiskt frirum" *Forskning om Utbildning*, no. 1.

Högskolevärlden No. 3–4.

Etzkowitz, H. and Lyedesdorff, L. (eds.) (1997) *Universities and the Global Knowledge Economy. A Triple Helix of University – Industry – Government Relations*. London: Pinter.

Garsten, C. and Jakobsson, K. (eds.) (2004) *Learning to be Employable*. London: Palgrave.

Habermas, J. (1962) *Strukturwandel der Öffentlichkeit*. Neuwied: Herman Luchterhand Verlag.

Hvid, H. and Hasle, P. (2002) *Human Development and working life. Work for welfare*. Aldershot: Ashgate.

Johannisson, B. (2003) *Iscensättande forskning som undersökningsmetod*. Paper for HSS 03 Högskolor och Samhälle i Samverkan. Ronneby.

Jungk, R. and Müllert, N. (1981) *Zukunftswerkstätten: Wege zur Wiederbelebung der Demokratie*, Hamburg: Hoffmann und Campe.

Karlsson, L-E and Svensson, L. (1995) *Tjänstemän i underläge: om fackets och den anställdes maktlöshet vid organisationsförändringar*. Stockholm: Carlssons.

KK-report 2003. *KK-stiftelsens företagsforskarskolor*. Stockholm: FBA Holding AB.

Korpi, W. (1978) *Arbetaren i välfärdskapitalismen*. Prisma: Stockholm.

Lather, P. & Smithies, C. (1997) *Troubling the Angels. Women Living with HIV/AIDS*. Boulder, CO: Westview Press.

Lewin, K. (1946) "Action Research and Minority Problems". *Journal of Social Issues*. Vol. 2, pp. 34–36.

Liedman, S-E (1998) *Mellan det triviala och det outsägliga*. Göteborg: Daidalos.

Limborg, H. J. (2002): *Den risikable fleksibilitet*. Copenhagen: Fryden-lund.

Lundvall, B-Å (ed.) (1992) *National Systems of Innovations. Towards a Theory of Innovative and Interactive Learning*. London: Pinter.

March, G. (1991) "Explanation and Exploration in Organizational Learning". *Organization Science*, 2, pp. 71–87.

Minnich, E. K. (1990) *Transforming Knowledge*. Philadelphia: Temple University Press.

Negt, O. (1969) *Soziologische Phantasie und Exemplarisches Lernen*. Frankfurt am Main: Suhrkamp Verlag.

Olsén, P., Steen Nielsen, B. and Aagaard Nielsen, K. (2003): *Demokrati og Bæredygtighed*. Roskilde: Roskilde Universitetsforlag.

Ribbens, J. & Edwards, R. (eds.) (1998) *Feminist Dilemmas in Qualitative Research*. Public Knowledge and Private Lives: London, Sage.

Sandberg, Å. (ed.) (1981) *Forskning för förändring*. Stockholm: Arbets-livscentrum

– (1982) "Från aktionsforskning till praxisforskning". *Sociologisk forskning*, No. 2–3, pp. 80–99.

Schön, D. (1983) *The Reflective Practitioner: How Professionals Think in Action*. London: Temple Smith.

Skjervheim, H. (1956) *Deltaker og Tilskodar*. Oslo: Oslo Universitet.

Svensson, L. and von Otter, C. (2001) *Projektarbete: teori och praktik*. Stockholm: Santérus Förlag.

Svensson, L. et al. (2002): *Interaktiv forskning: för utveckling av teori och praktik*. (Work Life in Transition No. 7). Stockholm: Arbetslivs-institutet.

Sørensen, Å. Bøttger (1992) "Aktionsforskning om og I Arbejdslivet" *Tidsskrift for Samfunnsforskning*, vol. 33.

Toulmin, S. (1996) "Concluding Methodological Reflections" in *Beyond Theory: Changing Organization through Participation,* Toulmin, S. and Gustavsen, B. (eds.) Amsterdam: John Benjamin Publishing.

Toulmin, S. and Gustavsen, B. (1996). *Beyond Theory: Changing Organization through Participation*. Amsterdam: John Benjamin Publishing.

Trist, E. L. and Bamforth, K. W. (1951) "Some Social and Psychological Consequences of the Longwall Method of Coalgetting" *Human Relations* No. 4, pp. 4–38.

Westlander, G. (1999) *Research Roles in Action Research*. (title in Swedish: Forskarroller i varianter av aktionsforskning) Research report TRITA-1999:24. Stockholm: Royal Institute of Technology.

GUNNELA WESTLANDER

3. Researcher Roles in Action Research

This chapter about Action Researcher roles overhauls the basic ideas and how they have developed and changed from Action Research in the late forties up to the present day. A number of methodological profiles are discernible concerning the role-taking of the researcher. The presentation is based on a critical reflective research concerning this topic as it has been published in scientific journal articles and books. Most of them conclude after thoughtful arguments with a call for a change. Different role-takings are recommended – and successively re-evaluated – as the Action Research area has developed. The chapter offers a methodological discussion of the role for the Action Researcher and why this role has changed over time. Contributions made on the international as well as Scandinavian scene are described.

3.1 Action Research – the original ideas

Action Research has gone through a great number of changes in terms of guiding conceptions, and its applications, mostly multi-disciplinary, are intended to solve a manifold of problems. The first articles appeared in the late forties, articles that have constantly been referred to in historical reviews of this research orientation.

The most famous texts from that time were written by psychologist Kurt Lewin (emigrant from Germany during the early thirties who thereafter worked in the field of social psychology at different universities in the United States until his death 1947. The last years of his life were spent at Massachusetts Institute of Technology). As Lewin is regarded by many as the father of Action Research (see e.g. Foster, 1973, p. 529) it is particularly interesting to draw attention to what kind of Action Research he advocates. Lewin wanted to create a research orientation the main purpose of which was "to help the practitioner" (Lewin, 1946, p. 32). His contacts during the time in the United States with institutions and industries convinced him of their incapability to solve practical problems, even if serious ambitions were espoused. Assumptions by stake holders in the organizations about how to realize their plans were built on too weaker grounds and their efforts stalled after the planning stage. There were no distinctive sub goals formulated to hold on to which might help to assess improvement empirically. Being without such "objective standards of achievement" one deprives, according to Lewin, the workers their legitimate claims to be evaluated on realistic grounds, which in turn leads to dissatisfaction. Nor can learning come about, as this implies possibilities to evaluate oneself against clear criteria.

Underlying Lewin's argumentation for an Action Research were his explicit values for a better society, a better working life, illustrated with his ideological declaration concerning this research approach: it should be used to defend and promote values of democratization. This outlook is quite visible in his article, published 1946, "Action Research and Minority Problems": "Minority problems are in fact majority problems" (op. cit. p. 44).

Lewin "could not be bothered with research only resulting in books" (his own expression. But he did not repudiate so-called basic research within the social sciences, which he on the contrary valued as deepening the insights into the laws underlying the social life. Basic research contributes by offering theoretical analyses of mathematical and conceptual problems. Consequently research should always embrace studies of concrete, specific situations, i.e. work place settings (see Chapter II:1), as well as conformity to laws.

Lewin's standpoint permeated his interpretation of the role of researcher in Action Research as well. Research is an activity and a knowledge-base of the Action Researcher him/herself, running parallel with his/her interactive involvement in the help-seeking client. His view is important to bear in mind when we later on in this chapter compare different variants of Action Research, as already mentioned in Chapter 1. Lewin was of the opinion that the researcher can take the following types of tasks: providing advice concerning alternative courses of actions, evaluation, design of investigations (if experimental), independently conducted research in a long-range knowledge-perspective.

Further Lewin launched the idea that "social management" can be operated according to a certain (step wise) pattern of planning, what he called *action in planned change* (see Fig. 1). In a first phase a proposed idea is jointly discussed in the light of resources *(means)* available and additional information that has to be gathered *(fact-finding)* in order to take a standpoint. If the decision is to continue an overall plan should be modelled with respect to goal-fulfilment. In the second phase the first step of this overall plan is realized and evaluated, and possibly re-evaluated, after which a third phase is planned in detail, and realized, and so on. Lewin summarizes: "Rational social management proceeds in a spiral of steps each of which is composed of a circle of planning, action and fact-finding about the result of action" (for an illustration, see Figure 2 in Lewin, 1947).

The Lewinian idea of this rationalistic layering between planning and action was adopted outside his own circle. It was spread all over the Western countries as "Action Research".

Another frequently cited researcher is Isidor Chein. Just as Lewin, he pointed to the duty of the Action Researcher to support the practitioner and the practice in improvement efforts. "Not only must he make discoveries, but he must see to it that his discoveries are properly applied" (Chein et al. 1948, p. 44). Discovering reality is achieved through *descriptive* research approaches. Searching for underlying or triggering factors, and to search for causes are a kind of studies that Chein calls *conditional*. The latter kind of studies offer results that challenge the researcher and force him/her to act by informing and helping to correct and influence factors behind that cause unsatisfactory states of affairs. In other words, research entails the responsibility to act.

Adam Curle (1949) also stresses the function of helping: "Action Research aims not only to discover facts, but to help in altering certain conditions experienced by the community as unsatisfactory." But his main theme is the researcher's own intentions. The researcher has to know in advance which kind of outcomes he/she wishes to attain and why. Further he/she must put effort into validating every new hypothesis that may arise and re-examine the preceding ones before they are rejected. To make value judgments and communicate them is an integral part of every Action Research process."

About twenty years later, Sanford (1970) made a retrospective of what had happened with Action Research after the first path-breaking and enthusiastic period. Obviously the aim was to give a picture of the development up to that time in the USA. Sanford himself had his base in the ideas propounded by Lewin on Action Research.

Sanford was of the opinion that Lewin's recommended steps (analysis, fact-finding, conceptualization, planning, execution, more fact-finding, evaluation) in the Action Research process had become widespread and adopted in the United States. On the other hand he found it difficult to make Lewin's idea heard about the distinction needed between the researcher's duty "to make research of the whole thing" and the practitioner's commitment to the change itself and making it effective. This was especially the case in the academic world of established social psychology (where Lewin belonged during his years in the USA). In other arenas, however, Sanford discovers many "programs clearly labelled Action Research" (op. cit. p. 5). Nearly all of these belong to activities in higher education, vocational guidance, on the job training, rehabilitation, that is to say domains concerning social welfare, community medicine, and public health. As a matter of fact, the resistances to Action Research emerged from two sides, from the academic establishment on one side, whose principal attitude (at that time) was that research activity and research results must be kept apart from practice and achievements, and from the practical businesses themselves on the other side, where research and its findings were considered as irrelevant and of no use for practical problem solving. "Academic resistance" was not casual. It returns from time to time even nowadays as pointed out by Sørensen (1992) referred to in the first Chapter of this book.

3.2   The researcher role reconsidered

There were indeed problems to be found in adopting Lewin's views on the sovereignty of science in Action Research. Sanford's own experiences of Lewin's methodological approach made him critical of the idea of the researcher having priority over the practitioner concerning problem definition as well as how to interpret, understand and theorize about the change processes. Such a role as researcher demonstrates, in Sanford's view, an authoritarian attitude to the world of practice world and moreover, it is grounded on a misunderstanding. One must admit that research "has direct consequences for its subjects" (Sandford, 1970, p. 11) and this applies to all of the Lewinian steps (see above). This consequence taken seriously is however not to be regarded as an embarrassing and unsolvable problem. Instead it should be developed to a deliberately collaborative approach. Researcher and practitioner (client) ought to find cooperative forms for each step. Action Research must take the form of a *collaborative inquiry* and leave Lewin's abstract categories for a more concrete direction of method refinement..

However, Sanford's account of the development of Action Research in the USA is mainly pessimistic. The account offered in many ways makes depressing reading and caused a certain consternation among the European researchers who had made efforts to develop Action Research. Michael Foster (1973) and Robert Rapoport (1970) who worked in the famous Tavistock Institute of Human Relations in London devoted themselves to describing above all the European activities within the field of Action Research – this main emphasis chosen partly as a reaction towards the lack of interest on behalf of the American colleagues for what was undertaken outside North America.

In Foster's *An introduction to the Theory and Practice of Action Research in Work Organizations* (1973) Lewin's school is described as "The Group Dynamics Stream". The work of the Centre for Group Dynamics emphasized individual and small group processes. It placed less emphasis than the Tavistock Institute on larger scale social systems. In addition, it was more academic and with closer links to experimental psychology" (op. cit. p. 531).

Like Sanford, Foster is bothered about the idea that Lewin persisted in concerning the content of the researcher role. Foster stated: "On looking back at what Lewin had to say, there is a glimpse of an experimenter/subject relationship which today would be considered manipulative. Values have shifted so that change agents have become more concerned to share with clients their own objectives (both research and action) as well as the ways and means they have in mind for activating them (op. cit. p. 531).

Moreover, Foster argues that Lewin is wrong in claiming that the development of practice is achieved by focusing on group processes and conflict solving. This is a far too narrow view. Social-psychological knowledge falls short and the intervention has to be broadened to include technological and structural conditions. This implies the need of an Action Researcher with a considerable multi-disciplinary competence or of a multi-disciplinary composed research team. That was the conclusion to be drawn of the rich experiences of difficulties and possibilities in doing Action Research.

The important distinction between Action Research and other kinds of research is the researcher's involvement in the whole action process. The Action Researcher becomes a *change agent*. Foster further emphasizes as unconditional that both the help-seeking client and the researcher intend to support the change and in the direction agreed upon *(change in direction)*. The description of Action Research was reformulated:

A type of applied social research differing from other varieties *in the immediacy* of the researcher involvement in the action process /and the intention of the parties, although with different roles, to be involved in a change process of the system itself/. It aims to contribute both to the practical concerns of people in an immediate problematic situation and to the goals of social science by joint collaboration with a mutually acceptable ethical framework.

(Foster, 1973, p. 534)

The fact that researchers engaged in Action Research more and more emphasized the collaborative relation with the practitioners implied a range of dilemmas to be solved. Rapoport discussed three kinds of dilemma experienced in Action Research studies conducted in the industrial sector (Rapoport, 1970). He has noticed three kinds of dilemma (that has to be solved):

- There are *ethical* considerations to handle
- Researcher and client have, at least in part, different *goals* implicit

in the Action Research proposal – and different interests – that
have to be faced and cleared out
- Too often the *initiatives* to an Action Research study emerge from
the practitioner side

The *ethical aspects* concern on one side the Action Researcher's own attitude to the ethical rules adopted by the practitioner (for example his/her
personnel policy, the nature of the products or services), and on another
side the trustworthiness to the Action Researcher in the eyes of the client (is it possible to keep confidentiality in relation to competitors? Is
he/she capable of preserving impartiality during the research process?)
Another matter is the client's choice of Action Researcher (may there be
a preference for "harmless" persons?).

Goal aspects have reference to the fact that the Action Researcher has
a helping function in relation to practice. Thereby he/she may be confronted with the contrary premises for on one side good research and on
the other side those for good practical solutions. How shall the Action
Researcher make the balance between his scientific interest and ambitions and the client's requests for prompt, direct and practical help to
solve the actual problem? This dilemma may be described as an opposition between the purely research-oriented line and that of the purely
service-oriented.

Good research would hopefully, according to Rapoport, be facilitated if the researcher negotiates for being allowed more space of time,
acquires financial means so that research assistants can do a part of the
work, and if he/she arranges external client support.

The initiative aspects deal with the collaborative relation Action
Researcher – client. It is the client who brings the problem and the
researcher who performs the studies leading to a solution. In other
words, the original initiative is with the clients, practitioners. On the
part of the Action Researcher this is the contrasting feature to academic
research tradition. The wording of the initial problem may however
change after the Action Researcher has made the first diagnostic analysis. In consequence there is a risk that he/she will be the one who takes
care of how the problem finally will be defined!

These value aspects are livelong and are continuously discussed (see
Chapter II:3).

How the problem successively undergoes revision during the Action Research period and by whom this is done, must be paid attention to, Rapoport recommends, that in order to understand the relation between the original client-problem and the result one finally ends up with.

The collaborative relationship, researcher – practitioner that got its foothold in the seventies – involved a number of interesting problems for the Action Research process that had to be handled. A bulky collection of articles appeared in two volumes, *The Quality of Working Life* (Davis and Cherns (eds.) 1975). They present Action Research projects, mostly from business industries in different parts of the world inter alia the Scandinavia.

3.2.1 *The Scandinavian contribution*

Among all the contributions in the above-mentioned anthology, the most relevant as an elucidation of the Action Researcher role came from the Norwegian social psychologist Einar Thorsrud. In his Chapter ("Collaborative Action Research to Enhance Quality of Working Life") Thorsrud concentrates his discussion, nearly exclusively on what is demanded of the Action Researcher. The fact that he/she enters a reality of practice where the understandings of the problem in fact are various, means that to begin with the researcher must be capable to bandy with alternatives and hypothetical problems which, each of them, firstly must be tested in order to arrive at a clearer picture of what the problem is about and how the planning process must be designed. The feedback of observations and findings that the researcher makes, entails further that he allows himself to be involved in how the changes are to be realized. The ongoing and final reporting within the organisation demands a sensibility for how to communicate in order to effectuate the best possible result on the organizational level.

Thorsrud was greatly occupied with specifying *researcher qualifications*. He made a distinction between project/program managers, project research members and novices who are to be trained in the difficult art of Action Research. His rather detailed scheme of education, training, participation and responsibility for different parts of the Action Research is grounded on his own and others' experience and has inspired to many subsequent, not least Scandinavian, efforts for industrial working life.

(Part II of this book offers some examples on how training in conducting Action Research is acquired today)

Among sociologists in Scandinavia an intensive debate continues on desirable and non-desirable development in the field (For a summary, see *Sociologisk Forskning* 1982, No. 2–3, Special issue: Action Research). The sociologists were particularly watchful on the ideologies and interests lying behind the various Action Research projects and how researchers' integrity and autonomy in relation to the client's needs would be maintained. Two research institutes were particularly involved in this debate: the Norwegian Arbeidsforskningsinstituttet and the Swedish Centre of Working Life.

The fact that the labour unions played an important role in the process of work life democratization in the Scandinavian countries was a reason for the Action Researchers taking great consideration to labour union opinion and participation. The term "practitioner" as used in Anglo-Saxon Action Research literature referred to simply "the company", whereas in Scandinavian thinking it was more associated with the employees and their affiliations.

3.2.2   *Action Research models applied in the field of OD consultancy*

Running parallel with developments of Action Research is the organizational development (OD) movement developed by consultants. French and Bell (1973) assert in their widely read book (followed by five revised editions) that the Action Research model is the platform used for most OD interventions. They bear upon the step wise procedure (analysis, fact-finding, conceptualization, planning, execution, more fact-finding, evaluation) proclaimed by Lewin.

It should be noted that French and Bell do not use the word "researcher" nor do they discuss how the relation between research and practical development/problem solving should look. Instead of the word consultant they use consistently that of *OD-practitioner*. It must be stressed that Action Research in the context of OD is a much more pragmatic business than Action Research applied by researchers.

Referring to French and Bell it becomes clear that in the context of Action Research researcher role and consultant role are quite different things. It is true that Action Research as a process may comprise mainly the same sequential pattern forward to the practical problem is solved. But the consultant may in her role fully devote herself to the helping function and the needs of the client. Are there any research results available that could be of advantage to the consultant's findings, she feels free to use them. On the contrary, being an Action Researcher implies a double task which is not easy to balance: to satisfy the needs of the client and at the same time combine this with research that could add to existent knowledge, some new and, if possible, generic knowledge open for a critical and reflective discussion (methodological and other) in the scientific community.

3.3   Researcher roles after 1980 – new directions

In what ways has the discussion developed regarding the tasks of the Action Researchers and what kind of academic knowledge should they use? Action Research promises contributions to facilitate problem solving in a practical context. This has been the characteristic since Lewin claimed his principles about how this should be done. Planning and action are the main elements.

But to solve problems is not necessarily the same as to promote development (industrial or other). Several authors who were starting to fear that the Action Research in certain industrial projects had had a far held this opinion too strong a focus on the matter of solving an acute problem. The initial diagnostic study seemed to absorb the researchers and their ambitions were disproportionately spent on analysing causalities around the problem and thinking of short-sighted solutions.

A suggested alternative was taking the *desired* future situation as a starting-point instead of the immediate problem. The planning phase should contain work to specify the *desired* conditions in terms of systems theory *(idealized design)* and according to them find out which means and resources should be used. The representation of the desirable future conditions (and not the present problem) should/ought to inspire and direct the choice of solution. The process should go from rather vague ideas of future and vague conceptions of ways to find more and more precise methods – a sharpening of an initially coarse means – goal thinking. From this kind of planning process *(interactive planning)* emerged a new form of meetings for joint, free searching *(Search Conferences)*.

What is essential is a proactive attitude directed to goals in several time perspectives and based on long-term values. Actions should be driven by a conception of desired future *(futures theory)*. The aim of the planning process is to reach a considerable degree of consensus concerning the desired future conditions and values to be defended. Norms agreed upon *(normative planning)* is a premise for a successful program realisation (Babüroglu & Ravn, 1992). Well-known spokesmen of this re-orientation of Action Research were Fred Emery and Eric Trist, Russel Ackoff, Hasan Ozbekan and the Scandinavians Einar Thorsrud, Björn Gustavsen, Per Engelstad.

All people involved in this type of Action Research have influence and responsibility for how successful the project will be. As regards the Action Researcher his/her contribution is important. It is about involving oneself into the planning phase (or phases) to make sure that they be carried out according to the above-mentioned lines. It is also about being attentive to and making others attentive to action possibilities and their consequences, in other words to develop *action knowledge* (Argyris & Schön, 1989). Researchers' accumulated experience may offer basic scientific material being analysed and summarized for a presentation of action patterns and their roles during the change process. It is argued that the situation-specific insights obtained from every Action Research project, will make researchers who frequently apply this approach owners of a considerable know-how.

Increasingly, Action Research is moving to a model of "full partnership" between researcher and practitioner, and practitioners are met not as help-seeking clients but as autonomous and even potentially self-developing persons. In the Scandinavian countries, embedded in a culture of democratization, this principle has been received (at least in theory) as natural. But that does not mean this emphasis has been accepted everywhere in Action Research projects conducted.

William Foote Whyte, Cornell University, sees himself as being inspired by Norwegian and Swedish Action Research. Whyte introduced the concept *Participatory Action Research* (not to mix up with Participatory Research, discussed later) and its acronym PAR. This variant of Action Research was designed and tested in a series of case studies within industrial and agricultural activities in the USA aiming at a fully developed *participatory* approach. At the same time he did not want participation to be a mandatory element in the research process. Catchwords were *co-learning, participation* and *organizational transforma-tion*. (Whyte, 1993). Here we have an illustration of a Mode II research (see Chapter 2, Table 1).

Learning (or co-learning) takes place in a local context where one has the possibilities to start *together*, researcher and personnel, in search-ing for the specific problem, and *together* decide upon how they shall be interpreted, and which ways would be most appropriate in order to solve them. In this throughout participatory process is also included to *jointly* find out how important concepts, such as for instance produc-tivity, should be assessed in a relevant manner and who the specialists in the organisation are that can contribute to project implementation success. Through his case studies Whyte and his group show how PAR can be shaped in different forms when it comes to the empirical work. Principally, the researcher is recommended to collaborate with a part of the personnel under the designation of "professional researcher". (op. cit. p. 514) in searching for information and ideas that may guide actions along the whole process from the first preliminary design to the presentation of results and their implications.

Whyte regards PAR as a contrast to an expert model where the research is controlled by the expert = the researcher In return PAR offers a model for high-grade collaboration aimed at growing stronger during an extended period of time. The goal is to direct the research process together. Chisholm and Elden (1993) described a whole spectrum of researcher roles. PAR could be positioned on the right side, see Fig. 4.

One of the tasks of the researcher is to analyse a more or less pluralis-tic pattern revealed thanks to the PAR-based performance of the project. Also each participant has the right to communicate the results from his own and others perspectives. In the publications on PAR-inspired Action Research the practitioners themselves allow much scope to writ-ten reports as well. Many applications in this spirit are made. Compared to other variants of Action Research, this is the case particularly in situ-ations where learning by participation (to share views and experiences) is a goal super ordinate to attaining certain specific conditions.

Whyte's idea of "professional researcher" in his PAR concept implies a highly interactive approach during the whole Action Research proc-

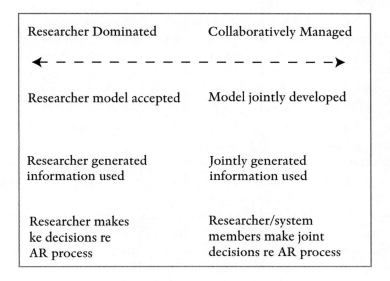

Researcher Dominated	Collaboratively Managed
← – – – – – – – – – – – – – – – –→	
Researcher model accepted	Model jointly developed
Researcher generated information used	Jointly generated information used
Researcher makes ke decisions re AR process	Researcher/system members make joint decisions re AR process

Figure 3.1. Researcher role in Action Research
(Source: Fig. 5 in Chisholm, R. F. & Elden, M. 1993)

ess on behalf of the researcher, and at the same time he/she has to be an analyst of what happens in the local context. A "third part" would be needed, someone who is allowed to study and analyse the pluralistic pattern of agents at some distance off in order to keep this kind of "Mode II research" on a level deserving to be called research. It has to be emphasized that in contrast to academic mainstream and to the initial Lewinian Action Research, the PAR-researchers start by accumulating local experiences from specific PAR-projects to successive theory-building and – if possible – generalized knowledge useful for colleagues and the scientific society as a whole.

There are many other forms of participation on the part of researcher and practitioner described in the Action Research literature. One form with particular features is found in the so-called *Participatory Research* (Brown & Tandon, 1983).

Participatory Research is a common name of a methodological approach that is put in the hands of the oppressed, powerless and thereby vulnerable groups in order to make them improve their situation. The task of the researcher is to participate in a way so that their powerlessness is finally cancelled and their control over work and life conditions are improved, and further to discuss with them their possibilities to externalize and communicate their life experiences. The duty of the researcher is to find out how to expand their knowledge and awareness about the outside world and in what specific ways their conditions differ from those groups of society having power.

This underdog situation of vulnerability places demands on an action-oriented researcher to place himself on the same side and in a genuine cooperation with the powerless and in via *dialogue* with them contribute in (a) elucidating their circumstances, (b) strengthening their self-esteem and (c) finding affirmative action plans for improvement. The researcher is participant on the same side as the oppressed/weak/powerless and contributes to develop a knowledge that is in the participants' perspective and interest (their *lived experience*) Knowledge is the crucial point and is to be regarded as an indispensable tool for emancipation. Useful knowledge means in the context of *Participatory Research* such knowledge that may be used in the service of one's own.

Compared to the former Participatory Action Research this variant, *Participatory Research*, is characterized by an even higher degree of responsibility on behalf of the participants themselves to keep the project vital at all times. The participants are doing research for their own sake and not for compromising with other stake holders in the society. The researcher on the other hand is rather an accompanist with certain academic qualifications that may be useful. Both parties are involved in a joint research task. Reflection is an important activity. Whereas moments of reflection are not explicitly inferred in the sequential Action Research model of the Lewinian tradition, these moments of reflection are in *Participatory Research* extremely essential. The emancipatory aim that directs this participative research approach determines which investigation methods can be the appropriate ones (McTaggart, 1991). It is not a question of research *about* people or groups, but of research conducted *by* human beings and about their common situation as they themselves perceive it.

As a contrast to the principles and ideas behind Participatory Research we finally mention *Cooperative experiential inquiry*, based on the idea about the professionals bearing rich experiences, and being capable of using these experiences and their potential abilities in a joint research form and – *without support from an external Action Researcher* (Reason, 1994). Coordinated in a network for this purpose the members are at the same time researchers (co-researchers) and study objects (co-subjects).

The commonly agreed highly interactive searching process is designed in a cyclical pattern and divided into phases. During the first phase the objective is to find a common, to all members relevant, research problem; conversation is focused on assumptions and hypotheses are worded connected to this problem. During the second phase each member's personal, everyday-experiences of the problem are collected and the discussion meeting circles around the evidence of the hypotheses. During the third phase one is digesting additional experiences acquired. Finally, in the fourth phase a reassembly takes place. Experiences are shared again and now in the light of the initial hypotheses behind the problem jointly suggested.

Different kinds of knowledge are developed in each phase. Propositional knowledge in the first and fourth, practical knowledge in the second and experiential knowledge in the third phase. The information gathered from cooperative experiential inquiry is mainly based on oral reporting in the frame of personal communication. *Cooperative experiential inquiry* has a design of rationality expecting participants who are highly motivated to fulfil the program. Professionals with academic education and trained in doing investigations could be especially well prepared for such an "Action Researcher-less" form of Action Research.

3.4   Concluding words

The variants of Action Research that has been discussed in this survey illustrate some different positions of the researcher's role taking. The researcher has an important task in reporting his/her own choice in the forthcoming projects. To be familiar with the different interactive modes will certainly strengthen the researcher's confidence to handle complicated situations during the Action Research process. To practice them is even more enriching.

Action Research is mostly carried out in the form of prospective case studies. A hard nut to crack for the Action Researcher is that in practice the course of events is to a great extent unpredictable, offers unexpected twists and turns, and that initial overall research planning is not possible to follow without striking out new paths. By the fact that each Action Research project is – or is perceived as being – to a great extent of unique, thus it seems difficult to make cross-comparisons.

The weakness in current Scandinavian Action Research is not the number of action projects going on, but the far too infrequent efforts to make such comparisons aimed at reaching a level of more general knowledge. Probably the main explanation is lack of resources in terms of time and financing such co-work, but it may also be a certain unawareness of that Action Research is something beyond specific projects no matter how exciting they may be to engage in or to read about. There are two strong prospects in contemporary Scandinavian Action Research. One is the increasing societal demand for research-based knowledge being used for improvement of health, effectiveness and sustainability and the other is the increasing interest among academics of different disciplines to learn from and take part in Action Research activities.

References

Argyris, C. & Schön, D. (1989) "Participatory Action Research and Action Science Compared". *American Behavioural Scientist*, Vol. 32, No. 5, pp. 612–623.

Babüroglu, O. N. and Ravn, I. "Normative Action Research" *Organization Studies,* Vol. 13, No. 1, pp. 19–34.

Brown, D. and Tandon, R. (1983) "Ideology and Political Economy in Inquiry: Action Research and Participatory Research". *The Journal of Applied Behavioral Science*, Vol. 19, No. 3, pp. 277–294.

Chein, I. (1948) "The Field of Action Research" *The American Psychologist*, Vol. 3, pp. 43–50.

Chisholm, R. F. and Elden, M. (1993) "Features of emerging Action Research" *Human Relations*, Vol. 46, No. 2, pp. 275–297

Curle, A. (1949) "A Theoretical Approach to Action Reseach" *Human Relations*, Vol. 2, pp. 269–280.

Davis, L. E., Cherns, A.B. and Associates (eds.) (1975) *The Quality of Working Life*. Vol I och II. New York: The Free Press, New York: Macmillan and London: Collier Macimillan Publishers.

Foster, M. (1973) "An Introduction to the Theory and practice of Action Research in Work organizations" *Human Relations*, Vol. 25, No. 6, pp. 529–556.

French, W. L., and Bell, C. H. (1973) *Organization Development. Behavioral science interventions for organization improvement*. Englewood Cliffs: Prentice Hall. (Rev. eds: 2nd 1978; 3rd 1982; 4th 1990; 5th 1995; 6th 1999).

Lewin, K. (1946) "Action Research and Minority Problems" *Journal of Social Issues*, Vol. 2. no, 4, pp. 34–46. Also in Lewin, K. (1948) *Resoving social conflicts*. New York: Harper & Row.

– (1947) "Group decision and social change" in *Readings in Social Psychology*, Newcomb, T. M. and Hartley, E. L. (eds.). New York: Henry Holt.

McTaggart, R. (1991) "Principles for Participatory Action Research" *Adult Education Quarterly*, Vol. 4, No. 3, pp. 168–187.

Rapoport, R. (1970) "Three Dilemmas in Action Research" *Human Relations*, Vol. 23, No. 6, pp. 499–513.

Reason, P. (1994). "Three Approaches to Participative Inquiry" in *Handbook of Qualitative Research*, Denzin, N.K. (ed.) London: Sage.

Sanford, N. (1970) "Whatever happened to Action" *Journal of Social Issues*, Vol. 26, No. 4, pp. 3–23.

Sandberg, Å. (1982) "Från aktionsforskning till praxisforskning". *Sociologisk forskning*, No. 2–3, pp. 80–99.

Sociologisk forskning, 1982, No. 2–3. Speecial issue about Action Research.

Thorsrud, E. (1975) "Collaborative Action Research to Enhance Quality of Working Life" Chapt 13, Vol. I in *The Quality of Working Life. Vol I and II*. Davis, L. E., Cherns, A. B. and Associates (eds.) New York: The Free Press, New York: Macmillan and London: Collier Macimillan.

Westlander, G. (2000) "Forskarroller i varianter av aktionsforskning" *Nordisk Psykologi*, Vol. 52 No. 3, pp. 197–216.

Whyte, W. F. (ed.) (1993) *Participatory Action Research*. Newbury Park: Sage.

KURT AAGAARD NIELSEN AND
BIRGER STEEN NIELSEN

4. Methodologies in Action Research

Action Research and Critical Theory

4.1 Abstract

The pluralistic landscape of Action Research will, in this article, be treated from a methodological perspective. We present Action Research traditions from an academic point of view. As an academic approach, we understand Action Research as being related to theory and to methodology.

We present controversies about ontological and epistemological aspects of the Action Research approach, and we only touch on specific forms of practices and techniques used by Action Researchers. Our approach to the different methodologies will be via a discussion of how Action Research has been established as a "democratic social science" or as knowledge creation based on democratic values. Starting with an interpretation of the methodological values expressed in Kurt Lewin's concept of Action Research, we follow two trends in Scandinavian Action Research: the pragmatic one represented by the dialog tradition, and the critical theoretical trend represented by the critical utopian Action Research. It is argued that the two trends have different concepts of society, and hence different criteria for knowledge and knowledge creation being democratic.

4.2 What is the problem?

The idea to relate Action Research to the concept of democracy was high on the intellectual agenda in the years around World War II. The reason was a necessity for self-critical reflection in academic research in a historical situation characterised by extremely authoritarian cultures both in the fascist regimes and in the democratic regimes. Popper (1945) formulated the theory of *The Open Society and its Enemies* in which he argues that research based knowledge is not the exclusive guarantee for truth, but all kinds of knowledge need to be accepted until you can prove them false. So for Popper, knowledge is seen as a necessarily pluralistic phenomenon or a non-authoritarian kind of knowledge; you can never prove what the right thing to do is by scientific means, or by the use of research. Democracy cannot be subordinated to research or science, which can lead into many directions.

Adorno and Horkheimer discuss the relation between democracy and research or scientific knowledge in more radical terms. They relate the positivist domination in the scientific community and in society as such to the authoritarian catastrophes. In *Dialectics of Enlightenment* (1947) they argue that the separation of science (and research) from values or culture that dominate the scientific community is a constitutive part of authoritarian society and culture. If science only deals with observable facts and science at the same time becomes incremental in societal development and planning, you exclude humanism and democratic values from essential dynamics. The society, and not only the culture, ends up in an authoritarian logic of development. Consequently, intellectuals must become *critical* not only concerning the principles of scientific research, but also of the material structures of society. A critical theorist considers, as the starting point of his or her reflection, reality as wrong or inhuman. Science and research as positively institutionalised practice is a part of that wrong reality. Therefore, to relate democracy to science or research you have to find methods to include a critique of undemocratic society in your research and reflection.

It was in the same historical era, around World War II, that Action Research was born and was presented as a practical effort to relate democracy and research. Action Research challenges the idea of a separation of culture and values from research. Involving ordinary people in the creation of (scientific) knowledge is also a reintegration of democratic values and culture in institutional change. But is this enough to overcome the profound authoritarian elements in modern society? Or is it only superficial modifications to the problems expressed by Adorno and Horkheimer, who saw the structural separation between democracy and science based social development as deeply embedded in industrialised social structures? Methodologies in Action Research deal with those historical problems as they have developed since the end of World War II. The general question is how Action Research – and research as such – can practice a necessary *critique of authoritarian or technocratic elements in society of today and tomorrow?*

4.3 The roots of Action Research

Kurt Lewin, like Adorno and Horkheimer, was in the group of German intellectuals who were exiled during the nazi-regime. During World War II, Kurt Lewin worked in the USA where he developed the idea of Action Research as a way of mobilising the social sciences against authoritarianism. Through the use of practical experiments, Lewin wanted to integrate research and education to enable the growth of a more democratic culture. He developed experiments with a combined purpose: in the experiments he trained participants in democratic group dynamics whilst concurrently developing new knowledge or social technology usable for solving problems and for creating better cooperation in organisations. Unlike Adorno and Horkheimer, he believed that social science was able to play a positive, reformist role without ending up being integrated into the existing alienated society.

Today's cultural and political landscapes look very different, but still social science in the main resists or hesitates to go in the direction of Action Research. All over the world, Action Research methodologies are becoming more accepted than they were just 10 years ago. At universities and in other research institutions, discussions on the so-called Mode II science have started, which is a way to produce relevant knowledge in a complicated world (see also Svensson and Nielsen Chapter 2 in this book). In Mode II, it is argued why there is a growing need for a combination of practical and theoretical knowledge in order to solve complicated problems and to develop technological innovations in a globalising world. But the general idea of strengthening democratic values and orientations, and the *critique* of social structures is outside the Mode II agenda. So something is missing in that general, new, paradigm of knowledge production.

In the following, we argue that Lewin's heritage should not be limited to the idea of a closer relation between theory and practice, but also the development of *democratic forms of knowledge and a critique of authoritarian structures and culture*. The impact of democracy on social science can, in our opinion, come to its optimal expression in the reception of Action Research in connection with Critical Theory. We will, however, also discuss the answers by the pragmatic oriented tradition and theory in relation to Critical Theory. In both methodological contexts, we find Action Researchers referring to Kurt Lewin's basic programs put forward in the forties. Here we will discuss the similarities and differences in greater detail.[1]

Action Research can be seen as a research tradition in which society is understood as being created in human action and, therefore, it can also be changed by human action; human beings are themselves creators of society and specific fields of society and are participants in the research and in the potential change processes, but of course, to paraphrase Marx, not under conditions they themselves have chosen (Marx 1969[1867]). In such expressions, we find the basic democratic idea of Action Research – namely the potentials of research when combined with democratic change: people try to change reality. Doing so, they gain experience and knowledge, not as a reflection on data but as a reflection and development of the social culture itself.

Culture and social experience is, of course, not automatically democratic. In everyday life, cultural knowledge is a result of domination and

---

1   In the US parts of Lewin's Action Researchers tradition "gradually degenerated into positivistic experimentation in which a few variables were manipulated and only tangible, quantitative variables were accepted as results." (Morten Levin 1999, p. 26) That part of Action Research which has been totally adopted into management-circles and without any democratic conscience will not be included in our presentation of Action Research methodologies. But we refer to the anti-positivistic or socio-technical tradition of Action Research as the mainstream tradition, at least in Scandinavian countries, for more than 50 years.

of reified conditions for social behaviour. The Action Researchers' role is to intervene normatively in social and cultural processes trying to organise them in the form of a knowledge creating process. It is important that the Action Researcher find tools to overcome domination and reification.[2] In doing so, the Action Researcher contributes (critically) to the creation of truth and solid cultural knowledge. The problem is how it can happen as a democratic process in itself; that is without ending in manipulation or new authoritarian interpretations.

Action Research in its democratic, normative meaning is a child of a hermeneutic philosophy of knowledge. Before he immigrated to the US, Kurt Lewin was situated in a German tradition of humanistic psychology. In the hermeneutic tradition, cultural and social phenomena are conceptualised through language. Hermeneutic dialogues create knowledge and meaning by changing the pre-understandings of the dialogue partners and so through dialogues the partners educate, and cultivate themselves. Lewin's experiments were based on cultivating dialogues but it was not until Hans Skjervheims' *Spectator and Participant* (1957) that a methodological reformulation of hermeneutic principles took place. Skjervheim argued that the interpretation of language and expressions in dialogues is only possible when the interpreter and the interpreted individuals (conscious or unconscious) share some kind of practical case or interest. Precisely in the question of interrelation between the interpreter and the interpreted individual, one finds the difference between classical hermeneutic philosophy and the hermeneutic ideas embedded in Action Research. Hermeneutics in Action Research is not primarily aimed at interpretation, but interpretation and shared action is, so to say, the same thing. The creation of meaning through language as a fundamental credo in hermeneutic philosophy is necessarily connected to organising social change. The dialogue before and after a social action cannot be separated from the action itself. In the so-called *pragmatic* direction of Action Research, the unity between

---

2   We use the concept reification as an important concept to express alienated relations in modern societies. Using the concept reification – and not alienated relations – we underline that we are not talking about a mental feeling, but we are talking about frozen realities which means a more objective reality attracting people to act instrumentally and obediently. Reification is a concept close to Marx` "Verdinglichung" which we find in his discussion of commodity fetishism in Capital Vol. I (Marx 1969 [1867]).

interpretation and action has become a basic belief. The pragmatists refer to Wittgenstein's argument that the meaning of words is the practical use of the words (Ø. Pålshaugen 1998, L. Wittgenstein 1953).

The direction of Action Research based on Critical Theory has a different interpretation of the hermeneutic dialogues. They are not necessarily understood either as cultivating processes or as development-oriented dialogues about practical issues. They are understood as scenes for critical re-orientations in a reified everyday life. Here action and dialogue is connected, but not unified. In symbolic dialogues developing social imagination new horizons can emerge and hence open up for a difficult criticism of "inescapable" powerful social structures as expressed in the absence of alternatives to the "reality principle" in everyday life.

In the following sections, we will explain those differences, first at an ontological level which means in relation to assumptions about what constitute social reality and second at a epistemological level which means in relation to assumptions about critical knowledge creation in society.

4.4 Ontology

It is not an easy task to characterise the ontological assumptions of Action Research. As mentioned above, Action Research has developed in many directions with huge differences in basic assumptions. However, we will try to trace those views, which are shared among most Action Researchers and those, which are not. By ontology, we mean assumptions concerning what constitutes social reality and the value implications ensconced in those assumptions. We see a constructive controversy in the discussion between a linguistic inspired Action Research and a materialistic and psychoanalytically inspired Action Research.

Kurt Lewin (1946) was the first to use the concept "Action Research". His scientific background was a critical attitude to the objectification found in experimental social research for example that practised in the

Hawthorne experiments.[3] That which in the Hawthorne experiment's reports was called a bias (and later called the Hawthorne effect) was in an Action Research perspective the real result: the researchers influenced the field and pushed it in a humanising direction. Lewin saw researchers' influence as something productive in the knowledge creating process. Experimental social science had and has problems ensuring its own validity. The answer to these problems was, for Lewin, to consider the field as something, which is in permanent social movement or change. At the same time, Lewin believed that objectification in (social) science was incremental in the authoritarian and undemocratic social orientations in contemporary modern societies. He understood that positivistic objectification of people in organisations or social systems (for example as practised in scientific management) contributed to an increasingly authoritarian culture. He was convinced that an organisational and cultural re-orientation aimed at giving people and employees more responsibility was an important cure for authoritarianism and that Action Research could play a role in this re-orientation towards a democratic society.

The idea of creating social responsibility on the shop floor or in the street by means of participation was a guideline for Lewin in his group experiments. He showed that you find no objective laws of behaviour in groups that could not be emancipated and restructured through democratic training and building responsibility. The same attitude guided his understanding of the research process. The research process should express a democratic orientation in the meaning that the researcher should share knowledge with practitioners in the formulation of problems and solutions.

Lewin was a practitioner and inventor of experimental research designs for Action Research. Hans Skjervheim (1957) developed, in philosophical terms, the ontological assumptions in Action Research.

---

3   The Hawthorne experiments were in a way the beginning of the human relations tradition. The experiments were implemented as positivist experiments. But they gave name to the Hawthorne effect and so to a long methodological discussion in relation to the role of researchers as being a part of the reality investigated. Gillespie (1993) presents a new interpretation of the Hawthorne experiments, he argues that the Hawthorne experiments were, from the very beginning, negotiations among dominant partners in the factories about reforms – and not as we read in all reports – scientific results coming out of measuring stimulus and response.

Hans Skjervheim connected Critical Theory and hermeneutic philoso-phy with a practical experimental approach to social science. Skjervheim wrote his most original contribution to the ontological basis of Action Research in his treatise published in 1957: *The Spectator and the Participant.* In the short but classic text, he developed the hermeneutic philosophy about commitment in scientific recognition as well as in actions in eve-ryday life: "We cannot choose the commitment – as human beings in the real world we are committed. Commitment is a basic structure of all kinds of human living." (Skjervheim 1957, p. 11).

A researcher trying to establish neutrality or independence can never reach his goal. The researcher is necessarily in the same ontological con-dition as everybody else. Relations to the other are built on requests or invitations to do something with him/her. It is the same basic ontology we find in classical hermeneutic sociology such as that of Max Weber. He also understands the researcher as being obliged to share the values and intentional meanings of the actor. Interactive relations are per definition not neutral; they are rooted in shared values connected to intentional orientations. But in contrast to Weber and hermeneutic sociology, Skjervheim denies the necessity for, or the reason in, try-ing to obtain neutrality or reduce commitment. If the researcher tries to obtain a neutral position, he ends up in a new social construction – a reality that is created for the purpose under investigation. So the traditional researcher *duplicates the reality*: what he/she investigates is an – for the purpose of research – established reality, and not the reality for the normal actor. This is, for example, the case in the classical con-trolled experiment, in the qualitative research interview or in surveys: the researcher creates situations, which only make sense because of the researchers' project. What is investigated is not the reality in constant movement or change but a frozen reality, suitable for the needs of the researchers. We reduce the truth about reality when the researchers perform their research as a construction with an exclusive or artificial purpose in the research process alone.

In all interactive relations, you always face an element of performa-tive commitments, which means an element of being on a way some-where. If the researcher avoids the performative dimension of reality in his or her striving for neutral observations, reality in itself becomes reified or frozen. For Skjervheim, reification is the undemocratic aspect of modern reality and positivism contributes to sustaining the reification. In all realities, you find reified relations and social structures; they are, so to speak, false but real. An Action Researcher should normatively or intentionally communicate with population in the field urging an overcoming of reification.

In his reformulation of hermeneutic philosophy, Skjervheim demands the researcher to become a direct participant in reality. In interactive processes between the researcher and the actors in the field you should find shared orientation towards practical issues. Researchers` normative participation in the investigated field becomes the basic virtue for the Action Researcher. So, the researcher should not only relate himself to the commitments made by the actors; in order to obtain valid observations, he or she should also make his or her own normative orientations explicit or articulated.

A consequence of Skjervheim's social philosophy is that it does not make sense to speak about universal rules or laws and that reality is always to be considered as *unfinished*; as something that can change in many directions – and hopefully determined by interactive decisions made by ordinary people. Perhaps reality seems directed by laws, but according to Skjervheim this is false and only an expression of the actual strength of reification. But reification is never absolute: you will always see unfinished interactive relations in any field. The Norwegian sociologist Dag Østerberg (1971) calls the unfinished elements of any social system or reality "the existentialist dimension of society". We can see Action Research as existentialism in social science.

The idea that people in modern societies live under reified circumstances but are capable of undertaking democratic actions, at all levels, to transform circumstances is close to Marxist materialism. When Marxists often see the reification in society at large, Action Researchers tend to be more aware of reification and possibilities to overcome reification on a small scale. For Marxists, and for Marx himself, the transformation and development of self-management culture and alternatives was difficult to realise unless actors unite as a class in a coordinated struggle. Skjervheim did not share that idea, and also most Action Researchers tend to act with a more naive interpretation within liberal democracy. We will come back to this issue below.

Most directions of Action Research share the ontological assumptions made above. Critical Theorists are closer to Marx in the interpretation of the strength of reified social structures while pragmatists are closer to Skjervheim in his interpretation of possibilities of democratic change within existing social structures. But it is not in the ontological assumptions we find the big difference between the directions. The normative idea that history can be made by human beings in democratic processes in everyday life is the strong value orientation among most Action Researchers. But in the pragmatic tradition, you find representatives who rarely identify reified social structures because the field of reflection is limited to an organisational reality.

Peter Reason (2002) extends Skjervheim's philosophy of participant research in his elaboration of the so-called "participative worldview". He also extends the concept of Action Research to an idea of *participatory research*. Reason includes relations to nature or biological realities in his participatory research. Researchers in the natural and technological sciences should also see themselves more as participants in nature or biological systems than as people who control or exploit nature through technology. "The participative worldview" replaces the positivist idea about nature as object for domination. Participatory research in the natural sciences makes you see the relation between man and nature as analogy to dialogues in the social world: nature has its own needs that you as a human being cannot dominate. Peter Reason also refers to the system-thinking of Gregory Bateson, who conceptualises human beings as being part of eco systems. With the phrase "patterns that connect" he also argues for a more humble – participative – nature relation (Bateson 1972).

In Critical Theory, too, the issue of man's relation to nature is part of a normative ontology. Adorno's pupil Rudolf zur Lippe sees the human-nature relation as being embedded in aesthetic knowledge and not just functional or practical knowledge. Aesthetic knowledge about nature expresses an interaction involving the nature and senses of man him/herself (Rudolf zur Lippe 1987). Only in the aesthetic relation to nature, that means in a relation expressing sensibilities like pleasure, irritation, happiness or despair, does the human being recognise and form (humanise) his or her own nature. Consequently, aesthetics has a special critical possibility in a modern world dominated by reification and lack of cultivation.

In the concept of a participatory world view Peter Reason is looking for a more profound normative orientation to both social and natural surroundings. This brings perceptions of *sustainable development* at local and global levels into Action Research's focus. We need to step into a direction that includes the natural scientist. Such steps are very new and we will not go further into the issue here. But we see a necessity to move Action Research away from being an exclusively social science perspective. In the coming years, this might be a very important methodological challenge.[4]

4.5 Epistemology

Epistemology means theories and assumptions about knowledge creation. For the Action Researcher epistemology is the key to understanding possibilities and conditions for creating new knowledge in a world we consider as always unfinished, and in which both researchers and ordinary people simultaneously find themselves in a reified and in an existential relation to the field of practice. Most Action Researchers would agree about the ontological assumptions we have presented above. In terms of epistemology, we see strong disputes among different schools of Action Research. We will present different epistemological approaches, but our focus on Action Research is from a Critical Theory point of view.

4.5.1 The socio-technical tradition

Action Researchers often characterise the knowledge creation process as a joint venture (for example Hans van Beinum et al. 1996, p. 182); researchers and the actors in the field develop a shared horizon of practical change, the creation of knowledge then takes place as an ongoing dialogue about the experimental implementation of actions. The

---

4 In spring 2006 we publish a book (in Danish) entitled *A Human Nature. Action Research for Sustainability and Political Culture*. Here we present our arguments about analogies between nature relations and social relations and we present a case story about *citizens' participation in nature conservation and in local sustainable development* as practical frame of reference for our arguments.

hermeneutic dialogues and interpretations are not only connected to texts or expressions, but to practical steps. Knowledge thus becomes the result of an embodied experience – also for the researcher.

The criteria for truth or new knowledge are not only a question of measuring collected data from the field, but more a question of creating experiences which can, potentially, change all participants' values and beliefs in the same process. Lewin's methodology was institutionalised in the tradition of socio-technical analysis. At the Tavistock Institute[5], the epistemology of socio-technical analysis was developed as an experimental practice in which researchers cooperated with practitioners in organisations to create development and problem solutions. The researchers were the initiators. The epistemological heart of the research was the experiment, design and testing of new forms of organisation and shared evaluation as a combination of subjective experience and objective results: did the experimental organisation lead to competitive new routines? In respect of traditional experimental science, the socio-technical researchers discussed possible generalisations from the results of experimental practice.

They struggled with a series of experiments, which went well in the short run, but broke down in the long run. A conclusion of the famous Norwegian experiments in "industrial democracy"[6] carried out in the eighties seemed to point in the direction of successful Action Research experiments as long as researchers are active in the field; but when researchers leave the organisation, it falls back into traditional forms of action. Experimental practice was not able to justify itself as general knowledge. Researchers started reflecting upon the nature of experimental Action Research: they questioned whether the classical experimental design was the best way to develop organisationally useful knowledge.

---

5   *The Tavistock Institute of Human Relations* is the most famous place for the direction in Action Research called socio-technical analysis. After World War II the Institute took Kurt Lewin's program as a kind of paradigm for organisational studies. Today the institute represents an important branch of Action Research – a system oriented therapeutic practice aiming at leadership education and organisational self management.

6   The Norwegian experiments in industrial democracy were guided by Fred Emery and E. Thorsrud. Emery came out of the Tavistock tradition and Thorsrud had roots in Norwegian hermeneutic sociology. (Emery and Thorsrud 1976)

Jürgen Habermas (1981 p. 167)[7] praised Skjervheim for bringing a concept of *practice* into hermeneutic interpretation. He also confirmed the importance of the researchers' normative intervention. For Habermas, it is part of the critical role of research to open up the possibility for seeing alternative social realities. But Habermas also criticized Skjervheim for going too far in the definition of researchers' participation in the field actions. Habermas argued that the researcher should restrict his commitment to normative participation at the level of the rules of discourse. The researcher should only involve him or her in the language game and not in instrumental or practical action processes. The reason behind the restriction is what Habermas calls a risk of being biased towards instrumentalism. Habermas finds a differentiation in participatory roles in the change process as necessary in a modern complicated world. Here you need to have a specialised eye on the language process and the development of general rules for discourse. Democracy through discourse ethics was Habermas' practical normative commitment. New knowledge could come out of creating an *evolutionary communicative culture*.

4.5.2   *The pragmatic turn in socio-technical tradition: Dialogues*

Since the eighties, developments among socio-technical Action Researchers tried to follow Habermas in his argumentation for a restriction of the researchers' commitment. Pålshaugen (1998) and Gustavsen (1992) both argue that Action Researchers should concentrate on methods and the construction of arenas for dialogues and not on designing experiments. Or as Pålshaugen says, "The Action Research strategy aims at reorganising the established pattern of communication in the enterprise by organising new forms of discussion and talks, dialogues, between people and groups who normally do not enter into such dialogues with each other within the traditional organisational form of the enterprise's discourse." (Pålshaugen 1998, pp. 21–22) As a consequence of the methodological turn, which also is a linguistic turn, research-

---

7   Jürgen Habermas is here presented in relation to pragmatic and socio-technical Action Research and less as a critical theorist. The reason is that Habermas was taken in by Action Researchers in order to reformulate socio-technical tradition, see Gustavsen 1992.

ers transformed socio-technical analyses into the dialogue tradition. Gustavsen and Pålshaugen had ambitions to reconstruct socio-technical analyses also on a level of methods and performing arenas. Pålshaugen uses the expression *reorganising discourses* as the linguistic formulation of the new aim of Action Research. It is still a normative intervention, but as you can only reach the organisational reality through language, the key to reform organisations has to be the language too. Making actors in organisations use other words is making them practice work in a different and more reflexive way. New research knowledge is knowledge of how to make reflexivity efficient and useful.

Behind this is an assumption that many dialogues and reflexivity in action lead to a less reified society or less traditional organisation. Pålshaugen and Gustavsen have formulated the theory of the *development organisation*. An "establishment of a development organisation is to a great extent an attempt to reorganise the company's discursive formation" (ibid p. 62). So a development organisation is, in contrast to the productive organisation running everyday business, an organisation, which takes care of change. A development organisation is a normative theory of procedures of how to improve democratic change in an organisation by including all interest groups inside and relevant interest groups or partners outside the organisation in a dialogue.

The Action Researchers and the actors in the developing organisation have different roles to play; however they all are players in the same game and with some kind of shared values. But generalised knowledge becomes possible – not as substantial knowledge about democratic productive organisation, but as methodological knowledge about how to manage reorganisation of discourses in the organisational world.

We will argue that Habermas' reformulation of Skjervheim's epistemology has some difficulties. And the difficulties also hit the pragmatic Action Research strategy. We will question the possibility in practical research processes of making a clear distinction between the communicative and the practical commitments. Can affections, emotional gestures and instrumentalist orientations expressed in language be separated from procedural principles and rules, which the researcher should exclusively care about?[8] In our opinion, the results of such Action Research do not meet the obligation of being critical. To be critical, the researchers have to draw attention to substantially excluded issues or suppressed subjectivity if he or she sees or feels it and creates space for expressions. If the researchers only concentrate on procedures for dialogue, they will not allow themselves to relate to excluded or dominated subjectivity. In our opinion, the researchers should actively support latent potentials and emerging tendencies of transcending domination and exclusion, and that requires a specific form of commitment and interactive performance that is more than procedural. We argue that the pragmatic turn in the socio-technical tradition ends up in a too formalistic definition of the role of researchers and a reduction of researchers' subjectivity involved in the Action Research process. That brings us to a discussion of subjectivity in Critical Theory. On this point, see also Eikeland's arguments for seeing the researcher as "a native" in Chapter 8 in this book.

4.5.3   Critical Theory as a background for Action Research

Habermas is, of course, a critical theorist. But he has developed Critical Theory in the direction of pragmatic philosophy. Another direction in Critical Theory is more faithful to classical or first generation Critical Theory (Max Horkheimer and Theodor Adorno). Below we will clarify how that direction of Critical Theory has inspired us, and our colleagues, towards what we call "critical utopian action research".

The name "Critical Theory" derives from its contrast with traditional theory. In traditional theory, concepts and knowledge express truth about "what is" and traditional theory systematically tries to avoid expressions about what we might wish or hope for. Critical Theory turns the meaning of theory upside down: theory as critical thinking should express an understanding of what is in light of what it "should be" (Adorno 1984 p. 206). Behind Critical Theories about phenomena or concepts about "what is" you can always trace a utopian otherness. The utopian otherness is not arbitrary wishes, it is embedded in the

---

8   In Oskar Negt (1988, p. 231) you find a critique of Habermas' pragmatic formalism. Negt argues that it is not rules for the communication you need in order to overcome domination and instrumentalism, but rather a reorganised time and space for expression of experiences. See also Kurt Aagaard Nielsen 1996, pp. 259–261.

classical bourgeois philosophy of the enlightenment in which people educate themselves and emancipate themselves from domination and stupidity. The utopian horizon is necessary in order to create critical knowledge. Only through the utopian categories can you understand human democratic possibilities in the existing reality. In other words, Critical Theory tries to conceptualise what is but in a subjective systematic relation to a classical utopian idea of an un-reified society articulated in the Philosophy of Enlightenment (Adorno 1963).

For Adorno and Horkheimer, Critical Theory represented an intellectual practice working with analyses of modern and classical philosophy, social science and culture. They did not enter into alternative social movements or alternative experiments. In fact, they made a virtue out of independency from institutionalised activities as they saw such commitments as carrying a risk of instrumentalism; you risk making the alternative or the experiment a purpose in itself. So they also stayed out of any connection to social movements or progressive political parties.

Critical Theory is in a way paradoxical. On the one side, the intellectuals or the researchers should outline a utopian dimension in society in order to deconstruct reification and rationalised culture. On the other side, the intellectuals or the researchers avoid practical or institutional commitments in movements or organisations working for alternatives; they do so in order to remain independent and able to deliver criticisms of all kinds of positive strategies.

From this paradox in Critical Theory, we bring the philosophy of utopian criticism into Action Research; the need to deconstruct frozen reality and culture by means of historical utopian categories. Action Research processes must, so to say, be followed by theoretical reflections of the societal nature around your field in the research project. This is a deconstruction process in the first case done by the researchers themselves, but of course the issues in the critical reflections of societal context can, during good Action Research projects, substantially become a part of a dialogue in the field. The deconstructing reflections are important for how to construct "time and space" – arenas – for participants and researchers doing and expressing experiences from every day life and expressing utopian ideas of a better life.

The tradition of classical Critical Theory was also connected to Freud's *Psycho-analysis*. From Psycho-analysis, the Critical Theorists bring in concepts of learning processes and of contradictions in socialisation and learning processes. Action Research always has an element of (social) learning. Actors do something from which they obtain experience. When individuals make experiences they do so within a socialised subjective structure. To make an Action Research process optimal is also to work with the subjective conditions for learning out of experience.

Critical Theory does not construct a general theory of subjectivity and neither do we as Action Researchers. But critical theorists observe contradictions in the socialisation processes in modern life. Such observations were used by psychoanalysts in a therapeutic context. In Action Research, such observations are useful and necessary in the construction of arenas and in the reflection of interrelations in practical projects. The individuals are not conceptualised as functional socialised identities or as a well-defined psychological structure. The individual creates him/herself in social and practical relations. Since relations are contradictory, *self-creation* is problematic. Because of authoritarian and reified social structures in everyday life, we develop ambivalences, which make social learning, and self determined cooperation difficult. The tragedy of socialization is not alone those difficulties, but the lack of conditions to make *experiences* out of practical complicated processes. In Action Research, it is important to construct arenas and processes that enable people to make experiences and social learning. We need new structures of time and space to stimulate development of experiences and social learning.

Social imagination is a key concept in the psychoanalytical dimension in Critical Theory. In our imagination we work with the contradictions and ambivalences. In our imagination we can open up the possibility for actions and change as possible answers to difficulties. But in our everyday life, we do not very often have the possibility systematically to develop social imagination. Action Research can create arenas – we call them "free spaces" – in which social imagination emerges in an easier and more productive way than what is possible in the structure of everyday life. We can create laboratories for social imagination.[9] Without such "free spaces" many practical actions or changes would never occur. They come out of a productive social imagination.

---

9 An important psychoanalytical inspiration is here D. W. Winnicott's considerations on playing, transitional phenomena and potential space (Winnicott 1971).

Such practical orientations were far from the ideas of Adorno and Horkheimer. Habermas rejected subject philosophy. Oskar Negt, however, took up the psychoanalytic interpretation of Critical Theory. He brought it close to Action Research even if he never uses the concept. Kurt Lewin and the early socio-technical Action Researchers were critical of Psycho-analysis; they found it too deterministic and unproductive in relation to social change and social learning (William Passmore 2001). In the eighties and eighties, Oskar Negt (1969), Alfred Lorenzer (1974) and Regina Becker-Schmidt et al. (1987) use the constellation of Critical Theory and Psycho-analysis to formulate a theory (and practice) of *social learning*. Doing so, they moved Critical Theory a step towards an Action Research issue: to connect imaginative processes to practical social change and to theory of societal development.

Oskar Negt was, in the eighties, the initiator of a research and social learning oriented project in cooperation with German trade unions. The project was called "Sociological imagination and exemplary learning."[10] In this project he and his colleagues took an important step towards making Critical Theory a practical oriented research. Essential for Negt's ideas of social learning processes is his critique of reified and authoritarian social structures in working life. He made experiments initiating time structures and space for workers' creation of social imagination as mediation of experiences from work and everyday life. Contradictions in life expectations are taken into an arena: a so-called proletarian public sphere.[11] In the creation of a proletarian public sphere, the participating workers tried out new forms of actions and learning processes making themselves self regulated both as individuals and as a group.

The projects resulted in new organisational forms in the unions and

---

10 Oskar Negt (1969). The project took place as a co-operation between IG Metall and a group of researchers. In the project researchers created dialogues and learning processes to develop traditional trade union orientations into a more societal union policy. The researchers created learning processes dealing with workers experiences from production as well as from reproductive life.

11 The concept is more systematically developed in Negt and Kluge (1972). Even if the word "proletarian" may today sound out of time the meaning in the book of Negt and Kluge is to come closer to an understanding of working class or employees as individuals and so to criticize a too collectivistic concept of class. In a way Negt and Kluge take a step towards contemporary class theories in which individualisation is an important aspect.

in a Critical Theory of learning in connection with practical reorganisations of union activities. In our Action Research we saw possibilities in Negt's understanding of learning through mediated experience from a life context. The learning and education of workers must overcome instrumentalism in daily work and express collective needs in modern workers' lives. Negt uses the concept *life context* to stress that learning is connected to identity for the entire person – and not only to roles in systems or organisations.

The role of researchers in the learning processes was partly to be responsible for creation of the "free space" for mediation of social imagination and partly to create a theoretical irritation of ideas in order to prevent an instrumentalist reduction. Negt's theories and methods also maintain the negative dimension of Adorno and Horkheimer and their Freudian inspired interpretation of identity building and learning. Negt never called his project Action Research. And he never saw such projects as harmonisation between theory and practice in research. We tend to agree in such hesitation to label Action Research as a highly integrated epistemology. And we find it important to work with the question of researchers' own creation of experience from his or her contradictory life context. The Action Researchers' substantial contribution to the development of knowledge and change depends on his or her own subjectivity and his or her subjective participation in a cooperating process with practitioners. Making this cooperation transparent is a big challenge to any Action Research process in order to give it democratic legitimacy, but also in order to anticipate democratic structures in the fields of society, where the researchers and scientists are involved.

To complete our presentation of an epistemology for critical utopian action research, we will finally present the ideas of a futures research philosopher, Robert Jungk (1913–1994). Robert Jungk invented tools and arenas for democratic change. We see his contribution to Action Research as very important for our *practical* interpretation of Critical Theory. Jungk did not belong to the group of academic Critical Theorists, but he was inspired by the same theoretical heritage. He worked most of his life in connection with new social movements that were emerging in the last part of the 20th century. He saw those movements as a new way of rethinking change and understanding political power structures. We introduce Robert Jungk's work because he, more than any other practical philosopher, underlined the importance of working with social imagination and utopian future oriented ideas and sketches as the essential link between critical analysis of authoritarian and instrumentalist culture and democratic change. It is difficult to point to the most important of Robert Jungk's books on futures research; at the practical end we shall, however, mention his 1981 book about *Future Creating Workshops* ("Zukunftwerkstätten") which was written together with Norbert Müllert, and his late treatise of *The Project of Encouraging* (Projekt Ermutigung) published in 1988.[12]

Robert Jungk's ideas about the importance of social imagination and utopian future orientation had roots in the Marxist philosopher Ernst Bloch (1885–1977). Bloch understood the history of society as being a materialistic history, but at the same time as a history of utopian culture – as flows of dreams, which have always characterised modern societies. Those dreams are essential to understanding conditions and methods for social change. For Bloch, Marxism had been too occupied with material history and too little with mental history or the history of imaginations and dreams. To create knowledge about modern societies is also to create knowledge about the utopian flows, only the utopian flows in everyday life can open up the possibility for social change. Jungk saw the rise of new social movements from the eighties as a new progressive utopian idea of democracy (utopian flows in history are not necessarily progressive). He encouraged the new utopian ideas and developed methods to strengthen the social imagination in social movements. Without a democratic utopian future horizon, the future will be dominated by technocratic planning. Jungk was critical of change and planning as something dominated by expert culture. In industrial and post-industrial societies future planning has increasingly become something defined by experts. In the future planning made by experts everything becomes too realistic. Qualitative change and renewal of basic social structures never occur in planning discussion.

To overcome this "reality power" (Marcuse 1941), Jungk has a practical ambition of developing a future oriented Action Research. He does not use the concept of Action Research – but rather *normative future*

---

12 Robert Jungk organised before he died the establishment of the "Bibliothek für Zukunftsfragen" in Salzburg. This library coordinates a lot of Action Research activities inspired from Robert Jungk from all parts of the world.

research, in which systematic work with social imagination and utopian sketches prepare experiments. But social imagination and the development of utopian sketches are not the goal of the normative future research. They are the heart of the reorientation of possible actions in every day life and in organisations. The future-creating workshop is an arena for the development of utopian sketches. In the Future Creating Workshop, you find space for the concretisation of utopian ideas in terms of action. If actions should be part of more extensive social change you have to prepare and create social experiments. Without social experiments it becomes impossible to improve radical change. "The greatest advantage of social experiments compared to traditional methods for social change, is the reduction of *fear* of social change. The fear of uncertainty about the consequences is always an important part of discussion when things you have never seen before are proposed. A social experiment followed by researchers cannot remove the fear, but it can reduce it importantly." (Jungk 1975). *(Translated by the authors.)*

The social experiment is an instrument for creating reversibility in processes of social change. Such reversibility is, in itself, a part of opening up your mind for the critical understanding of reality and encouragement to change. Through the experiment you gain new knowledge or experience with the existing reality. Systematic change in a reversible experiment can be useful in researching a field – not only for an instrumental change but also for a critical understanding of problems and inertia.

For Robert Jungk, the development of social imaginations and utopian sketches as well as initiation of social experiments was a kind of solution to the unpractical bias of classical Critical Theory. Jungk allows a start on "the wrong issues" and "the limited understandings", playing with them and opening them up for new experimental ideas and actions for a less authoritarian and instrumental world.

The normative future research can take place as activities in social movements or among members of institutions and organisations. But they can also take place as something supported by researchers. The researcher is a moderator of processes in workshops and in running social experiments. The researcher also has an obligation to discuss and make theoretical challenges to grassroots' proposals and sketches. And, first of all, the researcher has to support the awareness of the emerging *common* – general and universal – dimensions of the proposals and sketches, thus encouraging a break with the dominant narrow interest groups' perspectives. Such a break is, at the same time, a precondition for and a result of *social* imagination. For Jungk, the results of normative future research were a scientific and a political contribution to understanding future societal development as manifold – the more futures you can see as possibilities the more knowledge becomes democratic. The researcher is not seen as a guarantee for truth in living experiments, but as a cooperating partner with all kinds of actors in order to open up the possibility for democratic knowledge creation.

Researchers and experts are not privileged in knowledge creation; they are collaborators. Here we are back to basics in the definition of Action Research, but we have reconstructed methods and epistemological concepts inspired by Critical Theory. In Critical Theory the intellectuals or the critical researchers are a kind of advocate for a critique of general wrong (reified) social structures. In critical utopian action research, this negative role is supplemented by advocating the creation of proposals and constructions of new democratic common structures in society. Such constructions can only be born out of democratic co-operations in concrete fields of actions and experiments. In contrast to the Mode II paradigm of knowledge production, the role of critical utopian action researchers is to go beyond the local truth and local change – but to do it in co-operation with practitioners in shared projects. Practically it starts with strengthening public spheres around Action Research projects, asking for national and global implications and involvements in the local projects and movements. To ask for the general in the local is a special duty for Action Researchers.

4.6 Conclusion

In contrast to Habermas and pragmatic Action Research, the critical utopian action research inspired by Adorno, Horkheimer, Oskar Negt, Ernst Bloch, Regina Becker-Schmidt and Robert Jungk points to social imagination, experiments and sketching "alternative futures" to be discussed in public as the important elements in knowledge creation. Habermas and the pragmatic approach point out the dialogue and language as the primary medium for construction of new knowledge. In the two traditions, we find different concepts of critique – a strong and society based one in the heritage from Critical Theory and a more procedural and methodological concept of criticism in Action Research in the pragmatic tradition. Both are answers to an all too weak concept of criticism present in the socio-technical tradition. In a more technical or practical performance, the different approaches to Action Research have similarities and are able to cooperate. But in epistemological assumptions and reasons behind the tools and procedures you find different logics and perspectives. The discussion on epistemology is important for qualifying Action Research today. It is a way to bring in democratic values as a procedural and substantial element in the research process.

In spite of differences in basic methodological assumptions, Action Researchers share the idea that knowledge creation is not something exclusive for scientists or experts. Scientists and experts contribute as humble parts in a cooperative knowledge creation process. The idea of a knowledge society is – in contrast to actual conceptions of a knowledge society – a utopian idea of democratically cooperating people. The Action Researchers have a special task in creating of critical awareness about the necessity and possibility of democratic knowledge creation.

References

Adorno, T. (1963) *Eingriffe. Neun kritische Modelle.* Frankfurt am Main: Suhrkamp Verlag.

– (1984) "Soziologie und empirische Forschung" in Adorno, T. & Horkheimer, M. *Soziologica.* Frankfurt am Main: Syndicat/EVA.

– and Horkheimer, M. (1947): *Dialektik der Aufklärung.* Amsterdam: Querido

Bateson, G. (1972) *Steps to an Ecology of Mind.* San Francisco: Chandler.

Becker-Schmidt, R. and Axeli-Knapp, G. (1987) *Geschlechtertrennung: Geschlechterdifferenz. Suchbewegungen sozialen Lernens.* Bonn: Dietz.

van Beinum, H., Faucheux, C. and van der Vlist, R. (1996) "Reflections on the epigenetic Significance of Action Research" in Toulmin S. and Gustavsen B. (eds.) *Beyond Theory.* Amsterdam: John Benjamins publishing.

Emery, Fred; Thorsrud, Einar (1976): *Democracy at Work*. Leiden: Nijhoff.

Gillespie,W. (1993): *Manufacturing knowledge. A history of the Hawthorne experiments*. Cambridge: Cambridge University Press.

Gustavsen, Bjørn (1992): *Dialogue and development. Social science for social action*. Assen: Van Gorcum.

Gustavsen, Bjørn (1996): Development and the social sciences: An uneasy relationship. In S. Toulmin & B. Gustavsen (ed): *Beyond Theory: Changing Organization through Participation*. Amsterdam: John Benjamin Publishing.

Habermas, J. (1981) *Theorie des Kommunikativen Handelns*. Frankfurt am Main: Suhrkamp Verlag. (In English: *The theory of communicative action*. Boston 1984.)

Jungk, R. and Müllert, N. (1981) *Zukunftswerkstätten: Wege zur Wiederbelebung der Demokratie*. Hamburg: Hoffmann und Campe (In English: *Future workshops: how to create desirable futures*. Institute for Social Inventions 1987.)

Jungk, Robert (1975) "Vom Wort zu Versuch". Introduction to Meadows, D. et al. *Die Grenzen des Wachtums*. German edition of Meadows, D. et al. (1972). *Limits to Growth*, New York: Universe Books.

– (1988): *Projekt Ermutigung*. Berlin: Rotbuch Verlag

Lewin, K. (1948): *Resolving social conflicts*. New York: Harper and Row

Levin, M. (1999) "Action Research Paradigms" in *Action Research*, Greenwood, D. J. (ed.). Amsterdam/Philadelphia: John Benjamins Publishing.

zur Lippe, R. (1987): *Sinnenbewusstsein*, Reinbek: Rowolt.

Lorenzer, A. (1974) *Die Wahrheit der psychoanalytischen Erkenntniss*, Franfurt am Main: Suhrkamp.

Marx, K. (1969 [1867]) *Das Kapital. Kritik der Politischen Ökonomie. Erster Band*, Berlin: Dietz Verlag

Marcuse, H. (1941) "Some implications of Modern Technology" in *Studies in Philosophy and Social science*, Vol. 9 No. 3.

Negt, O. (1969) *Soziologische Phantasie und examplarisches Lernen*, Franfurt am Main: Eur. Verlagsanstalt.

– (1988) *Modernisierung – Im Zeichen des Drachens*. Frankfurt am Main: Fischer Taschenbuch.

Negt, O. and Kluge, A. (1972) *Öffentlichkeit und Erfahrung*. Frankfurt am Main: Suhrkamp. English version: *Public Sphere and Experience: Towards* an *Analyses of the Bourgeois and Proletarian Public Sphere*, Minneapolis: University of Minnesota Press 1993.

Nielsen, K. Aagaard (1996) *Arbejdets sociale orientering*, København: Forlaget Sociologi.

Nielsen, B. Steen and Nielsen, K. Aagaard (2006): *En menneskelig Natur. Aktionsforskning for bæredygtighed og politisk kultur*, København: Forlaget Frydenlund.

Passmore, W. (2001) "Action Research in the Workplace: The socio-technical Perspective" in *Handbook of Action Research*, Reason, P. and Bradbury, H. (eds.) London: Sage.

Popper, K. (1945) *The open society and its enemies*, 1. Edition, London: Routledge.

Pålshaugen, Ø. (1998) *The end of Organization Theory*, Amsterdam: John Benjamins Publishing.

Reason, P. (2002) "Justice, sustainability, and participation: Inaugural professorial lecture" in *Concepts and Transformation Vol. 7 number 1*.

Skjervheim, H. (1957) *Deltaker og Tilskodar*, Oslo: Oslo University Press. (In English: *Objectivism and the study of Man*. Oslo 1959.)

Winnicott, D. W. (1971) *Playing and reality*, London: Tavistock Publications.

Wittgenstein, L. (1953) *Philosophical Investigation*, Oxford: Blackwell.

Østerberg, D. (1971) *Metasociologisk Essay*, Oslo: Pax.

LISE DREWES NIELSEN

5. The Methods and Implications of Action Research

A Comparative Approach to Search Conferences, Dialogue Conferences and Future Workshops

5.1   Introduction

Action Research has produced several different approaches (schools) all of which have developed their specific methods or rules for creating the interface between research and practise. Some researchers have created "schools" of Action Research methods; other researchers have developed methods based on each other's experiences. The discussions, which take place across the various methodological approaches, keep the Action Research field alive and vital.

The success of these methods is to be found in the increasing demand for (1) methods able to handle the growing complexity and insecurity present in modern societies (2) the need to develop democratic dialogue about the development of organizations, enterprises and communities (3) the need for Action Research where researchers and actors produce knowledge and change together.

This Chapter will present three of the methods, which have been most widely used during the last 40 years in three Scandinavian countries namely Norway, Sweden and Denmark. These methods have been specifically linked to conferences and workshops that have taken place in these countries, namely the Search Conference (mainly in Norway), the Dialogue Conference (in Sweden and Norway) and the Future and Scenario Workshop (mainly in Denmark). The methods have seen extensive use not just in the Nordic countries but also beyond. They represent three (or more) different approaches, different time spans and different local contexts, but they all have a common ground, and a common influence on Scandinavian Action Research perspectives.

This article seeks to describe the history, methodology, and principles and orientation of each method. The final section will attempt to list the similarities and differences of the three approaches based on a conceptual approach to classification.

5.2   The Search Conferences

5.2.3   History and extent

The Search Conferences originated from the work undertaken by Eric Trist and Fred Emery in sixties at The Tavistock Institute of Human Relations in Great Britain. Their task was to merge two aircraft engine manufacturers and in doing so they developed their Search Conference methodology by adding a set of psychological criteria for effective dialogue and discourse, this was inspired by the work of Asch (1952).[1] The name Search Conference was introduced because the conference's primary function was to allow mere possibilities to surface.

> "In searching for meaning in these emerging possibilities, the participants are usually confronted with unexpected new directions and new ways of approaching old ideas."
> (Quote from Fred Emery in Emery and Purser 1996, p. 283).

Fred Emery was Australian and he introduced and further developed the methodology in the UK (1960–70). From 1970–82 Fred and Merrelyn Emery's concept of Search Conferences was used between 300 and 400 times in community planning, organizations, education etc. in Australia. Since then Fred Emery's widow Merrelyn Emery has continued the work with the methodology in the US (Emery and Purser, 1996; Emery 1999).

---

1   In Emery and Purser (1996), the Search Conference Methodology is described in detail. The history of the Search Conference is presented in the book's Appendix, which includes an interesting interview with Fred Emery about the history and development of the conference.

In Scandinavia, the Search Conference was an element in the industrial democratisation experiments conducted by Emery and Thorsrud. (Emery and Thorsrud 1976). In the period from 1964 to 1969, the Norwegian Industrial Democracy Project was undertaken in Norway. It was a collaborative project between the Norwegian Federation of Trade Unions (LO) and the Norwegian Employers' Federation (NAF), and ran four demonstration projects. The idea was to develop experimental sites as action oriented socio-technical experiments, where new principles of organising work and new principles of communication were implemented in order to maintain the continuous learning and diffusion of results from the experiments. There was little diffusion of all the socio-technical experiments, but the ideas spread and were adopted in other Scandinavian countries in different projects providing inspiration for those who focused on strategies for democratic changes and the self-management of work in organisations.

5.2.4   Methods

"A Search Conference is a participative event that enables a large group to collectively create a plan that its members themselves will implement." (Emery and Purser, 1996, p. 4).

The Search Conference methodology consists of exercises in collective problem identification, discussions and changes. The Search Conference moved towards new structures for conferences away from bureaucratic structures towards democratic ones, in the same way as the socio-technical experiments had moved work organisations towards new principles.

In relation to work, Fred Emery's original intention was to develop methods that could break tendencies of deskilling and apathy in industrial work. Through influence and responsibility in work conditions, the methodology intended to improve industrial democracy and the working environment. This could be achieved through changes in industrial design, where workers in self-managing groups develop responsibilities for coordination, control and outcomes. The new "learning organisations" in the production process with self-managing groups, which had responsibility for their own coordination and control, was one outcome of the experiments.

These principles taken from the socio-technical experiments were directly transformed to the principles of the participative conference (the Search Conference), where the participants take responsibility for the content and the outcome of the conference. The designers and managers of the conference only take responsibility for the design and management of the learning environment and process. Over the duration of the conference, participants also assume increasing responsibility for the process (Emery 1999).[2]

The point of departure for the conference was a focus on the principles of organisational industrial democracy. The use of the methodology has, moved into areas other than industry, such as planning and community development. The success of the approach was due to the failure of traditional controlled, exclusionary and hierarchical planning methodologies to include citizens' local knowledge. The need for more democratic principles was a platform for the success.

The Search Conference is a participative planning method, which enables people to develop a plan for the most desirable future for their community or organisation. The plan is developed during the conference in collaboration between the participants. During the conference, the participants – citizens, planners, politicians, managers, and workers – create their own community of planners and implementers. As a collaborative community, the Search Conference facilitates knowledge sharing, knowledge production and knowledge utilisation. Search Conferences emphasise the importance of face-to-face interaction between stake holders in order to create a new community with the purpose of creating future strategies on the basis of different ideas.

The Search Conference produces a plan for the future system of knowledge and learning among the participants together with agreements on obligations to work for the implementation of the plan.

A typical Search Conference has 20–40 participants from the company, and community etc. The selection of the participants is a collaborative process between the facilitators and the system. There is enormous

---

2   The theoretical ground of the search conference is described in detail in Merrelyn Emery (1999): Searching. The Theory and practice of making cultural change.

variation in the meaning of "participation" depending on the type of participants at different conferences. Sometimes a Search Conference seeks to ensure the representation of different stake holders at the conference; sometimes the goal is just to select the "right" people for the purpose of the conference.

The conference normal takes place over two or more days and is offsite. The dialogue is formed in plenum, and group work is only used for specific purposes like speeding up the conference or discussing vital details (Emery 1999). The conference is based on the knowledge and experience of the participants, and in its original form no experts with specific knowledge were invited as lecturers or to make presentations, as is the case in normal expert driven conferences.

The conference will include the following generic stages (Emery 1999, p. 172):

Phase 1. The future in the past and present. What is happening in the social environment?

Phase 2. The past in the present. Where did we come from?

Phase 3. The past and present in the future. What is desirable?

Phase 4. Creating a desirable Future. Action plans incorporating the best of the past, present and future.

Phase 5. The future in Action. Action creates diffusion.

Normally, the time-use at the conference is divided into thirds: one third for the uncertain and turbulent environment, one third for the search for the systems past and present in order to develop the most desirable system, and the last third for action planning.

The Search Conference is an intensive period in a much longer process with at least three stages a) Preparation and planning and the selection of participants, b) The Search Conference, and c) Implementation.

The principles of democracy in the Search Conference are as follows: First, the form of the conference makes it different from bureaucratic conferences where the agenda is established before the conference by the conference organisers and the dialogue is one-way. Second, the Search Conference establishes a democratic dialogue in which all participants can join. Third, the Search Conference, as a training laboratory for democratic dialogue, establishes training in democratic dialogue among the participants.

The conference has further been instrumentalised in the concept of the Future Search Conference (www.futuresearch.net). The Future Search Conference is designed around four basic principles:

- Getting the whole system in one room
- Developing desired future scenarios rather than problem solving
- Working together on a series of structural tasks
- Working as peers and equals in small self-managed groups.

A Future Search Conference normally has 30–72 participants and lasts for two to three days in order to produce a consensus or common grounds for the desired future. All parts of the system are represented. The generic process of the Search Conference is followed. The participants work with posters, mind mapping, changes in groups in mix of difference and unity.

The Future Search Conference has been instrumentalised as closed events offered by the consultancy conference industry, where the experimental and alternative development of the ideals of the conference seem to disappear as well as a long lasting and close development project or experiment with a limited number of local actors.

5.2.5 Principles and orientations

The Search Conference was originally developed on the basis of ideas for creating democratic experiments and learning organisations as alternatives to the bureaucratic ones. As such, the Search Conference's purpose is to produce critical alternatives based on democracy and shared responsibility for the outcome, but also on an explicit critique of traditional bureaucratic structures in organisations and in dialogues at conferences.

The Search Conference has a clear future perspective. The conference is seen as an integrated part of a change process in the organisation or the community it is a part of.

The Search Conference is based on theory and concepts developed by Emery concerning ecological system development where an organisation or community could be analysed in relation to its surroundings (Emery and Purser 1996, p. 40). Another fundamental idea was that of dialogue.

While the socio-technical experimental ideas and the Search Conference were expert and research driven, there has always been a high degree of involvement through democratic dialogues.

It is not the intention that a Search Conference can stand alone; it is incorporated in sequences of developmental events in order to ensure actions that are in the line with the outcomes of the conference.

The Future Search Conference, which was developed later, has changed the purpose in two ways. First the purpose is not to stimulate changes, but to create dialogues across different actor groups. Second the conference is established normally as a shut, and not as an integrated part of a series of events. You might say that the concept in Future Search Conference has moved far away from the ideas of the originally Search Conference.

5.3   The Dialogue Conference

5.3.1   History and extent

In Norway, the social partners decided, in their 1982 revision of the Basic Agreement, to make agreements especially dealing with development. These were based on the fact that the diffusion of the experiments from 1960 to 1970 was not as successful as expected and new organisational development was needed.

> "In these agreements focus was placed not on content but on procedures: on how to deal with such issues as work organisation and local co-operation." (Gustavsen 2001, p. 18).

In the 1982, the Norwegian Agreement, the *Conference* was introduced, which means meeting places for discussions of goals, ideas and visions. By the end of 1985, about 200 enterprises in Norway had used the Conference as a tool in developmental organisational activities (Gustavsen and Engelstad 1986).[3] This was the baseline for the metho-

---

3   The Dialogue Conference and its principles is described clearly in Gustavsen and Engelstad 1986. Later the conference is described in Pålshaugen 1998.

dology called the Dialogue Conferences, developed by Gustavsen and Engelstad. The Dialogue Conferences were loosened from the setting of experiments related to the Search Conference and had a purpose of (re) establishing cooperation between labour market parties; a cooperation which in according to Gustavsen was lost in the turbulent years of the seventies (Gustavsen 2001). Many authors have described the Dialogue Conference as a continuation of the experiences from the Search Conference, which was developed from the socio-technical experiments and from the growing interest for the communication based on the participants' experiences (van Beinum 1996, p. 22).[4] But as we shall see, there are some major differences.

The Dialogue Conferences were also introduced in Sweden in the Swedish national program, Leadership, Organisation and Co-determination (LOM) that lasted from 1985 to 1990, which involved about 150 enterprises and public institutions and 60 researchers. The LOM programme moved from an intra-organisational to an inter-organisational perspective with a focus on a network perspective (Gustavsen 1992, p. 92). The central concepts of the LOM programme were networking, learning and democratic dialogue. In the period from 1983 to 1991 about 450 conferences were organised in the LOM programme. The tendencies in the topics of the conferences were to expand the topics from linear processes inside each enterprise and to expand the view on organisations to external views. This development ran through the programme and the focus shifted from on organisational/enterprise approach to a network approach.

In the nineties conferences developed further, thus in 1994 the Enterprise Development program 2000 (ED 2000) was launched in Norway. The core aim of the program was to initiate new processes of organisational development in Norwegian enterprises across the globalised economy and traditions of labour market co-operation and employee participation. About 100 enterprises joined the program and a larger number was indirectly linked through network relations. About 100 researchers joined the program; thus 40 to 50 people were

---

4 It is however interesting that the main actors in the field of Search Conferences (Emery and Emery) and the main actor in the fields of Dialogue Conferences (Gustavsen) makes seldom reference to each others methodologies with clear descriptions of the mutual learning, inspiration or differentiation across the two types of conferences.

closely involved (Gustavsen and Finne and Oscarsson 2001, p. 14).

In 2001, a new program was started in Norway, namely Value Creation 2010 (VC 2010), its focus was on how to create innovations in networks not through diffusion of knowledge via networks, but by organising new groups of enterprises in networks and create regional partnerships (Gustavsen 2004, p. 29).

In 1996, in Sweden, the so-called Learning Region programme also used the Dialogue Conferences in order to create regional cooperation around learning and development.

5.3.2   Methods

The Dialogue Conference is an integrated part of an Action Research tool used in the above programs, which also consist of a variety of methods like conferences, workshops, project groups, meetings etc. (Gustavsen 1996, p. 20). The conference is founded on active participation in discussions based primarily on group work with short reports in plenary. The conference draws on experiences from the participants in fluid and shifting relations to others. One of the purposes is to create platforms for future cooperation based on future new practises (Gustavsen 2001, p. 22). The conference is not a traditional conference with lectures, long stories told in monologue, mediation through a select group ("managers") or agreed-on general declarations or plans binding to all participants.

The characteristics of the Dialogue Conferences follow from the design criteria and from the ways in which the participants tend to act (Gustavsen 2001, p. 18). Within the development conferences the following "criteria" for dialogue (later called "orientational directives") were:

- Dialogue is based on principles of give and take, not one way communication
- All concerned with the issue under discussion should have the possibilities of participating
- Participants are under obligation to help other participants be active in the dialogue
- All participants have the same status in the dialogue arenas

- Work experience is the point of departure for participation
- Some of the experience the participants have when entering the dialogue must be seen as relevant
- It must be possible for all participants to gain an understanding of the topics under discussion
- An argument can be rejected only after an investigation
- All arguments that are to enter the dialogue must be represented by actors present
- All participants are obliged to accept that other participants may have arguments better that their own
- Among the issues that can make the subject of discussion are the ordinary work roles of the participants – no one is exempt from such a discussion
- The dialogue should be able to integrate a degree of disagreement
- The dialogue should continuously generate decisions that provide a platform for joint action

The Dialogue Conferences were originally (as in the LOM project) an integrated part of communicative instruments used in a "development organisation". The instruments are a mix of conferences, project groups, permanent units, meetings, strategy forums, etc. The rules and stages of the instruments are organized in accordance with principles of participation, extension of development tasks and communication. The conferences consequences are also to establish "internal public spaces of dialogue" in the organisations (Räftegaard 1998, p. 285). Later the conferences changed the focus and somehow also the content (see below).

A Dialogue Conference is established with specific rules that require 1) that the communicative modes are primarily based on dialogues 2) that the discussions are guided by development task requirements; and 3) that the discussions are organized in such a way that all members of the organisation can actively participate on equal footing. The Dialogue Conference requirements were developed so that the three requirements could be met for a large number of participants; between 80 and 90.

The Dialogue Conferences are used as a generic tool in different phases of each project and are part of a sequence of events (start up conference, intermediate conferences and follow up conferences) facilitated under the same principles or requirements. The Dialogue Conference sessions, which are common to all Dialogue Conferences, are based on the following three-stage work procedure (Engelstad 1996, p. 112):

1. Brief instructions provided by the conference managers during the plenary with respect to topic, group composition (homogeneous or heterogeneous) and work procedures
2. Participants spend the majority of each session (the number of sessions vary in accordance with the duration of the conference; normally one of two days) within small groups. All groups engage in the same topics and democratic dialogues are encouraged through specific rules
3. Rapporteurs, selected by the group itself from among the participants make brief presentations in plenary, assisted by visual aids. There are no discussions in plenary except for the final session.

The managers of the conference collaborate with a mixture of researchers and representatives from the companies. They decide about three elements in the conference: the questions for discussion at the conference, the order in which the questions are handled at the conference and the mix of group members (Räftegaard 1998, p. 287).

The Dialogue Conferences are used as a part of a communicative apparatus needed to bring the enterprise through a change cycle. In the early stages, the Dialogue Conferences were closely linked to the concept of "the development organization" with a focus on how cooperation inside the organisation could improve development. The focus changed during the eighties to include external relations to enterprises in networks and shifted in the nineties towards network relations between enterprises as a platform for innovation and later also to regional development. The original point of departure on the work environment and organisational development was, over the two decades, transformed to concepts of enterprise development through innovation, networks and regional partnerships. As such, the Action Research changes its focus from the critical action oriented changes of organisations towards market driven business innovation in networks and regions, but still with a focus on dialogue based democratic development.

5.3.3 Principles and orientations

The Dialogue Conference focuses on enterprise and has developed from an inside out perspective. Even if the conference is used at regional levels, the focus is on improving enterprise development through dialogue. The aim is to generate processes of development for organisations and networks through dialogues and using collaboration to innovate ideas about the future in enterprises and regions. The critical orientation is not at the forefront. The idea coming from the experiments and from the Search Conferences of transforming the enterprise to produce better conditions through democracy and changing the system, job design etc. in a critical orientation towards work organisation and bureaucratic principles has now changed.

Originally, a Dialogue Conference was based on theoretical ideas concerning dialogue and organisational development. Later, the aim was to focus on practise and neglect theories (Gustavsen 2001, p. 19). After the LOM programme, the Dialogue Conference changed to concentrating on discourses and innovation in networks, but with a denial of theoretical driven development of the associated Action Research perspective. Action Research is understood as a practical tool and not theory induced change oriented research. The main idea of developing the methods is one of scale.

> "If there is any meta-idea that can be said to guide this kind of development it is the idea of being able to maximise the number and quality of the ideas that can be created and made real."
> (Gustavsen 2001, p. 24).

The principles of democracy created through Dialogue Conferences have however not changed:

> "If our purpose is to build social relationships that can embody a principle of equality for all participants, the choice that offers itself is democracy, taken as a set of historically validated practices that we can enter into and make our own." (Gustavsen 2001, p. 25).

The Dialogue Conference's use in bigger programmes is often seen as the main success criteria for this methodology; is a question of scale; of producing extended networks, high levels of activity and a variety of ideas. The focus on scale is, from an Action Researcher's point of view, a shift from the more classical Action Researcher position which is closely related to changes in the social context in close collaboration with the participants in the changes: local communities, companies, groups and now to facilitate development and innovation through a variety of actors in greater network settings.

The Action Researcher's role changes in the Dialogue Conferences as the facilitator of changes in relationships or networks across many experiences from different institutions, organisations or regions. The influence of the researcher on the actions in the field changes too, the researcher changes to a facilitator of interactions and innovations across networks (enterprises and regional) and leaves the role of research focus on the internal "development organisation" in a classical way.

5.4   The Future workshop

5.4.1   *History and extent*

The future workshop is a participatory process "which enables people to get together to explore any issue, which concerns them, and to develop creative approaches, which please them. It releases people's resourceful-ness and invites them to take part in creating the kind of future they want." (www.globalideasbank.org.).

The future workshop has been developed and used by Robert Jungk from the late fifties onwards (Jungk and Müllert 1981). In the late sixties initiatives by the public concerning influence and decision making in the political processes from the "bottom up" used the Future Workshop meth-odology to a great extent in Germany, and the idea spread across countries in the following decades. The methodology was used in local communi-ties, organisations and also in technology assessments. In Denmark, a wave of future workshops started in the late eighties. Local communities, grassroots movements, NGO:s and unions introduced the methodology and thousands of people became used to employing the methodology. Since then it has also been integrated into Action Research.

In Denmark, we never experienced an Action Research development related to big programs initiated by collaboration or agreements between labour market organisations and research, as was the case in Norway and Sweden. Although the Danish research was closely linked to, and inspired by, developments in the other Nordic countries, the methods used in Action Research never expanded in an institutionalised manner as they did in Norway and Sweden. Action Research in Denmark is thus on a smaller scale compared to the two other Nordic countries (Aagaard Nielsen 1996a).

However, the Future Workshops and the principles behind them found a platform in Denmark. Researchers, consultancies and students in Denmark have used the methodology in such diverse areas as industrial sociology, local community studies, urban ecology and business development. In relation to demonstrating its use and influence in Action Research two selections can illustrate the influence of the methodology in different settings in Denmark. One was the social experiment called "Industry and Happiness" developed by Kurt Aagaard Nielsen, Birger Steen Nielsen and Peter Olsén (Aagaard Nielsen 1996; Nielsen 1999; Olsén 2003). Another was the development of the methodology "Scenario workshops" developed by the Danish Board of Technology.

5.4.2   Future Workshop Methodology

The future workshop was developed as a critical methodology, which could be employed to prevent disastrous results arising from decisions that could result from people's experience of powerlessness.

> "At present the future is being colonised by a tiny group of people with citizens moving into a future shaped by this elite. I believe that we should not go blindly into this future"
> (quote from Jungk on www.globalideasbank.org).

The future workshop is linked to the theory of Action Research, where local actors or stake holders are involved in the production of future visions, actions and scenario building. The methodology of the workshop is related closely to the methodology developed originally by Jungk and Müllert (1981).

Future Workshops can last from a few hours to two days. The workshop is often arranged off-site at places away from people's daily routines in order to create mentally and physically free spaces for learning.

The future workshop is a mix of three methodologies. First, it is an action-oriented approach where local stake holders are involved in the processes of change and development. Secondly, the workshop is facilitated by specific rules of communication in order to create communication on an equal base and eliminate the influence of power relations in the communication between the participants. Thirdly, the workshop is facilitated through specific rules of visualization and creativity.

The workshop is organized with alternating plenum and group sessions. All statements from the plenum sessions are documented on posters. Also, the groups' work is presented and commented upon by using posters. The workshop has three phases

Phase 1, the *Critique Phase*. The headline of this phase is: *We are consequently negative*. This phase is run as a brainstorming session, following three principles a) short statements, written on posters by the facilitators b) no discussion of statements and c) all statements are allowed. After the brainstorming, the participants are asked to vote for the statements, they find most important. The participants normally have three or five votes each. They can vote with all their votes for one single statement or give votes to several statements.

After the voting, the facilitators count the points and form a list of prioritised themes. The most, four to five, prioritised themes form the basis for four to five visualization groups. After a short period of group work (10 minutes), the groups present their theme (with no use of words) in plenum. The plenum reflects on the visualization and the comments are written on the posters.

Phase 2, the *Utopia Phase*. The headline of this phase is: *Reality is out of function. We are situated in a perfect world, where everything is possible*. This phase starts with a brainstorm that follows the same principles as phase 1. After the voting the facilitators counts the points and makes a list of prioritised themes. Groups are formed around the four to five themes with the highest number of votes. The main purpose of these utopia groups is to develop the utopia and include as many relevant ideas from the brainstorming as possible. After a longer period of group work, the utopias are presented in plenum and discussed with all participants.

Phase 3, the *Realization Phase*. The headline of this phase is: *We keep our wishes and dreams, how can they become reality*. The realization phase can be divided into two parts: First the utopia groups continue their work of bringing the utopia orientations closer to reality. After a longer group work session, the results are presented in plenum and reflected upon. Subsequently, the groups are asked to make agreements to continue the work with the realizations of different plans of action after the workshop and arrangements around the work to be done after the workshop ended.

The outcomes of the workshops were:

- A typed protocol of the posters was handed out to the participants within two weeks after the workshop, including photos from the workshop. The protocol forms the collective platform for further group work, strategies, scenario building, discussion etc. At the same time the individual participant can use it to memorize the context, the ideas and discussions.
- The research team analysed the results of the workshop by focusing on the utopias, their foundation in the criticisms, and their influence on the scenarios and the future events/actions.
- The participants can use the shared knowledge to produce new strategies in their daily routines after the workshop.
- The results can be used in concept development, in general analyses of the sector and in future research and scenario building at the business, industry, organization and society levels.

5.4.3 Future workshop and "Industry and Happiness" – a social experiment

The project "Industry and Happiness" was designed as a social experiment with extended use of Future Workshop methodology. The project ran from 1989 to 1996. The methodologies and intentions of Future Workshops were used for two purposes a) a systematic work with utopian perspectives as done in the Future Workshops was intended to be the driving perspective in the project and b) to develop democratic industrial production loosened from everyday enterprise strategies. As such, the project was designed in contrast to previous action methods and experiments (also the ones mentioned above in this article). (Aagaard Nielsen 1996, p. 277).

The project was run as a two-sided sequence:

1. Future Workshops with workers in the fishing industry (13 women and four men). The headline was here "The future of the fishing industry" with concrete references to the relation between work and life as a referendum for critique, utopian and realization.
2. A series of science workshops (a new invented methodology in the project) where workers, technicians and researchers worked together on ways of improving democracy in industry.

The project produced a vision for a future fishing industry on the basis of utopian visions mixing work and everyday life experiences. The requirements concerning the "Factory of wishes" were of the products (socially useful), of the work (planned democratically), of work routines (based on human rhythms and needs, of knowledge (product and technical development produced in collaboration) and of society (based on a new consensus). The experiment resulted in a new fishing factory in Esbjerg, which however closed down after one year.

As an interesting and visionary experiment it has had a huge influence on Action Research and on debates around the production and implementing of democratic visions in working life (his is because of the researchers' deep documentation and dissemination of the processes and results[5] of the experiments). In particular, the requirements from the future workshop developed by the workers in the fishing industry have created inputs to the discussion about the content of sustainable working life.

The workers' ideas and need for knowledge was the main driver behind the project, which was in line with the idea of democracy, which was present during the whole experiment. The workers, in order to make progress in the process, used the researchers' expert knowledge about organization, fishing technologies, etc. The knowledge was drawn into the project through the science workshops but on the conditions

---

5   Several books and articles have focussed on different aspects of the experiment like sustainability, learning, and the social orientation in work. (Aagaard Nielsen 1996; Nielsen 1999; Olsén 2003)

put forward by the workers. In this way, the project, in its experimental stage too, broke with the Emery and Thorsrud experiments in Norway, which were based on expert driven experimental ideas.

5.4.4   Principles and orientation

Future Workshops have a clear theoretical foundation in Critical Theory centring on the notion of emancipation. Some workshops also have a clear experimental aim where researchers and participants in common take the responsibility for future changes. It is however far from all workshops, which have this close relationship between the workshop dialogue and subsequent action.

The Future Workshop's principle of communication is very restricted in order to establish a dialogue, where power structures that exist outside the workshop are forbidden during the workshop. This opens up the possibility for placing value on all the participants in the workshop experiences, and providing an atmosphere of collaboration on every idea. Few other methodologies intervene as directly in the communicative power structure as the Future Workshop.

The Future Workshop has an explicit focus on a utopian perspective and allows creative and visionary thinking about future emancipation from the ties of everyday life in organizations and home. To work with dreams is often mentioned as a main outcome of participating in the workshop, which far exceeds the material outcome of joining the workshop. As one of the workers in the project described her lessons she learnt from the project: *"Once in a while you must believe in your dreams"* Rigmor Pedersen.[6] Another positive evaluation often seen from the experiences gained from the workshops is that the workshop is, in itself, a learning process about how to deal with utopian ideas and their transformation to action plans.

The democratic orientation, understood as giving voices to participants in Action Research, is like other Action Research method, built into the methodology of Future Workshops. But the Future Workshop has, on top of this, a strict design that also guarantees a democratic process of selecting topics, creating groups and steering the discussions.

---

6   Lecture by Kurt Aagaard Nielsen, Roskilde University, 2005.

All selections of topics and all group formations are based on individual wishes and preferences during the quoting resulting from the quota system or selection through personal preferences.

As mentioned above, the Future Workshop has been used as an extended praxis in Denmark in a lot of different settings. There are, however, only a few examples of experiments resulting from Future Workshops. Nonetheless, there is a growing interest among researchers and students at Roskilde University in employing these methods as a result of a critique of other qualitative methods and their lack of action orientation and connectedness to practical changes in society.

5.4.5   Future Scenario Workshops

The scenario workshop consists of two parts: Qualitative scenarios and a workshop run after the principles of the Future Workshop. The methodology was originally developed by the Danish Board of Technology in a project called "Barriers to urban ecology" (Andersen and Jæger 1999), and has been used in a variety of projects in other EU projects such as Fleximodo (www.cittadellascienza.it/fleximodo). It has also been used within Transport Research in Denmark (Drewes, Nielsen and Jespersen and Hartmann-Petersen 2004).

The idea of combining the principles of action oriented research and future research in the Scenario Workshops was to overcome the problem of "desktop research" in which researchers produce future visions without any links to practice or to contributing to the development of new methodologies including both science and practice. The main challenge was formulated as follows: How is it possible to develop future studies through involvement and dialogue with the actors in the sector? How is it possible to create spaces for learning and the production of visions and actions by involving knowledge produced and created in daily practices?

Qualitative scenarios. "Scenarios try to describe some hypothetical series of occurrences. By using a relatively comprehensive scenario, the analyst is able to get in touch with occurrences and turning points demanding a critical choice. Afterwards these turning points can be examined more or less systematically. But the scenarios should not be used to "prove" anything. They are literary and/or educational aids rather than tools for rigorous analysis. They should be used to stimulate, illustrate and learn, they should provide us with precision and richness in communication and to check details (our transla-tion)" (Selstad 1991, p. 163). *The process of building scenarios begins with the search for driving forces, the forces that influence the outcome(s) of events:* "*Thus, in writing scenarios, we spin myths – old and new – that will be important in the future ... These myths about [obviously if this is as in the original, it should not be changed] scenarios help us come to grips with forces and feelings that would not otherwise exist in concrete form. They help us describe them, envision them, bring them to life – in a way that helps us make use of them.*" (Schwartz 1999, p. 43).

The scenario workshop is run in accordance with the principles of the Futures Workshop as described above, but with one exception. In the workshop, the researchers introduced some scenarios or dimensions of scenarios. This is typically done in the beginning of the realization phase. In some workshops that were developed later, the researchers also asked the utopia groups to draw time lines from the present towards the utopia, and describe events necessary to make the utopia come real by the year 2030.

5.4.6   Principles and orientations

The Scenario Workshop has mainly been used in community develop-ment and planning (urban ecology and transport). The setting around the workshops creates "free spaces" across actors and science and is a fruitful example of the development of science towards transgressivity across science and society. The participants represent different interest groups around the topic: managers, workers, citizens, NGO:s, politi-cal parties, consultancy, research, government, local municipalities, etc.

The workshops create processes of learning among the actors. They create common understandings of the borderlines between consensus and conflicts, but also common metaphors and languages for solving prob-lems in the future. The workshops create free spaces of "communication', where participants can feel free to join the processes of creativity and are not bounded by the restrictions normally induced by relationships to the political and power structures. The methodology is able to produce visions of business and policy strategies as well as input to scenario build-ing and desires concerning acts and events.

The experiences from the workshops are that the borderlines between consensus and conflict are moved through the dialogue and the creative processes that take place within the workshop. The consciousness of more commonly shared utopian horizons might be a good platform for changing directions or orientations and overcoming present conflicts. Furthermore, the dialogue and activities during the workshop decreased the mistrust that was sometimes present before the workshop. Workshops will often break down communicative barriers among different actors because the workshops aim to find a common consensus. However, there is no intention to break fundamental differences in orientation and interest even after the workshop.

5.5 Comparison between the methodologies

The literature about these methodologies, their intensions, reflections among the users, and the evaluation of the results are enormous. It is sometimes difficult to find out exactly what has happened in the contexts where the methods have been used. It is said that the literature around the methods is much more focused on the processes of the methods than on the results or outcomes of the methods (Rasmussen 2004, p. 23). What do the participants feel about the methods, what results have they produced, and so on?

If we are going to select among the catalogue of methods we need to go another way round to find out whether the methodology is in line with the purpose of our Action Research and compare it also to our own resources and normativity. What outcome do we want and what scale of resources do we possess? What relation to theory, practice and change do we claim?

Action Researchers have to different degrees used different methodologies and even used a mix of different methodologies. Tendencies towards more informal/non-formalised uses of methodologies the so-called "open space" approaches to processes of action have expanded. This article has been aware of these tendencies, but still finds it useful to analyse Action Research methodologies along the lines of main typologies developed with specific institutional, theoretical and methodological story lines.

Figure 1 was created with an awareness of the criticism about over generalising an attempt to compare the four methodologies in order to find similarities and differences. Six criteria for comparison as selection criteria for this purpose were selected:

1. Field of problem
2. Theory
3. Communicative orientation
4. Future orientation
5. Democratic orientation
6. Extend and use

The figure gives an overview of the main similarities and differences in the methodologies and thus gives an overview of the content of this article.

The figure is shown on the opposite page.

5.6 Conclusion

This Chapter has presented and compared three of the most widely used methods in Action Research during the last 40 years in three Scandinavian countries namely Norway, Sweden and Denmark: The Search Conference (mainly in Norway), the Dialogue Conference (in Sweden and Norway) and the Future and Scenario Workshop (mainly in Denmark).

The comparison has focused on criteria like: Field of problem, Theory, Communicative orientation, Future orientation, Democratic orientation and Extend and use.

In relation to some of the main questions posed in this book, the result of the analysis can be stated as follows:

How can theory and practice be integrated in Action Research? Will a focus on the practical usefulness of Action Research lead to a neglect of theoretical knowledge? The Chapter shows that in the Scandinavian methodologies, theory and practice in different ways and to different extents are integrated. Where the Search Conferences and the Future workshops integrate elements from Critical Theory, the Dialogue Conferences, on

	Search Conferences	Dialogue Conferences	Future Experimental Workshops	Future Scenario Workshops
Field of problem	Early versions: Work organisation Experimental changes Later versions: Processes of democratic development in organizations, communities etc.	Early versions: Support to democratic development of "development organisation" Later versions: Development of innovative net-works of enter-prises Regional development	Reaction towards the expert driven colonialisation of society Development from "bottom up"	Alternative future studies and scenario methods by involving Actors as opposed to the expert driven future studies
Theory	Theories of democratic dialogue, ecological systems and experimental development	Early versions: Theories of dialogue and democracy Later versions: Non theoretical focus (focus on practice) Implicit theory: discourses learning networks innovation regions	Critical Theory Emancipation Experiments	Actor involvement Future studies Scenario methods Backcasting
Communi-cative orientation	Theories of dialogue	Theories of discourses	Theories of equal communication	Theories of equal communication
Future orientation	Radical changes through experiments Strong future orientation	Incremental changes through the "development orga-nization" or innovative network alliances	Radical changes formed through utopian thinking	Gradually changes stimulated by scenario development and utopian thinking
Democratic orientation	Democratic develop-ment facilitated by research	Democratic develop-ment facilitated by research	Democratic develop-ment facilitated by workers and stimulated by research	Democratic develop-ment facilitated by research
Extend and use	Social experiments Communities Organizations	Enterprise innovation Enterprises in networks Enterprises in regions	Social experiments Communities Organisations	Actor involvement in future studies Communities Organizations

Figure 5.1. Comparing Action Research Methodologies

the other hand, have moved towards a non-theoretical focus, although they include elements of implicit theoretical inspiration. The Chapter also illustrates that the discussion about theory – whether it is a choice or not- seems fruitful in order to gain a deeper understanding of the epistemology of different actions research approaches and the norma-tivity of their point of departure.

The comparison results also in a denial that the practical useful-ness will neglect theoretical knowledge as is often stated as a critique of Action Research. The theoretical awareness of Action Research is an integrated part of the discipline and its history although theory in Action Research has a quite different position compared to the deduc-tive use of theory in other areas of social science. In Action Research, theory is an element in the research processes in line with processes of abductive reflections between theory and the empirical field in the same way as in other areas of qualitative social sciences.

Is the ambition of Action Research to produce generalised knowledge? The answer is both no and yes. It always depends on which level of gen-eralised knowledge the science (scientists) want to produce, and the level it is produced at. The researcher selects hers/his level of gener-alisation whether empirical, analytical or theoretical generalisations. Against the background of the methodologies analysed in this article, all methodologies select at least to produce local useful knowledge in the first run. But the ambition of producing more generalised knowledge is also in the ambitions of the methodologies, but in different ways. The social experiments related both to Search Conferences and Future Workshops clearly includes an ambition of transferring the knowledge to other social contexts, an ambition of external validity of their results and of analytical generalisation. The latest version of the Dialogue Conferences, on the other hand, seem to neglect this ambition with the focus only on the practical and context bound knowledge production.

Another type of generalisation is bound into the methodologies. All four methodologies that have been selected have established specific sets of rules and have ambitions to make these methodologies transferable to other Action Research projects. This is an ambition of external valida-tion and thus generalisation, not on the results of the Action Research project, but on the usefulness of the methodology. This level of gener-alisation about the methodology is a criterion in front in several of the selected methodologies, with the most explicit formulation in the latest versions of the Dialogue Conference, where the question of the extent and scale of the conferences is a main criterion of success.

How should Action Research be organised and will the Mode II knowledge production take over? Action Research is produced in relations with the stake holders and Action Research can fruitfully be analysed in the line of criteria of Mode II knowledge production. Action Research has its roots in science, but has also to great extent been transferred outside the Universities.

The four methodologies analysed here have a mixed history of institutional development in Universities, R&D institutions related to the Working Life and private consultancy. In Sweden and Norway, R&D institutions related to Working Life have been the main users of the methodologies. In Denmark, where these R&D institutions in Working life never developed, the institutional platform for Action Research has been Danish Board of Technology and Roskilde University, both institutions having long traditions of transdisciplinarity.

References

Asch, S. (1952) *Social Psykologi*. Englewood Cliffs, N.J: Prentice-Hall.

van Beinum, H. (1996) "Om aktionsforskningens udvikling i Europa, et perspektiv" in *Aktionsforskning: medarbejderindflydelse på forskning og udvikling i arbejdsmiljøet*, Nielsen, K. Aagaard and Vogelius, P. (eds.), Copenhagen: Arbejdsmiljøfondet.

Drewes Nielsen, L. and Gjesing Hansen, L. (1997) "Involving Citizens in Sustainable Development: Scenario Workshop on Sustainable Mobility", *Journal of Advanced Transportation*, Vol. 31, No. 2, 1997, pp. 159–170.

Drewes Nielsen, L. and Jespersen, P. H. (2003) "The Use of Action Research Methods in Scenario Construction", *Sevilla Workshop, Institute for Prospective Technologies: EU Joint Research Centres (IPTS), May 2003*.

Drewes Nielsen, L., Jespersen, P. Homann and Hartmann-Pedersen, K. (2004) "Future Workshops on Freight Transport: a Methodology for Involvement", *World Transport Politics & Practise*, Vol. 10.

Emery, F. E. and Thorsrud, E. (1976) *Democracy at work*, Leiden: Martinus Nijhoff.

Emery, M. (1999) *Searching. The Theory and practice of making cultural change*, Volume 4, (Dialogues on Work and Innovation), Amsterdam: John Benjamins Publishing.

Emery, M. and Purser, R. (1996) *The Search Conference: A Powerful Method for Planned Organisational Change and Community Action*, San Francisco: Jossey Bass.

Engelstad, P. H. (1996) "The Development Organization as Communicative Instrumentation: Experiences from Karlstad program" in *Beyond Theory: Changing Organization through Participation,* Toulmin, S. and Gustavsen, B. (eds.), Amsterdam: John Benjamin Publishing.

Fleximodo: www.cittadellascienza.it/fleximodo

Gustavsen, B. (1990) *Strategier for utvikling av arbeidslivet,* Oslo: TANO.

– (1992) *Dialogue and Development Action Research and the Restructuring of Working Life,* Stockholm: The Swedish Center for Working Life.

– (1996) "Development and the Social Sciences. An uneasy relationship" in *Beyond Theory: Changing Organization through Participation,* Toulmin, S. and Gustavsen, B. (eds.), Amsterdam: John Benjamin Publishing.

– (2001) "Theory and Practice: the Mediating Discourse" in *Handbook in Action Research,* Reason, P. and Bradbury, H. (eds.), London: Sage.

– (2004) "Participation and local organisation" in *Action Research in Workplace Innovation and Regional Development,* Fricke, W. and Totterdill, P. (eds.), (Dialogues on Work and Innovation, Vol. 15), Amsterdam: John Benjamins Publishing.

Gustavsen, B. and Engelstad, P. H. (1986) "The design of conferences and the Evolving Role of Democratic Dialogue in Changing Working Life", *Human Relations* Vol. 39, No. 2, pp. 101–116.

Gustavsen, B., Finne, H. and Oscarsson, B. (2001) *Creating Connectedness. The role of social research in innovation policy,* (Dialogues on Work and Innovation), Amsterdam: John Benjamins Publishing.

Jungk, R. and Müllert, N. R. (1981) *Zukunftswerkstätten, Wege zur Wiederbelebung der Demokratie* (Danish version) (1984) *Håndbog i Fremtidsværksteder,* København: Politisk Revy) (English version: *Future workshops: How to create desirable futures,* London: Institute for Social Inventions).

Nielsen K. Aagaard. (1996a) "Aktionsforskning i Denmark" in *Aktionsforskning: medarbejderindflydelse på forskning og udvikling i arbejdsmiljøet,* Nielsen, K. Aagaard and Vogelius, P. (eds.), Copenhagen: Arbejdsmiljøfondet.

– (1996b) *Arbejdets sociale orientering,* Copenhagen: Forlaget Sociologi.

Nielsen, B. Steen, Nielsen, K. Aagaard and Olsén, P. (1999) *Demokrati som læreprocess,* Roskilde: Roskilde Universitetsforlag.

Olsén, P., Nielsen, B. Steeen and Nielsen, K. Aagaard (2003) *Demokrati og Bæredygtighed. Social fantasi og samfundsmæssig rigdomsproduktion,* Roskilde: Roskilde Universitetsforlag.

Pålshaugen, Ø. (1992) "Aksjonsforskning: En nyttig vitenskap?" *Tidsskrift for samfunnsforskning,* No. 33, pp. 231–251.

– (1998): *The end of organization Theory?* (Dialogues on Work and Innovation), Amsterdam: John Benjamins Publishing.

Rasmussen, L. B. (2004) "Action Research – Scandinavian experiences" in *AI & Society,* Vol. 18.

Reason, P. and Bradbury, H. (2001) *Handbook in Action Research,* London: Sage.

Räftegaard, C. (1998) *Pratet som demokratisk verktyg. Om möjligheten till en kommunikativ demokrati,* Hedemora: Gidlunds.

Schwartz, P. (1999) *The Art of the Long View. Planning for the Future in an Uncertain World,* London: John Wiley

Selstad, T. (1991) *Med krystallkule og computer. Prognoser og scenarier i samfunnsplanleggingen,* Oslo: Universitetsforlaget.

http://www.audiencedialogue.org/books.html

www.peopleincharge.org

www.ccnr.net/searchconf

http://www.futuresearch.net/the_method/overview/history_theory.cfm

EWA GUNNARSSON[1]

6. The Snake and the Apple in the Common Paradise

Challenging the balance between surface and depth in qualifying Action Research and feminist research on a common arena

Can contemporary feminist research be used as a critical potential for qualifying contemporary Action Research and vice versa? Firstly, are there common epistemological and ontological grounds in relation to knowledge production for developing a qualifying discussion for both approaches? Secondly, what aspects of knowledge production and dilemmas in the two approaches can be used to increase scientific "robustness"?[2] These are the key questions that I will unfold in this Chapter and to which I will give some contributions.

Conceptual models and qualitative methods developed within the field of gender and feminist research that focus reflexive research processes generally, the researcher – participant relation and the researcher subjectivity are discussed as means of achieving an increased robustness in Action Research. Developing an increased articulation and contextualisation in incorporating gender research on a meso-micro level, in the tension between structure and agency, is seen as a tool for qualifying

---

1   I gratefully acknowledge the critical comments and suggestions of Ulrika Björk, Stine Hee Pedersen, Lennart Svensson, Susanne Andersson, Inga-Britt Drejhammar and Hanna Westberg. A special thanks to Keith Pringle for his suggestions to improve the English language.

2   The concepts robustness and robust knowledge are used with reference to Nowotny, Scott and Gibbons (2001) discussion on validity.

Action Research. On the other hand to incorporate the idea of a common praxis with a more extended Interactive Research process with the participants could qualify gender and feminist research in a new way.

6.1. The common Nordic – and in particular the Swedish – arena.

The Nordic context is the main frame for the discussions and research referred to in this Chapter; my own research and lived experience within the field of working life studied from a feminist perspective from the eighties until today is another situating frame.[3] In this introduction I will give a short background to what I see as interesting parallel developments between gender and feminist research and Action Research. I will relate it to the introduction and Chapter 2 in the anthology but also to the discussion on validity or knowledge robustness that Eikeland develops in Chapter 8. I find the distinction that Eikeland makes between validity *of* and *in* science particularly interesting. Looking back the common development traits between the two traditions are seldom emerging at the same time but could be used as a ground for a joint critical discussion. I see two major general discussions:

– Firstly, the question of integration or separation in relation to mainstream science. This is a tactic and strategic discussion that gender and feminist researchers have struggled with since the beginning of the eighties with shifting standpoints in relation to historical phase, the type of research environment, within policy driven research environments or within the academy, and depending on the academic discipline. The integration process of gender and feminist research into mainstream science could therefore be characterized as an uneven and complex development process.

– Secondly, the dilemmas of scientific validity in multidisciplinary policy driven research environments and in the role that gender and feminist research has played in the political gender equity discourse in society. Dilemmas that have parallels, as I see it, to Action Research

---

3   My own history is a combined experience from; policy driven research environments outside the academy, development projects focusing gender and from centres for gender studies within the academy.

in relation to the pressures from an increased Mode II research. These parallels could serve as a common ground for a critical discussion and development of an extended validity concept in science. I will also argue for the necessity to develop a validity concept that embodies a dimension of an articulated *"external"* validity. The contribution by Nowotny, Scott and Gibbons (2004) on achieving social robustness through contextualisation is here interesting and could be linked to feminist discussions (see p. 129).

Gender and feminist researchers have argued for a need to carry out research in separate research environments, both outside and within academy. Within the academy this has been a claim since the eighties. The argument behind this claim was the need to develop the knowledge of the "other" (women's experiences and interests) without being included and subordinated in mainstream science. Today a majority of gender and feminist researchers would argue that both separate research environments are needed as well as an integration in mainstream science.

There would have been no gender studies or research without feminism as a driving force. But whereas gender studies or research is a field of knowledge and research, feminism is both a political movement and a field of knowledge and research, the latter being called feminist research or feminist theory. Gender studies or research is a generic term for the field as a whole, including a large range of orientations.[4] [5] I will in this chapter use the concept gender research for the whole field and the concept feminist research for the stream within the field of gender research

---

4   For an overview of the field of gender research see The Swedish Research Council's report *Gender research: Questions, conditions and challenges* (Thurén, 2003) or the English short version; *Gender Studies: A Summary from The Swedish Research Council's Committee on Gender Research* (2005).

5   Some common elements upon which the different orientations within gender research can agree are for example; The theoretical frame incorporates a theory about the gender order in society. Often but not by definition, relations of power in the gender order are expressed through a male superordination and a female subordination on a structural level. The relations of power between the sexes are central for understanding gender on all analytical levels. Gender is created in a continuous social and cultural construction process in which the individual, organisational and societal levels interact with each other. Science is also permeated by the gender order and therefore a critical perspective on gender-blindness in theories is developed. The actual gender order is often automatically reproduced due to the fact that the gap between discourses and practices is not problematised (Thurén, 2003, *my translation*)

that also emphasizes the need for a normative change and action. In relation to Action or Interactive Research what will then be the best corresponding concept to use? I find both concepts attractive but in different ways. Spontaneously, Action Research seems the best alternative due to its more outspoken idea of a normative change and action. On the other hand, in the Swedish tradition it is historically strongly linked to a research stream of doing research "for" practitioners instead of co-researching (Svensson, 2002) In the feminist policy driven research stream during the eighties the element of co-research with participants had a stronger emphasis than the Action Research tradition had at the same time. Maybe that was partly the reason why we did not name it feminist Action Research. I will here use the concept Action Research, but stressing the meaning of co-research with participants instead of doing research for participants. Changes of names often reflect a deeper conceptual change in meanings and research focus[6]

A strong argument in gender research during the eighties was that men's experiences, interests and privilege of interpretation was reflected more or less implicitly in most theories, models and methods. This is often referred to as the privilege of the male norm in science and politics. This led to a deconstruction of old concepts and methods and construction of new concepts and models. Aino Saarinen (1989) describes these phases from the late seventies as a phase of deconstruction, followed by a phase of construction and then by the end of the eighties a phase of the intervention project (or phase of integration). During the phase of deconstruction, the main aim was to make visible how women were made invisible and marginalised within science. In the construction phase, women's own privilege of interpretation and their creation of new concepts based on women's experience and every-day life were put in focus. In the phase of integration, gender is then seen as a basic structuring dimension in society including the relation between women and men.

6.1.1   *A view from somewhere*

As a researcher in a policy-driven research organisation with a focus on

---

6   See also the overview of different development streams in Action Research in this book Chapter 2 by Aagaard Nielsen and Svensson.

working life and democracy during the eighties – the Swedish Center for Working Life – and part of the programme entitled Women's Working Lives[7], I could say that at that time I was a "twin-sister" to the male (rarely female) Action Researchers there. However, we did not name it as Action Research, but as women studies or feminist research with the same vision of creating a more robust knowledge by including women's experiences in science. We also shared the critical epistemological position in relation to the dominant Western tradition on knowledge production based on the experiences and interests of a particular group of privileged men (see part 6.2 in this Chapter).

The work we did was in many respects very similar to Action Research in the close and interactive relation with participants, local unions etc. with a main focus, though, on work-life conditions in female-dominated branches and so called "low skilled" professions. But there was very little in-depth theoretical or methodological discussion between the Action Researchers and the feminist researchers. One explanation is the tension at that time between feminist and Marxist traditions, popularly expressed as class first and then if necessary gender.

Reflecting back, you could say that the commonly experienced subordination in society, felt by the feminist researchers as well as the participants created a specific consciousness about power relations in general and particularly between the researcher and the participant. In this sense, I think feminist research was closer to the current co-research idea than Action Research at that time. Academic research practices were heavily criticised for being hierarchical, privileging men and therefore undemocratic. A question in focus was: how to achieve a close, interactive and non-hierarchical interview situation, based on a subject – subject relation between the researcher and the participant? A new methodological stream emerged that focused the interview situation and this in turn led to new concepts like the *"solidaristic interview"* by Karen Davies and Johanna Esseveld (1989). Ann Oakley (1981) used the concept *"non hierarchical interview"*. The extensive Nordic bulk of methodological work during the eighties and in the beginning of the nineties in gender research is in many respects still useful and could serve as a

---

7 For an overview of the research done in the programme see – *Women's Working Lives: Visions and research for a better working life* (Baude et al. 1987).

source of inspiration for today' s feminist and Action Researchers.

The need for creating a more "democratic" knowledge production, including women in science as well as women's experiences and interests in general, and thereby achieving a normative change in science, has since the beginning of gender and feminist research been a "double" aim. Closely related to these aspirations of inclusion and democracy is the idea that this will result in an increased validity both *of* and *in* science, to use Eikeland's typology (see Chapter 8). In the next part I will use the work of some feminist philosophers to show how these arguments for inclusion and democracy relate to a critical feminist position to traditional Western science. A position, with its similarities to the Action Research position, offers a challenging ground for both traditions to talk to each other.

6.2. Transforming the boundaries of the privileged and limited arena for knowledge production

Feminist philosophers like Elizabeth Kamarck Minnich (1990) have strongly inspired feminist researchers with a democratic and liberating aspiration.[8] In her book *Transforming Knowledge* she criticizes the dominant Western tradition and summarizes its *"root problem"* in the following way:

> "The problem we still have today in thinking well about the rich diversity of humankind is expressed by the observation that, at the beginning of the dominant Western tradition, a particular group of privileged men took themselves to be the inclusive term or kind, the norm, and the ideal for all, a 'mistaking' that is locked into our thinking primarily in the form of faulty generalizations, circular reasoning, mystified concepts that results from the former errors, and the partial (in both senses of the term) knowledge that frames such concepts." (Minnich, 1990, p. 2)

Partial knowledge that is not recognized as such, Minnich writes, but

---

8 See also Sandra Harding (1987 and 1991). For an overview of critical feminist contributions see Evelyn Fox Keller and Helen E. Longino (1996).

sets the standards for "sound" knowledge. In my view, Minnich's critical position could serve as a good point of departure for a common epistemological discussion between feminist research traditions and Action Research traditions. It is in the vision around change, democracy and liberating research practices and processes, by including women's and the participant's experiences in science that these two traditions meet each other. From different entrances both traditions emphasize the necessity to move from a partial *"exclusive limited arena"* for knowledge production to an *"inclusive extended arena"* for knowledge production. These aspirations also point at a common need for an *"extended"* conceptualisation of validity in relation to knowledge production (see also the discussion by Eikeland in Chapter 8).

Both feminist research and Action Research problemize social power relations. Feminist research does it by opening up this exclusive space to include women, women's experiences and everyday life and practices, so as to create a more objective (socially robust) and general knowledge. In the Action Research perspective, the argument is that the equal relations between participants and researchers can, through a common praxis, generate a qualitatively different and more "democratic" knowledge that ideally promotes a liberating process for the people involved. Knowledge is also here understood as having its material roots in the participants' and researchers' everyday practices. With respect to the roots of knowledge there are strong similarities between the two traditions.[9] On the other hand, the Action Research perspective has, to a much higher extent than gender and feminist research, stressed the necessity to also involve the participants in a reflexive research process, from the initial phase of formulating the problem, co-researching and analysing to the final distribution of knowledge To incorporate the idea of a "common praxis" and the benefits from knowledge produced in an Interactive Research process in gender and feminist research could qualify it in a

---

9   The work done by Dorothy Smith on a feminist sociological method with its point of departure in women's everyday life and the concept "relations of ruling" has informed many Nordic feminist researchers (Smith, 1987). In her new book *Institutional Ethnography: A sociology for people* (Smith, 2005) she develops an inquiry for people incorporating an alternative understanding of experience as dialogue. She then comes closer to the Action Research approach than in earlier work.

new way.[10] The focus though on a too unproblemised gender neutral "common praxis" has from a feminist standpoint been heavily criticised for neglecting and marginalising the impact of gender in a more serious way (see for example Maguire, 2002).

The feminist perspective could be used by Action Research as a qualifying potential for transcending the boundaries of a too unarticulated and unproblemised "common praxis" and make visible more in-depth social power relations other than in the researcher – participant relation. As a constant dimension that cuts into the very marrow of every day life experiences and practices for both researchers and participants gender has to be problemize as such. Here I see a key issue in the discussion with Action Researchers: namely, how to find a balance between surface and depth, commonalities and differences between and within categories, without drowning in a paralysing relativism? Leaving gender out though is not an option; and neither is leaving the interaction with participants out.

The Snake and the Apple in the common paradise is in the title used as a metaphor to illustrate the dilemma between the "common and the diverse" or expressed as the dilemma of "balancing between surface and depth" that both traditions have to solve but from different entrances. For feminist research the common is representing the snake and for Action Research social power dimensions like gender, class, ethnicity and sexuality becomes the snake. The question is: Could both traditions incorporate and merge in theory and praxis, in various ways both the benefits of a "common praxis" and at the same time the integration of the knowledge of strong social divisions such as gender? Or is the solution to be found in a partly shared common paradise and a necessary partly separate paradise of one's own?

To solve the problem of a missing gender perspective by the method of *"adding women and stir"*, as Minnich (1990) formulates it, is therefore not good enough to strengthen the gender perspective in Action Research. This is because it remains within a system built on principles of exclusion and characterized by the conceptual errors those principles necessitate and perpetuate (Minnich, 1990). Adding the gender dimen-

---

10 Lisa Heldke (1989) labels this the "co-responsible option" (i.e. a common responsibility for the inquiry) and she stresses the similarities between the epistemological projects of John Dewey and Evelyn Fox Keller.

sion is a transformation that creates more upheaval than this, from the beginning leading to consequences around formulating the research question and the field throughout the whole research process. It stirs up questions about the objectivity of science; and it questions the seductive and comfortable position in the dominant western tradition of seeing the researcher as neutral, free from values, bodies and emotions. To bring the dimension of gender into discussions of subjectivity and the researcher's practices creates a better ground to produce a less subjective and more objective knowledge production (Skeggs, 2002).

A critical potential in the gender and feminist perspective lies in its potential to act as a *"sensitizing and consciousness raising tool"*, making different forms of power relations visible not only in relation to gender but also in relation to class, ethnicity and sexuality for example. These are social power relations that are embedded and active not only in the research field and in interactive reflexive research processes but are also embedded and normative within the researchers and participants themselves and in the relations between them. Here the new stream within gender research: *Critical Studies on Men* is contributing in a fruitful and challenging way in naming men as men and as such being explicitly gendered (see for example Hearn, 2002).

6.2.1   The unequal dichotomy researcher – practitioner[11]

The unarticulated dichotomy researcher – practitioner in Action Research creates a dilemma, not only from a gender perspective as mentioned earlier. The dichotomy disguises important relations of power but is also an unequal dichotomy in other ways. It is associated with philosophers like Aristotle and Kant (Lloyd, 1984) who systemized the existing dichotomous thinking into a distinction between theoretical and practical reason that is questionable in our knowledge society. It relates to the dichotomy of head and hand and a traditional view of industrial work and crafts versus more "intellectual" work. Both categories are too broad and unarticulated, as I see it. The dichotomy reproduces and reflects the separation between theory and practice that Action Research argues

---

11 I use the concept participants unless I am not referring directly to work by Action Research using the concept practitioner.

must be avoided. In my own work with participants like claims adjusters, technical advisers and ICT consultants they felt very uncomfortable being called practitioners and could not easily identify themselves with that category. Using the dichotomy researcher – practitioner still reflects a normative privilege of interpretation in favour of the researcher. A privilege, often given to the researcher by the practitioners, that reflects the status of science in our society. The researcher is also a "researcher practitioner or participant", with practices grounded in our society and in the everyday-life we all live; and cannot be dealt with as a detached part of it. See also the related discussion in Eva Amundsdotter's Chapter 11 and Eikeland's Chapter 8 in this book.

Eikeland argues that:

"The relationship between research and practice is hardly a relationship between complementary parts within a division of labour any more than thinking and acting is ... Such a division contributes to the invalidation of knowledge, and to host difficulties in the production, transfer, and communication of knowledge."
(Eikeland, Chapter 8).

His way of solving the problem is to compare it to the master – apprentice relationship where he sees this relationship as a dynamic relationship based on sharing, because it is designed to make the apprentice into a master, where both researchers and participants incorporate both positions. So far I agree, but the way the conceptualisation master – apprentice has been used in practice it is not good enough as I as a feminist researcher see it. From a feminist perspective the conceptualisation of master – apprentice has been strongly criticised for disguising social power relations such as gender but also differences within the category of class. The use in practise of master – apprentice is closely linked to the history of male guilds and therefore permeated by a male norm. The conceptualisation of master – apprentice has been deconstructed during the eighties by many feminists doing research on qualifications and skills. In my own work this has been problemized both in relation to female dominated "unskilled work" but also in relation to the hierarchy between skilled and unskilled male industrial workers. The research we did showed clearly that the underlying norm in "skilled and qualified" was a "qualified" male industrial worker, in occupations strongly incorporating a male guild tradition. A norm that marginalised skills and qualifications in female dominated occupations (Gunnarsson, 1994). This was also shown when different work evaluation systems were deconstructed in the nineties. I cannot suggest a fruitful way to transcend the stereotypical and hierarchical thinking embedded in the researcher – practitioner dichotomy, but I see it as a necessary focus for a broad discussion where also different categories of participants have to be involved. However, if a dichotomy has to be used, the new concepts must reflect a more equal value and position in terms of both knowledge contribution and power relations.

Dichotomisation reflects a strong tradition in science that I find problematic. Due to its tradition of questioning stereotypical dichotomies like, reason and emotion, rational and irrational, social and biology, strength and weakness, etc, gender research could contribute to make visible the limitations of dichotomies.[12] Dichotomies could be fruitful as *"thought positions"* highlighting some important elements but they are very limited as analytical tools in practice and tend to reproduce old and new stereotypes (Gunnarsson, 1994). See also the related discussion under the heading *Between closeness and distance (p. 136)*. Fortunately, by virtue of their variability, real life and practice constantly challenge and transcend our dichotomies.

6.2.2   *Generalisation – contextualisation as a questioning companion*

If women's common experience and lived everyday life was a central cornerstone in gender and feminist research as in the feminist standpoint position that dominated in the Nordic countries during the eighties, the problem of generalisation has today become an *"inseparable questioning companion"*. Women's "common" experience and interest has been discussed since the eighties among feminist researchers particularly in relation to other powerful social dimensions such as class, ethnicity and sexuality. Expressed in another way; how strong is the gender dimen-

---

12 For an overview of how different philosophers and philosophical traditions have used dichotomies, see The Man of Reason by Genevieve Lloyd (1984). At the same time as dichotomies has been questioned within Western philosophy the interest for emotions and feelings has increased (Morwenna Griffiths, 1988 and Ulrika Björk, 2005).

sion in different local contexts? The discussions in gender research have from the eighties shifted grounds from seeing the category of women and men as two homogeneous categories to a discussion around differences within the categories and also seeing them as relational. This discussion is today expressed in the current development of theories on intersectionality, incorporating the intersection of gender with other major social dimensions such as class, ethnicity, age and sexuality.[13]

An interesting contribution is given by Britt-Marie Thurén (1996) in her way of developing new analytical and comparative tools for analysing the gender dimension. She proposes three concepts that differentiate between aspects of gendering: *force, scope and hierarchy. Force* deals with the importance of gender. Is gender-governed behaviour well defined? Are there sanctions for those who break the gendered patterns of behaviour? *Scope* deals with the number of areas that are affected by gendering (divisions of labour, life styles, interests, body dynamics, etc). *Hierarchy* has to do with power and assessment of value. Is one gender more powerful or considered more valuable than another? These concepts are useful to contextualise and ground gender in relation to class, ethnicity and sexuality and thereby achieve a more robust knowledge. This can be associated to the argumentation by Nowotny, Scott and Gibbons who stress that: *The more strongly contextualized a scientific field or research domain is the more socially robust is the knowledge it is like to produce* (Nowotny, Scott and Gibbons, 2004 p. 167). They understand social robustness as a relational and not a relativistic or absolute idea and add therefore a special quality in grounding and extending the conceptualisation of validity in going beyond the relativistic post-modern idea about "situated knowledge" (Harraway, 1991).[14]

In the next part I will return to the Nordic arena and present some structural concepts that have influenced Nordic gender research since the eighties. These concepts could be seen as important contextualising frames that increase robustness in the research process. As structural frames they are important to highlight today when gender structures are disguised in the strong discourse of individualisation in society.

---

13 Intersectionality is by no means a new discussion. A classical article is Doing Difference, by Candace West and Sarah Fenstermaker 1995, where they develop an understanding of the intersection of gender, class and race.

14 An interesting postmodern discussion on validity is presented by Scheurich (1997).

6.2.3   The Nordic context as local and situated

To understand why, how and what type of knowledge production is found within the gender and feminist research field of the Nordic countries, it is necessary to highlight some important "local frames" that have informed the research field in Scandinavia. The strong Nordic political discourse on gender equity in society, stressing the necessity for both women and men to contribute and take part in paid work as well as in unpaid care and household work has influenced gender and feminist research in two major ways:

Firstly, it has led to a strong research tradition since the eighties until today, particularly in Norway and Sweden, of so called policy-driven research stressing the necessity for a close link between researchers, different political actors and practitioners. This policy driven *"demand based research"* has been to a large extent financed by the state through different research organisations and funds and have had a more outspoken requirement of "usefulness" than traditional academic research. In a way this demand based research struggles with similar validity problems as Action Research does when linked to Mode II research. On the other hand it has probably played a decisive role for the access we have had to work places and for the development of a unique Nordic bulk of empirical gender and feminist research with high social robustness in work life research.

The strong discourse of gender equity in combination with the policy driven research in the Nordic countries has also forced gender and feminist researchers to defend the scientific standards of their work in the public political arena. Gender and feminist researchers has since a long time been right in the middle of the transformation that Nowotnoy, Scott and Gibbons describe when arguing that: … *the great conceptual, and organizational, categories of the modern world – state, market, culture and science – have become highly permeable, even transgressive. They are ceasing to be recognizable distinct domains. As a result, common sense distinctions between the "internal" and the "external" are becoming increasingly problematic, a change which has radical implications for demarcations between science and non-science and for notions of professional identity and scientific expertise* (Nowotny, Scott and Gibbons, 2004, p. 166). This transformation stresses by consequence the need for an extended conceptualisation of traditional academic validity. This position could be discussed as a critical potential for both action and feminist research.

Secondly, a majority of Nordic women, including also female research-ers, have the experience in their everyday lives to combine reproductive and productive work, as well as being in general the main person respon-sible for solving everyday problems when conflicting requirements from the productive and the reproductive spheres occur. This lived reality of shifting between the requirements from the productive and the repro-ductive sphere has led to a unique Nordic development of theories, con-cepts and methods in research to understand the relation between the two spheres and to make a broader life context visible in research.

I will here present some structural concepts that embody a more holistic view in incorporating the relation between the productive and the reproductive sphere. Furthermore, they are contributions that in different ways are trying to catch and problemize the transformation between the general and the local level. The concepts can be used as *"reflexive gender reminders"* in general and as methodological tools in a reflexive research process to increase gender robustness in research.

One of the most radical theoretical contributions during the eight-ies that had a strong influence on the development on contemporary Nordic research was the coining of the concept *"responsible* or *care ration-ality"* by the Norwegian researchers Bjørg Aase Sørensen (1982), Hildur Ve (1994) and Kari Waerness (1984). This development of Weber's concept of rationality made women's paid work with children, elderly and sick people visible in a new way as well as unpaid care work. The focus on care work also made visible important forms of emotion work and opened up for an expansion of the traditional work concept. The embedded aspect of power in the concept gave a basis for understand-ing gendered meanings in relation to different forms of rationality in society. Using the concept of rationality, women were seen as rational beings with agency, defining rational goals both in paid and unpaid work, in opposition to the earlier more passive sex-role theory. Today, rationality has been contextualised in different ways incorporating both positions and professional differences (Gunnarsson, 1998).

Another informing concept is the *"Gender Contract"* that has been coined by Nordic researchers to describe the sex-segregated division of labour (paid as well as unpaid). Here, aspects of power and negotia-tions are important elements. The idea of the concept is to highlight different structural and normative frames that are restricting women's (and men's) space of action. Gender contracts are expressed on different levels: on an overall structural level in society in the relation between paid and unpaid work; at the work-place, in the vertical, horizontal and time sex-segregation; and within the family expressed as a segregation in the allocation of work tasks (Haavind, 1985). Using indicators of sex-segregation in the labour market, as well as the degree to which care for children and elderly persons is solved within the enlarged family, Gunnel Forsberg (1998 and 2006) makes visible regional variations in gender contracts in Sweden. These regional variations in gender contracts provide informative "locally situated" frames for understanding limits and variations of spaces of action for women and men.

Finally I will mention a concept created by Hanne Haavind (1985) the so-called *"relative subordination of women"*. A concept highlighting a generally accepted normative and structural difference between women and men in society, commonly illustrated by the example of giving an "accepted smaller" but significantly lower salary for women doing the same work as men. The concept of relative subordination could serve as a reflexive gender reminder along the research process for making sometimes self-evident power relations between women and men more visible.

6.3 Is there a distinctive feminist method of inquiry?

A strong argument in gender and feminist research during the eighties was, as mentioned before, that a male norm in science was more or less explicitly reflected in theories, models, concepts and methods. This led to a deconstruction of many traditional concepts and models followed by a construction of new ones. A dilemma in practice when new concepts and models are created, where I see a parallel for Action Research, is to incorporate the new knowledge of "the other" into mainstream knowledge without *getting lost in translation*. During the eighties I was involved in policy driven research on making skills and qualifications visible in female dominated so called low skilled occupations. The research we did together with participants, in this case secretaries and assistants, resulted in new knowledge and new concepts. We then found ourselves in the dilemma of not being able to negotiate these concepts in relation to existing qualification models and work evaluation systems. In practice there is a dilemma in not only adjusting the new knowledge to existing models or theories but also to initiate a real transformation of mainstream knowledge. However, the research that we carried out at that time started a process within the involved local unions that contributed to the development of new work evaluation systems that were gaining ground and accepted in the nineties.

From the nineties and until today, when gender and feminist research have been in an integration phase in relation to mainstream science the answer to the question whether the epistemological position or not is reflected in concepts and methods is more complex and there are large variations between disciplines and research environments.

There is today an increased need for a development of more contextualised (local or situated) multiple methods approaches due partly to a general expansion of local multi-disciplinary research environments but also the due to the growth of Mode II research. In an ongoing change project with the aim to achieve a *sustainable gender conscious and acting organisation* an Action Research approach is combined with a feminist approach using multiple methods. An Action Research approach was chosen to obtain an increased sustainability in the change process. Four researchers and 15 participants in the organisation, *gender equity actors*, worked together to initiate and develop various change and learning processes focusing the integration of gender equity and increase gender competence in the organisation.[15]

A common practice for both feminist and Action Research could be to develop a conceptual frame and a multi-method model for how to organise interactive reflexive research processes incorporating a gender dimension. Researcher as well as participant subjectivity in relation to gender is here an aspect that has to be emphasized. I will here give some examples from gender and feminist research that I find useful for a combined feminist and Action Research approach.

---

15 The project is a 3 years research and development project with a twofold aim; to strengthen the gender equity integration in the organisation, and to increase gender competence in formulation of programme areas, policy documents and evaluation of research applications (Gunnarsson and Westberg, 2003). The final research report will be published 2006.

6. *The Snake and the Apple ...*

6.3.1   Reflexive research processes

In the Nordic countries a specific contribution has been made in the development of "grounded" qualitative methods that focus reflexive research processes and aspects of the researcher subjectivity (See for example; Berge and Ve, 2000 Davies, 1999 Drejhammar, 2001, Gunnarsson, et al. 2003, Haavind, 2000, Korvajärvi, 1998 and Widerberg, 1999 and 2002). It is in this field that gender research offers a particularly challenging contribution to Action Research. I will here give some examples of methods useful at a meso/micro level that can increase robustness in the knowledge production. Eva Amundsdotter's Chapter 11 in this anthology is also contributing to new knowledge within this field.

New more grounded methodological work is today part of several Swedish doctoral student's work within the field of Action Research.[16] These are contributions that will give a deeper understanding of an Interactive Research process. Their work will contribute to answer critical questions such as; how, when and where are the moments of transformed knowledge to be found? And how could this knowledge then be conceptualised to meet academic standards in order to strengthen the Action Research perspective and also qualify feminist research? The lack of a conceptual and methodological articulation on this meso/micro level has probably contributed to a marginalisation of Action Research in academy.

6.3.2   Researcher subjectivity

A basic assumption in qualitative gender and feminist research is that it must incorporate reflexive knowledge processes and the researcher subjectivity is here an important aspect. It is particularly this point – i.e. the researcher's position in knowledge production – that is too unarticulated and critically analysed in Action Research. A strong criticism from feminist researchers is also to be found in the argument: that not incorporating reflexivity on gender in relation to Interactive Research processes and particularly on researcher subjectivity, still means partly taking a com-

---

16 For example by Swedish doctoral students at the National Institute for Working Life, linked to Söderhamn's and Apel, Lindesberg's research stations.

fortable positivistic standpoint (see for example Maguire, 2002). This has also been highlighted in Critical Studies on Men (Hearn, 2002).

To incorporate the researcher' s conditions as a context in scientific knowledge production processes: conceptualising and understanding the researcher both as a practitioner and a subject, opens up a different and enlarged discussion incorporating contextual conditions that are also part of the researcher subjectivity (Hee Pedersen and Gunnarsson, 2004). To work with and reflect upon this "condition" in a systematic and analytic way is a praxis that in itself gives the opportunity to understand more in-depth social power relations such as gender. But at the same time it implies that the single researcher puts her/himself in a risky position, particularly in relation to legitimacy in her/his research field. However, if we do not want to fall into the same trap as science dominated by positivistic ideas about objective knowledge and science which both Action Research and feminist research are criticizing for viewing the researcher as neutral (without gender, class, emotions and bodies), then especially Action Research have to confront this challenge.

Contemporary post-modern research is adding new empirical work incorporating the gendered meaning of body and emotions in the knowledge production process (Dorte Marie Søndergaard, 1996 and 1999, and Jo Krøjer, 2003). With a focus on the body, produced as a subject in relation to the spatial landscape in the work place, Jo Krøjer offers a new and creative method of so called *"embodied reading"* to make the meaning of the gendered body more visible.

Karin Widerberg highlights a different but very relevant aspect when she argues that: "Critical qualitative research is always about developing methods and methodology, but a basic fault is that qualitative research is thought and taught as being free from a positivistic inheritance that is still often implicitly embedded".[17] My own experience is that remnants of this positivistic position is often unconsciously embedded and given priority in both the researchers and the participants practices and will continue to be so if not an increased consciousness will be built into the research process and the researcher's reflexivity.

The lack of reflexivity among participants with reference to gender

---

17 An argument stressed at a doctoral course at the National Institute for Working Life held in the spring of 2005.

(but also, class, ethnicity and sexuality) has to be problemized and dealt with in a similar way. Questions must be raised about hierarchies within the category of participants as well as equity in relation to the contribution of experiences to the common praxis. A development is needed on how this can be organised in practice in different local settings.

The method of memory-work, as Karin Widerberg develops it, offers a fruitful means for consciousness-raising (Widerberg, 1999 and 2002). The method destabilises researcher (and participants) subjectivity by making visible alternative understandings of the multiple "I" parting from a personal experience, told as a story. A particular theme and situation is chosen, for example: experiences of exclusion in work-life, written as anonymous stories, partly to enrich the interpretation process. These stories are then worked with in collective settings like workshops and no one is allowed to claim ownership of the story. Meanings, normativity and implications of the multiple "I" with reference to gender, class and ethnicity are then made very visible often in a very uncomfortable and thoughtful way. The method is useful in different phases in an Interactive Research process but particularly in the initial phase of formulation. Used in the initial research phase it opens up for a more serious understanding and incorporation of dimensions of gender but also age, ethnicity, sexuality and not "adding them" later on in the process.

Some of my colleges and I have developed a very easy method to make visible the researchers and participants subjectivity in relation to gender, position/class and ethnicity. We started to use original quotations on constructions of skills and competence made by women and men in a male dominated industry. We then changed the I making three new quotations with the same content but another subject; another sex, ethnicity and position. It resulted in a very interesting experience. The quotations became funny but very absurd in many cases and quite horrifying particularly when we changed the I from a white man to a coloured woman. A conclusion we, researchers and participants, drew from that work-shop experience was that gender bias was understood as conceptions but ethnic bias was understood as prejudice. We intend to develop this method more thoroughly together with different categories of participants and in different local contexts.

An increased reflexivity concerning the researcher's own gap between, *"the gender we think and the gender we do"*, to quote Sylvia Gherardi and

Barbara Poggio (2001), is a necessary research practice today to become more legitimate and trustworthy as a researcher. The gap between what we think, say and do has often been highlighted by feminist researchers in relation to male researchers' practices particularly in the academy. It is still very relevant, due to men's general privilege of interpretation over women, but has also become relevant for female researchers in their strengthened position in the academy. Today, the privilege of interpretation is also given to feminist researchers particularly in relation to participants. Also feminist female researchers have to be more critical, as I see it, about this gap as well as the meanings and implications of their own class position. Helena Aarseth and Bente Marianne Olsen (2004) have developed a method that by focusing the field of tension between subjectivity and the structural dimension of men's lives opens up for a potential for change. The method can probably be developed and used also for categories of women.

Doing or constructing gender is, as I see it; a relational process where men's superordination of women, is closely linked to women' s subordination and therefore has to be conceptualised in relation to each other, without marginalising men's general superordination over women on a structural level. Eva Amundsdotter has in her research together with the participants developed the concept: *"women's comfortable subordination"* to illustrate this (Amundsdotter, 2004, see also Chapter 11). Britt-Marie Berge and Hildur Ve show in an Action Research project for gender equity in the classroom how this comfortable subordination was maintained in practice by some of the female teachers (Berge and Ve, 2000). These teachers carried out what Gherardi and Poggio name *"remedial work"*, i.e. recreating the traditional gender order (Gherardi and Poggio, 2001).

6.3.3 *Between closeness and distance*

The rotation of the researcher position of being either close to or detached from the participants in the research processes has been problemized in both action and feminist research. Karen Davies (1999) discusses this rotation of positions in relation to participatory observation. She argues that participatory observation is a fruitful means of reaching other ways of knowing. In Eikeland's and Amundsdotter's chapter they argue that it is more relevant to talk about participatory experience in relation to the Interactive Research process. When the solidaristic or democratic interview method was developed during the eighties (see p. 121) the element of an interactive exchange of experiences between the researcher and the participant in the interview situation was part of its democratic idea. It is in practice an example of when Eikeland argues that the use of personal experience must move from periphery to the centre of the research process. Davies also discusses problems of integrity and objectivity when the researcher is close to the participants. In the discussion of close or detached, I find it unsatisfying to create this kind of dichotomy and prefer to see these two positions as simultaneously present but with a shift in focus in relation to different phases in the research process. A different way to conceptualise it is done by the philosopher Martha Nussbaum (1995) when she describes the characteristics of a qualified researcher in encompassing both the sharpness of feeling and the empathy of thought. In contemporary feminist research emotions and body are today on the agenda to fill the unsatisfactory lack of knowledge in these fields. Emotions seen as a mode of understanding and reaching other ways of knowing has from a philosophical perspective been developed in the thesis of Katarina Elam (2001). Simon Williams is in his work exploring the position and research of emotion in social theory (Williams, 2001).

The praxis of being close and distanced (not completely detached) at the same time has been developed within many professional groups in the reproductive sphere. Researchers have much to learn from these professionals. So, for example, this was an important element in the claim adjusters' work in relation to injured "customers". To be close but professionally distanced meant according to them to take a professional responsibility for the closeness or intimacy created in different situations. The boundaries of what they named *"professional empathy"* were discussed among colleagues as an everyday praxis (Gunnarsson, 1998). To be close but not transcending a professional boundary was by them seen as an important professional characteristic.

6.4 Concluding considerations

The Snake and the Apple in the common paradise is in the title used as a metaphor to illustrate the balance between surface and depth that both action and feminist traditions have to solve but from different entrances. The question I initially asked myself was: Could both traditions incorporate and merge in theory and praxis the benefits of a "common praxis" and at the same time integrate a strong social division such as gender? I do think that there is a partly common paradise where action and feminist research could meet and qualify each other. One field for a fruitful exchange of experiences could be in "grounding and contextualising" research to achieve an increased social robustness in the knowledge production. Here I see a shared need for action and feminist research to together with the participants develop an extended concept for scientific robustness. Another field for a common exchange of knowledge and experience is in relation to interactive reflexive research processes; how should these processes be organised in practice to include gender?

Finally, a common "snake" in the paradise is, as I see it, the expanding idea that scientific quality and excellence is measured preferably by positivistic quantitative measures. This development threatens to marginalise a major part of action and feminist research.[18]

References

Amundsdotter, Eva (2004) *Strategier för förändring: på väg mot den jämställda arbetsplatsen*, Växtkraft Mål 3 Svenska ESF-rådet.

Antony, Louise (1992) "Quine as feminist: The radical import of naturalized epistemology". In *A Mind of Ones's Own: Feminist Essays on Reason and Objectivity*. Antony, Louise and Witt, Charlotte (eds.) Boulder: Westview Press.

Aarseth, Helene och Olsen, Bente Marianne (2004) "Maskulinitet,

---

18 For a discussion on gender and excellence see Margo Browns (2004) and proceedings from the conference "Reaching for scientific excellence in gender research" organised by The Swedish Research Council's Committee on Gender, October 2005.

imagination och livssammanhang. Att nå förändringspotentialer hos män", *Kvinnovetenskaplig Tidskrift*, No. 1–2, 2004.

Baude, Annika et al. (1987) "Women's Working Lives: Visions and research for a better working life", Stockholm: The Swedish Center for Working Life.

Berge, Britt-Marie & Ve, Hildur (2000) *Action Research for Gender Equity*, Buckingham: Open University Press.

Björk, Ulrika (2005) "Enhet och tvetydighet i känslornas sfär", In *Filosofisk tidskrift* No. 2 May 2005.

Brouns, Margo (2004) "Gender and the assessment of scientific quality", In *Gender and Excellence in the Making*, Directorate-General for Research EUR 2122, European Commission.

Davies, Karen (1999) "Närhet och gränsdragning – att nå andra sorters kunskaper genom deltagande observation", In *Mer än kalla fakta: Kvalitativ forskning i praktiken* Sjöberg, Katarina (ed.), Lund: Studentlitteratur.

Drejhammar, Inga-Britt (2001) *Organisationsutveckling jämställdhet: En studie i tre företag*, Lund: Studentlitteratur.

Elam, Katarina (2001) *Emotions as a Mode of Understanding: An Essay in Philosophical Aesthetics*, Uppsala: Uppsala University.

Forsberg, Gunnel (1998) "Regional Variations in the Gender Contract: Gendered Relations in Labour Markets, Local Politics and Everyday Life in Swedish Regions". *Innovation*. Vol. 11 No. 2, 1998.

Forsberg, Gunnnel (2006) "Storstadsplanering för jämställdhet – går det?" In *Kors och tvärs: intersektionalitet i storstadens arbetsliv*, Gunnarsson, E., Neergaard, A. and Nilsson, A. (eds.) Stockholm: Normal Förlag.

Fox Keller, Evelyn and Longino, Helen, E. (eds.) (1996) *Feminism and Science*, Oxford: Oxford University Press.

Gherardi, Sylvia and Poggio, B. (2001), "Creating and Recreating Gender Order in Organizations", *Journal of Business* 36 (3).

Griffith, Morwenna (1988) "Feminism, Feelings and Philosophy" In *Feminist Perspectives in Philosophy*, Griffith, Morwenna and Whitford, Margret (eds.), Basingtoke: Macmillan.

Gunnarsson, Ewa (1994) *Att våga väga jämnt!: Om kvalifikationer och kvinnliga förhållningssätt i ett tekniskt industriarbete*, (*Daring to be equal: on qualifications and skills and wome's ways of relating to work in a technical industrial field*), Diss. Luleå: Luleå Tekniska Universitet.

– (1998) "Könsperspektiv på yrkeskunskaper på personskadereglerare",

("A Gender Perspective on Claim Adjusters Skills"). In Gunnarsson, Ewa, Andersson, Susanne och Westberg, Hanna *Känsla och regelverk i balans*, Stockholm: Arbetslivsinstitutet/Folksam.

– (2003) "Disguised in the Shadows of Symbol Discourses: an Attempt at Developing a Multiple Tool Analysis Approach among 'Nomads' and 'Groundeds' in Flexible and Network Oriented Organisations", In *Where Have All the Structures Gone? Doing gender in Organisations, Examples from Finland, Norway and Sweden* Gunnarsson, Ewa et al. (ed.), Stockholm: The Center for Women's Studies, University of Stockholm.

– et al. (ed.) (2003) *Where Have All the Structures Gone? Doing Gender in Organisations, Examples from Finland, Norway and Sweden*, Stockholm: The Center for Women's Studies, University of Stockholm.

Gunnarsson, Ewa och Westberg, Hanna (2003) Jämställdhet och genusvetenskap: ett integrerings- och kompetenshöjningsprojekt inom Vinnovas organisation och verksamhetsfält. Projektplan. Stockholm: Arbetslivsinstitutet.

Haavind, Hanne (1985) "Förändringar i förhållandet mellan kvinnor och män", *Kvinnovetenskaplig tidskrift*, No. 3:17–28

– (ed.) (2000) *Kønn og Tolkning: Metodiska møjligheter i kvalitativ forskning (Gender and Interpretation: Methodological possibilities in qualitative methods*, Stockholm: Natur och Kultur.

Harding, Sandra, (ed.) (1987) *Feminism and Methodology*, Milton Keynes: Open University Press.

– (1991) *Whose Science Whose Knowledge: Thinking from Wome's Lives*, New York: Cornell University Press.

Harraway, Donna (1991) "Situated Knowledges: The science question in feminism and the privilege of partial perspective", In Harraway, Donna, *Simians, Cyborgs, and Women: The Reinvention of Nature*. New York: Routledge.

Hearn, Jeff (2002) "Epistemologies for Studying Men", In *Developing Studies on Men in the Nordic Context*, Helsinki: Ministry of Social Affaires and health, Council for gender Equality, 2003.

Hee Pedersen, Stine & Gunnarsson, Ewa (2005) "Hoovedbrud: menns vi gör feministiske forskningsstrategier i organisationen", *Kvinder, køn och forskning*, No. 4, 2004.

Heldke, Lisa (1989) "John Dewey and Evelyn Fox Keller: A shared epistemological tradition", In *Feminism and Science*, Tuana, N. (ed.) Bloomington: Indiana University Press.

Kamarck Minnich, Elisabeth (1990) *Transforming Knowledge*, Philadelphia: Temple University Press.

Korvajärvi, Päivi (1998) *Gendering Dynamics in White-collar Work Organizations*, Academic dissertation, Acta Universitatis Tamperensis 600, Tempere: University of Tampere

Krøjer, Jo (2003) *Det mærkede sted. Køn, krop og arbejdspladsrelationer.* Roskilde: Roskilde Universitetsforlag.

Lloyd, Genevieve (1984) *The Man of Reason: "Male" and "Female" in Western philosophy.* London: Methuen.

Maguire, Patricia (2001) "Uneven Ground: Feminisms and Action Research", In *Handbook of Action Research: Participative Inquiry and Practice*, Reason, Peter and Bradbury, Hilary (eds.) London: Sage.

Nowotny, Helga, Scott, Peter and Gibbons (2001) *Re-Thinking Science Knowledge and the Public in an Age of Uncertainity*, Cambridge: Polity Press.

Nussbaum, Martha, C. (1995) *Känslans skärpa, tankens inlevelse: Essäer om etik och politik.* Stockholm/Stehag: Symposion.

Oakley, Ann (1981) "Interviewing Women: A Contradiction in Terms", In *Doing Feminist Research* Roberts, Helen (ed.) London: Routledge and Kegan Paul.

Rolin, Kristina (2002) "Commentary on 'Epistemologies for Studying Men' by Jeff Hearn", in *Developing Studies on Men in the Nordic Context,* Helsinki: Ministry of Social Affaires and health, Council for gender Equality 2003.

Saarinen, Aino (1989) "Kvinnoforskningens interventionsprojekt: problem och utmaningar", *Kvinnovetenskaplig Tidskrift,* No. 3–4, 1989.

Scheurich, James, J. (1997) *Research Method in the Postmodern*, London: Routledge.

Skeggs, Beverly (1997) *Att bli respektabel: konstruktioner av klass och kön,* (Formations of Class and Gender. Becoming Respectable). Göteborg: Daidalos.

Smith, Dorothy, E. (1987) *The Everyday World AS Problematic: A Feminist Sociology,* Boston: Northeastern University Press.

– (2005) *Institutional Ethnography – A Sociology for People,* New York: Alta Mira Press, Rowman and Littlefield Publishers.

Svensson, Lennart (2002) "Bakgrund och utgångspunkter" In *Interaktiv forskning: för utveckling av teori och praktik,* Svensson, Lennart et al. (eds.) (Arbetsliv i omvandling 2002:7), Stockholm: Arbetslivsinstitutet.

Søndergaard, Dorte Marie (1996) *Tegnet på kroppen. Kön: Koder og konstruktioner blandt unge voksne i akademia,* Copenhagen: Tusculanum.

– (1999) Destabilising Discourse Analysis, approaches to poststructuralist empirical research, *Kön i den akademiske organisation,* Arbejdspapir No. 7. København

Sørensen, Bjørg-Aase (1982) "Ansvarsrationalitet: Om mål-middeltenkning blant kvinner". In *Kvinner i Felleskap.* Holter, Harriet (ed.) Kvinners levevillkor og livsløp. Oslo: Universitetsförlaget.

The Swedish Research Council's Committee on Gender (2005) *Gender Studies: A Summary,* Stockholm.

Thurén, Britt-Marie (1996) "Om styrka, räckvidd och hierarki, samt andra genusteoretiska begrepp", *Kvinnovetenskaplig Tidskrift,* No. 3-4, 1996.

– (2003) *Genusforskning: Frågor, villkor och utmaningar,* Stockholm: Vetenskapsrådet.

Ve, Hildur (1994) "Gender Differences in Rationality, the Concept of Praxis Knowledge and Future Trends", In *Feminist Voices on Gender, Technology and Ethics,* Gunnarsson, Ewa and Trojer, Lena (eds.) Luleå: Centre for Women's Studies, Luleå University of Technology.

Wærness, Kari (1984) "The Rationality of Caring". *Economic and Industrial Democracy.* London: Sage.

West, Candace and Fenstermaker, Sarah (1995) "Doing Difference", *Gender and Society,* No. 1. 1995

Widerberg, Karin (1999) "Alternative Methods: Alternative Understandings: Exploring the Social and the Multiple 'I' through Memory-Work", *Sociologisk Tidskrift,* No. 2, 1999.

– (2002) *Kvalitativ forskning i praktiken,* (Qualitative Research in Practice) Lund: Studentlitteratur.

Williams, Simon (2001) *Emotion and social theory,* London: Sage.

THOMAS TYDÉN (ED.)

7. Aspects of Interactive Research in the Nordic Countries

A Historical Perspective

7.1 Introduction

Action Research has a long and rather strong history in the Nordic countries with a peak in the seventies. Looking back over the past thirty years, we can see a growing interest in Action Research though with peaks and troughs. However, this trend can be difficult to detect as the name of the research method has changed during the years. "Action Research" is nowadays not the most commonly used name for this method, which basically implies a meeting between science and practice, a meeting that is characterized by respect for your own knowledge and competence, and at the same time a humble attitude towards the knowledge and competence of the other. This meeting between science and practice has many names: Collaborative Research, Synthesis Pedagogic, Interactive Research, Participatory Research, Mode II and so on. The development of this method to create new knowledge through the interplay of different actors has been described in many textbooks where *The New Production of Knowledge* (Gibbons et al. 1994) and *Rethinking Science* (Nowotny et al. 2001) are the two most widely used concepts.

It is interesting to notice that for example in Sweden there is a growing interest from those funding research in contributing to this way of conducting research. Organizations funding Action Research have a practical interest for different public sectors such as infrastructure and communications, social care, energy production and use. But there are also research funders in the industrial sector that show interest in these research methods. Behind this interest lies a very pragmatic view, as those funding the research can see that the money spent on such research that is conducted in this way seems to lead to a better use in the society. That means that they find they get better returns on their investments.

The development of Action Research and its followers is described in this chapter that is divided into four separate sections each relating to one of the four Nordic countries, namely Denmark, Finland, Norway and Sweden. The development of Interactive Research has not been the same in the four countries as Denmark differs from the other three as such research almost came to a halt in the eighties. The extent of Interactive Research in Finland is not so large, but its pace has been steadier then in the neighbouring countries. It interesting to see what impact the Swedish LOM-program has had on the development of Interactive Research, which is reflected in the contributions. The development of regional research milieus concerning the public sector and with Interactive Research methods almost as a business concept has been rapidly growing in Sweden but its roots lie in Norway. And so do many other initiatives concerning Action Research. These are outlined in the Norwegian contribution.

The contributions have different foci. The section concerning Denmark discusses the theoretical development of the research methods. The Finnish paper focuses on the organizational development of the Action Research in Finland using examples from workplace research. While the Swedish paper discusses the political development of Interactive Research in the Swedish public sector.

The section concerning Denmark was written by Steen Elsborg from the Learning Lab at The Danish University of Education. Tuomo Alasoini, Project Manager at the Ministry of Labour and Docent at the University of Helsinki and Elise Ramstad, M.Ed.Sc. and PhD student at the Helsinki University of Technology has written the contribution from Finland. The Norwegian part was written by Morten Levin professor at the Institute for Industrial Economics and Technology Management at the Norwegian University of Science and Technology (NTNU) and the Swedish contribution was written by Thomas Tydén, Professor and the Director of Dalarna Research Institute.

References

Gibbons et al. (1994), *The new production of knowledge*. London: Sage
Nowotny H, et al. (2001), *Re-Thinking Science*. Cambridge: Polity Press

7.2 Action Research in Denmark by Steen Elsborg

For the past two decades, Action Research has been more or less ignored by the political and academic communities in Denmark. Since the turn of the century, however, we have seen a renewed interest in this field: applicable research is now at the top of the political wish list, and this has won new prestige for Action Research among the academic circles in this country.

This rekindled interest in Action Research has already led to several innovative measures. For one thing, we see the establishment of "labs' at the research institutions, laboratories where the production of knowledge is based on innovative experiments. Another example is that in 2002, the first Danish academic network for Action Research was established, a network which has Roskilde University, Ålborg University and Learning Lab Denmark in the steering group.

The effort to integrate science and development and to create quality in theoretical as well as practical work is not without opposition. Criticism includes the argument that the political agenda may become unbalanced to the point where research becomes a tool in itself, and the argument from academic circles that Action Research is incompatible with the basic tenets of scientific research.

Action Research was introduced in Denmark in the eighties, was applied in the eighties and early eighties, and was more or less ignored from the late eighties until recently.

The following is my attempt to provide a general account of the current situation in the Danish research environment. Danish Action Research is tightly wound up with the Scandinavian tradition for Action Research, primarily the Norwegian. The inspiration for the Danish Action Research mainly came from Norway, and therefore I shall start my account of the Danish Action Research with an explanation of the nature of this inspiration.

7.2.1 The socio-technical tradition

Cooperation experiments in Norway in the eighties were rooted in the conviction that democracy and competitiveness are mutually dependent. Sociologists, employees and managers collaborated to develop new (corporate) organisational structures. The specific aim was to establish democracies in organisations, and the socio-technical approach set the framework. At the same time, the collaboration experiments had a much wider aim: To contribute to a further democratisation of society through introducing democracy in the organisational design of each workplace.

Fundamentally, the focus on the socio-technical approach has been to create an interplay between operation and development – based on the belief that the starting point in optimising the production will also develop the employees involved both personally and collectively by giving them responsibility and decision-making power (see also the Norwegian part by Morten Levin).

The socio-technique developed along two tracks, both of which influenced the situation in Denmark. One track came to us directly from Norway, and, later on, from Sweden, and was aimed at establishing developing work routines for the employees. While the second track was the result of the American development of the socio-technical principles aimed at optimising the application of human resources, managerial and otherwise, through the establishment of a learning organisation.

The second of the two was developed when the socio-technical approach arrived from the United States and corporate consultants combined it with organisational theory. This led to the development of the concepts underlying "Action Learning" and later also "The Learning Organisation". In Denmark, this track took root at Copenhagen Business School, from which it has since spread to become a household name in applied organisational and management development. Whether or not to classify this track as Action Research is, however, still a topic of debate in Denmark, since the track in its simplistic forms is aimed at short-term optimisation without incorporating opportunities for the involved employees to pursue their own agenda and take active part in knowledge creation (see: Senge (1999) and Illeris (2004)).

The direct socio-technical inspiration of the collaboration experiments in Norway showed up in Denmark in the shape of individual projects involving students and/or researchers from the Technical University of Denmark (DTU) and Roskilde University (RUC). In the eighties, this track was picked up by the Danish Technological Institute, which conducted several projects with individual companies. Later on, Action Researchers in Sweden collaborated with the Swedish Trade Union Confederation (LO) to develop this track for the launch of the strategy concerning "The Good Work" and later on "The Developing Work". In Denmark, this track was picked up by the Confederation of Trade Unions, which used this approach as a basic strategy through the eighties (Hvid, 1999). The approach is still in use in the labour unions, now under the headline "The Sustainable Workplace".

Autonomous groups were, and are, a variation of the socio-technical principle, but the principle of employee involvement has rather more far-reaching aspects than this concept, because it generally stresses the fact that the employees must be involved in the design of the work organisation. In hindsight, we can see that there used to be a tendency to identify the establishment of autonomous groups with the socio-technical philosophy.

Experience has shown, however, that there were and still are a number of problems with the original socio-technical approach, not least the fact that it has turned out to be problematic to distribute even successful development projects both internally in the organisation and externally to other companies. This was also concluded from the Nordic collaboration experiments, where the immediate effect was significant, but when the researchers returned five years later, they found that the organisations had reverted back to their former ways.

The question was and is therefore whether Thorsrud's claim, made in 1960, that democracy and competitive power, driven by values and profit respectively, are really interdependent? So far we seem to lack solid evidence that democratisation and optimization walk hand in hand. In the eighties in Norway, this led to a critical stance against the validity of the collaboration experiments; this criticism had a huge impact on the Danish Action Research community. The radical Norwegian

Action Researchers (such as Mathiesen and Nygård) pointed out that the collapse was the responsibility of the employers and that history had shown that employers wouldn't support the process after all. This led to the development in Norway of a branch in the academic Action Research community, which insisted that Action Research was by its very nature a counterbalance to the existing power structure. In opposition to Thorsrud's and Emery's consensus-line, this branch stressed the conflict of interests, and so the radical Action Researchers decided to undertake research on behalf of the employees – a sort of unilateral research. Whereas researchers in the collaboration experiments served as chairmen and evaluators both of the process and of the results, the critics argued that researchers would have to take an active stance in order to promote a democratisation process.

This criticism of the socio-technology's orientation towards consensus had a major impact on the development of the academic research community in Denmark, where the prevailing notion was that Action Research should provide not only an epistemological alternative to the unpopular positivism, but also provide an ontological alternative, with the aim that participation in the change and knowledge creation processes could mobilise less resourceful groups and contribute to a new distribution of power on a societal level. The then newly founded Roskilde University was an important player in the formation of strategic partnerships between researchers, students and professional and unskilled labour. Students' reports and research projects were conducted, but at the same time the collaboration aimed to mobilise workers in a class struggle.

In the early eighties saw the so-called "external branch critical reports" concerning painters, the butchers and the breweries, reports that were aimed at improving the work environment as the strategic aim, and which were based on Action Research. The criticism caught the public's eye and was supplemented with traditional documentation, but in Denmark it became almost synonymous with Action Research anyway. The critical community for each discipline was, among other things, maintained through study groups comprising both workers and academics. Another activity in this respect was the establishment of the AAA; the "Action group Workers and Academics", which also had mobilisation through study groups as a goal, and which had a huge influence on the shared knowledge production between workers and academics during this period.

Thus, in the eighties, the labour movement and the student movement considered Action Research a mean to a joint mobilisation for the reformation of society, and the system with study groups was developed in this period as a uniquely Danish element of the Nordic Action Research. The content mainly concerned working environment and technological development, education of the workers and informal education. Various geographically separated academic communities in Denmark collaborated on this, with Roskilde University being the leading one among them.

The DUE-project (Democracy, development and IT) grew to become the primary project in relation to technological development in Denmark. The DUE-project was based on an existing collaboration between students and shop stewards at the University of Århus, and on a collaboration project involving unilateral research in Sweden and Norway, respectively. The DUE-project was conducted as collaboration between union offices in a number of companies that worked with the students and researchers to determine how employees could gain influence on the introduction of new technology. The work form here was also the study group, where the theoretical knowledge of the academics as well as the practical insights of the workers was discussed in the group. Employers rejected the DUE-project and this meant that the project had no direct impact on the companies that were involved. The project did, however, have an influence on the wording of technology-agreements in Danish companies, it helped call attention to new models of collaboration for the Danish unions, and it served to position the Danish study-group Action Research internationally (Christian Clausen, 1988).

In terms of formal and informal education of the workers, probably the most significant Action Research project was conducted as a long-term collaboration between researchers and students from Roskilde University and brewery workers from Tuborg and Carlsberg. The collaboration centred on the development of new corporation-wide production systems and the impact this had on the industry and on society in general. The joint production of knowledge had a specific impact on the workplaces, and led to a general competence development among workers, students and researchers alike (Salling Olesen, 1985).

By the late eighties and early eighties, Action Research was increasingly replaced by traditional positivistic research in which the researchers came to serve as experts in their collaboration with the unions, and where workers were increasingly ignored in connection with knowledge production. With the advent of the eighties, the introduction of Japanese production organisation brought with it a new demand for workers to think of themselves as belonging to an organisation with a shared set of values, which again resulted in a political pressure for research to design collaboration-based projects aimed at improvements, rather than innovation. The socio-technical enclave of Action Research was, by the mid-eighties, reduced to more or less invisible micro-communities.

7.2.2 The process orientation

In another attempt to remedy the lack of impact of the collaboration experiments in Norway, focus was shifted from a milieu that was dominated by experts to a milieu focusing the communication. Socio-technology was basically abandoned in favour of a process-oriented focus. The concept of discourse entered Action Research – the so-called "Linguistic Turn". In this branch of science, the primary task of the Action Researcher was and is to ensure a democratic dialogue. Networks and coalitions became the societal aspects of this branch, and results were sought passed on through comprehensive projects, which included the public sector. From the mid-eighties onwards, this branch grew to dominate both Norway's and Sweden's Action Research communities. Among the practical upshots were development of the Search and Dialogue Conferences, but the Linguistic Turn never broke through in Denmark.

In Denmark, the (remaining) Action Research community criticised the Linguistic Turn as being naive in relation to the power structures of society. As opposed to Norway, Denmark never saw the development of a firm belief that an non-hierarchical space was realisable in a capitalist society – which "Habermas could be operationalised through concepts for democratic dialogue" – as it had been done and still is with Bjørn Gustavsen as the front figure in Norway and Sweden.

The Linguistic Turn did not go unopposed in Norway or Sweden either, but a widely spread consensus was developed around the constructionistic focus on dialogue as being the best attainable goal. This was a highly experimental objective, but the focus was on the process rather than on the result. The Danish Action Research community rejected this philosophy as being far too moored in the existing societal structures.

And yet, Danish Action Research was influenced by the period's widespread focus on processes and methods. Also in Denmark in the eighties and eighties, the attempts by Action Research to establish a team spirit with the participants were to some degree replaced by the Action Researchers' quality control of the methods and taking care of the processes. In the eighties and eighties, researchers at Roskilde University developed the Danish tradition for conducting Action Research in Future Creating Workshops in reply to the Search and Dialogue Conferences.

As opposed to the Search and Dialogue Conferences, the Future Creating Workshops take into account the fact that the capitalist power structures generate an inherent conflict of interest, which cannot be neglected. Using Critical Theory, the Future Creating Workshops are aimed at transcending existing relations – to encourage and facilitate the development of a collective sociological fantasy, and thereby to call attention to the fact that society can be organised differently. This is, perhaps not surprisingly, not an ambition of, the frequently publicly co-funded, Search and Dialogue Conferences in Norway and Sweden. The most important Action Research project in Denmark in this respect is "Industry and Happiness", conducted as a collaboration between Action Researchers from Roskilde University, the DTU and female workers at a fish processing plant (see: Olsén, Nielsen og Nielsen (2003)). This project was rooted in Oscar Negt's Critical Theory and was originally planned at the now closed Institute for Sociology at the University of Copenhagen.

7.2.3 The criticism of Action Research from the scientific community

The Danish Action Research's focus on defending the rights of those who in terms of influence cannot fend for themselves resulted in a general rejection of Action Research by the Danish scientific community.

The question was, and is, whether the criticism was based on unilateral solidarity among the scientific community or it was against the epistemological basis of Action Research. But the argumentation was unmistakeable: Action Research was considered developmental work lacking the necessary firm rooting in the established foundation of science.

In Denmark, the criticism of Action Research made both acceptance in the scientific community and obtaining funds extremely difficult for those who styled themselves Action Researchers. Not surprisingly, many refrained from calling themselves this, even when Action Research was what they did. Kurt Aagaard Nielsen described this process as a "name drain" in Danish Action Research (Aagaard Nielsen, 1996).

To add insult to injury, the insistence from Roskilde University that the democratisation of knowledge creation was the central aspect of Action Research made the academic world snub Action Research as biased and claim that Action Research was really nothing but research FOR the participants. This was another reason why Action Research lost headway in the Danish scientific community in the eighties and eighties.

The criticism of Action Research did, however, also lead to constructive improvements in Denmark. In the eighties, introspection within the Danish Action Research community engendered the realisation that not enough effort had been spent on consciously and explicitly accounting for the innovative projects in terms of what was to be learned, what the path to success was, and on the process of result verification. This process of introspection pointed to the fact that innovation projects must be designed in such a way that they can meet resistance, and that knowledge creation must be both explicit and transparent.

In the eighties and the 2000's, Danish Action Research gradually came to realise the importance of a much closer and qualified communication with the established scientific community, not least because this communication will challenge the Action Researchers' theoretical standpoints, a challenge that reflects positively on the practical aspects of the research. This is a new response to the criticism of Action Research; the Action Researcher applies his or her own professionalism to represent a context-independent knowledge about society, knowledge which the researcher actively puts into play to influence the current agenda; this is an alternative contact point with society based on the normative role of the researcher.

The Swedish branch of Action Research, so-called Interactive Research, should be viewed in this light. The societal aspect here is the research's affiliation to the research community; the Action Researcher's results must be tested by the academic community, and thereby ensure increased societal relevance. This is a branch of Action Research, which has a large influence on the present Danish Action Research.

7.2.4 Ålborg University

At Ålborg University (AAU), Action Research has been a particularly popular method among the social sciences. The Norwegian Action Researcher, Tore Hegland has been the seminal character in this community. Hegland came to Denmark in the eighties, and was among the first to introduce the epistemology of Action Research at the University of Copenhagen, and later at AAU. To Hegland, the change projects – the action and the changes – are the true objectives of Action Research; knowledge production takes second place (Hegland 1981).

In later years, the AAU Action Research community has been greatly influenced by the notion of first person research as the key point in Action Research; to develop the basis of the democratic processes by explicitly registering and reflecting on one's own practice (Reason and Bradbury, 2002).

Another prominent character in the AAU community is Bent Flyvberg. It is debatable whether to call his research "Action Research", but it is beyond discussion that he has inspired Action Researchers at home and abroad with his theories about the particular and the context-dependent. As do Reason and Bradbury, Flyvberg points out that as a researcher one has to shape the values that one's research will be measured against (Flyvberg, 1999). On a more practical level, Flyvberg has had a concrete influence in the area of traffic planning, an area where an Action Research environment during the last few years has emerged around the researcher Lise Drewes Nielsen at Roskilde University.

7.2.5 Management research

To complete the picture of the prevalence of Action Research in Denmark the existing alternatives within management research to the previously mentioned environments that focus on action learning and the learning organisation, must be included. From the eighties onwards, smaller environments influenced by Peter Reason's Cooperative inquiry approach to Action Research were developed (Maalø (1998), Kristensen and Bloch-Poulsen (2004)). In this connection it is also worth mentioning that management orientated Action Research has been carried out at DTI (Danish Technological Institute[1]) inspired by the LOM-project. In Denmark, this has been the Action Research environment where the dialogue tradition has been the most used approach.

7.2.6 From 2000 onwards

The Danish government is currently channelling money into applied research, research that addresses practical issues, that actively engages in development processes and which focuses on opportunities. This has increased the potential for an eventual acceptance of Action Research as the research method that preserves society through the epistemological notion that "to understand reality, one must take part in changing this reality".

It is beyond doubt that Action Research's insights into and ability to facilitate interplay between change, learning and science now has a unique opportunity to step out of the practical and scientific shadows and make a mark on the agenda of today's Denmark. The Action Research communities mentioned above are key in this dissemination of Action Research, but at the same time, the renewed interest has led to the establishment of new Danish Action Research communities.

7.2.7 Learning Lab Denmark

One of the primary efforts in this respect is the publicly funded Learning Lab Denmark (LLD). LLD was founded in 2000 to be an interdisciplinary laboratory for experiments concerning learning in the knowledge society – in the educational sector as well as in public and private organisations. LLD's epistemological starting point is Action Research – onto-

---

1 Danish Technological Institute is an independent, not-for-profit institution approved by the Danish authorities to provide technological services to businesses and the community.

logically speaking, the aim is a wide scope. From its founding, LLD was physically located at the Danish University of Education (DPU), and from 1 January 2005, LLD has been an institute at the DPU.

LLD considers itself to be a Mode II organisation characterised, among other things, by insisting that research and communication must go hand in hand throughout the research process. It will be interesting to observe in the next few years whether its self-perception as a Mode II-organisation means that LLD's research will be influenced by a notion of interest-consensus, and whether the focus will shift away from Action Research's democratisation of the research process towards communication.

7.2.8 Danish Action Research network

In 2002, the Danish Action Research Network was established. The aim of the network is to facilitate the reintroduction of Action Research as a scientific approach in Denmark. The network is the first Action Research network operating on a national level in Denmark, and the network's activities revolve around an annual conference, which includes a PhD seminar.

As mentioned in the opening chapter of this textbook, Danish Action Research Network defines Action Research as follows:

"Action Research is understood as a scientific method for conducting research. It highlights the connection between understanding and change between theory and practice and facilitates active cooperation between researchers and the participants in the production of new knowledge"

"... active cooperation between researchers and the participants in the production of new knowledge" is a formulation which goes against the previously dominant perceptions of Action Research in Denmark, because it does not emphasise democratic knowledge generation as more important than other elements of Action Research.

It has, in my view, been a problem (and has led to a "name loss") that the very definition of Action Research has been normative[2]. The pre-defined normativity has far too often meant that the aim has been to bring about this or that particular development, while the research aspect has been neglected – and this has to become more balanced if Action Research is to really become influential in Denmark!

The definition above enables us to conduct Action Research characterised by practitioners being invited to participate in knowledge creation, meaning that we are dealing with three levels of learning; the learning among researchers, the learning among practitioners and finally the learning that takes place in the interplay between practitioners and researchers. Each is legitimate and must be spelled out in detail.

In this process, it is vital for the Action Researcher, in order to obtain quality, to maintain a fine balance between intimacy and distance. Intimacy generates a contextual understanding, which cannot be obtained in any other way, while distance allows for reflection and an overview that can be difficult to obtain or maintain in the context.

7.2.9 Past and present

I have, in broad terms, demonstrated that Danish Action Research, by its insistence on a perspective including the reformation of society, for better or for worse, differs from the development of Action Research in Norway and Sweden. For better, because Action Research thereby avoided becoming an instrument for improving existing structures, but for worse because this has led to the marginalization of Action Research in Denmark.

As methodology, Action Research comprises the expertise in just the kind of research which is currently in increasing demand in Denmark. In the Danish Action Research Network, it is a matter of debate how to best bring this expertise into play. The consensus seems to be that the main challenge lies in ensuring that the researchers and participants involved must, together, design and conduct the intended change- and knowledge creation processes, which must facilitate learning for everyone involved: researchers, participants, organisations and society. These

---

2   Each change project is of course, by its very nature, normative. Normativity emerges through specifics.

are not easily balanced objectives, but the network seems to be in agreement on the fact that if we manage to do this explicitly and in a reflected manner, the potential is absolutely amazing.

7.2.10 References

Clausen, Christian et al. (1992): *Deltagelse i Teknologisk Udvikling*. Copenhagen: Fremad.

Eikeland, Olav and Finsrud, Henrik Dons (1995*): Forskning og handling: søkelys på aksjonsforskning*. Oslo: Arbejdsforskningsinstituttets skriftserie (AFI)

Eikeland, Olav and Fossestøl, Knut (eds.) (1995): *Kunnskab og handling: aksjonforskningens metodologiske og vitenskabsteoretiske status*. Rapport fra en nordisk konference. Arbejdsforskningsinstituttet (AFI)

Hvid, Helge (ed.) (1999): *Ressourcer og velfærd i arbejdslivet*. Copenhagen: Frydenlund.

Illeris, Knud (ed.) (2004*): Læring i arbejdslivet*. Copenhagen: Roskilde Universitetsforlag.

Jungk, Robert and Müllert Norbert (1984): *Håndbog i fremtidsværksteder*. Copenhagen: Politisk Revy.

Kristiansen, M. and Bloch-Poulsen, J. (2004): "Self-referentiality as a power mechanism: Towards dialogic Action Research". *Action Research* 2004; 2: 371–388.

Greenwood, Davydd J. and Levin, Morten. (1998): *Introduction to Action Research: Social Research for Social Change*. London: Sage.

Maaløe, E. (1998): *The Employee Owner: Organisational and Individual Change within Manufactory Companies as Participation and Sharing Growth and Expand*. Copenhagen: Academic Press.

Nielsen, Kurt Aagaard and Vogelius, Peter (1996): *Aktionsforsknin: medarbejderindflydelse på forskning og udvikling i arbejdsmiljøet*. Copenhagen: Arbejdsmiljøfondet

Nielsen, Kurt Aagard (1996b): *Arbejdets sociale orientering*. Copenhagen: Forlaget Sociologi.

Olesen, Henning Salling (1985): *Voksenundervisning: hverdagsliv og erfaring*. Viborg: Unge Pædagoger.

Olsén, Peter, Nielsen, Birger Steen og Nielsen, Kurt Aagaard (2003): *Demokrati og bæredygtighed*. Fredriksberg. Roskilde Universitetsforlag.

Senge, Peter M. (1990): *Den femte disciplin: den lærende organisations teori og praksis*. Copenhagen: Klim.

Thorsrud, Einar and Emery, Fred (1970): *Nye samarbejdsformer i industrien*. Copenhagen: Gyldendal.

Toulmin, Stephen and Gustavsen, Bjørn (1996): *Beyond theory: changing organizations through participation*. (Dialogues on work and innovation). Amsterdam/Philadelphia: John Benjamins Publishing.

7.3 Interactive Research in Finland: Workplace research from the 1940's to the present day by Elise Ramstad and Tuomo Alasoini

Workplace research was pursued only on a small scale in Finland up until the Second World War. It was not until the war and the early post-war era that companies and government authorities began to take more of an interest in the research and development of working and production methods, management and supervision, and occupational health. The Finnish Institute of Occupational Health, founded in 1945, was the first institution in Finland to conduct research on the work and health of the working-age population in Finland. To begin with, the Institute's operations were based mainly on medical, engineering and psychological expertise. Another important reform was the introduction of industrial psychology as a teaching subject at Helsinki University of Technology in 1947. Four years later, the University of Technology was given Finland's first professorship in industrial psychology and work supervision studies.

Workplace research became more varied in Finland from the 1950's to the eighties. The higher education system expanded as new university units were founded and existing ones were decentralized, and during this time subjects such as administrative and social sciences, economics and legal science began to take more of an interest in workplace issues. At this stage, the role of the universities was still limited to traditional research. The operations of the Finnish Institute of Occupational Health also expanded in the eighties with the establishment of five regional Institutes.

In the eighties, the Government began to take a more active role in guiding workplace research. The strengthening of the labour market organizations in political decision-making influenced this above all, and as a consequence, a number of important legislative reforms were carried out in the eighties, focusing on areas such as occupational health and safety, occupational health care and co-determination in companies. Research began to be used more systematically as a means of monitoring the impact of these reforms and predicting the need for legislative reforms. In 1973, workplace research also became a part of science policy. The Government made research on working life and working conditions one of the most important areas of research for public funding. The responsibility for coordinating funding was given to the Academy of Finland.

During the eighties and the early eighties, the role of workplace research based on social and behavioural science grew in Finland, while multidisciplinary approaches and action-oriented research became more common. At the end of the eighties, some universities began to set up units, which specialized in workplace research. They include the Work Research Unit at the University of Jyväskylä (1986), the Work Research Centre at the University of Tampere (1988), and the Center For Activity Theory and Developmental Work Research at the University of Helsinki (1993). The operations of existing units such as the Finnish Institute of Occupational Health, the Laboratory of Work Psychology and Leadership at Helsinki University of Technology and the Technical Research Centre of Finland (VTT) also began to expand into social and educational sciences.

The Finnish Work Environment Fund was founded in 1979, and it became the biggest funding body for workplace research in Finland. Initially, the Fund supported research, training and information provision, which aimed at improving only occupational safety and health, but its purview was expanded in 1988 to include industrial relations and then in 1995 productivity issues. Research funding by the Academy of Finland and the Institute of Occupational Health also grew in the eighties, and the Ministry of Labour, which was founded in 1989 to handle issues concerning the working environment and occupational safety and health, soon became an increasingly important coordinator and funding body for workplace research.

By the start of the eighties, workplace research and development had acquired a relatively strong institutional and funding base in Finland. Over the past ten years or so, that base has grown even more solid as a consequence to science and education policy reforms, companies' increased interest in development, tripartite workplace development programmes and Finland's accession to the EU in 1995.

The operating environment of work organizations in Finland has changed rapidly over the past few years as a result of the deep economic recession in the early eighties and the subsequent period of rapid economic growth. As the economy has become more globalised, companies have focused on their core competence in the hope of cutting costs, and this has helped boost their interest in external cooperation on research, development and training. A new concept of learning and innovations, which focuses on the social nature of innovations and the importance of cooperation networks, has also contributed to increased cooperation between companies and researchers.

Science and technology policy in Finland has been guided since the early eighties by the national innovation system as a frame of reference, which has initiated discussion about a more extensive concept of innovation policy (Science and Technology Policy Council of Finland 2003). This change contains the idea of what is referred to as the "third task" of the universities, i.e. to reinforce the social effectiveness of their operations and their interaction with working and business life. Many universities and other educational organizations have, in fact, stepped up their cooperation accordingly and founded special service units dedicated to cooperation with the business sector. Another important science policy reform in Finland was the introduction of regional polytechnics, which began in the eighties and was completed in 2000. According to new legislation which came into force in 2003, the polytechnics are charged with a statutory research and development duty to serve teaching, working life and regional development. The founding of a new academic society for workplace researchers and a scientific journal for workplace research in 2003 could be considered a third major advance in this area.

The Government has also attempted to influence the changes in working life and the reinforcement of Interactive Research through programme-based development. The National Productivity Programme was started in 1993 on a tripartite basis and acted as a source of funding for research and development aimed at improving productivity and quality. The Finnish Workplace Development Programme (TYKE) was started in 1996 and funded the development of work organizations and workplace researcher training. A third programme, the Well-being at Work Programme, was launched in 2000. All three of these programmes, which were included in the relevant Government Programmes, terminated at the end of 2003. As a continuation, the Ministry of Labour has started a new Workplace Development Programme (TYKES) for the period 2004–09. The new programme supports the development of work organizations, the development of development methods, learning networks and researcher training. The vision of the new programme is that by 2009, Finland should have a network of expertise, which gives the country a competitive edge in the development of work organizations. As a consequence of these programmes, direct investment by central government in workplace research and development has grown considerably. The Ministry of Labour and the labour market organizations have proposed that the TYKES programme should have a total budget of €87 million.

Finland's accession to the European Union has also reinforced the funding base of workplace research and development and boosted international cooperation on research and development. Workplace development projects have also been funded through the European Social Fund (ESF). As a consequence, the Employment and Economic Development Centres, which are in charge of most of Finland's ESF funding, have become sources of funding for regional workplace development. The 15 Employment and Economic Development Centres were set up in 1997, when the regional units of the Ministry of Trade and Industry, Ministry of Labour and the Ministry of Agriculture and Forestry were merged. In addition to funding, they offer advisory and development services to SMEs in their region at various stages of the companies' lifespan.

7.3.1 The organization of workplace research

In Finland, research policy is the responsibility chiefly of the Ministry of Education and the Ministry of Trade and Industry. The former is in charge of science policy, including administration of the higher education sector, while the latter is in charge of technology policy. The higher education sector consists of 20 universities and 31 polytechnics. Both have separate units in a number of localities, for instance the polytechnics have 60 such units all over Finland. In 2001, polytechnics accounted for a mere five per cent of R&D operations in the higher education sector, but the percentage is growing. The funding structure for R&D at universities and polytechnics is also different in the sense that the percentage of external funding is clearly lower at universities (55 per cent compared with 75 per cent at polytechnics) (Oksanen et al. 2003).

Each ministry is responsible for research, which serves development in its own sector. There are 20 research institutes, which operate within the administrative sectors of the ministries. The Technical Research Centre of Finland (VTT), which operates under the Ministry of Trade and Industry, is the largest by far, and it alone accounts for 40 per cent of the R&D funding for research institutes. The institutes are very different in terms of funding structure. The bulk of VTT's R&D funding (75 per cent) is external, while external funding accounts for a maximum of half the funding of the other research institutes.

The proportion of R&D expenditure out of Finland's GDP has been growing throughout the eighties and the early 2000's. It stood at 3.5 per cent or €4.8 billion in 2002. Businesses accounted for just over 70 per cent of this while the government accounted for about a quarter. The percentage of funding for workplace R&D is only a small fraction of the total, despite the fact that the funding has been developing very favourably over the past 10–15 years. The total funding was between €17–20 million in the early eighties, but is estimated to be at least twice that today.

According to data from Statistics Finland (2000), there are some 30,000 researchers working in the tertiary education sector and the public sector combined. According to a study by Ramstad (2002), 123 R&D units reported that they were engaged in workplace research or development in 2001. They had a total staff of nearly 1,700, which worked in various duties involving workplace research, development, consulting and training. The units represented a variety of organizations such as universities, polytechnics, research institutes, vocational colleges and adult education centres. The number of R&D staff had increased at almost all these units between 1996 and 2001, and it was estimated that staff numbers would continue to grow.

In Ramstad's study, the total number of workplace research and development staff in the tertiary education sector and at research institutes was estimated to be about 1,000. In the tertiary education sector, 14 universities have about 40 units involved in workplace R&D activities. On average, these units are fairly small, since only five of them (the Laboratory of Work Psychology and Leadership and the BIT (Business Innovation Technology) research centre at Helsinki University of Technology, the Center For Activity Theory and Developmental Work Research at the University of Helsinki, the Organisation and Management Unit at the Helsinki School of Economics and Business Administration, and the Work Research Centre at the University of Tampere) had over 20 employees involved in workplace R&D in 2001. In addition, two Continuing Education Centres belonging to two universities fell into this size category. Ramstad's study also showed that about half of the polytechnics were actively involved in workplace R&D, with most polytechnics having some kind of involvement. Where research institutes were concerned, the Institute of Occupational Health was the biggest institution by far to be involved in workplace R&D in Finland. Aside from these, workplace R&D is pursued only at three other state research institutes.

There are a wide variety of problems in the workplace and working life, so they touch on a number of different scientific fields. Studies show that workplace research is conducted in Finland at a number of different university departments and that there are also a number of multidisciplinary units (Ramstad 2002). Most units employed representatives of many different disciplines. Technical or engineering science training is the common background for researchers and developers, followed by economics, social sciences or educational sciences.

In terms of regional distribution, Uusimaa and Pirkanmaa (Tampere region) are the two strongest areas in Finland, when it comes to R&D in general and workplace research in particular. There are seven universities in the Helsinki metropolitan area, several state research institutes and nine polytechnics. The most significant workplace R&D organizations in the area are the University of Helsinki, Helsinki University of Technology, the Helsinki School of Economics and Business Administration, the Institute of Occupational Health and VTT Industrial Systems. The Helsinki metropolitan area accounts for as much as 40 per cent of the total number of workplace R&D staff at universities, polytechnics and research institutes. The corresponding figure for Pirkanmaa is about 15 per cent. Aside from the University of Tampere, the noteworthy workplace R&D organizations in the Pirkanmaa area are Tampere University of Technology, VTT Industrial Systems (of which part is located in the Helsinki metropolitan area and part in Oulu), the Regional Institute of Occupational Health and two big polytechnics.

The other regions are left in the shadow of the Helsinki metropolitan area and Tampere. There are concentrations of a couple of dozen workplace R&D staff in Jyväskylä, Kokkola, Kuopio, Lahti, Lappeenranta, Oulu, Pori, Seinäjoki, Turku and Vaasa.

The conclusion from all this would be that workplace research and development in Finland is dispersed, lively and varied. The dispersal brings both advantages and disadvantages. One of the advantages is that support for research and development is available to work organizations in different areas. A certain separation also enables the regions to retain their own particular characteristics, which bring a welcome variety to research. Meetings between universities, polytechnics and other educational institutions with working life also create interesting potential for new combinations in research and development. However, one of the disadvantages of isolation is that theoretical and methodological development becomes more difficult. Teaching and research are often pursued as part of other scientific activity. Systematic further training is provided in industrial psychology, education, labour law and public health studies, but in, for instance, sociology and economics, training is provided alongside other teaching.

7.3.2 Key actors in interactive workplace research

In practice, Interactive Research has emerged over the past 20 years in Finland. Before this, the universities tended to adhere to their traditional, purely academic role for the most part. Practice-oriented units such as the Finnish Institute of Occupational Health and the universities of technology traditionally tended to take the role of "percolating" expert knowledge through to businesses.

Nieminen and Kaukonen (2001) studied companies' interest in cooperation on innovation activity with different partners in a questionnaire, which comprised 374 companies in industry and knowledge-intensive business services in the Oulu, Tampere and Turku regions. According to this study, the companies were most likely to consider cooperation with research institutes such as VTT as important. This was the answer given by 31 per cent of respondents. The figure for universities of technology and technical departments of universities was 23 per cent of respondents, with 21 per cent for polytechnics, a mere 12 per cent for universities and a surprising 3 per cent for schools of economics and business administration. What this tells us is that the companies still place more confidence in the usefulness of R&D cooperation in the field of technology than in any other area. It also indicates that, from the companies' point of view, innovation is seen quite prominently as the promotion of technological innovations.

In the light of what has been said above, it is easy to see that Interactive Research is not a mainstream approach in Finland when it comes to cooperation between companies and R&D units. In fact, Interactive Research in Finland is largely based on fixed-term funding of individual research groups, projects and networks, with the funding deriving from the Workplace Development Programme, the Finnish Work Environment Fund or ESF. The following is a concise overview of some of the foremost networks and clusters of expertise in Interactive Research in Finland.

The most internationally distinctive approach within Interactive Research in Finland is Developmental Work Research (DWR), which emerged in the eighties. It is based on a cultural-historical activity theory originally developed by Russian psychologists, and its main theoretical tool is a model of the activity system. This branch of research is interested in expansive learning. This means that development does not apply just to "how things are done" but also to the focus of the operations (the object of activity) — what makes learning expansive is the expansion of the object of activity (Engeström 1987). The most widely distributed application of the DWR approach is the Change Laboratory® method. It means that the members of a *de facto* work unit develop their work activities in close proximity to their actual workspace, with the aid of varied empirical material consisting of disruptions and problems in their work (Virkkunen et al. 1997). The method was developed in 1996, and since then it and versions of it have been applied to dozens of work organizations ranging from ICT companies to schools and hospitals. Instructors trained to use the method have also been trained for several work organizations. The best-known representative of this approach is the Center for Activity Theory and Developmental Work Research at the University of Helsinki, which has a graduate school, based on this approach and maintains a learning network for research and development staff that uses the Change Laboratory method. The learning network is funded by the TYKES programme. The network supports development of the method and development work by those who use it in work organizations. The network includes researchers, instructors, consultants and people in workplace development positions, who represent a multitude of scientific disciplines and occupational backgrounds. The Merikoski Rehabilitation and Research Centre in Oulu is an active member of the network and apply the Change Laboratory method in northern Finland.

The LOM project, which was implemented in Sweden (1985–90), has been a particularly important source of inspiration for Interactive Research in Finland. In 1991, the Work Research Centre at the University of Tampere started a three-year project on quality in the municipal sector with funding from the Finnish Work Environment Fund. 21 work units from 13 municipalities took part in the project, which was the largest Action Research study to be started in Finland at the time. Solutions to making municipal service-provision more effective and improving the quality of working life was sought through improving the employees' opportunities for participation in accordance with the principles of democratic dialogue and the OA tradition from the USA, rather than more "traditional" methods such as management by result and work rationalization. The project resulted in several new projects in the municipal sector that continued after the original project ended and resulted in a cooperation network for researchers and consultants using the democratic dialogue and work conference methods. The network is coordinated by the Commission for Local Authority Employers and the Work Research Centre is in charge of its academic expertise. The network included an exceptionally wide range of representatives from municipal employer and employee organizations and the municipal organizations. Over the years, the methodology of the researchers in the network has become more diverse and various local adaptations of the democratic dialogue method have been developed (Kalliola and Nakari 1999). The experts in the network have performed development work using the work conference method in some 50 municipalities and joint municipal boards, and in more than 500 work units within them. Many other experts, including the consultants and instructors of some trade unions, have also applied the method to workplace development projects.

VTT Industrial Systems has been working on a new development approach called experimental development research since the end of the eighties (Hyötyläinen 2000). It is based on Developmental Work Research, Action Research and a Grounded Theory approach. Development activity is guided by the concept of a development cycle, which progresses from a basic analysis of the existing modes of operation to planning, testing and introducing new, more developed modes of operation. The staff of the company in question takes part in creating a new mode of operation using the tools introduced to the process by the researchers; the aim is that the theoretical models and practical tools created during the planning and testing phase can be introduced to everyday work in the workplace. The first projects carried out with VTT's new approach involved a transition to flexible production automation and networked teamwork. Since then, the method has been applied particularly to the creation of multilateral and innovation-focused business networks within a number of development projects.

The Laboratory of Work Psychology and Leadership at Helsinki University of Technology is a multidisciplinary unit employing more than 50 researchers and four professors. The staff has academic degrees in engineering, psychology, economics and adult education, and they form several research teams. The aim of the Laboratory's operations is to coordinate people, work, knowledge, organizations and the work environment in an optimal fashion, and thus to improve productivity and human well-being. Research at the Laboratory is divided into four focus areas: management and organizational development, communication and interaction in management, development tools and well-being and workloads. The Laboratory was one of the first institutions in Finland to start practical development actions in companies by means of a participatory approach to development in the early eighties. The development of work processes is based on a multidisciplinary socio-technical model and long-term studies in understanding and managing processes of change. Where development projects are concerned, the research approach has been Action Research based on case studies. Theories and models of organizational behaviour, business development and organizational structures also feature in the background. In recent years, the Laboratory has been pursuing long-term work to develop reward schemes and strategy procedures. Learning networks in these fields were set up this year with support from the Workplace Development Programme. Both networks include several R&D units and various work organizations.

The above are only some of the main learning networks in workplace development in Finland at present. According to a questionnaire sent out by the Workplace Development Programme, there were 45 active workplace development-learning networks in Finland in 2003. The learning networks were usually held together by a specific theme such as development of work organizations and work processes, management systems, improvement of the work environment and occupational safety and health or the development of indicators and tools. Other factors, which might unite networks, included companies in the same sector (industry, social welfare and health, the municipal sector, training and education) and improvement of workplace cooperation structures and occupational training. Networks were only rarely based on regional development, which has been a significant source of motivation for founding networks elsewhere in the Nordic countries. This difference between workplace research in Finland and the other Nordic countries has been recognized for some time. Then again, there is a great deal of regional development work in Finland, but it has not been adopted as part of workplace research and development, but is instead considered to be part of the regional and economic policy pursued by the Ministry of Trade and Industry and the Ministry of the Interior. Examples include 22 technology centres and 35 regional centres of expertise, which cover all provinces in Finland. It seems likely that the regional perspective will take on more importance in Finland, too, as regional innovation strategies and innovation environments attract more attention.

7.3.3 References

Engeström, Y. (1987) *Learning by Expanding: An Activity-Theoretical Approach to Developmental Research.* Helsinki: Orienta-Konsultit.

Hyötyläinen, R. (2000) *Development Mechanism of Strategic Enterprise Networks: Learning and Innovation in Networks.* Technical Research Centre of Finland (VTT Publications 417). Espoo: Technical Research Centre of Finland.

Kalliola, S. and Nakari, R. (eds.) (1999) *Resources for Renewal: A Participatory Approach to the Modernization of Municipal Organizations in Finland.* Amsterdam/Philadelphia: John Benjamins.

Nieminen, M. and Kaukonen, E. (2001) *Universities and R&D Networking in a Knowledge-Based Economy: A Glance at Finnish Developments.* (Sitra Reports series 11). Helsinki: Sitra.

Oksanen, T., Lehvo, A. and Nuutinen, A. (2003) *Scientific Research in Finland: A Review of Its Quality and Impact in the Early 2000's.* (Publications of the Academy of Finland 10/03). Helsinki: Academy of Finland.

Ramstad, E. (2002) *Työelämän tutkimuksen ja kehittämisen asiantuntijaresurssit 2001* [Research and Development on Working Life: Expert Resources in 2001]. (Finnish Workplace Development Programme Reports 23). Helsinki: Ministry of Labour.

Science and Technology Policy Council of Finland (2003) *Knowledge, Innovation and Internationalisation.* Helsinki: Science and Technology Policy Council of Finland.

Tilastokeskus. *Tutkimus-ja kehittämistoiminta.* Tilastokeskus Statfin 30.4.2004.

Virkkunen, J. et al. (1997) "The Change Laboratory: A Tool for Transforming Work". In *Workplace Innovations: A Way of Promoting Competitiveness, Welfare and Employment.* Alasoini, T., Kasvio, A. and Kyllönen, M. (eds.) (Finnish Workplace Development Programme Reports 3). Helsinki: Ministry of Labour, pp. 157–174.

7.4 Action Research in Norway by Morten Levin

The history of Norwegian Action Research is approximately as long, complex and intricate as the history of sociology, anthropology and social geography. The social sciences invaded Norway from the West. It was in England and USA that the founding Norwegian fathers found their inspiration. Burning souls were intellectually stimulated through exchange with broader academic communities in such a way that they returned to Norway as missionaries for new professions. Action Research represented no exception in terms of understanding how it was rooted in Norway. The history of Action Research in Norway can be dated back to the middle of the fifties and is closely related to Einar Thorsrud.

In the foreplay of the creation of the Institute of Social Research in Industry (IFIM) on the premises of the Norwegian Institute of Technology (Later to become The Norwegian University of Science and Technology- NTNU) the then director of personal, Einar Thorsrud at the Freia chocolate factory, came in contact with the intellectual environment at the Tavistock Institute of Human relations in England. Many prominent researchers had created a stimulating environment that gradually challenged the established research paradigms in social sciences. The two dominating intellectuals were the Englishman Eric Trist and the Australian Fred Emery. Their major concern was to create a closer link between theory and practice and to shape a knowledge generating process that could create practical results. Democracy at work was also one of the important issues they wanted to promote through active engagement in industrial change processes. The Tavistock Institute was also heavily engaged in the rebuilding of British Industry after the erosion caused by the devastating Second World War.

These modern concepts of organizational change and democracy at work were diffused to Norway through this contact. The CEO of Freia Chocolate factory took the initiative to create a freestanding institute (IFIM) at the Norwegian Institute of technology in Trondheim through an endowment. This also made it possible for the Norwegian Research Council for Science and Technology (NTNF) to grant money that made it possible to inaugurate IFIM in 1958. It seems reasonable to date Norwegian Action Research back to May 1958.

The dominating project in this first phase was the Norwegian Democracy Project. The idea was to create field experiments that could create a different and non-Tayloristic work organization. Those ideas had been floating in the Tavistock environment for some time, but it turned out that they were impossible to implement under the conditions of British working life at that time. The hostility and lack of trust between trade unions and employers could not create a common ground for experimentation. The situation in Norwegian working life was very different. Trade unions and employers were on negotiating terms: a well-regulated relationship created a trustful situation where it was possible to live with the coexistence and cooperation and conflict. In fact, the chairman of the trade union council (LO) and the president of the confederation of employers (NAF) were on good speaking terms. When ideas floated in from England, it was possible for the social partners to agree on participating in what? It is also worth noting that the state, which was under a long period of social democratic government in practice, became the third social partner.

The Industrial Democracy project was located at IFIM in Trondheim, and the field experiments were spread among six different companies all over Southern Norway (Thorsrud and Emery, 1968). The Industrial democracy project was built on a core assumption that democracy would go "hand in hand" with concretely improving efficiency and modernization of Norwegian work life. Increased democracy at work (Heavily influenced by the conceptualisation of Pâté man's (1970) book *Participation and Industrial Democracy*) could be enhanced parallel to the creation of an effective and competitive work organization. In a European perspective, this was a very ambitious project.

The Industrial democracy project was founded on socio-technical thinking. The idea was, first, that technology impacted working conditions, which meant that creating a new organization had to take technology into account. Technology formed constraints as well as opportunities. In short, no clever change in working life could be made smartly unless the interrelationships between technology and organization were seriously considered. The thinking on democracy at work was rooted in the same socio-technical perspective. Without understanding the implications of technology, work could not be constructed in a way that would enhance democracy at work. The simultaneous design of work and technology was seen as the only possible road to both support democracy at work and an efficient work organization. The conceptualisation of good working conditions was heavily influenced by humanistic psychology (Maslow, 1954). The leading lights for design of work were coined in psychological job demands and defined a set of design criteria (Emery and Thorsrud, 1976). Emerging from this work was also a strong interest in group-based work. The concept "self regulating work groups" represented the point of departure for strands of thinking that later were known as team based working. This innovation is probably the most significant contribution from Norwegian international social science to date (Lindø, 1993)

In the early phases of the Industrial Democracy project, the activity was highly dominated the great amount of influence the participating researchers held. The participating researchers applied the methodological apparatus defined by the socio-technical approach. The analysis of the working conditions based on the socio-technical understanding of the ideas concerning re-design of work was almost totally in the hands and minds of the "expert" researchers. Gradually, this strategy changed as the approach departed from the thinking of Action Research as a "natural experiment" and moved towards the more active involvement of the participants. Elden (1979) suggests three different generations of research into work. It started as expert driven activity (the sleeping bag generation), had an interim phase where the researchers prepared methods and structures for change activities (the tool kit generation) and finally the third phase where the researchers took the role of supporting local initiatives (the do-it-your self generation).

It is obvious that the Industrial democracy Project represented the initial steps of work research in Norway. With a few important exceptions (for example Lysgaard 1967), work research in the eighties and eighties was the arena for Action Research. Action Research in Norway is now approaching 50 and can celebrate half a century of existence together with sociology and anthropology. Action Research became one of several voices that shaped the discourse of Norwegian social science.

The research group that Einar Thorsrud set up at NTNU in Trondheim was gradually considered by the members not to be localized at an ideal location. The cooperation with the Norwegian Institute of Technology had its ups and downs and the distance to the political and administrative centre in the capital Oslo was seen as problematic. In the middle of 1964, most of the researchers packed their cases and moved to Oslo. A new government funded Institute was created – the Work Research Institute (WRI). In doing this, the Action Research activity basically disconnected itself from its strong presence on the academic arena. A lot of attention and energy was paid to be close to important political and administrative processes. The close connection to the state bureaucracy and to the social partners in working life (trade unions and confederation of employers) ensured an important social and political position for WRI. For many years, they benefited from these close contacts, as they shaped the ground for sustained Action Research funding. In this perspective, Norway stands out as one of the bastions where Action Research could be funded.

An offspring of this activity was seen in a cooperative agreement between employers and trade unions aiming to support participative efforts for change at company level. This activity was institutionalized through a supplementary attachment to the main national agreement between employers and trade unions. In this regard it represented a quasi-public institutionalization of Action Research modes of organizational change. It is important to see that this activity departed from mainstream US based organizational development activity as it was strongly rooted in participation. In fact, we can see that mainstream US textbooks gradually picked up the participative issues in a very instrumental way clearly disconnected from the larger aspects of political economy (See for example Cummins and Worley, 1993).

In the aftermath of the Industrial Democracy Experiment, the methodological discussions in Action Research evolved substantially. The original socio-technical approach invited to a strong expert dominance. Methods and conceptual models were advocated and controlled by the researchers, and even if the intention was to invite broad participation, the methodological apparatus was quite limited in terms of participation. Searching for new models that could encourage higher degree of participant involvement being put on the agenda. The quest for broad based participation led the researchers to develop more collective problem solving methods. At WRI, the focus soon was turned towards large-scale conferences. The idea was to bring all participants together for a joint definition of the problem, planning and execution activity. In order to achieve this, the Dialogue Conference was created. The theoretical constructs underpinning this activity were borrowed from Habermas (Gustavsen 1992, Gustavsen and Engelstad, 1986). The specific form that was developed at WRI was named "Dialogue Conferences". An important feature of these conferences was how the design could support participation and leave the staff (researchers) with the task of being the "democratic police" responsible for keeping the process going and ensuring that everyone had the right and opportunity to speak out. A typical Dialogue Conference took two days, and was usually run away from the actual company site. The outcome was usually a set of plans for the improvement of work and increased efficiency. These plans were then expected to be acted on later. The Dialogue Conference was the contribution from the WRI .

On the other hand, this was not the first effort to organize Action Research in the form of conferences. In the late eighties, the Search Conference made its inroad to Norway. Inspiration was found in some Australian experiments (Emery, 1981). This conference model was called "Search Conferences" and aimed at a collective definition of the problem, searching for a desired future, and to develop action plans to reach those desired goals. The first Norwegian experiment was conducted in a North Norwegian fishing town of Skjervøy (Herbst, 1980). It opened up the possibility for community development activity and represented as such an Action Research outreached to local community development. In addition, Search Conferences could well be applied in more conventional organizational settings.

The theoretical conceptualisations at the WRI moved in the direction of conceptualizing and legitimating Action Research on dialogue based discourse ethics. Important theoretical inspirations were found in the works of Habermas and Wittgenstein. We can see these positions in the works of Gustavsen and Engelstad (1986), Pålshaugen (1998). But the WRI did not totally lock into this line of thinking, even if it dominated. The traditional socio-technical thinking was still the main theoretical formulation held by Qvale (1982) and the foundation of Action Research based on Aristotelian thoughts supported the work of Eikeland (1990).

In Trondheim, IFIM barely survived the move of the WRI to Oslo. At one critical stage, the board had a discussion on closing it permanently, but arguments for IFIM's importance to promote social aspects of work in a dominantly engineering culture won the battle. IFIM did not return to the limelight as a pure Action Research environment. Quite the contrary, quite a lot of the activity at IFIM turned out to be conventional applied research. On the other hand, Action Research was still the research paradigm for a group of IFIM researchers. Through contacts hold by Max Elden a link to Cornell University in USA was established. Bill Whyte had created a group at Cornell (Programs for Employment and Work Place Systems – PEWS) and it held some parallel thoughts to the Action Researchers at IFIM. This connection came to have a decisive influence on the theoretical and practical thinking both at NTNU and at Cornell. The joint work of Greenwood and Levin (1998) resulted in a book laying out an epistemological and methodological argumentation for Action Research based on American pragmatist philosophical thinking. In the eighties, the local university was gradually more open to including social science teaching as part of the engineering education. Max Elden was appointed professor, later to be followed by Morten Levin. This created a bridgehead for teaching Action Research at graduate and undergraduate level, as it lent opportunities for creating PhD programs in Action Research. Three PhD programs based on Action Research were established (Levin, 2004) and quite a few of these graduates now play an important role in Norwegian Action Research. In fact, here is no longer any discussion as to whether or not Action Research is accepted as one way of doing research and Action Research has accordingly a fair degree of legitimacy and standing at the university.

This very short and brief story of Norwegian Action Research shows how this professional activity has developed on the local soil following the US and British influence. Kurt Lewin's work in the period around the Second World War and the Tavistock Institute of Human Relations post WWII engagement in Action Research were the pillars upon which the Norwegian Action Research was built. The inspirations did not only affect the early efforts, but it is typical that a close and in depth international cooperation has been a trademark. It is clearly so that Norwegian researchers have held a firm place in international networks. This has been important for the continued agility of the national activity. The international cutting edge activity has always had Norwegians in key positions on the editorial boards of key journals and other relevant publications (handbooks etc.). This international presence has hardly been met by any other Norwegian science community.

In addition to this WRI and IFIM based Action Research, there have been fragments of other forms. Habermas' critical thinking, both theoretically and methodologically has for example, inspired the inspiration . The focus for these projects has to a very high degree been on supporting underprivileged groups' ability to increase their control over their own situation. In this perspective, the point of departure is quite similar to the Industrial Democracy Project. One such project was the North Odal's project, which had a focus on how to improve the commuters' life situation. North Odal is a valley some 90 kilometres North of Oslo. As most commuters to larger metropolitan areas, these people have to get up extraordinary early in the morning and returned home late at night. All kinds of family , health and social problems were linked to the life as commuters. These were the problems that were in focus and the project caught a lot of public attention, both relating to the issues at stake and to the research strategy. The clear activist role that the researchers took provoked many orthodox social scientists.

Another important and influential strand of reflective practice that can be labelled Action Research was Tomas Mathiesen's work with criminal re-establishment systems (KROM). The intention with this long term "project" was to shape a process that bridges the transitions between being an inmate to becoming a citizen. We would also find examples of Action Research in health care and social services. These efforts are interesting because of their focus, but they have contributed very moderately to the advancement of models and methods in Action Research.

The development of Norwegian Action Research has, from the initial Industrial Democracy Project onwards, been closely linked to large-scale national programs. The Industrial Democracy Projects were a key area in which to root Action Research as a strand of professional activity. They also created a sustained interest of the social partners in working life. This project had summoned enough economic and intellectual resources to create a large enough group to withstand attacks and challenges from orthodox social science. On the other hand, there have been remarkably few direct confrontations between conventional social scientists and Action Researchers. In the wake of the Industrial Democracy Project, there was an attempt to debate the epistemological and methodological approaches in Action Research (Moxness, 1981), but this can almost considered to be a rare one off event. A more important debate followed the evaluation that was commissioned by the Norwegian Research Council in 1991. Both IFIM and the WRI were evaluated. The conclusions from these evaluations created the foundations for a discourse in the Norwegian Social Science Journal (*Tidsskrift for samfunnsforskning*). Unfortunately, this debate died out after just one paper written by one of the evaluators (Sørensen, 1992) and a response from the Action Research environment at the WRI written by Pålshaugen (1992).

In recent year, two large national programs have pulled Action Research in Norway. Enterprise development that ran from 1995 to 2000 supported the development of Action Research groups that did research on working life and enterprise development. Through this project research teams have been developed at Rogalend Research in Stavanger and Agder Research in Kristiansand. In addition, a group was created at the University of Tromsø. In Trondheim, a new group was formed that mainly had a focus on working life and a strong inclination to use Action Research. These researchers had formerly been working at IFIM. This group also has close relations to the university department for Industrial Economics and Technology Management. These two groups cooperate intimately and represent an important national point of gravity in Action Research.

7.4.1 References

Cooper, G. L. and Mumford, E. (eds.) (1979): *The Quality of working life in Western Europe*, London: Associated Business Press.

Cummin, T. G. and Worley, C. G. (1993): *Organizational Development and Change*, Fifth ed., New York: West Publishing Company.

Greenwood, D. J. and Levin, M. (1998*): Introduction to Action Research, Social Science for Social Change*, Thousand Oaks: Sage.

Gustavsen, B. (1992): *Dialogue and Development*, Assen: Van Gorcum.

Gustavsen, B. and Engelstad, P. H. (1986): "The design of conferences and the evolving role of democratic dialogue", *Human Relations*, 39(2), pp. 101–116.

Eikeland, O. (1990): *Erfaring, Dialogikk og Politikk*, (Experiences, dialogics and politics) Oslo: WRI.

Elden, M. (1979): "Three generations of work-democracy experiments in Norway". In *The Quality of Working Life in Western and Eastern Europe.* Cooper, C. L. and Mumford, E. (eds.) London: Assoc. Business P.

Emery, M. (1981): *Searching: For New Directions, in New Ways, for New Times.* Canberra: Centre for Continuing Education, Australian National University.

Herbst, P. (1980) "Community Conference design: Skjervøy, to day and tomorrow", *Human Futures,* (2), 1–6.

Levin, M. (ed.) (2002): *Researching Enterprise Development Action Research and the cooperation between management and labour in Norway,* Amsterdam: John Benjamins.

– (2004): "PhD program in Action Research: Can they be housed in universities?" *Concepts and Transformation,* 8:3, pp. 219–238.

Lindø, P. H. (1993): *Internkontroll: Krysspress mellom byråkratisk kontroll og aktiv medvirkning,* PhD Diss. (Internal control – crosspress between buereacratic control and active participation) Institutt for organisasjons- og arbeidslivsfag, NTNU.

Lysgaard, S. (1961): *Arbeiderkollektivet (Workers Collective),* Oslo: Universitetsforlaget.

Maslow, A. H. (1954): *A Theory of Human Motivation,* New York: Harper.

Moxness, P. (1981): "Hvordan gikk det med Samarbeidsprosjektet LO/ N.A.F.?" (What happende to the IIndustrial democracy Project?). *Tidsskrift for samfunnsforskning,* 22(4), pp. 331–340.

Pateman, C. (1979): *Participation and Democratic Theory,* London: Cambridge University Press.

Pålshaugen, Ø. (1992): "Aksjonsforskning: en nyttig vitenskap", (Action resaerch is useful sceince). *Tidsskrift for samfunnsforskning,* 33, pp. 231–251.

Pålshaugen, E. (1998): *The End of Organization Theory?* Amsterdam: John Benjamins.

Quale, T. (1982): "Oljeboring, ville vesten I Nordsjøen – eller vanlig norsk industri", *Tidsskrift for samfunnsforskning,* 5/6, pp. 535–557.

Sørensen, Å. B. (1992): "Aktionsforskning i om arbejdslivet", (Action Research in work life) *Tidsskrift for samfunnsforskning,* 33, pp. 213–230.

Thorsrud, E. and Emery, F. (1970): *Mot en ny bedriftsorganisasjon,* (Towards a new work organization) Oslo: Tanum.

7.5 Interactive Research growing from the grassroots in the Swedish Public Sector by Thomas Tydén

7.5.1 Introduction

A major part of local and county authorities work is ultimately concerned with encounters between people: between teacher and pupil, social worker and client, health care staff and patient. The success of such meetings depends on a high degree of professional skill, often based on years of professional experience. Professionalism is generally not something that can be taught through schools and training courses, but rather something that each person laboriously acquires in the course of day-to-day work, in which theories confront and complement practice and the individual's own personal qualities. The secret of professionalism is to some extent hidden within the unique make-up of each individual, but certain generalisations are nevertheless possible. To understand these practitioners and the nature of their professional qualities, the skills they have acquired through experience must be brought to light and as far as possible put into words. And a greater degree of understanding is needed to make better use of these experiences and to give new colleagues the opportunity of putting these experiences to use in their own practical work. Ultimately it is a question of using limited resources to the best advantage. And the sums of money involved are huge, given that these professional groups account for what is by far the largest part of the public economy.

Research on the practical work of these professional groups requires special tools to get to the essence of their professional skills. One factor that complicates this is that the concept of research is not problemized: instead it is used as if there was general agreement as to what it is. But the issue is not as simple as that. There are a number of research traditions that may well, in varying degrees, play a part in the development of community work practice. Earlier studies clearly indicate the importance to active professionals of reflections based on practical experience, stories and examples given by colleagues (Tydén et al. 2000). The more experienced among them call for a more systematic analysis of work experience, and they often expressed a need to provide this kind of reflection themselves. The academic world may not always be the obvious answer to their needs.

The above gives an indication of the risk involved in the introduction within certain professions of a research approach traditionally found to work for others, before it has been made clear what the preconditions are for such an introduction. Gunbjörg Erlingsdottir (1999) discusses this phenomenon in her thesis with the help of the story of Pandora's box. According to one version of this myth, all that was good in the box was turned to evil when it was opened in the wrong place. Good intentions are transformed into negative consequences when put into practice in the wrong context. Erlingsdottir's thesis dealt with ideas taken from industry being applied to health care, but the example may well be applied to the tendency to follow traditional academic thinking in attempting to make science of social work, teaching, care work etc. However, the picture is not a straightforward one, since we have seen an alternative research approach beginning to appear during recent years, with a clear practical orientation, in which the focus is on knowledge and practical work and the interplay between the experiences of researchers and practicians is a central issue. Concepts such as participatory research and Interactive Research constitute attempts to define this research approach. Many of the researchers involved in this kind of research collaboration with active professionals in the public sector are not to be found within the traditional institutions at the country's universities: instead they are attached to a rapidly growing flora of practically-orientated research institutes that are more or less independent of the university world (Bergström et al. 2000, Tydén 1997, Samuelsson 1999)

In this section on Interactive Research in Sweden, I have chosen to give a detailed presentation of these new research environments in which interactivity is not just a trademark but also a necessity if they are to meet the demands made by public institutions in the local areas in which their research is conducted.

This section highlights the development of Interactive Research as it has been manifested in the various research environments built up by local and county authorities in Sweden.

Beginning with the development of Swedish research policy since the eighties, it will examine how this led successively to the development of a regional research policy as well as to the organisation of research on a regional basis. But, first a word or two about the history of learning in local and county councils.

7.5.2   A historical perspective on learning

Learning has always been an important part of the work of local and county authorities. The county council ordinance of 1862 named teaching as one of the matters which regional councils had the right to discuss and make decisions about. Questions of knowledge and competence have gone hand in hand with the development of county authorities during the 150 years of their existence. During different phases of their development these concerns have expressed themselves in different ways, among these being the growth of various educational institutions run by county authorities themselves or with their support. Examples of these are the "folk high schools" and schools of agricultural and domestic science. Various kinds of health care training programmes have also been started and run by regional authorities. The local authorities and, earlier on, parish councils ran schools on their own initiative, and this work too was regulated by law in the middle of the 19th century.

The central position accorded by local and county authorities to learning was not something unique to these public institutions. On the contrary, it is clear that the development of local and county authorities was paralleled by other significant tendencies in society. When the county councils were created, Sweden was moving rapidly towards industrialisation: a new society that posed challenges to existing structures. The industrial society demanded a disciplined, not to say servile, work force, which nevertheless possessed a particular kind of competence – above all literacy. The 1842 school law may be seen as society's answer to the demands of industry. In its first form this law entailed six years' compulsory schooling for all children in Sweden. The main subjects were reading and writing exercises and arithmetic, along with Christianity. The pupils were to have a certain level of basic skills in these subjects. Christianity was another subject intended to give certain basic skills, as well as implanting moral values in relation to work and society. Fixed school hours with timetables for lessons schooled pupils in punctuality and regularity to meet the demands of the industrial society.

A new type of educational method began to appear, mainly determined by the enclosed spaces that were a consequence of compulsory schooling for all. Learning was to become something separate from children's daily life – their practical experience. Before the introduction of compulsory schooling, learning was an integral part of day-to-day life for ordinary children. For the better off there were cathedral schools, tutors and other forms of private teaching. But for the majority there was no formal education. Nor, perhaps, was there any need of such a thing for the kind of work that the children of the period could look forward to doing in the future – often the same as their parents did. Industrial society was to mean a shift from problem-based learning that arose from concrete incidents in everyday life to fact-based learning determined by what others – not the pupils themselves – judged to be the competence they needed. The written word took over as a medium for learning, which resulted in certain limitations. Written texts are only a channel of communication between a writer and a reader, and too much emphasis on written material can eclipse other important sensations that influence learning, such as sensual impressions and the pupil's own practical experience. A similar development took place in other areas of society such as the armed forces, where learning and education around the turn of the 19th–20th century moved from the old exercise grounds to the barracks. Barracks teaching was to take over at the expense of more practically orientated training. Later in this chapter we shall see how local and county authorities during the past decades have gradually begun to approach a synthesis between written, factual knowledge and practical skills.

The work of local and county authorities during the past century was characterised, among other things, by a number of measures taken to reinforce and improve the competence of staff. What has happened during recent decades has been a conscious effort, as well as experiments with, among other things, different types of research and development in the field of further education and enhancement of competence. These will be described in greater detail in the next section.

7.5.3   Focus on research and learning

7.5.3.1 Developments in Sweden

Research policy in the eighties was outlined in the government bill 1959:105. This spelled out what was expected of research as a motive force for development in society. In the words of the bill:

> "Research is the most dynamic force in the development of society. Research results constantly create new, previously unimagined possibilities for material and cultural progress. Without a doubt the present period is one in which substantial support for research is one of the main preconditions for the preservation and continuing development of the welfare state in the true sense of the expression, and in which research on an increasingly internationalised basis constitutes one of the best foundations for improved unity and cooperation. Even though investments made for the advancement of research may not always give immediate returns from the point of view of the national economy, such investments will inevitably be an increasingly important factor in the long-term planning required for well-balanced social development."

Sandström (1994) notes that this laid the foundations of a generous attitude towards research and research committees, in spite of the fact that the government did not specify how research was to be utilised. In 1962 a working committee on research was instituted, consisting of representatives from government and from research committees. According to Sandström (ibid), this meant that a point of contact had been created between politics and research, one that was to be characterised by a continuity that had previously been lacking. Research was to be used to an increasing extent as a basis for planning in the various sectors of society.

But research issues were still dealt with on a national level, with departments and national research committees exerting powerful influence. It was not until twenty years later that this positive attitude to research clearly and manifestly made its mark on local and county authority work on a regional level.

There are several reasons why Swedish research policy, as well as educational policy, underwent such a rapid development in the eighties. If we consider events in a wider, international context, we can see that Sweden was affected by a larger wave of interest in education that swept over Western Europe and, above all, the USA. Some would explain the forces behind this wave by means of the "Sputnik effect". The background to this was the fact that the Soviet Union, in 1957, managed to launch a space rocket called the Sputnik. This was the first man-made object ever to orbit the earth. The event had a profound effect on the USA, where there was a sense of having been beaten into second place.

The countermeasures taken were above all to take the form of enormous investments in the entire educational system, along with a gigantic research and development project run by those who had ordered it, the so-called Apollo Project. The goal as formulated by President John F Kennedy was for the USA to have sent an American to the moon before the end of the eighties. Education, as well as research and development, were to become central themes in American politics during this period, a fact that affected European politics, Swedish politics and, of course, also local politics, although in different stages. As was noted at the beginning of this section, local and county councils were influenced by world events as early as in 1862, when the county councils were created, and this picture has not changed in the 150 years of the county councils' existence. If anything, dependence on the outside world has increased.

7.5.4 Research in different regions of the country

7.5.4.1 The regionalisation of the universities and colleges of further education

In the course of the last half century, the education system in Sweden has been the subject of a number of reports and reforms. The education report of 1968, U68, recommended fixed courses of study to increase efficiency and job-orientation in further education. This reform was partly carried out in 1969 when a system of streaming, complemented by a selection of individual courses, was introduced. In 1977, a further education reform based on U68 was carried out with a view to increasing the availability of education still more, broadening and differentiating the total amount of education on offer, and democratising the organisation of education. Moreover, education was to be conducted on a scientific basis, to give training in critical thinking and to provide adequate professional training. The result of this reform was that the concept of further education was broadened to encompass all education beyond the high school/secondary school level, dividing it into five sectors: technical professions; administrative, financial and social professions; health care; teaching; and professions involving the arts and information.

The major change was the creation of a number of new colleges, mainly small to medium-sized further education colleges as well as nursing schools. Eventually the latter were to be incorporated into the further education colleges. This, however, was not accompanied by a fixed state budget for research, and for the first ten years or so research and development work was very limited. This limitation was in turn one of several factors influencing local and county councils in the creation of research institutions of their own, as will be discussed in greater detail in the next section.

From the school year 1993–94 onwards, yet another further education reform came into force, in which the main issue was deregulation and decentralisation, chiefly by affording wider scope to decision-makers at the various colleges and universities . During the past decade, research activity at regional colleges has intensified dramatically, thanks to a conscious research policy on the part of the state, followed up by financial support for research from both the state and other actors, the most important of these being the Knowledge Foundation.

7.5.4.2 Regionalisation of research

As was pointed out earlier, the state had plenty of scope for directing research. The general control exercised by means of the government, parliament, authorities and other state bodies, was able to influence the direction taken by research both in the short and the long term. The report of the research committee of 1977 (SOU 1977:52) states that control …

"is exercised by means of power over the structure and extent of state research organisations, and by means of the power to initiate and order research within the given framework."

At this time, the end of the eighties, there were also other interested parties within the public sector – the local and county councils – who needed research and development and who also had some scope for ordering, initiating or themselves conducting research and development. But the councils had not done anything like as much as the state in the way of carrying out and financing research. Uncertainty as to how far research could be regarded as the business of local authorities might partially explain the lack of initiative shown by Swedish regional and municipal authorities. Another explanation may have been the fact that the regional councils' finances kept them from getting involved in research work. At the same time, it became more and more apparent that the councils had become increasingly dependent on research, and that they themselves had to put more and more effort into various forms of development work in direct connection to their own activities.

The report of the research committee stated that:

"information from institutes, organisations, businesses and authorities indicates that local councils are acting as financiers in connection with various kinds of research and development work. Some of the money for research jobs accounted for by universities and colleges also comes from local authorities. Some councils also contribute in the form of research subsidies to projects at the universities, and a number of councils allocate grants for, among other things, research. Larger local authorities run their own research and development work in different fields."

Although the research committee's report shows that individual councils were to a certain extent committed to promoting research, its conclusion is that neither local nor county authorities are particularly active in initiating major research and development efforts. The report points out that there is *"scope for taking collective initiatives"* on problems that local and county authorities have in common, and it also emphasises that

"the efforts made by research committees, state authorities, delegations, boards etc are to some extent determined by their idea of the extent of research and development projects and the number of interested parties on the committee. There is therefore good reason for more local and county authorities, both as parties interested in research and development and as initiators of research and development work of their own, to make their voices heard."

It may be concluded that these reports and the work simultaneously in progress of building up regional colleges of further education to be linked to the world of research are instances of state authorities preparing the ground for local and county government initiatives in starting research and development work of their own. A further supporting factor was the generally positive attitude to research and development that, as we have seen above, was rapidly spreading around the country.

7.5.5 At the flashpoint between research and practice: regional research and development environments begin to appear

During the last twenty years, a large number of regional research environments have come into being in Sweden. In an inventory of publicly financed research and development organisations that were not affiliated to universities and colleges, carried out by the Dalarna Research Institute in 2000, a budding flora of research activity could be discerned. 82 organisations were listed, mainly active either in health care or the social services (Bergström *et al.* 2000). These were organisations not mentioned either in national research policy discussions or in the regional growth agreements. This is a growing sector of the research world, at the same time as it is still to a large extent hidden from the public eye.

The majority of the organisations listed do the bulk of their work in areas central to the business of local and county authorities, such as health care and the social services. They reflect a growing commitment to research and development on the part of these authorities. This is in all probability the first stage of an evolution, which will make local and county authorities increasingly important actors in this field. Judging by the information in the inventory, they are primarily interested in creating research and development centres within – or in close proximity to – their own fields of activity. This often means interdisciplinary or applied research rather than work within a single discipline.

It is noteworthy that these environments have been created at the same time as the university and college system has expanded. There are often links between them as well. In other words, these are complementary rather than competing organisations. It is perhaps natural to regard the growth of these new research and development organisations as a consequence of the universities' and colleges' partial inability to deal with problems raised in the course of public-sector work. Sörlin (2004) is of the opinion that research done at universities takes place according to a system of academic norms and with the object of developing basic knowledge in close contact with teaching. He further feels that it should not be taken for granted that this kind of research furthers economic growth in the same way as research done in close contact with businesses and authorities and geared to satisfying a demand for knowledge originating in the commercial market.

Similar thoughts were expressed in the research strategy document compiled by the Swedish Association of Local Authorities and the Federation of Swedish County Councils during the preparation of the research policy proposal of 2004. (Svenska kommunförbundet and Landstingsförbundet, Stockholm 2003). In the background material I contributed to the strategy document, I argued in terms of the prepositions applied to research (Tydén 2003). I discussed how research affecting local and county councils may be organised so as to benefit their work. One aspect of this is that research and development around council work should chiefly, or to a greater degree, take place in collaboration with representatives from this sphere of activity. Research about councils is conducted in varying measure at Swedish colleges and universities. What is required to a much greater extent is research with local and county councils. These prepositions embody the necessary, complementary ingredients involved in conducting research relevant to local authority work. In what follows, the emphasis will be placed on the preposition with, since it represents a neglected area of state research policy.

The importance of research for improvement and renewal is often dependent on how research is organised in terms of dialogue with representatives from the work area involved, mutual respect for each other's skills and continual interaction. Expressions such as research-based development work or researcher-supported development work may be seen as attempts to capture the essence of this aspect of improvement work.

In the strategy document referred to above, the council associations emphasised that it is therefore important for the coming proposal to make it clear that there is an area separate from research, and also separate from administration, an area whose task is innovation/development – let us say an innovation system – in which research and knowledge play an important part, as do teaching methods, organisational development and administration. It is of course important that the national system accords legitimacy to this area and gives it a measure of financial support without stipulating any form of state control.

Yet another explanation for the appearance of these regional research centres outside the traditional academic institutions may be a theoretical discussion about new knowledge production that is currently taking place, as well as a debate about the universities and the ways in which the quest for knowledge is organised. Important new research issues and fields of research have to an increasing extent obliged researchers to work across the boundaries delineated by their own scientific disciplines.

Another conclusion is that these new research and development organisations produce new knowledge just as other research organisations do, but that what they create above all is research environments. These environments comprise both researchers and practitioners, and they highlight the dialogue between these groups and stress the importance of interdisciplinary learning and the combination of different kinds of competence.

It was noted at the beginning of this chapter how the school law of 1842 led to a change in teaching methods from a form of learning based on experience and concrete problems to teaching tied to written texts. Learning and production environments had to be separated, and the written word took the place of the production environment. For 150 years the emphasis in learning was to be placed on *catalogue* knowledge (terminology) and *analogue* knowledge (knowledge of texts) (Dahlgren 2001). But such things as the advent of research environments promoting close collaboration between research and practice, and drawing on co-operation and an exchange of experience between these, lead to what may be termed *dialogue* knowledge (discussion/exchange/interplay between instrument and human being, or between human beings).

We are now beginning to approach a synthesis of these three kinds of knowledge, although the first two are still to a large extent dominant. It takes time to adapt education to new needs. The tendency is always to carry on in the old ways even though surroundings and purposes change. An analogy may serve as an instance of this. When the first cars began to be produced in the 1880's, they looked strikingly like horse-drawn carriages, and it was several decades before car manufacturers had freed themselves from this left-over of history and started to design cars on the basis of their particular function rather than harking back to the epoch of the horse-drawn carriage. In our case the challenge is to develop research and learning on the basis of post-industrial conditions and free ourselves from the old Taylorist factory ideal.

It is in this context that local and county authorities, by creating new research environments of the kind mentioned above, have been in the forefront of a pioneering development. This new development highlights the dialogue between researcher and practitioner, and emphasises the need for collaboration on an equal basis. Earlier in this section we noted how local and county councils in their policies have been dependent on and influenced by international and national trends and policy developments. But as regards the development of new local and regional research environments we can assert that the local and county councils have not been following any trend. On the contrary, Swedish local and regional authorities have been the instigators and to some extent the promoters of this trend in the early, decisive and long-term commitment they have shown on these issues, by creating and developing regional research and development environments where Interactive Research has a natural environment in which to thrive and develop.

7.5.6   References

Bergström, E. et al. (2000), *Det dolda universitetet. Framväxten av nya FoU-miljöer utanför universitet och högskolor.* (DFR-rapport 2000:2) Falun: Dalarnas forskningsråd.

Dahlgren, L-O (2001), http://www.fryx.vasteras.se/LOD.htm

Erlingsdottir,G.(1999),*Förförandeidéer:Kvalitetssäkringihälso-ochsjukvården.* Lund: Företagsekonomiska institutionen, Lunds Universitet.

Proposition 1959:105, p. 39.

Sandström, U. (1994), *Mellan politik och forskning: Staten och byggforskningen 1960–1992*. Stockholm: Byggforskningsrådet.

SOU 1977:52.

Tydén, T., Josefsson, C. and Messing, J. (2000), *Socialsekreterare och kunskapsbildning*. Stockholm: Socialstyrelsen.

Tydén, T. (2003), "Forskning och offentlig sector". In *En forskningsstrategi för kommuner, landsting och regioner*. Stockholm: Svenska kommunförbundet & Landstingsförbundet.

OLAV EIKELAND

8. The Validity *of* Action Research – Validity *in* Action Research[1]

My theme, validity and Action Research raises several questions. What is validity? What is Action Research? Are they unequivocal concepts? Are they relevant for each other, or compatible? An overall objective of this book is to relate and integrate discussions about Action Research better with discussions within more mainstream research traditions, rather than presenting Action Research as a parallel and unmediated alternative, a separate paradigm, or discourse, "out of touch" with mainstream social research[2]. Since the concept of validity in social research was both conceived and born from within mainstream research, it is important to review the mainstream discussions, to assess the relevance of "validity" for Action Research. Hence, I will discuss the concept of validity and its historical entanglement with different methodological approaches and paradigms, followed by a critical review of some concepts of Action Research, in order to sort out aspects of validity relevant for Action Research. But the following can only be selective suggestions and summaries, maybe representative in a holographic way. References serve mostly as positions presenting validity challenges Action Research approaches must solve and transcend.

The strongest justification for Action Research is produced by showing that what most distinctively characterizes Action Research cannot

---

1 Discussions with Richard Winter, Benedicte Brøgger, and Lars Klemsdal have contributed to improve the quality of this text. So has feedback from the editors.

2 Preventing separation, without conflating distinctions, is an important concern of mine. See Eikeland (1985), (1995), (1998), (2001). Paalshaugen (1992) explicitly defends Action Research as an incommensurable paradigm.

be a) reduced to a mere combination for utilitarian purposes of applied theories and techniques, borrowed from other research approaches (e.g. Spjelkavik; 1995). Instead, b) Action Research represents a core element *of* those other approaches, not sufficiently articulated (i.e. tacit) within mainstream presentations. Hence, c) Action Research, when developed and justified properly in this way, could contribute importantly to solving some inherent contradictions, impasses, and validity-problems bothering mainstream social research. This situation makes other approaches intuitively approximate Action Research, labelling it a "practical turn", "turn to practice" (Schatzki and Knorr-Cetina, 2001; Gherardi, 2000; Nicolini et al. 2003), "participative approach", "practical reflexivity" (Cunliffe and Easterby-Smith, 2004), and similar things. I try to show – *in outline* – a movement from a) to b) and c), both from within mainstream approaches, and from within Action Research since the forties.

Hence, mainstream validity challenges cannot be ignored by Action Research, and relegated to other parallel disciplinary discourses. Instead, they should be used to "mainstream" Action Research itself, within an emerging socially distributed mode of knowledge production in need of new research practices, and a new understanding of different ways of knowing (Cf. Gibbons et al. (1994), Nowotny et al. (2001), Eikeland (1999a), (1999b), Eikeland & Fossestøl (ed.) (1998).

8.1   Approaches, paradigms, and trajectories

I will write about three "ways of accessing data" in mainstream social research, through: (1) observation, (2) asking questions, and (3) experimentation. They are not mutually exclusive, but often presented as distinct. More basically, I describe different "paradigm-relationships" between researchers and the researched, based on ways of knowing extracted from the thoughts of Aristotle as presented in Eikeland (1997a; 1998b; 1999b; 2001; forthcoming): (I) a spectator-astronomer (*spectas*) paradigm, (II) a manipulator-user (*manipus*) paradigm, (III) a stranger-visitor (*stravis*) paradigm, and (IV) a native-performer-community (*napeco*) paradigm. Each paradigm means striving to live up to different ideal standards of research practice. Hence, the same "way of accessing data" may still be different within different "model-relationships". Finally, I refer to different historical, developmental trajectories of disciplines and approaches.

Observation (1) and questioning (2) have been the main bases for sociology and anthropology, while experimentation (3) has had a stronger base in psychology. Both (1) and (3) treat subjects studied as external ("natural") objects, whose changes are to be explained, predicted, and sometimes provoked, modified, and controlled, by the researchers. Communication, "normal" interaction, and mutual influence between researchers and researched are minimized and controlled, in order not to invalidate findings. Questioning (2) breaks the separation of researchers and researched, but brings with it a host of potentially invalidating "researcher-effects" and "reactivities" of the encounter, which should be "controlled for".

Still, these approaches are *all* in the "othering-business" of studying what *they* – the others – do, based on a division of labour, and a distinct separation, between the researcher and the researched. The researchers move in (on the others), and stay temporarily, observing, asking questions, or administering treatment, while taking notes, or recording. Then they move out from "the field", leave "the others" behind, and report their "findings" – their empirical "experience" – with their interpretations and explanations, to a separate community of researchers, different from the observed, where knowledge about them is supposed to be accumulated. This self-conceptualisation has not changed much over the last 50 years, regardless of all the discussions about how the observers are observed (observational reciprocity, relativity of perspectives), the reactivity-effects of the research processes, the potential arbitrariness of the conceptual framing of observations, interpretations, and explanations, and other difficulties (Cf. Eikeland, 1985b; 1995). Attempts at modelling social research on natural science have tried to accommodate to a *spectas* paradigm (I) (observing and explaining, without intervening), or to a *manipus* paradigm (II) (controlled, experimental intervention). Qualitative social research remains mostly within a *stravis* paradigm (III) (questioning and close observation with minimum intervention). But although they approach things from different starting points, their trajectories seem to converge, bringing them to a similar intellectual "terminus" of "theory-pluralism" among an unlimited series of differently positioned, reciprocal observers, doing research *on* each other (see Chapter 2).

Action Research has a different trajectory. It developed from within the experimental *manipus* paradigm (II), emerging, transcending, and separating from it gradually, and not always very consciously. Quasi-experimentation grew into a parallel trajectory from the same roots, Don Campbell (1916–1996) being a major figure. Still, Campbell (1978) explicitly acknowledges his relationship and affinity with the Action Research tradition. The acknowledged founder of Action Research, Kurt Lewin (1890–1947), was an experimental psychologist, and John Dewey's (1859–1952) philosophy was all about the expansion and diffusion of the experimental method and attitude, from insulated laboratories to everyday activities in communities, schools, and organisations.

In a way, Action Research was born in 1946 by transforming the social field-experiment practically from within, when, one evening, the subjects of research were invited to join in the interpretation of the findings (French; 1985, French and Bell; 1990:25, Benne et al.; 1975:1–6, Lippitt; 1949). This practical "*Aufhebung*" of the controlled and manipulative experiment, changed the relationship between the knower and the known, both principally and practically, breaking the division of labour between the researchers and the researched. Treatment was no longer to be administered by researchers on "blinded" subjects. But still, experimentation (3) should not be abandoned. It should be transformed. Action Research should not remain within the horizon of a *manipus* paradigm (II), however. It should adapt to a *napeco* paradigm (IV), doing research *with*, not *on* others, searching for actual commonalities we relate to as competent, native performers, even when borrowing techniques developed within other paradigms (e.g. 3–IV).

The very separation – through divisions of labour and allocation of tasks – between researcher and researched, the knower and the known, contributes much to the invalidation of knowledge, for either epistemological, ethical, or both reasons. Some current Action Research, however, seem to be stuck in the ruins of a *stravis* paradigm, a *manipus* paradigm, or both, speaking uncritically about "interventions" to create changes in the reality of people they visit. With only vague ideas about any *napeco* paradigm, they keep fighting against an older *spectas* paradigm.

8.2 Validity in general

According to *Webster's Unabridged Dictionary* "*valid*" derives from Latin "*validus*", meaning "strong" or "powerful". Among several meanings, the one that claims validity as something "sound", i.e. well grounded on principles or evidence, and able to withstand criticism or objection, seems to be the most relevant meaning for research in general. Descriptions, arguments, inferences, interpretations, justifications, insights, explanations, predictions, and conclusions would all seem to need validity in this sense. Why is research supported as a common good by political decision-makers? Why should it be? Probably because they, and most people, still believe that research produces valid results in this sense, which are somehow better than dogmatic, or just any stray, opinion or belief, and better than unexamined habit and tradition. Presumably, research produces unbiased and adequate, or, at least improved, knowledge of some "thing" known.

This prevalent "enlightened" *doxa* is basic to the legitimacy of modern institutions. Arbitrary, uninformed, or dogmatic public bureaucracies, "professionals", or "mob rule", acting only in their private interest, are intolerable. If "science" cannot deliver valid knowledge and competence, most people will feel an urge to find something *better* (more valid). An important reason is this: Why should I listen to, and learn from, whatever anyone tells me? Provided you cannot force, manipulate, or seduce me, probably most of all because your observations, arguments, or inferences are better (more valid) than mine, or your knowledge and competence is better (more valid).

Validity, then, concerns the *status* of research, or, of *any* arguments and points of view, or, of any practice, competence, and skill, as somehow providing *better* insight into, or mastery of, something, than any arbitrary habit or opinion. Hence, validity is not arbitrary or just descriptive, merely registering what happens to count – *de facto* – as current opinion accepted by some people in some context. Validity needs justifications, legitimacy, and competence. It is normative, prescriptive, and argumentative (*discoursive*), specifying what should count rightfully as standards of truth, justice, fairness, beauty, and similar normative questions. It says (simplified): trust, believe, or learn this, *for these reasons*! Even relativist attempts at abandoning or deconstructing truth and objectivity, (do and must) say the same thing *about their own deconstructive claims*. So, validity, in the broad sense, seems unavoidable for any activity or opinion posing as science or research, or claiming to understand, know, or master anything. Since Action Research does all of this, *"we must make sure we are not kidding ourselves"* (and others), as Reason and Rowan (1981:243) have formulated it on behalf of Action Research.

8.3 Mainstream special validities

But "validity" also has a more restricted sense within social research, as a technical term associated with *testing* and *measuring* social phenomena. In this sense, it worked like a Procrustean measuring rod in the middle of the 20th century, dismissing as unscientific, knowledge that did not "measure up" to technical definitions of it. Measuring and testing spring from the tendency in the natural sciences since the 17th century, to quantify and measure all things (Cf. e.g. Porter; 1995 and Crosby; 1997). It also springs from the social practice of *testing* individuals, to find out if they were of a certain desirable or undesirable kind, or possessed similar properties, for example "witches" in early modern Europe, or, "fitted for mandarin-work" in the administration of the Chinese emperors of old (Cf. Wainer & Braun, 1988: xviii). Fused, these traditions surfaced in a modernised, Western scientific guise, in the aftermath of soldier testing in World War 1, as part of a broad, burgeoning "test-industry" or movement, according to Cronbach (1916–2001) (1970:9), for 50 years the most central figure internationally in psychometrics. Tests try to find or invent *observable* measures for *non*-observable entities like intelligence, attitude, "status", etc. As *indicators*, results immediately raise questions like: "Are we measuring what we think we are measuring?" (Kerlinger (1973:457) or, "is this a *valid* measure"?

8.3.1 Construct validity

According to Cherryholmes (1988:421), "Social research methodology entered adolescence, if not maturity, in July 1955." Angoff (1988) shows that testers had mostly been concerned with *pragmatic* validation, i.e. the mere predictive power of tests, *useful* for certain purposes, like finding "mandarinability". They had been less concerned with providing consistent theoretical explanations, giving better insight and understanding, and a broader legitimacy for the use of tests. In order to provide tests with scientific validity and legitimacy, and to improve the interpretation and explanation of results, Cronbach and Meehl (1955) argued that "construct validity" was the primary kind, decisive also for other kinds of validity. "Constructs" are conceptual parts of *theories*, not operationally defined, i.e. non-observables such as. "witchiness". Cronbach (1970:142) illustrates: A reading test may *predict* poor "school performance" of a child. But without high "construct validity" in interpreting the results – i.e. a valid explanation – the test *results* will not tell us *why*, whether it is caused by an emotional disturbance, mental ability, organic speech deficiency, cultural or sub-cultural conceptual differences (ethnic, class, gender, etc.), witchcraft, or combinations, thereby also obfuscating adequate action to remedy the situation.

Construct validity is primarily necessary for *practical* purposes, not predictive. But, Cronbach (1970:123 and 142) continues, "Construct validation is more complex than other types of validation". "*Predictive* validity is examined in a single experiment", comparing it with other *concurrent* measures of the same, or with real time *criteria*, while "Construct validity is established through a long-continued interplay between observation, reasoning, and imagination". Mishler (1990:436 & 418–419), summarizing subsequent discussions, sees convergence among "prominent validity theorists on the primacy of *construct* validity". Cronbach (1970:142) concludes that the "Process of construct validation is *the same* as that by which scientific theories are developed".

Developments in social theory and methodology since 1970 have shown (Cherryholmes; 1988) that the admission that a) "*All* validation is (ultimately) construct validation", b) "The end goal of validation is explanation and understanding" (Cronbach (1984) in Mishler (1990:418)), and c) validation processes are identical to theory development, was like opening Pandora's box (Latour; 1999:23) – i.e. the floodgates of phenomenology, hermeneutics, Marxism, feminism, science studies, post-structuralism, and deconstruction – on the discussions about validity. The flood of critique shifts the emphasis from technical measures to "choice" or the development of an interpretive horizon, i.e.

to what the researchers bring along to the "thing" studied. As recognised by Cronbach (1988 & 1989), it shifts the horizon from a disciplinary psychometric discussion, to the general horizon of philosophy of science, epistemology, and methodology, and even wider, to discussions about power, politics, knowledge forms, and the institutional, cultural, and historical formation and embeddedness of knowing, i.e. to questions about the validity of all the built in preconditions, preconceptions, and presuppositions of certain forms of science and research. It deconstructs, *from within*, the restricted concepts of "predictive", "concurrent", and "criteria" validity. But in order to retain a critical sense of direction – not drown in the flood, and let all things pass – an obsession with validity seems necessary (Cf. Lather; 1993). From here, there is no *valid* "turning back" along the road that brought us. Naïveté is over, enter nativeness. For survivors from the flood, and from the "evils" of Pandora's box, flooded lands are fertile.

8.3.2   Whose constructs?

These discussions about validity worked in the border zone between a *spectas* (I) and a *manipus* (II) paradigm. Their "constructs" were made and defined, not by "natives", but by a segregated group of researchers, either trying to minimize intervention and all reactivity of research methods, or administering controlled treatments, trying to predict and control, through "blindfolding / blind-testing" subjected participants. Behind their somewhat artificial precautions, are several presuppositions, hardly self-evidently valid, but still central for maintaining both *internal* and *external* validity for this kind of research. *Internal* validity is the assumption that the "independent variable", introduced and varied by experimenting researchers, is what actually causes the registered changes in "dependent variables", *not* some uncontrolled and unknown intermediate, or complementary, cooperating cause, making results like "x causes y" valid at least for those exactly specified experimental conditions.

External validity is the assumption, granted internal validity, that the introduction of "the same" independent variable as in the experiment, will have the same effect when introduced under similar non-experimental conditions (Mishler (1990:417). This arrangement of research seems to presuppose, *first of all*, that there are "natural states" of communities and organisations, or of any people studied, to be approached by researchers. These states are supposedly their working mode *without* the presence of researchers intervening and studying them, making "unobtrusiveness" and self-obliteration a research ideal. *Secondly*, that what is observed can be trusted to represent adequately the things observed, not only what the observers bring as preconceptions and prejudices from their point of view. This seems to require observation through a perspective from "nowhere-in-particular", without any selective "filters" or coloured lenses. And *thirdly*, that human events are controlled by efficient *causes-and-effects*, which can be separated, isolated, manipulated, and controlled. *Finally*, along with these, and as a consequence, looms the ethically dubious practice of treating other human beings merely as external, natural objects.

But, *first of all*, people are influenced continuously by the state of their own bodies, by each other, by the institutions framing and directing their activity. Why eliminate only the researcher-effects? What makes the rest more "natural", and desirable as a subject of study? *Secondly*, all observations must be "filtered", "framed" and "coloured" by whatever cultural-cognitive "instruments" the observer brings to the observation, making it thoroughly *interpreted*. To perceive is to perceive something *as something*, and always *some* things, never *no* thing, or *every* thing. And, *thirdly*, since people are different, "the same cause" may produce one reaction in one individual, culture, institutional setting, organisation, or community, a different one in another one, depending on how "the cause" is interpreted, or handled, by the ones "affected", and on whatever other causes are influencing them. Physical, chemical, and biological agents may have effects evading human, cultural filters, but we are mostly *not* merely physical, chemical, or biological to each other. Statistical correlations may, of course, be valid on an aggregated level, but it is, by definition, not possible to deduce from these alone, anything about any new individual case encountered. Statistics is a "spectator sport", as Jaeger (1990) appropriately points out.

In spite of this complexity, social life as lived experience is not arbitrary, random, and chaotic, and somehow *not* knowing and handling these complicated facts of social life, would imply *not* knowing how to participate competently in everyday activities. Since most of us participate, and find our ways around, somehow, most, or at least many of us, must know already. What we perceive, and how we interpret it, is determined by who we are, our background, our position, our interests, etc. There are no simple operations to perform in order to reach an unbiased "view from nowhere". Also, technical interventions have low validity, if any, in social settings, except, maybe, statistically, in introducing large-scale measures. What *must* be known by performing natives appears too complicated to catch for this kind of science. Hence, learning what competent natives must know already, acting and interacting in their societies, seems a more promising subject of study than externalised "quasi-natural" states of societies, *without* researchers, or with "researcher-effects" eliminated. Maybe "researchers-as-native-apprentices" is a better idea (cf. Coy (ed.), 1989).

8.3.3   Watch the natives (turning against you)!

Phenomenologists break the frameworks set by the spectators-*cum*-manipulators' paradigms, according to Cherryholmes (1988:430ff.). Natives have advanced and complex competencies, not merely based on detached observation, technical manipulation, or pragmatic considerations of usefulness. Hence, the phenomenologists want to take seriously the "constructs" of the "natives" by finding out what they are, understanding them, and using them as starting points for developing theory. The prototypical discipline for doing this remains anthropology. Its conventional practice of studying far-away cultures makes it clear, however, that this is a move from a *spectas* and *manipus* paradigm, to a *stravis* paradigm. Although even the discipline and practice of psychometrics could be considered a strange, native culture to be visited and observed by anthropologists, the phenomenologists are still segregated researchers (Cf. e.g. Latour and Woolgar (1979), Latour (1987) and Knorr-Cetina and Mulkay (1983). To remain or "go native" is considered a threat to validity (opening the floodgates), since we presumably then acquire certain "interests", and invest "emotions" in the practices of the natives, become moved by limitless, uncontrollable influences, and come to see things *too much* as the natives do. By "going native" we presumably lose interest in, and the ability to do, research, and stop reporting back to the separated research community. We become biased, and unable to be disinterested and "objective". Hence, "participant observation" *is*, quite deliberately and consciously, being a stranger and visitor, not yet a native-apprentice, since true apprentices aim to be masters themselves.

But the emphasis on construct validity does give the floor to anthropologists like Geertz (1973). Like many, Geertz abandons all belief in "data", i.e. in anything presumably "given" as "uncultured", or "theory free". Cultural "findings" are always already designed, selected, and interpreted by the natives, and must next be selected and interpreted by the anthropologist observers, creating Giddens' (1973) famous "double hermeneutic". Hence, the primary business of anthropology (Geertz: 1973: 9ff.) is not measurement, but interpretation and explication of meaning. The researchers' business is to understand "the natives". Participant observation has, however, conventionally been understood as *observation*, avoiding, as much as possible, intervention and influencing events. Hence, "participation" remains a way of closing in on the observed. Schatzman and Strauss (1973:13f.) still share the presuppositions of the *spectas* paradigm about "unobtrusiveness", comparing themselves to zoologists and archaeologists, merely "observing events in a natural situation", instead of the supposedly contrived artificiality of experimental laboratory research.

But what we perceive depends on who and what we are, and reactivity is pervasive. Geertz' (1973:16) validity-question cannot be avoided: "*How* can you tell a better account from a worse one"? and, "what *basis* do we have for our interpretation"? Observation based interpretations may say more about the observers, transferring their personal and private contexts, than it says about the observed, since what the observed is interpreted *as*, must be something the observers bring along, and presumably understand. We cannot just say; "I saw it", or, "I heard it", without *understanding* it.

Is it possible at all for interpretations to be based on close, but non-intervening and unaffected observation through preconceptions brought along from "theory" or "home culture" alone? Currently, there is a tendency to rest content with stranger-visitor researchers providing *their* interpretations, since *both* explanation *and* understanding appear to require more than what seems possible to provide, and reasonable to expect, from participant observation. At least this emphasizes that whatever is concluded is done *by* the researchers, not by the researched, although the aim of the phenomenological approach was to understand and base their theories on *native* constructs. Instead the *stravis* researchers are thrown back at their own presuppositions and preconceptions, all "threats to validity" produced by the division of labour itself between the observer and the observed.

If even interpretations made by pure, unbiased, and uncontaminated observers say more about the observers, than they do about the observed, then privileged "points of view" seem hard to defend as starting points for gaining access to "the things" studied. What interpretive framework to use no longer depends on what "fits the facts" either. There are strict, logical reasons for concluding that the same observations may be explained and interpreted within an unlimited number of frameworks, since any number of false premises may produce true conclusions. "This whale is warm-blooded" is a true conclusion that is correctly deduced from the false major premise that "all *fishes* (Xs) are warm-blooded", and from the false minor premise that "this whale is a *fish* (or, an X)".[3]

Once more, the gates seem to open up to all kinds of motives or justifications for *choosing* one explanatory framework before another, strategic, political, religious, ethical, pragmatically useful, selfish, emotional, etc. I have my theories, motives, and justifications, while you have yours, and those who happen to share similar preferences, world-views, and causes join the same gangs! But we also seem to be approaching a common terminal station for the trajectories based on the separation of researcher and researched, the ultimate, and generalised "othering-station". At this terminal, then, all the separated researchers seem to agree in an indifferent, "hen-tropic", and "caco-*phóney*" theory-pluralism among an unlimited, and stalemated series of "free", equal, and reciprocal observers, using theories too as useful instruments, chosen for any preferred purpose.

---

3   Cf. Eikeland (1985b). To find the right middle term (fish, mammal, or some other X) was Aristotle's great challenge. If there is no right one, anything goes. This is also why neither *induction* (neither the plebeian, nor aristocratic one of Larry Laudan (1981), nor Peirce's *abduction* (1868 and 1878) will work in a non-arbitrary way.

8.3.4   *Watch Yourself! Or, Who's a Native?*

In turning the attention away from the observed, towards the observers, at least the researchers regain colour, and become visible. There are no rock bottom, uncultured, and theory-free "data". But neither can researchers pretend to be colourless, transparent, invisible, and unobtrusive (unbiased, neutral) media for the perspectives of any others, observed or interviewed. Instead, we *all* become colourful, opaque, situated, and prejudiced observers, no matter from what distance we observe each other. All perspectives and aspects are different but equally valid in this absolution of the scientific observer. Anything goes! Such equality in difference invites absolute indifference too, however.

To transcend the terminal state of indifferent theory-pluralism, and let the *napeco* paradigm emerge as interpretive horizon, we have to realize two things. *First*, deep-seated prejudices, basic assumptions, preconceptions, and presuppositions brought along to every observation as "instruments of perception", are not *chosen*. Modern theories, and other "head-stuff", are like superficial opinions, *words*, easy to remove, change, or exchange. But prejudices, etc. are not like declarations. They are not merely "espoused theories" (Argyris and Schön; 1978), or theories at all. They are subconscious and tacit, merged with or submerged in our practices and routines, in our acquired experience, and in the gradual, constitutional formation of our knower-subjectivities, stored in deep layers of emotional and habitual reactive-perceptive patterns. Changing *them* is not like changing a theory or opinion. What we see and understand *through*, both as knowers-researchers and as natives, is our acquired *habitus* (Bourdieu, 1972; 1980), inscribed and cast in historical forms, institutional divisions, and practical categories.

Secondly, all observers do *more* than merely observe each other. If we only see them *observing*, the turn "inward", towards the observers, may come to a superficial halt in the endless row of subjective meanings, partial aspects, and perspectives. But more than observation becomes common if we move beyond the merely observational stance, and ask questions about the formation of our presuppositions, basic assumptions, preconceptions, and prejudices as observers, in line with the *transcendental*, or "Copernican", turn of Immanuel Kant (1724–1804). We may even ask, in line with the *existential* turn of Martin Heidegger

(1889–1976) and Ludwig Wittgenstein (1889–1951), what the necessary preconditions are for the complex performative and communicative competence implied in our everyday native practices. Then we can use the turn consciously to transcend the stalemated and indifferent cacophony of theory-pluralism. What do we as actors always already have to know and do in order to do what we actually do, in our sophisticated everyday practices? This is what the phenomenological researchers were looking for. But now we change positions. The natives are no longer "the others". *We* have ourselves become the natives. The basis for our interpretations is no longer merely what we *see* the others do, or our recordings of what the others tell us on the basis of *their* acquired experience. The relevant "empirical" experience transforms from hard-to-get, illusionary "data" *about* the others, accessed at validity's peril, to our own acquired, personal experience, in a sense always already accessed. The ways and means of doing, or not doing things, accumulated in the personal experience and competence (*habitus*) of any one of us as practitioner-knower-researcher, adjusted to the realities of lived practical experience, becomes the entrance door to more adequate knowledge, and to more adequate concepts of knowledge. We are all natives, and the natives' competence no longer simply skews, biases, and distorts cognition in ways to be eliminated and controlled for. It is a *sine qua non* of any cognition.

Our witnesses to this transforming move beyond observation will be Devereux (1967), Hammersley and Atkinson (1987), and Hastrup (1995). They work from within a *stravis* paradigm. But in the determination of fieldwork as no longer modelled on unbiased, and unobtrusive observation, they represent transitional figures towards Action Research, from within an interpretive, stranger-visitor approach. Devereux, a psychoanalyst-anthropologist, turns his critical gaze at himself, and at other researchers, as participant observers, using psychoanalytical concepts like "transference" and "counter-transference" in order to understand the relationship between observer and observed (1967:41–42f.). His reflections focus on how technical research methods can be used as psychological defences against anxiety in the researchers, and how untreated psychological traumas and neuroses in the researchers work as projections and counter-transference towards what is observed. As with analysts in Psychoanalysis, the prejudices can be controlled, according to Devereux, through a compulsory apprentice-didactic Psychoanalysis. Basically, however, *any* unattended difference between the researcher and the researched, or rather between *any* two people, may be projected or transferred as a distorting interpretive framework (both ways). But apprenticeship is retained as a necessary way of getting through the jungle of projections.

Hammersley and Atkinson (1987), while sticking strictly to the distinction between researchers and researched, have stopped trying to eliminate reactivity, i.e. the effects on the researched of researchers interacting with the field. Instead, they recommend using reactivity and researcher effects as sources of information, aligning, in spite of themselves, the researchers with the researched in their mutual affective relationships, since this interactive reactivity is outside any controlled research method. And what the researchers can do, the natives can do too. Researchers are natives, and *vice versa*. Hastrup (1995) has consciously abandoned trying to assimilate what goes on during an anthropologist's fieldwork to any models of observation, recognizing fully the weaknesses inherent in observation, and purging the *stravis* paradigm of any *spectas* remains. Instead, she uses her own participant *experience*, no longer reducible to observation or technical "data", as a starting point for theorizing. But her participant experience is hardly different in kind from other participants' experience, once more equalizing the researchers and the researched. As native-novice she becomes an apprentice, but under conditions hardly adjusted to learning. Instead of the assumed "culture-adequate" and culturally specific results of observation, the knowledge-generating process as such, based in gradually acquired personal experience and emerging insights, moves to the centre of her attention.

But still, none of these authors write much about *how* their "self-study" proceeds, although it clearly cannot be merely by conventional empirical methods. The methods of their methodological studies are not presented in any detail. Studying themselves, not as imprisoned in private and subjective selves, or in language, but as the way to get to know human life and social realities more object-adequately, adjusted to the nature of the studied object at hand, i.e. "objectively", their primary methods can no longer be observing, interviewing, or experimenting *on* the others. Instead, they have to "theorize *through* practice" (Zalewski;

2000), as methodologists and practitioner researchers do. What they, as natives, or as researching practitioners, have to adjust their practical conduct to, i.e. whatever they must take into consideration in doing what they do without failing or stumbling, and thereby accumulate as normative experience, *is* the social reality sought for. If not, why heed it, why adjust to it, why care about it, as we do? The only trouble is that these adjustments are often done tacitly and subconsciously. So, how can they be grasped and articulated? What does "theorizing-through-practice" mean? How is it done? At least it must mean remembering that we are all natives, and that we have to start wherever we are.

For natives, or native-apprentices, the old, Delphic-Socratic "know thyself" emerges as relevant, and unavoidable. Once we realize that what is to be recollected in the analysis of our selves, are not primarily private fears, inwards-looking, and empty emotional subjectivities, reminiscences of former lives, or a separate world of ideas, Socratic midwifery and recollection work becomes relevant as a modern, empirical research method (cf. Eikeland; 1998b). Recollection concerns conscious and subconscious "memories" and tacit knowing, the collection and integration of which constitutes experience. In recollection work we do not study others in analogy to external objects moving and changing, with hypothesized inner, subjective wills and motives. We study our own *habitus*; i.e. "ways-of-doing-things" – "what-does-it-mean-to-do-x-or-be-y?" – and what is implied in these different ways, through critical examinations of our own native-performer experience and competence, their adequacy or inadequacy. Prejudices and presuppositions are not simply chosen, but formed experientially through interaction and practice. We, the natives, are not atoms that remain self-identical if abstracted from history, circumstances, past personal experiences, and hopes and expectations for the future. We carry them all in our selves, individually and collectively, as our socially formed selves. If we critically inspect our own prejudices, presuppositions, and practices, then, and what these in fact take into consideration and are adjusted to, the outcome will not be merely "subjectively chosen", private, theoretical frameworks, but historically and culturally – practically – formed conceptions, or even, occasionally, "object-adequate" skills as prejudices – ways-of-doing-things that really work – among expert or virtuoso performers, i.e. what science has always been hunting for.

What emerges through recollection, then, are things we have in common *qua* certain kinds of practitioners. For detached, non-participants, observing from a distance, language, social skills, norms, traditions, power relations, inner wills and motives, even organisations, and similar "entities" are invisible and intangible, not something necessarily taken into consideration in order to perform their observations. Native practitioners, on the other hand, must heed and handle entities as these practically, in order to manage at all, although not always competently. In order to manage practically, we must know the language, power relations, and traditions, and how to deal with different kinds of situations and people. But "the lens" of mainstream research only lets us "see" the "brute facts" of externally observable events, as Salner (1989:49) formulates it. Anything "inside", or "between", things occupying a physical space, is invisible.

Social researchers not immersed as participants may either operate with extraneous mathematical models, or with conjectured subjective meanings and motives, ascribed to observable individuals in order to prevent their theoretical reduction to mechanical, machine-like objects. But language, norms, social skills, traditions, power relations etc. remain "theoretical constructs", and projecting specific "wills" and "motives" remains a moral obligation, not a practical necessity. For native practitioners, however, they are experiential reality, common, hard-hitting "powers" in their lives, which they have to handle, or fail. Even without knowing them, they *feel* them. To experience their reality, we must participate as native practitioners. Hence, if there is a *privileged* position here, it is the native's. What we as natives have in common, are habits, standards of competence, language, tradition, norms, and ways-of-doing-things. These are the bases for the "common meanings" of Charles Taylor (1971), unattainable by anyone extraneous to the collective as anything but conjectures and hypotheses.

Research based on the separation and difference between researchers and the researched, recognizes and appeals to certain forms of evidence and "data". It ignores, and renders suspect the practical experience of native performers, readers, thinkers, speakers, and writers, or, it is unable to attain to native experiences because it doesn't analyse *its own* nativeness, i.e. the prejudices, etc. of its own *habitus*. But nativeness cannot be eliminated from research. Research must go *through* native experience.

Hence, the validation and use of practical, personal experience must move from periphery to centre of any research process, transforming it in the movement. The "whats" and "hows" of this process *is* Action Research. Hence, a critical review of validity challenges in mainstream research points to a strong Action Research, tested by developing answers to validity challenges of mainstream approaches. Validity *requires* an Action Research where action and research are united in a reflective native approach studying what-it-means-to-be-and-act-as-a-native, what is implied and presupposed in ways-of-doing-things the native-performative way. But can current shades of "really extant" Action Research (REAR) – more often than not performed as unmediated alternatives in segregated and fortified opposition to mainstream research – live up to the standards of an Action Research emerging in and from "enemy country", developed and tested "in battle"?

8.4 "Really Extant" Action Research – various validities in varieties of REAR

Since the seventies, Action Research has become a diverse, and worldwide community, documented in many publications.[4] How does it relate to the content of the preceding paragraphs? What Kvale (1989:73) says about qualitative social research could be said about Action Research as well:

> It has been an exception rather than the rule, that a qualitative research report includes a discussion of the reliability and validity of the results. If such concepts are mentioned, it may be to dismiss them as positivist reifications.

Validity has not been a central concern in the REAR communities. In a sense, Gustavsen (1986:152f. & 1988:234f.), central in Scandinavian Action Research over the last 35 years, has "dismissed" the discussion by

---

4   See e.g. O'Hanlon (ed.) (1996), Toulmin & Gustavsen (eds.) (1997), Hollingsworth (ed.) (1997), McTaggart (ed.) (1997), Reason & Bradbury (eds.) (2001), Winter & Munn-Giddings (2001), Day et al. (eds.) (2002). These collections mostly represent what I call "second wave AR" below.

pointing out that Action Research may not have high validity, neither internally nor externally, but mainstream research does not really fare much better, and at least Action Research is relevant for practitioners and develops theory democratically. But even if this were true, leaving it at that would be insufficient. Neither Action Research nor validity can simply be reduced to democratic procedures.

Below, I outline some Action Research-approaches in order to clarify differences concealed behind the label of Action Research. Validity questions are not identical for all kinds. I mention several strands without discussing all. In approximately temporal succession, they are: 1) the re-location and transfer of experimentation, 2) feedback of results, 3) results and research expertise used in political activism, 4) researcher-practitioner collaboration in OD-work, 5) research useful for practitioners, 6) counter-cultures of indigenous knowing, and practitioner-research, and, finally, 7) immanent critique. These are not separate and mutually exclusive approaches, but shades of Action Research, often intermingled. No. 2, 3, and 5 are mentioned without elaboration in section 4.1. In section 4.2, no. 1, 6, and 7 are presented together. As an influential current of Action Research in Scandinavia, no. 4 receives a separate discussion in 4.3.

8.4.1 Action Research as "applied research"

In the 1940's and 1950's, survey feedback research was perceived by established social science in the USA as a break with mainstream attempts at keeping research activities segregated from society. It was launched as an early Action Research approach (Cf. French; 1985, French and Bell; 1990). As indicated by the designation, research-results are fed back to the researched for application or discussion. The research processes – data collection and data analysis – remain the conventional ones, however, not necessarily limited to surveys, but still based on a division of labour and separation of researchers and researched. Feedback research is a kind of "applied research", applying mainstream research techniques for ulterior practical purposes. It doesn't raise specific validity questions beyond those concerning conventional mainstream methods.

From 1965 to 1980, many Scandinavians saw Action Research as putting "politically correct" themes on the research agenda, and as the use of research results in political activism. Researchers considered themselves a kind of counter-expertise. No research could be neutral in its choice of questions to research. Most contemporary, mainstream research was conceived to be working as "servants of power" (Baritz; 1960). Hence, inversely, the legitimacy of using research as a tool serving underprivileged groups in society could not really be questioned. But this too is a kind of applied research, based on a division between facts and values, and between means and ends inherited from Max Weber (1904). Research techniques, as instruments, are considered neutral "facts" or means beyond value-disagreements[5]. This approach does not question methods any more than feed back research does. Neither does it raise specific validity questions beyond the mainstream approaches reviewed. "Research action", or "researcher activism", rather than "Action Research", might be better designations for this, as well as for feedback research.

A diluted cumulative effect of these "researcher activism" variants is the now prevalent attitude both in Action Research communities and in broader circles, that, since it cannot be neutral, and since the "ivory tower" is crumbling anyway, research should be useful and relevant for practitioners. Research is evaluated in moral and political terms according to how immediately applicable it is, according to how easily it can be understood by practitioners, and according to how appealing it is to people who are primarily concerned with getting things done, i.e. who do not have the time and patience to elaborate too thoroughly. The legitimacy of the practitioners' interests is usually not questioned. This attitude borrows legitimacy from the also prevalent attitude that "science" has been deconstructed with "positivism", by the flooding of research validity by apparently insurmountable challenges referred to earlier sections, and that science has lost both its validity and its reliability.

8.4.2   *Action Research as radically different ways of doing research*
The approaches in 4.1 do not really question the validity of the what, how, and why of mainstream research methods. In a way they remain

---

5   Brox (1990) represents such an approach.

naïve. Their criticism and indignation with established research is moral and political, directed at "wrong" applications of "neutral" instruments. The Action Research-variants below are related in that their opposition and critique towards established, mainstream research is not merely moral and political. It concerns the research instruments themselves. Research methods are not neutral, and Action Research is not merely using the same instruments for different, politically correct purposes.

8.4.2.1 First wave of Action Research

This is continuous with the birth of Action Research in the forties, through the double step of a) moving experimentation from the laboratories into the field, and, more radically, b) inviting the subjects of research to join the community of researchers in the primary interpretation of findings.[6] Re-locating experimentation and expanding the community of inquiry is different from participant observation, interviewing, and conventional experimentation, although these may be parts. Transferring experimental research *from* insulated laboratories based on a division of labour between researchers and subjects (as objects), *to* experimentation in everyday settings in workplaces, communities, and organisations as communities of inquiry, transforms it.

In the transfer, the division of labour is suspended and principally overcome. This suspension transforms the experiment from technical manipulation and spectator theories, to a development of common and shared knowledge and competence, from using others as "guinea pigs", to experimenting *together*. It does make experiments "uncontrollable", but at the same time, it makes the objects known into co-researchers (knowers), departing from continued attempts at retaining control in the "quasi-experimental" tradition. Ultimately, then, this transformation changes the kind of knowledge sought for.

The first wave of Action Research did not break with the self-interpretation of mainstream research, however. It conceived of itself as a continuation and expansion of attitudes and practices of a unified science. It was simply "scientific". For different reasons, this first wave of Action Research in the forties, and the fifties, petered out or was redirected as

---

6 As representatives of first wave AR, cf. e.g. Collier (1945), Lewin (1946), Chein, Cook and Harding (1948a) & (1948b), Lippitt (1949), Corey (1953), Shumsky (1958), Whyte and Hamilton (1964), and Marrow (1964).

organisational development-work (OD), program evaluation, and sensitivity training during the sixties (Sanford; 1970, Campbell; 1978).

8.4.2.2 Second wave of Action Research

The second wave of Action Research rose in the seventies as part of a politically radicalised and counter-cultural climate, both in industrialised and third world countries. It developed as parallel counter-cultures of "alternative", "indigenous" knowledge and practitioner research, independently in many different places, and often without any clear continuity with or knowledge about the first wave of Action Research.

"Practitioner research", "teacher research", etc. belong in this counter-cultural second wave too, although these terms sometimes mean just practitioners using conventional research techniques. Islands of Action Research were parallel to each other but also to mainstream research, i.e. without really relating to, or interacting with mainstream research. But "counter-cultural" Action Research uses the results of science criticism to justify doing something different, and still call it research. Since mainstream research is "rotten", we have to rid ourselves of it, and do something completely different.

Instead of working as spectator-astronomers, manipulator-users, or stranger-visitors, counter-cultural Action Research has mainly worked by gathering people in dialogue about their experience as professionals or as native members of different communities. Neither observing others, nor the manipulation of, nor the intervention into, their realities, but these experience-focused dialogues, as such, constitute the Action Research processes. Professional researchers participate fully in, and often facilitate these processes, and other practitioners participate as co-researchers, making the research process open and shared among all practitioner-participants, in line with the first wave break-through in the forties.

Hence, counter-cultural Action Research has preached and practised dialogue, but hardly with mainstream research, giving counter-cultural Action Research a somewhat "sectarian" image in the institutionalised research world. And some babies were undoubtedly thrown out with the dirty mainstream water.

8.4.2.3 Third way of Action Research

Finally, there is Action Research as immanent critique.[7] This is a way of doing Action Research, but hardly a wave. The approach shares features with both first and second wave Action Research. With the first it shares an obligation to start from within mainstream research practices, and by insisting on a critical dialogue with *anyone* as the way forward, eventually transcending given starting points. It shares the obligation to experiment in real social settings with practitioners as members of peer groups of inquiry and interpretation. But it does not share any obligation to retain and defend the three conventional paradigms of social research (I, II, and III above) with their institutional arrangements.

The first wave had no real understanding of profoundly different approaches in a unified, still expansive, scientific movement. With the second wave the third way shares the obligation to develop "indigenous" knowledge *as* natives, and *with* natives. It also shares the participatory research practices. But it does not share its separatist inclinations opposing mainstream research. Mainstream social research is one of the most interesting native tribes, not because it is right, but because it is wrong in most interesting ways. Ways I have tried to indicate in the first part of this article. The third way does not share any obligation to defend and preserve, separate, substantial cultures uncritically as they are, if they obstruct the pursuit of its final, and strongest obligation towards some very old and traditional, higher ideals of intellectual activity and individual autonomy, searching for truth within open and critical groups of peers, whose community of practice is constituted primarily through this "trans-cultural" or "super-cultural" obligation and inquiry in itself. This highest obligation to "cultivation" is a precondition for diversity.

What makes immanent critique into Action Research is its insistence on thinking through personal practices of both researchers and natives, searching for patterns and inconsistencies within things said and done. It is obsessed with validity (cf. Lather; 1993), and this obsession pulls it ahead in all fields and directions. Immanent critique is not separate or different from any other position or practice. It unfolds and develops

---

7 Cf. Eikeland (1985), (1998a), (2001). See also Antonio (1981) on the concept of immanent critique.

inherent tendencies in any practice, position, or perspective, to the point where they transform themselves, and new patterns emerge and can be articulated. Hence, immanent critique is transforming Action Research, and transforming mainstream research, as well. This chapter tries to emulate this approach, by starting where it does, the way it does.

8.4.3 Action Research as researchers and practitioners collaborating in OD work

Still another approach must be presented and examined. It figures as an important "second-wave" current of Action Research, but there are significant differences that should be addressed. It contains the dominant tradition at the Work Research Institute (WRI) in Oslo, which has had a clear influence on ways of doing Action Research in Sweden and Denmark since around 1970. Since the second half of the sixties researchers at the WRI have assisted and written about OD projects in Norwegian work life, private and public.

Since the first half of the eighties, this activity has been called Action Research.[8] The projects have mostly worked with participatory methods involving whole departments, or small and medium sized enterprises, to establish organisational structures allowing increased participation in daily work. But since I am not writing history, only certain aspects of one dominant WRI approach will be discussed here, concerning the relationship between the researchers and the field. My own work has also been based at the WRI since 1985, since 1987 with developing and building systematic learning capacities – permanently interlaced Action Research-spirals as learning systems – into organisations, using distinctions and alternations between a) "on-stage-*performance*" in "work organisations", b) temporary "project organisations", and c) "back-

---

8   In spite of this, it is one of the few in the second wave with continuity connecting it to the first wave of AR. Although the label AR was not used before the beginning of the seventies, Einar Thorsrud, the founder of the WRI, had personal contacts since the late fifties with Eric Trist, Fred Emery, and Philip Herbst at the Tavistock Institute, and with Chris Argyris, and Don Schön in the USA. Trist, Emery, and Herbst became important figures in Norwegian developments from the first half of the sixties.

stage-*reflections*" in "development organisations".[9] A distinction with a similar origin between "development organisation" and "work organisation" is more widely diffused through the work of P.H. Engelstad, Ø. Paalshaugen, and B. Gustavsen. The similarity springs from the close collaboration from 1986 to 1990, between the two first mentioned, myself, and B. Bernhardsen, in an Action Research-project among car dealers and repair shops, where the distinction was first circulated (Cf. Eikeland, 1987; Paalshaugen, 1988). Practices appear similar, but interpretations differ. A basic nexus indicated by the concepts of "immanent critique" and "counter-public spheres", exists between my own Action Research-work, and the strong justification suggested in the first part of this article. This nexus will emerge more clearly at the end.

8.4.3.1 Complementarity?

The dominant WRI-approach is based on a division of labour between researchers and field-participants, in a way recognizing these as different cultures and discourses. The division is construed as "complementary", each party bringing contributions from different discourses into OD-work in organisations. According to this view, no one is privileged or "above" the other, although the researchers often speak of what they are doing as their "interventions" in the organisations of others in order to create changes. In the theoretical elaborations, however, the researchers remain principally distinct and separated, as complementary parts.[10] But the model itself does not originate with the relations of researchers to a field of research different from themselves, inquiring into "the others". Its origin lies in the model of a cooperative team in practical project work (Thorsrud; 1976), with a defined division of labour and complementary roles between specialists in different fields. Still, I don't think it really challenges fundamental presumptions of modern institutionalised research.

---

9 See Eikeland and Berg (1997). The whole approach has clear similarities to the "free space" thinking presented in the article in this book by K. Aa. Nielsen and B. S. Nielsen (2006), mainly due to similar inspirational sources.

10 Gustavsen (1990), Engelstad (1995), Paalshaugen (1991). Greenwood and Levin (1998) emphasize "co-generative" learning between "natives" and external researchers in a democratic process, but do not use the term "complementary" to describe this.

Starting from and accepting a division of labour between "researchers" and "practitioners", then, this approach frequently raises questions about the role or contribution of research/ers in development work. The loci of the collaborative development work are never the researchers own work places or tasks, however, but the work places of "the others". The researchers move out into the social realities of the others, not vice versa. The loci are where the field participants are natives, not the researchers. Hence, I will keep writing about "the natives" in this context.

The "role of research" is normally described as bringing in research perspectives to assist the development processes. But this role does not usually or necessarily mean doing tasks specific to any distinct and identifiable research process. Hence, the basis for the "researchers' perspectives" is unclear, since conventional research is constantly challenged verbally. The research/ers' role usually means anything individuals with formal positions as researchers might contribute to a project with practical objectives, often tasks hard to separate from what management consultants normally do, as e.g. planning and leading a conference or seminar, project management of some kind, taking notes and writing summaries, teaching, "applying" theoretical or empirical research results, or even far more menial tasks. This appears to be what being "action oriented" means, contributing to getting things done.

But the details of the research processes as such, e.g. of "data-collection", "data-analysis", "theory-development", or of whatever else might identify research as a kind of activity different from other activities, somehow get mysteriously lost, or they merge (are conflated, de-specified) completely with *anything* people designated as "researchers" might do, making them into researchers formally, but not necessarily *de facto* by doing specified research work. Research tends to be reduced to an intended "side-effect" of "interventions" to create changes in the reality of people the researchers visit and collaborate with, and of contributing to project and development work. But "intervening", "creating changes", and "getting things done" in a project – without anything in addition – hardly qualifies as research in itself, unless getting things done anywhere and in any way at all does. And the "research addition" cannot be merely systematic observation, questioning, or conventional experimentation, with pitfalls indicated in the first sections of this article.

Core Action Research competence is *not* equal to "getting things done", *plus* systematic observation, questioning, and experimentation. Turning the gaze of "close-up" spectators more intensely towards the "practice" of others is *not* equal to an epistemological "turn to practice". It is important to keep in mind that A) doing whatever is required for the purpose of acquiring knowledge and understanding, is different from B) doing whatever is required for the purpose of changing a social system or individuals, no matter how much we may "have to change it in order to understand it". A) and B) may overlap. A) may require changing something and somebody, and it certainly requires practical experience, as the previous sections of this article has tried to show. B) may require learning and searching for new knowledge related to intended changes.

But the ultimate objectives of the two are different, making the practical requirements different too in spite of accidental overlaps, since they move at different rhythms and velocities, go through different stages, and search for different ends. Research methods are not automatically methods for making changes, nor are methods of change necessarily research methods. A) changes things *in order to* understand. B) understands as much as necessary *in order to* change something. So, is Action Research an A)-kind of method, or a B)-kind? The WRI tradition usually thinks of it as a B)-kind. Hence, they do things *with* others, but do they do *research with* the others?

In this approach researchers participate in development processes among "the natives", where researchers "intervene". The planned change and development processes are not among the researchers. The natives are only to a quite limited degree invited into the research-processes of the researchers. The differences and the separation of cultures and discourses between the natives and the researchers are maintained. The research processes remain mostly closed country (black box), even to other researchers. Exactly such an invitation to the natives to take part in the specific research processes – opening them up – was what launched Action Research in the forties, however. Later on, in the counter-cultural second wave of Action Research, collaboration in con-scientization-work, specifically, has been central. What distinguished Action Research at the start, and made it "revolutionary", was not col-laboration, or broad participation, around any project objectives whatever, where "researchers" participate as complementary team specialists. Within second-wave Action Research, researchers have acted as facilitators in groups *sharing* research and learning processes, as presumed experts in such processes, where dialogue has become a central way of working.

The WRI-approach has also been promoted as a *dialogical* approach since the middle of the eighties (Gustavsen; 1984 & 1985). But "dialogue" is hardly distinguished from other ways of conversing like e.g. deliberation or negotiation. The main "dialogue" is not between researchers and field participants joining hands in processes with the clear and specific purpose of learning or research. In the WRI-tradition the researchers are mostly organisers, administrators, and instructors of conversational processes, "restructuring" the discourses in organisations on behalf of the native others, processes the others – the natives – go through, not the researchers. In addition, these conversational processes, mostly arranged as so-called "Dialogue Conferences" *presumed* to be dialogical, since the researchers mostly do not participate in the group work, are not primarily research processes of the A)-kind, but mainly preliminary steps in designing practical development projects, securing ownership and support for processes and results. Project planning, designing participation, is also said to be done "in dialogue" with representatives of employers and employees in organisations. But when any kind of conversation for any purpose, performed in any way, becomes "dialogue", and anything done is "Action Research", important differences disappear, and without differences, understanding is hard. Indifference rules, and everything is equally valid, or invalid.

In order to understand, it is important to keep in mind, that just like the concept of complementarity, the concept of dialogue promoted by the WRI-approach does not, like many other concepts of dialogue, have its origin primarily in the critical elaboration and development of specific research or learning processes. Most other concepts of dialogue currently in circulation, not merely colloquial, get their inspiration either from ancient dialogical philosophy in Plato (428–347 BC) and Aristotle (384–322 BC), from Martin Buber (1878–1965), from Karl-Otto Apel (1922–) and Jürgen Habermas (1929–), or from David Bohm (1917–1992). But the primary, and practical, origin of the WRI concept of dialogue lies with processes of *negotiation* between employers associations and workers unions (Cf. Engelstad, 1983; Engelstad and Gustavsen, 1983). These parleys, established in Norwegian work life since the 1930's, are what many projects in Norway during the eighties tried to expand and develop to include collaboration in organizational development. In 1982 they finally succeeded in getting the expansion included in general agreements between the major work life organisations (LO and NAF/NHO). These expanded negotiations and the resulting compromises about specific steps of action or general arrangements, then, are what were attempted infused with Habermasian concepts of "ideal communication" in the eighties (Gustavsen; 1984, 1985, 1987 & 1990).

During the eighties the division of labour within this current of Action Research has been described as going between process and content in development processes, researchers designing the processes, e.g. of Dialogue Conferences, while the field participants – the real conference participants – provide the content from their work experiences. This relationship is called complementary. But it is hardly an ordinary complementary relationship. What does complementarity mean? As in a jigsaw puzzle or in a machine, each complementary part fills in the gaps, or completes the lacunas of the others by providing what the others lack reciprocally, i.e. producing a kind of whole together (*com-plere /-plenus = full, or whole together*). But even if complementary parts were fluid and flexible, continuously adapting to changes in the others, each part would remain what it is as part without merging with the others or gradually becoming identical to them. Merging or identical parts are hardly complementary. Complementary parts retain separate tasks and roles, separate functions. In many ways complementarity freezes the relationships in divisions of labour between producers and consumers, between merchants and customers, between tasks in work organisations, or generally between roles in social systems. Together they make up a whole society, work organisation, or whatever. But what kind of whole or totality is this relationship between researchers and field-practitioners part of?

8.4.3.2 Masters and Apprentices Going the Same Way

The relationship between thinking and acting is not like other technical or social divisions of labour between farmers, shoemakers, tailors, etc.

The relationship between research and practice is hardly complementary any more than thinking and acting is. Thinking without acting is empty. Acting without thinking is blind. To the extent that this division has become part of historically entrenched social divisions of labour, its legitimacy is highly questionable. As indicated, such a division of labour allocating thinking and reflecting to certain individuals or groups, and mere execution to others, contributes to a host of difficulties in the production, transfer, and communication of knowledge, and ultimately it contributes to the invalidation of knowledge. It is *the* main problem within mainstream research, trying to assimilate "the others" as subjects of study, to objects or to instruments. This division is one of the major difficulties with many models of organisations and societies when it is not a temporary and technical part of a system of rotation, but made permanent as part of a social and structural division of labour. The complementarity model reproduces this without challenging it. Hence, a different, and I think more fertile way of construing the relations between research and performance in different social fields, which takes account of the practical revolutions made by Action Research, and the differences in competence, is to compare it to a master-apprentice, rather than to a complementary producer-receiver relationship[11]. Who, then, are masters, and who the apprentices?

We met an apprenticeship model in the *stravis* paradigm above. Validity considerations "forced" researchers to participate and observe, not as unobtrusive "astronomers", but as apprentices in cultural practices. Devereux (1967) gave the model prominence as a way of learning to pass through the impasses of mutually transferred projections between spectators. This time, field participants are not external moving objects to be described, predicted, and explained, nor are they material to be formed and changed, or instruments to be used, nor are they strangers to visit. Nor are they specialised partners in a team with partial, complementary roles, executing the "meta-designs" of "researchers". If theory and practice, thinking and doing, reflecting and performing, are to be united, the same people must participate in both, as in alternating – cyclic – phases and levels of the same process. This is what the

---

11 On apprenticeship see Coy (ed.) (1989), Rogoff (1990), Lave and Wenger (1991), Caldwell and Carter (eds.) (1993), Ainley and Rainbird (eds.) (1999), Nielsen and Kvale (eds.) (1999) & (2003).

well-known Action Research-spirals are all about, alternating between reflecting and acting within open, experimenting, collaborative, research processes. Masters and apprentices must go through the same processes over and over, together, bringing them all closer to mastery through practice and a learning, inquiring dialogue.

In contrast to the complementarity model, the master-apprentice relationship is a dynamic learning relationship based on full sharing, because it is designed to make a master of the apprentice. In building capacity for organisational learning in organisations, this is the objective, to transfer and re-locate research and learning skills to the others, but not merely didactically. The apprentices must be fully initiated into the "secret" tricks of the trade, although through several stages and levels. There cannot be a permanent division of labour. An apprentice does not have a partial role. S/he is on the way to mastery, as is the master. A didactic, class-room, teacher-student relationship *is* complementary in a certain sense, since, there, the student is not on his way to become a teacher. A didactic teacher is not primarily a practical role model for the student, unless the student is becoming a teacher. Hence, what these teachers convey is "pure theory" separated from experience, to be received *as* theory by listening students. Didactic teaching is based on listening and remembering, not on imitation, experimentation, and practical guidance. In apprenticeship the master is a practical role model. Although masters might teach systematically, instruct, and "give orders", most exchanges have to be more dialogical, based on questions and answers explicating what is going on and being done, how and why, here-and-now, *in practice*[12].

Masters and apprentices are not complementary. They share common standards for what they are doing, striving towards the same to attain them. Their performances and skills are at different distances in different directions from realizing them, masters closer, apprentices farther away. Where you are, practically, in relation to standards of performance and to the ability to articulate this, decides whether you are a master or an apprentice, not formal positions, titles, or distinctions. The master is the servant of the other's learning. If an unequal relationship

---

12 As a normative standard for learning relationships, apprenticeship implies more than the "undesigned" legitimate peripheral participation (LPP) and "learning-by-hanging-around" of Lave and Wenger (1991).

is petrified as part of a social structure, it becomes conservative. But apprenticeship is not necessarily part of an unchanging, hierarchical, social structure. *Qua* learning relationship it cannot be, since formally locked positions of authority and subordination are detrimental to the "masterly" autonomy to be learned. Hence, the core learning relationship comes more appropriately to its own when liberated from fixations to social structure and status.

Both the dynamism and the commonality within it are emphasized when underscoring that the role of master and apprentice is not formally determined nor permanently allocated between participants. It changes and alternates continuously. It rotates, increasingly as advanced levels are attained. All involved in the relationship are on their way, at different places along the same way, changing, moving, and transforming, approaching the same standards of performance. In such a liberated apprenticeship everybody's prejudices are on trial all the time, through a searching and inquiring dialogue, as Plato's Socrates – a master, if anyone is – pointed out a long time ago.

But this kind of critical dialogue for learning and research is *not* the same as negotiating and compromising on coordinated steps of action, or on general agreements on rules of conduct. Neither does a complementary relationship have this transformative dynamism of mutual criticism between individuals moving forward along, and in, the same way. Complementarity stifles the relationship between the different parts.

In the *stravis* paradigm, the researcher is the apprentice (at best), not merely an extraneous, close-up observer. In the *napeco* paradigm, those who know the most and best in practice, or those who provide the better arguments, are "masters". Authority is not predetermined. But most research practices are still forced to work within given institutional divisions of labour. Could professional researchers be "masters", then, while the natives are apprentices, without reproducing the pitfalls of separate roles traversed above, and of didactic, top down instruction? They could, in the research processes (the dialogical commons), and in all the difficulties of methodology, i.e. in the methods of methodology. These are things all practitioners observing and categorizing need to know in order to act competently. And, both masters and apprentices are members of the same community of inquiry. Since not even masters are perfect, the common way of progress constitutes the community, i.e. they all have the learning and inquiring way of relating to their own practices and to each other, in common. An apprentice is a trainee, and we are all permanently apprentices, but alternate as masters. The common way of developing an emerging mastery *is* the real community. Hence, a group of "masters" and "apprentices", released from being part of a social structure, is a group of peers, and a community of inquiry (Torbert, 1976).

Participants may have complementary fields of activity and expertise, substantially different. In the way of researching and inquiring into these complementary experiences – its specific processes and activities – they are still similar or alike. Experts in processes of inquiry are masters some times, having a greater knowledge and awareness of pitfalls of methodology, while experts in substantial fields of activity are masters at other times, carrying in their own embodied experience and *habitus* the criteria for deciding the appropriateness of emerging conceptualisations. The merging of research processes with practices, and the open sharing among participants in the inquiry, is what constituted Action Research in the forties. The same fusion is needed to overcome the validity challenges of mainstream research. The aim of becoming like the other in certain respects (skills, knowledge, and understanding) is what constitutes apprenticeship. Validity needs a researcher to learn what a native knows by becoming a reflective *native*. It also needs a native to learn what a researcher knows by becoming a *reflective* native. Native researchers are what learning organisations need, and it is also what has to be preserved in order for the core of Action Research to unfold. If anything or anyone in this is complementary, it is a merging complementarity in total flux.

But are dialogical apprenticeship-approaches *interventions*? A municipality read my book, and invited me. I provided supervision-through-dialogue in order for them to understand better, and to develop ways of cultivating "learning by doing" more systematically in their organisations. This was not intervention. It was not administering technical treatment as causes, to get calculated, artificial changes as effects. If what I provide generates improved understanding, this produces development. Principally, this is more similar to a therapeutic non-intervention against subjects, protecting them against interferences and interventions from obstructing surroundings and extraneous influences. Extraneous obstructions and influences intervene as efficient causes. Bringing my own practices to consciousness, making me *see* things previously invisible, in order to perfect them, does not. Unfolding developments and emerging patterns differ from interventions. They approximate the Aristotelian relationship between praxis (doing it), and eupraxía (doing it well). A sprouting bud or blooming flower does not intervene into its former way of being. It fulfils it. Stopping the bud is intervention! Masters provide practical forms as elucidations of a model. Apprentices approximate, and train themselves by imitation, experimentation, dialogue, and supervision, into the same form or pattern, *not* identical to a particular master, of course. The form or pattern of a *common* standard – "die Sache", "saken", or the "what-it-means-to-do-or-be-something" – is separable in thinking, and, as such, separate from any individual master. It is common to and shared by masters and apprentices. When apprentices apprehend it, they develop into masters autonomously, without interventions.

8.5 Immanent critique and dialogical validity – Exposing threats to validity

Earlier, I claimed a basic nexus between the strong justification for Action Research presented, and a certain Action Research-practice of alternating between "on-stage-*performance*" in "work organisations", and "back-stage-*reflections*" in "development organisations", indicated by the concepts of "immanent critique" and "counter-public spheres". I will try to clarify and conclude.

8.5.1   Counter-public spheres and immanent critique

Immanent critique generates development and transformation by exposing inner insufficiencies, tensions, and contradictions – logical and pragmatic – in the practices of positions, paradigms, cultures, discourse formations, etc. in relation to their own proper objectives, also carried internally, tacitly or explicitly. It tries to bring thought, speech, and act into mutual accord. As an activity, immanent critique needs, not just a *public* sphere in organisations as indicated by Paalshaugen (2002), but a *counter*-public sphere.[13]

Although there are obvious barriers (psychological, social, cultural etc.), different in size and quality for people in different positions, a democratic public sphere is *in principle* open, and free for all to join the way they like. But all kinds of openness and freedom are not equally conducive when it comes to inquiry into and exposure of internal insufficiencies etc. nor equally conducive to learning and development. Exposure and speech, and even silence, can be confused, oppressive, abusive, abrupt, seductive, concealing, manipulative, strategic, injurious, gossipy, formalistic, etc. A democratic public sphere must allow for this, and rhetoric is its art of mastery. But openness uncovers, and leaves unprotected, vulnerable layers of experience, emotions, and practices.

A counter-public sphere must, of course, be open for all kinds of utterances emerging from and expressing personal experiences. But it must simultaneously somehow protect individuals against "power-talk". "Power-talk" and talk that obscures are often unavoidable and necessary starting points. But they must be gradually and as far as possible prevented, suspended, and eliminated in order to aid the articulation of experience. So must psychological, social, and other barriers preventing access and participation. Open, critical, and constructive dialogue is necessary. It must gradually suspend, not difference, disagreement, or conflict, but the kinds of talk and oppressive silence just mentioned, and the barriers against participating and contributing as well. The art of doing this must be learned, by doing, i.e. by practising.

Creating a public sphere requires mainly the removal of restrictions. Creating a counter-public sphere requires the acquisition of skills in exposing and deconstructing power-talk, obscure talk, and the barriers preventing individuals from taking part. Hence, a public sphere can be established by decree backed by power, a counter-public sphere cannot. It establishes itself by critically exposing power-talk and obscure talk, and by creating protective back-stage spaces where critical reflection and immanent critique is allowed. When personal and collective learning and inquiry is the objective, power-talk is exposed and suspended.

---

13 Paalshaugen (2002) is a re-interpretation of "development organisations". This re-interpretation really brings the concept back to square one. Cf. the call for permanent, local public spheres in Eikeland (1985a).

Immanent critique and counter-public spheres are two sides of the same coin, and constitutive for peer groups of inquiry among masters and apprentices.

Above, I have tried to promote critical development and transformation towards valid social knowledge, by exposing insufficiencies, etc. both in mainstream research methods, and in some really extant Action Research approaches. The two trajectories – transformed mainstream research, and a mildly transformed Action Research – converge towards what I think is a conceptually and practically strong – valid – form of "mainstreamed" Action Research. The spectator-astronomer (*spectas*) paradigm, the manipulator-user (*manipus*) paradigm, and the stranger-visitor (*stravis*) paradigm are all insufficient, with serious inherent invalidities. Although we are all spectators, manipulators, users, strangers, or visitors in relation to others some times during our lives, and these ways of knowing are unavoidable, we all carry with us preconditions from elsewhere in doing these things competently, preconditions which – for a number of historical reasons – mainstream social research has been very good at neglecting. This "somewhere else" is our native-ness – the personal "me" and the "I" – which are not merely private or psychological, but historical, social, institutional, transcendental, etc. This "somewhere else" is where Action Research has to start, and the native-performer-community (*napeco*) paradigm emerges as the "always-already-there" of the other paradigms as well, when we start focusing critically on <u>praxis</u> – our own "ways-of-doing-things" – as the basis for understanding.

The Action Research-review ended up with a model of permanent apprenticeship, supporting and supported by the *napeco*-paradigm. We are all always already native apprentices in different national, social, and local tribes, and in professional tribes of psychometricians, anthropologists, Action Researchers, etc. When we start investigating and inquiring into them through immanent critique, they transform. The question is: What do natives need in order to develop their skills as reflective natives, practitioner researchers, and apprentices? Hardly more *spectas*, *manipus*, or *stravis* researchers! We need to organise our common ways of learning and inquiry, the Action Research cycles of reflection and action, the master-apprentice communities of practice and inquiry. The alternation between "on-stage-*performance*" in "work organisations", and "back-stage-*reflections*" in "development organisations" is designed to organise – provide space for – such learning activities, and facilitate "learning-to-learn". On stage, we perform our roles and appointed tasks. Back stage, we discuss and analyse critically experiences from performing on stage, we practice to improve, we switch roles and plays, etc. Thus, the Action Research-cycles shifting between reflecting and acting receive organisational form.

The space back stage must become a counter-public sphere, protecting people from rhetorical forces at work in the public sphere. As indicated, this must be done by consciously giving space to dialogue, where dialogical aspects of language use are distinguished from negotiating practical compromises, from persuasive and seductive rhetoric, from instructive didactics, from formal syllogisms, and from merely soothing and comforting speech.[14] Critical dialogue makes the subconscious conscious, the submerged and merged emerge, the implicit explicit, the enfolded unfold, by bringing context into the explicit "text", and keeping the dialogue focused on and springing from acquired personal, participant experience, articulating tacit presuppositions, preconceptions, prejudices, ways-of-doing-things, and basic assumptions of participants.

Focusing the dialogue both on the acquired practical experience (empeiría/*Erfahrung*), and on particular experiences (páthos/*Erlebnis*) of the participants, brings their *habitus* and its institutional inscriptions to the centre of attention. In this way we can also clarify the "back-pack" of mutual expectations we, as individuals "trapped" in institutionalised researcher roles, encounter "field practitioners" with. At first encounters, we are *never* primarily "personal" individuals, but group-role individuals representing cultures, institutions, or organisations, confronting each other through our own prejudices transferred and projected. We are not personal "I"s, but socialised and habituated "me"s. The *personal* encounter, where the habitual "me-roles" can be gradually "stepped out of", made visible, and discussed, is for the "back-stage" space that must be created and secured as "development organisation". In principle, Action Research invites everyone to dialogue as equals "back stage".

---

14 I have tried to clarify these distinctions in Eikeland in (1997a), (1998b), (2001a), and (forthcoming).

Mainstream social research does not, but remains "off-stage", as interpreting audience and spectators.

8.5.2 Action Research, generalisation, and "Kontextaufhebung"

Spectas, *manipus*, and *stravis* research de-contextualises knowledge by taking aspects of a situation out of it (abstracting), importing them into their theories and models. Thus re-contextualisation becomes a problem in the application and adjustment of theories and models in new situations. The practico-dialogical Action Research suggested here proceeds differently. It does not de-contextualise in the first place. It works by – what cannot easily be expressed in English, hence German must be used – *Kontextaufhebung*, i.e. by bringing elements of the context, hitherto not verbalised (tacit), into the explicit "text", or dialogue, and thereby changing the situation (expanding it), but still keeping it intact (retaining, suspending, and transcending it). Instead of merely speaking and acting *in* the situation, defined by it, we speak *about* the same situation, transcending it and redefining it. This – *Kontextaufhebung* – is what bringing sub-conscious, tacit, implicit habits and skills into explicit, articulated, consciousness is all about. It is not just horizontal problem solving, but vertically raising consciousness without loosing foothold on the ground. It's like growing taller. You see more of the surrounding context than when you are smaller, more submerged, and sunk into wherever you have your feet. Immanent critique and "*Kontextaufhebung*" is Action Research because it is not a) spectator based observation, not b) experimentation *on* others as causally, culturally, or socially, determined objects, not c) interviewing anyone. It works dialogically and critically with personal, practically acquired experience, focusing on *habitus*. Like experimentation and Action Research, "*Kontextaufhebung*" *changes* its subject of study when it submerges itself into it, and makes all the preconceptions, assumptions, and prejudices explicit.

Spectas, *manipus*, and *stravis* research also have problems with generalisation, since they study the distribution of properties of the others as natural objects. By starting with our own native competencies and their preconditions – *habitus* – as human beings, as members of specific cultures, as members of professional groups, and representatives of institutions, etc., *napeco* research starts by searching for what we always already have in common, i.e. commonalities or generalities at work in what we do in particular times and places. In their competent forms and patterns, common "ways-of-doing-things" are simultaneously empirical, normative, and general. This is no paradox or impossibility from within an Aristotelian concept of experience.[15] The point is to bring people to an awareness and consciousness of what generalities or universals are always already at work in their own practice and context as "basic historical concepts" (Koselleck, 2002, 2004).

8.5.3 Dialogical opening

As several writers emphasize (Cf. Merriam 1998:199), the most important rule for securing validity is making all practical moves, the component parts of what is done, their connections and presuppositions, and anything disturbing the generation of insight and understanding, visible, exposed and understood, bringing it all *into* the dialogue, *opening* the research process, or any process, up for inspection. Action Research was conceived by doing this in the forties. The *method of methodology*, i.e. the tribe of mainstream social researchers examining their own ways-of-doing-things, also contributes importantly to making the moves, presumptions, and preconditions of research processes visible. Hence, an important provision for securing validity is discussing and exposing all known, possible, and relevant threats to validity, a practice initiated by Francis Bacon's (1561–1626) discussion of idols, and emphasized by e.g. Campbell (1988, pp. 264–265). Disclosing and revealing these things implies exposing and making conscious, increasingly wider contexts, bringing these into dialogical Action Research-spirals of learning.[16]

Some think of validity as *trustworthiness* and credibility of research results, i.e. how others can have confidence in research results (Cf. Merriam (1998:198f.), Guba and Lincoln (1989), and Mishler (1990:417). But people trust widely different things. Many are too credulous. Therefore, there is a *dialectical* aspect to this, and a *rhetorical* aspect. The difference between persuading (rhetorically), convincing or proving (didactically,

---

15 Aristotle's concept of experience is the theme in Eikeland (1997a)

16 Cf. Winter (1987), who has an excellent discussion of validity. Winter's ultimate requirement appears to be that AR must include reflections on its own preconditions to achieve validity.

or demonstratively), and showing (dialogically) disappear in Mishler's (1990:420) conclusion that "validation is the social discourse through which trustworthiness is established". Validity cannot be reduced to just any such social discourse. Without the distinctions, it opens for a normative reading of Latour's (1987) "science in action", letting anything go, getting support by any means!

The primary purpose of an Action Research process is hardly to find out whether whatever is *said* also gets *done* either, as Paalshaugen (1991) implies, but rather to find out whether what actually gets *done* (or not done) by Action Researchers and others, is also what is *said*, not "covered up" in some way by language. In order to secure validity, research processes must be opened up, not covered up. It may be a problem for project work that people, for a number of reasons, do not always do what they say. But it certainly is a serious problem for research, and for the common understanding of human activity at all, that people more often than not, do not reveal and say what they actually do, but cover it up, or stash it up, in order to make it look nicer, prettier, more rational (rationalization), more politically correct, more innovative etc., than it is.

Hence, Action Research is normative, and requires *one* specific kind of change in social systems above all else: its own preconditions, the realization of the social and psychological pre-requisites and preconditions enabling people – without danger – to *observe, tell, understand,* and *change* what is *actually done* by *power, neighbours, colleagues, themselves,* or anyone, not only espoused declarations of values, but the details of *actual* practices and events, i.e. a critical counter-public sphere, and the possibility to learn individually and collectively. Building the capacity to systematically alternate between performing "on stage", and reflecting critically "back stage", may challenge organisations stifled by routines and habits, or led by power and rhetoric. But this is what research validity needs. It is what organisational learning needs. It is also what innovation and competitiveness requires. Its potential is enhanced by emerging "new modes of knowledge production" (Gibbons et al. 1994, Nowotny et al. 2001), and by emerging new relations between academic institutions for research and learning, and a knowledge-based work life.

References

Ainley, Patrick & Rainbird, Helen (eds.) (1999): *Apprenticeship – Towards a New Paradigm of Learning*, London: Kogan Page.

Altheide, David L. & Johnson, John M. (1994): "Criteria for Assessing Interpretive Validity in Qualitative Research", pp. 485–499 in *Handbook of Qualitative Research*, Denzin, Norman K. & Lincoln, Yvonna S. (eds.) London: Sage.

Altrichter, Herbert; Posch, Peter & Somekh, Bridget (1993): *Teachers investigate their Work . An introduction to the methods of Action Research*, London & New York: Routledge.

Anderson, Gary L., Herr, Kathryn & Nihlen, Ann Sigrid (1994): *Studying your own school: An Educator's Guide to Qualitative Practitioner Research*, Thousand Oaks: Corwin Press.

Antonio, Robert J. (1981): "Immanent Critique as the Core of Critical Theory: Its Origins and Developments in Hegel, Marx and Contemporary Thought", pp. 330–345 in *The British Journal of Sociology*, Vol. 32, No. 3.

Argyris, Chris & Schön, Don (1978): *Organizational Learning: A theory of action perspective*, Reading, MA: Addison-Wesley Publishing Company, New Edition: (1996): *Organizational Learning II: Theory, Method and Practice*, Reading, MA: Addison-Wesley Publishing Company.

Baritz, Loren (1960): *The Servants of Power: A History of the Use of Social Science in American Industry*, reprinted by Greenwood Press Publishers, Westport, Connecticut

Benne, Kenneth D.; Bradford, Leland P.; Gibb, Jack R. & Lippitt, Ronald O. (1975): *The Laboratory Method of Changing and Learning*, Palo Alto, CA: Science and Behavior Books.

Bourdieu, Pierre (1977) *Outline of a Theory of Practice*, Cambridge: Cambridge University Press (French original 1972).

Bourdieu, Pierre (1990) *The Logic of Practice*, Cambridge: Polity Press (French original 1980).

Bray, John N. et al. (2000): *Collaborative Inquiry in Practice: Action, Reflection and Making Meaning*, Thousand Oaks: Sage.

Brox, Ottar (1990): *Praktisk Samfunnsvitenskap*, Oslo: Universitetsforlaget

Caldwell, Brian J. & Carter, Earl M.A. (eds.) (1993): *The Return of the Mentor: Strategies for Workplace Learning*, London: The Falmer Press.

Campbell, Donald T. (1978): *Qualitative Knowing in Action Research*, pp. 184–209 in Brenner, Michael, Marsh, Peter & Brenner, Marilyn (eds.) (1978): *The Social Contexts of Method*, London: Croom Helm.

Cherryholmes, Cleo H. (1988): "Construct Validity and the Discourses of Research", *American Journal of Education*, Vol. 96, pp. 421–457.

Collier, John (1945): "United States Indian Administration as a Laboratory of Ethnic Relations", pp. 265–303 in *Social research*, Vol.12, No.3.

Corey, Stephen M. (1953): *Action Research to Improve School Practices*, New York: Teachers College, Columbia University.

Coy, Michael W. (ed.) (1989): *Apprenticeship: From Theory to Method, and Back Again*, Albany: State University of New York Press.

Cronbach, Lee J. (1970): *Essentials of Psychological Testing*, Third Edition, New York, Evanston, and London: Harper & Row.

Cronbach, Lee J. (1988): "Five Perspectives on Validity Argument", pp. 3–17 in *Test Validity*. Wainer, Howard & Braun, Henry I. (eds.) Hillsdale, NJ: Lawrence Erlbaum.

Cronbach, Lee J. (1989): "Construct Validation After Thirty Years", pp. 147–171 in *Intelligence: Measurement, Theory, and Public Policy*. Linn, Robert L. (ed.) Urbana and Chicago: University of Illinois Press.

Cronbach, Lee J. & Meehl, P.E. (1955): "Construct Validity in psychological tests", *Psychological Bulletin*, Vol. 52, pp. 281–302.

Crosby, Alfred W. (1997): *The Measure of Reality: Quantification and Western Society 1250–1600*, Cambridge & New York: Cambridge University Press.

Cunliffe, Ann L. & Easterby-Smith, Mark (2004): "From Reflection to Practical Reflexivity: Experiential Learning as Lived Experience", pp. 30–46 in *Organizing Reflection*. Reynolds, Michael & Vince, Russ (eds.) (2004) Aldershot: Ashgate Publishing.

Devereux, George (1967): *From Anxiety to Method in the Behavioral Sciences*, The Hague & Paris: Mouton & Co.

Dewey, John (1938): *Erfaring og opdragelse*, Oslo & København: Dreyer & Christian Ejlers forlag, 1974

Eikeland, Olav (1985a): "Jobbskaping i lokalmiljø: perspektiver og muligheter", pp.12–13 in *Studienytt*, No. 4

– (1985b): "H.W.Smith og jakten på den skjulte mening eller: the

actual meaning of triangulation", pp. 173–208 i *Sosiologisk Årbok 1985.*
Østerberg, Dag & Otnes, Per (eds.) Oslo: Institutt for Sosiologi,
UiO.

– (1987): *Rapport til Hovedavtalens bedriftsutviklingstiltak (HABUT);
Bilbransjeprosjektet,* AFI-notat 31/87, Oslo: Arbeidsforskningsinstitut
tet.

– (1996): *Kunnskapsproduksjon i endring: to bidrag,* AFI-notat 8/96, Oslo:
Arbeidsforskningsinstituttet.

– (1997a): *Erfaring, dialogikk og politick: Den antikke dialogfilosofiens betydn-
ing for rekonstruksjonen av moderne empirisk samfunnsvitenskap. Et begrep-
shistorisk og filosofisk bidrag,* 3rd Ed., Oslo: Universitetsforlaget.

– (1997b): *Demokrati og medvirkning under et nytt kunnskapsforvaltningsregime: tre foredrag,* AFI-notat 5/97, Oslo: Arbeidsforskningsinstituttet.

– (1998a): *Faglige metamorfoser og immanente konvergenser: opptakt til et nytt
kunnskapsforvaltningsregime,* AFI-notat 5/98, Oslo: Arbeidsforsknings
instituttet.

– (1998b): "Anámnêsis: Dialogisk erindringsarbeid som empirisk forskn-
ingsmetode", pp. 95–136 in *Kunnskapsproduksjon i endring: nye erfarings-
og organisasjonsformer* Eikeland, Olav & Fossestøl, Knut (eds.) Oslo:
Arbeidsforskningsinstituttet.

– (1999a): *From Training to Learning: New Trends and Future Perspectives,*
AFI-notat 3/99, Arbeidsforskningsinstituttet, Oslo.

– (1999b): *Mot et nytt kunnskapsforvaltningsregime?* AFI-notat 7/99, Oslo:
Arbeidsforskningsinstituttet.

– (2001a): "Action Research as the Hidden Curriculum of the Western
Tradition", pp. 145–155 in *Handbook of Action Research: Participative
Inquiry and Practice.* Reason, Peter & Bradbury, Hilary (eds.) (2001)
London: Sage.

– (forthcoming): *The Ways of Aristotle: Aristotelian Phrónêsis, Aristotelian
Philosophy, and Action Research, or Why Aristotle Insists on Letting Phrónêsis
Deliberate About Means Only,* Book manuscript

Eikeland, Olav & Finsrud, Henrik D. (ed.) (1995): *Research in Action:
Forskning og handling, Søkelys på aksjonsforskning,* (AFIs skriftserie 1),
Oslo: Work Research Institute.

Engelstad Per H. (1983): *Skotfos mot strømmen: Industriell omstilling,* Skien:
Skien Næringsråd.

– (1995): "Fra dialogkonferanser til utviklingsorganisasjon", pp. 161–210 in *Forskning og handling: søkelys på aksjonsforskning.* Eikeland, Olav & Finsrud, Henrik D. (ed.) (1995) Arbeidsforskningsinstituttet, Oslo.

Engelstad, Per H. & Gustavsen, Bjørn (1983): "Mot en ny bedriftsorganisasjon 15 år etter", pp. 18–30 in *Teori i praksis: Festskrift til Einar Thorsrud.* Blichfeldt, Jon Frode & Qvale, Thoralf U. (ed.) (1983) Oslo: Tanum-Norli.

French, Wendell L. (1985): "The emergence and Early History of Organization Development with Reference to Influences Upon and Interactions Among Some of the Key Actors", pp. 12–27 in *Contemporary Organization Development: Current Thinking and Applications.* Warrick, D. D. (ed.) Glenview, Illinois & London, UK: Scott, Foresman & Company.

French, Wendell L. & Bell Jr., Cecil H. (1990): *Organization Development: Behavioral Science Interventions for Organization Improvement,* Fourth Edition, Englewood Cliffs, NJ: Prentice-Hall.

Geertz, Clifford (1973): *The Interpretation of Cultures,* New York: Basic Books.

Gherardi, Silvia (2000): "Practice-based Theorizing on Learning and Knowing in Organizations", *Organization,* 7 (2): 211–223

Giddens , Anthony (1973): *New Rules of Sociological Method,* London: Hutchinson.

Greenwood, Davydd J. & Levin, Morten (1998): *Introduction to Action Research: Social Research for Social Change,* Thousand Oaks, London & New Dehli: Sage.

Guba, Egon G. & Lincoln, Yvonna S. (1989): *Fourth Generation Evaluation,* Newbury Park, London & New Dehli: Sage.

Gustavsen, Bjørn (1984): "Forskning og utvikling – Problemer og erfaringer", pp. 11–28 in *Förändringsprogram i arbetslivet – Några svenska och internationella erfarenheter av forskningsmedverkan.* Gustavsen, Bjørn & Sandberg, Åke (ed.) (Varia rapport no. 47) Stockholm: Arbetlivscentrum.

– (1985): "Workplace Reform and Democratic Dialogue", pp. 461–479 in *Economic and Industrial Democracy,* Vol. 6, No. 4

– (1986): "Social Research as Participative Dialogue", pp. 143–156 in *The Use and Abuse of Social Science.* Heller, Frank (ed.) London: Sage Publications.

– (1987): "Reformer på arbetsplatsen och demokratisk dialog", pp.

25–45 in *Arbetets retionaliteter – om framtidens arbetsliv*. Odhnoff, Jan & Von Otter, Casten (1987) Stockholm: Arbetslivscentrum.

– (1988): "Noen trekk ved utviklingen av 'Aksjonsforskning' i arbeidslivet", pp. 215–238 in *Sosiologisk Årbok*, Oslo: Institutt for Sosiologi, Universitetet i Oslo.

– (1990): *Strategier for utvikling i arbeidslivet*, Oslo: Tano.

Habermas, Jürgen (1962): *Borgerlig offentlighet*, Oslo: Gyldendal Norsk Forlag, 1971.

Hammersley, Martyn & Atkinson, Paul (1987): *Feltmetodikk – grunnlaget for feltarbeid og feltforskning*, Oslo: Gyldendal Norsk Forlag.

Hastrup, Kirsten (1995): *A Passage to Anthropology: Between Experience and Theory*, London & New York: Routledge.

Heider, K. G. (1988): "The Rashomon Effect: When Ethnographers Disagree", *American Anthropologist*, Vol. 90: 73–81

Heron, John (1996): *Co-operative inquiry: Research Into the Human Condition*, London, Thousand Oaks, New Dehli: Sage.

Jahoda, Marie, Deutsch, Morton and Cook, Sturt W. (1951): *Research methods in social relations: with especial reference to prejudice*, New York

Kerlinger, Fred N. (1973): *Foundations of Behavioral Research*, Second Edition, Holt-Saunders International Editions, New York: Holt, Rinehart and Winston Inc.

Knorr-Cetina, Karin D. & Mulkay, Michael (eds.) (1983): *Science Observed: Perspectives on the Social Study of Science*, Beverly Hills, London & New Dehli: Sage.

Koselleck, Reinhart (2002): *The Practice of Conceptual History: Timing History, Spacing Concepts*, Stanford, CA: Stanford University Press.

Koselleck, Reinhart (2004): *Futures Past: On the Semantics of Historical Time*, New York: Columbia University Press.

Kvale, Steinar (ed.) (1989): *Issues of Validity in Qualitative Research*, Lund: Studentlitteratur.

Lather, Patti (1993): "Fertile Obsession: Validity after Poststructuralism", *The Sociological Quarterly*, Vol. 34, No. 4, pp. 673–693.

Latour, Bruno (1987): *Science in Action*, Milton Keynes: Open University Press.

Latour, Bruno & Woolgar, Steve (1979): *Laboratory Life: The Social Construction of Scientific Facts*, Beverly Hills & London: Sage.

Laudan, Larry (1981): *Science and Hypothesis: Historical essays on Scientific*

Methodology, Dordrecht, Holland & Boston, MA: D.Reidel Publishing Company.

Lave, Jane & Wenger, Etienne (1991): *Situated Learning: Legitimate Peripheral Participation*, Cambridge: Cambridge University Press.

Lewin, Kurt (1946): *Action Research and Minority Problems*, reprinted pp. 201–216 in Lewin (1973)

– (1973): *Resolving Social Conflicts*, London: Souvenir Press.

Lippitt, Ronald (1949): *Training in Community Relations: A Research Exploration Toward New Group Skills*, New York: Harpers & Brothers Publishers.

Marrow, Alfred J. (1964): "Risks and Uncertainties in Action Research", Kurt Lewin Memorial Award Address 1964, pp. 5–20 in *Journal of Social Issues*, Vol. 20, No. 3.

Merriam, Sharan B. (1998): *Qualitative Research and Case Study Applications in Education*, San Francisco: Jossey-Bass.

Mishler, Elliot G. (1990): "Validation in Inquiry-Guided Research", *Harvard Educational Review*, Vol. 60, No. 4, pp. 415–442.

Negt, Oskar (1971): *Sociologisk fantasi og eksemplarisk indlæring: Til teori og praksis i arbejderuddannelsen*, Roskilde: Roskilde Universitetsforlag, 1975

Negt, Oskar & Kluge, Alexander (1972): *Offentlighet og erfaring: Til organisasjonsanalysen av borgerlig og proletarisk offentlighet*, (Nordisk Sommeruniversitets skriftserie No. 3, 1974)

Nicolini, Davide et al. (2003): *Knowing in Organizations: A Practice-Based Approach*, London: M.E.Sharpe.

Nielsen, Klaus & Kvale, Steinar (1999): *Mesterlære – Læring som social praksis*, København: Hans Reitzels Forlag.

Nielsen, Klaus & Kvale, Steinar (1999): *Praktikkens læringslandskab – at lære gennem arbeijde*, København: Akademisk Forlag.

Nielsen Kurt Aagaard & Nielsen, Birger Steen (200x): Methodologies in Action Research, pp. xx–yy in this book

Peirce, Charles Sanders (1868) & (1878): "Some Consequences of Four Incapacities" (1868), "Deduction, Induction, and Hypothesis" (1878), both in *The Essential Peirce – Selected Philosophical Writings, Vol. 1. (1863–1893)*. Houser, Nathan & Kloesel, Christian (eds.) (1992) Bloomington & Indianapolis: Indiana University Press.

Porter, Theodore M. (1995): *Trust in Numbers: The Pursuit of Objectivity in Science and Public Life*, Princeton, NJ: Princeton University Press.

Paalshaugen, Øyvind (1988): "A Norwegian Programme of Action Research for Participative Democracy", pp. 125–160 in Eikeland, Olav & Finsrud, Henrik D. (ed.) (1995), First published in German translation pp. 83–113 in *Sozialwissenschaften und Industrielle Demokratie*. Fricke, Werner & Jäger, Wieland (ed.) (1988) Bonn: Verlag Neue Gesellschaft.

– (1991): *Som sagt, så gjort? Språket som virkemiddel i organisasjonsutvikling og aksjonsforskning*, Oslo: Novus Forlag.

– (1992): "Aksjonsforskning: En nyttig vitenskap? Et innspill i fire satser", pp. 231–252 in *Tidsskrift for samfunnsforskning*, Vol. 33, No.3.

– (2002): "Discourse Democracy at Work: On public spheres in private enterprises", pp. 141–192 in *Concepts and Transformation*, Vol. 7, No. 2.

Reason, Peter & Rowan, John (eds.) (1981): *Human Inquiry: A Sourcebook of New Paradigm Inquiry*, Chichester & New York: John Wiley & Sons.

Reason, Peter (ed.) (1994): *Participation in Human Inquiry*, London: Sage.

Reason, Peter & Bradbury, Hilary (eds.) (2001): *Action Research: Participatory Inquiry & Practice*, London: Sage.

Rogoff, Barbara (1990): *Apprenticeship in Thinking: Cognitive Development in Social Context*, New York & London: Oxford university Press.

Salner, Marcia (1989): "Validity in Human Science Research", pp. 47–72 in Kvale (ed.) (1989).

Sanford, Nevitt (1970): "Whatever happened to Action Research?", pp. 3–24 in *The Journal of Social Issues*, Vol. 26, No. 4.

Schatzki, Theodor et al. (2001): *The Practice Turn in Contemporary Theory*, London: Routledge.

Schein, Edgar H. (1987): *The Clinical Perspective in Fieldwork*, Qualitative Research Methods, Vol. 5, Newbury Park, London, New Dehli: Sage.

Schwalbach, Eileen M. (2003): *Value and Validity in Action Research: A Guidebook for Reflective practitioners*, Lanham: Scarecrow Education.

Shipman, Marten (1981): *The Limitations of Social Research*, London & New York: Longman.

Shumsky, Abraham (1958): *The Action Research Way of Learning*, New York: Bureau of Publications, Teachers College, Columbia University.

Spjelkavik, Øystein (1995): "Applied Research or Action Research?", pp. 269–296 in Eikeland, Olav & Finsrud, Henrik D. (eds.) (1995)

Stacey, Ralph D.; Griffin, Douglas & Shaw, Patricia (2000): *Complexity and Management: Fad or Radical Challenge to Systems Thinking?*, London and New York: Routledge – Taylor & Francis Group.

Taylor, Charles (1971): "Interpretation and the Sciences of Man", reprinted pp. 15–57 in *Philosophical Papers 2: Philosophy and the Human Sciences*, Cambridge University Press, Cambridge, 1985

Thorsrud, Einar (1976): "Complementary Roles in Action Research", pp. 77–90 in *Experimenting with Organizational Life – The Action Research Approach*, Clark, Alfred W. (ed.) New York & London: Plenum Press.

Torbert, William R. (1976): *Creating a Community of Inquiry: Conflict, Collaboration, Transformation*, London/New York: John Wiley & Sons.

Weber, Max (1904): "Die 'Objektivität' sozialwissenschaftlicher und sozialpolitischer Erkenntnis", pp. 146–214 in *Gesammelte Aufsätze zur Wissenschaftslehre*, 6th Ed., Tübingen: J.C.B. Mohr (Paul Siebeck) 1985.

Whyte, William Foote & Hamilton, Edith Lentz (1964): *Action Research for Management: A Case Report on Research and Action in Industry*, Homewood, Illinois: Richard D. Irwin Inc. and the Dorsey Press.

Winter, Richard (1987): *Action-Research and the Nature of Social Inquiry*, Aldershot: Avebury.

Winter, Richard & Munn-Giddings, Carol (2001): *Action Research in Health and Social Care*, London & New York: Routledge.

Zalewski, Marysia (2000): *Feminism After Postmodernism: Theorising through Practice*, London & New York: Routledge.

ANN-CHRISTINE LARSSON

9. Interactive Research
– Methods and conditions for joint analysis

9.1   Introduction

Which methods you choose in a research process, has a lot to do with what problem you are going to analyse and what knowledge you want to achieve. If you choose an Interactive Research design you have to reflect over the following questions:

- Will involvement by the participants give an added value to the research process?
- What resources will be needed in terms of time and money? And what kind of supporting structures do you need?
- Are you, as a researcher, prepared to be *a part* of a joint learning process together *with* the participants?

The aim of this chapter is to discuss the usefulness of Interactive Research methods and the conditions that make the use of such methods possible. When I talk about Interactive Research, I mean a research *process* characterised by *joint learning* together with the participants in the study, this starts with the definition of the research problem and continues to the analysis and dissemination of the results (see Chapter 2). This definition points to an important difference between Interactive Research and Action Research. In Action Research (Reason and Bradbury, 2001), the participants seldom have an active role in the analysis of the data, in the construction of new theories or in the development of new concepts. The case study, which is described below, illustrates joint learning and some of the necessary conditions for making this joint learning process possible.

I will focus on how participants of an EQUAL-project, who were on long-term sick leave, became involved in the analysis of the data throughout the entire research process. My methodology was based on that of *critical realism* (see Bhaskar, 1978). I wanted to go beyond a mere *understanding* of the participants' experiences and try to *explain* the causes of their situation. I was interested in finding underlying structures, patterns and mechanisms on different "levels'. The usefulness of Action Research in getting a deeper understanding is well documented (Reason and Bradbury, 2001), but the involvement of the participants in the analytical work is not often dealt with in the Action Research literature.

My conclusion is that the use of interactive methods gave me better opportunities for carrying out research that combined a deep understanding with a critical and theoretical analysis of the participants' situation. The participants were helpful in the theoretical work in different ways, namely in finding the explanations and causes of the exclusion processes, in defining new concepts, in producing theoretical models, and so on.

But it is not an easy task to use an Interactive Research design. There is a need for supportive structures, especially when it comes to the developmental work. Otherwise there is a risk that the researcher will spend her/his time solving a lot of practical problems instead of focusing on the research question. The researcher runs the risk of becoming a consultant. In Interactive Research there is a division of labour between the project leader and the researcher. In this R&D project I worked close together with two project leaders and a coordinator who were responsible for the developmental work.

9.1.1 *What was the research about and how was it organised?*

The European Social Fund (ESF) funded the R&D project. It was an EQUAL project which intended to test new ways of tackling discrimination and inequalities in the labour market. *Empowerment* is one of the key principles of the EQUAL programme; it goes hand in hand with an objective to change structures that inhibit the empowerment process for the groups, which are excluded from the labour market. This part of the EQUAL programme[1] consisted of three projects with different target groups and was carried out over three years. The budget for the whole programme was four million Euros. In the project I followed the target group were people who were on long-term sick leave.

It was an R&D project with a combined interest in promoting change and in conducting research at the same time. The developmental part of the project was organised by a learning centre in a small municipality. The organisation of the change process was not one of the researcher's responsibilities, but for the project manager and a coordinator. I followed the developmental process closely and participated in different activities arranged by the project.

The project management accepted this, but this decision had also to be taken by the participants – individually and jointly. Participation in Interactive Research must be voluntary and, therefore, the first thing you have to do is to get consent from the people involved (Herr and Anderson 2005). I was invited to a group meeting and presented the objectives and the ideas behind an Interactive Research approach. The group later discussed, on their own, whether or not to participate in the research project. The answer was positive.

My research focused on two groups of employees – employees from the public sector and a few unemployed. I started my research with the first group, which consisted of eleven women and one man, and I followed their activities closely from the very beginning of the project. The next step in the research process was to invite the second group (twelve women and one man) to a meeting, and to introduce the two groups to each other. Not all the participants took part in our meetings, depending on their other activities. The meeting between these two groups led to a learning process between them in terms of a joint understanding and explanation of their problems, because of their different status in regaining health and trying to get back to working life. It was soon evident that the main reason for their sick leave was stress related – having to deal with heavy demands, both in their working and private lives.

---

1 For more information about the programme, see www.esf.se and for more information about the project see www.people.nu

In the EQUAL programme *empowerment* is a main objective, but it is also meant to be a method for ensuring the inclusion of groups that are discriminated on the labour market. My research ambition was to find out how empowerment could be understood from the participants' perspective, but also critically analysed from a theoretical perspective.

The question, *"Is it possible to measure empowerment and how can we understand and explain the concept?"* was discussed with the participants at an early stage. To try to answer such a complicated question I used an Interactive Research design, which will be described below.

9.2   The Interactive Research design

Interactive Research cannot be described solely in terms of the methods used. Interactive Research is more of a perspective – a certain way of understanding and conducting research. The involvement of the participants in the *analytical* work is the essence of an interactive approach. Different methods can be used depending on the situation and the research question. The combinations of qualitative and quantitative methods will strengthen the research findings.

In Figure 1, I have illustrated joint learning as a focal point in an Interactive Research approach. The participants and the researcher enter this process with different experiences and anticipations. These differences must be articulated and discussed before the learning process can take place in an open and trustful atmosphere. The joint learning should (in an ideal situation) continue throughout the whole research process – from the definition of the problem to the presentation of the results. But what happens to the role of the researcher in this joint learning approach? Is every participant a researcher? Both yes and no! In seeking for new explanations the participants have a similar role to that of the researcher. But the motives for being involved may differ. The participants approach the joint learning process with different motives and anticipations. The outcome of the joint learning process will also differ – academic results on the one hand and practical usefulness on the other. The participants are seldom interested in gaining academic merits, but in finding new explanations and practical solutions (see Figure 1).

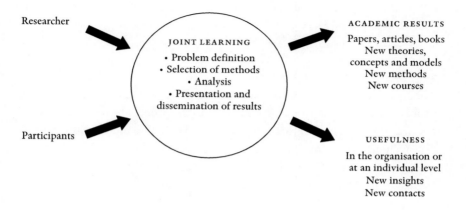

Researcher

ACADEMIC RESULTS

JOINT LEARNING
• Problem definition
• Selection of methods
• Analysis
• Presentation and
dissemination of results

Papers, articles, books
New theories,
concepts and models
New methods
New courses

Participants

USEFULNESS

In the organisation or
at an individual level
New insights
New contacts

Figure 9.1. An illustration of an Interactive Research process with different roles and interests (Svensson, see Chapter 1)

Interactive Research should not or could not be used everywhere. Joint learning is a time-consuming process, especially for the participants (see Chapter 15). A necessary thrust must be established (Herr and Anderson 2005) and the researcher must feel comfortable with having such a close relationship with the participants. There must also be a room for a critique of the situation and the organisation, which is being investigated. A supportive structure is therefore necessary (see below and Chapter 11).

In my case study, many of these requirements were present or established in advance. The use of an Interactive Research approach was thus a natural choice for me. The participants had a lot of time to be engaged in the joint learning process. They were on sick leave and often found the meetings stimulating and encouraging. The project leaders accepted a critical approach, which sometimes led to a development in the project activities. I was free to use the data and to present it in my own way. It is important that the entry process is anchored at all levels in the project. Personally, I preferred to treat the participants as subjects in the whole research process – especially in the presentation of the data. I enjoyed the informal contacts, which to some extent will probably continue after the research is completed. The research process is to a very high degree collaborative (illustrated below), but the dissertation process is an individual enterprise (Herr and Anderson, 2005).

9.2.1 Research design in the case study

The involvement of the participants makes it difficult to plan the research process in advance. Instead, it will be an open process in which decisions about different methods are taken step-by-step. The methods used were not decided in advance, but were decided upon and developed together with the participants based on the joint experiences made over time.

The following methods were used:

1) A questionnaire, which was developed together with the participants (during a total six meetings)
2) Group meetings (in total 41) – for a joint analysis and discussions of the data. Most of these meetings were organised by me and some by the project leaders
3) Thematic writing with participants (eleven meetings, sometimes during a weekend)
4) Individual interviews at the participants' workplaces
5) Presentation of preliminary findings in seminars, conferences and workplaces together with the participants. (14 meetings so far[2])
6) Meetings and seminars at APeL, the R&D centre, which was the organiser of the programme (see www.apel.nu). I carried out participant observations in different project meetings/settings (98 meetings/occasions[3])
7) Meetings and seminars in the university context (21 meetings so far).

The description of the methods used gives a static impression of the research approach, but in reality it was a very flexible and open process. The development of the research process is illustrated in a schematic form in Figure 2. The different phases in the research process are illus-

---

2 Co-presentations have been made for students at the university, for local, national and transnational partnership, but also at research conferences.

3 This includes meetings at ESF-seminars and (local, national and transnational) partnership meetings. Some of the meetings lasted for two days.

PROCESSES		RESULTS	PARTICIPANTS
1. Forming the overall research question		Work place learning and empowerment	Mainly the researcher
2. Gathering data	A	Modification of the research question. Developing a questionnaire.	Joint responsibilities
3. A deeper understanding.	N	Getting behind the scene[4]	Joint responsibility
Together with participants		Creating trust	Joint responsibility
Together with other researchers	A	Theoretical discussions	Mainly the researcher
4. Explanation		Modification of research question. Empowerment in terms of different resources?	Joint responsibility
	L	Writing a book about the participants' experiences	Joint responsibility
5. Theoretical orientation	Y	Empowerment as authorization/to enable[5]/ increased resources.	Mainly the researcher
6. Operationalisation of theory		Seven aspects of recources	Joint responsibility
7. "Testing" the operationalisation	S	Validation of theory	Separate and joint processes
8. Theoretical development	I	Papers, articles and a dissertation	Mainly the researcher
9. Dissemination	S	Dialogue seminars	Joint responsibility

Figure 9.2. Some phases in the research process with the results and participants involved.

trated as well as the results and the roles of the participants in the different phases.

The research process, which is illustrated in Figure 2, can be used to describe the development of the theoretical concept *empowerment*

---

4   This is Goffmans' (1959/1990) concept based on his dramaturgical perspective on social interaction.

5   See for example Jonsson Ahl and Florin Samuelsson (2000)

employed in my study. Empowerment was a central concept in the EQUAL programme, but in this policy context, the concept was used in different ways without any clear definition.

The use of different methods made the research design flexible and open for continuous change. The results from the questionnaire (phases 2–3) produced some basic facts which could be used in the joint analysis. In the early phases of the research process (phases 3–4), we discussed different theoretical understandings of the concept of empowerment. The participants made the following reflection based on the definitions presented, *"How is it possible to even talk about empowerment, when you are suffering from an extreme fatigue that most of us are doing?"* This comment pointed to a shortage in the conception of empowerment, namely the omission of the physiological aspect.

Together we created an understanding of the outcome of empowerment processes as *increased individual and collective resources* (phase 6). The resources for empowerment were seen as composed of the following elements:

- Social resources – that is friends and belongingness to different networks
- Knowledge or competence that the individual possesses
- Economic resources
- Institutional resources (social, cultural or symbolic[6])
- Physical resources
- The individual's feeling of self-esteem, self-confidence or self-efficacy.
- Emotional resources (included in all resources).

We also tried to assess some indicators for each of these resources (phase 7). In the discussions we tried to analyse how the participants' resources had been affected by the different activities in the project. This joint analysis led us to a modification of the original research question in the following way: *Could the outcome of empowerment processes become sustainable in an extremely rationalized working life, which causes stress among the*

---

6   These aspects of resources are similar to Bourdieu's (1985) definition of symbolic/cultural power.

employees? The new questions indicate a shift in focus – from the short-term outcomes of the activities in the project towards the long-term effects of strong mechanisms on the labour market.

One limitation with the use of the resource theory is an individual bias and the exclusion of a dimension of power – both on organisational and societal levels. Empowerment should be seen as a relational concept. This means that to empower someone, you have to disempower someone else.[7] This critical element in empowerment was not clear to the participants from the beginning, but it became very clear to me during a PhD-course later on.[8] This lack of critical reflections in our joint learning process points to a weakness in the interactive approach. It runs the risk of becoming too close and to near to the experiences of the participants. It is necessary to have access to an academic milieu to get a distance to what is going on in a group (Herr and Anderson 2005). This new perspective was later brought back to the group as an input in the joint analysis.

The example indicates that a concept has to be open to new definitions. The characteristics of an empowered person are hard to define once and for all; they depend on where a person started (Rappaport, 1987). Empowerment can begin at the individual level and can, at the next stage, take a more collective expression (Cameron and Cadell, 1999).

The dissemination process was parallel to the development of the theory. The dissemination of the research findings was an ongoing process within the project. The research findings were discussed in seminars and different meetings with the job centre, the social insurance office, the learning centre, and with the employers involved in the project. At the national level, the dissemination process has just started. A preliminary plan has been developed with the participants, this includes the following activities:

---

7   Williams et al. (1994) discusses see the idea of "power" as at the root of empowerment. Rowlands (1995) sees empowerment as a bottom-up process. Eade and Williams (1995) mean that empowerment is about challenging oppression and inequality.

8   It was a PhD-course in Interactive Research methods were I presented the different phases in my research process and the use of the resource model. As a feedback I got questions about what will happen when the individuals meet the society outside of the project. We discussed how empowerment must be seen as a relational concept put in a wider societal context.

1. Writing a book together. The target groups for this book are people on long-term sick leave, but also decision-makers, union representatives and politicians.
2. Organising dialogue-seminars for employees on long-term sick leave based on the research findings.
3. Organising meetings with the decision-makers in the municipality involved in the project to try to accomplish a more focused intervention.

Another part of the dissemination process was directed to the research communities. The participants have taken part in different meetings with researchers – in conferences, seminars, informal groups etc. In the conferences we made a joint presentation of the research findings. I have also been invited to one of the participants' work places to present the research findings together with the participants.

The dissemination process is thus organised as a joint learning process. It has been a way of challenging the strong division of labour between the researchers and practitioners. The involvement of the participants in this dissemination process has proven to be very fruitful. It was a manifestation of the success of the interactive approach and at the same time a way to make the academic society less exclusive.

9.3 Some conditions for constructive Interactive Research

If an Interactive Research approach is useful in producing "better' theoretical and practical knowledge, why does not everyone use it? The Interactive Research approach has been useful for me in my study. But Interactive Research does not work for everyone and in all situations. Some necessary conditions have to be present. I will describe some of the conditions that were established in the R&D project I was taking part in.

The first of these are related to the role of the researcher, namely competence in organising a joint learning process, the researcher's interest in using this method, his/her social competence in establishing a close relationship with the participants. The second set of conditions for Interactive Research have to do with the existence of a supportive structure in terms of developmental support, a strong project organisation, time and money for R&D assistance.

9.3.1 *The role of the researcher*

The role of the Interactive Researcher must be developed in a situation where there is enough time to develop a close and trustful relationship between the researcher and the participants. A *reflexive trust,* which is distinct from a more unreflective confidence (Gustafsson, 2004), is something that has to be worked out in a joint process. An unreflective confidence can be introduced "from above" by a resourceful group in society, while reflexive trust must be developed "from below" based on equality, critical reflection and an open dialogue.[9]

Reflexive trust is dependent on a "win-win" situation, which is necessary for genuine engagement. In such a situation, the participants can decide whom they should trust, on what grounds, and for what reasons. Trust can be established in *co-creative meetings*, which are based on joint work and mutual interaction (Perneman, 1997). These meetings are characterised by change-orientation, genuine participation and an honest dialogue. As a participant/practitioner you are not simply a problem solver, but you are also a researcher critically committed to examine your practice. As a researcher, you also have to critically examine your own scientific practice (Friedman, 2001).

In the role of an Interactive Researcher, you are in a vulnerable position because you are more dependent on your participants compared to a "traditional" researcher. You also have to be more open and flexible in planning your research. But critical research cannot only be undertaken in close relationships (Davies, 1999; Chapter 5 and 10). One risk for a researcher is to be too close to the participants and to be too involved in the change process (Davies, 1999; Smith, 1987). The researcher, and the participants, must be able to distance her/him/their self/ves, to be able to see the mechanisms and patterns that are often invisible in a

---

9 This kind of open dialogue is often referred to in the literature. Senge and Schamer (2001) say that it is a main element in the community Action Research Gustavsen (2002) talks about a *democratic dialogue*. Van Maanen (1988) talks about a "jointly told tale". Schön (1983) uses the term a *reflective community*.

contextual setting. In order not to stay "native", it is necessary to have a research group, which can provide continuous discussion and support.

What is needed to become an Interactive Researcher? My experience shows that it is important to have both theoretical and methodological competence. In this way, you can understand the research process and the selections of methods in different contexts. You can guide and support the participants in the joint learning process. As a researcher you cannot have the same role as the participants in the learning process. The participants must work to expose the taken-for-granted aspects of their context, while the researcher has to understand what it is to be an "insider" without losing the perspective of being an "outsider" (Herr and Anderson, 2005). It is when different understandings meet that interesting and exciting learning processes take place.

Is it possible to create a joint learning process that is based on equality? The issue of power is always present in the research relations – in terms of gender, race, class and age (Reynolds, 2002). These differences cannot be excluded. But in an interactive situation you can create a mutual respect for each other's knowledge and a mutual understanding of different ways to solve a (research) problem.

Interactive Research intends to give a voice to knowledge, which is often tacit (see Chapter 2). Friedman (2001) terms this building "theories in practice", which is an attempt to make theories explicit. In this way, the "hidden" theories can be critically examined and they make a contribution to the overall theory building. But the formulation of new theories is a subtle process, which should be organised by the researcher.

But how do we know that we have organised a joint learning process in my study? One indication is the strong involvement the participants have shown in the meetings during the more than two years. Another indication is the dynamic and intense group process where the participants wanted to find out and explore, practically and theoretically, about their situation. For example, the participants have invited feminist researchers to discuss gender issues with them. We could see that part of their problem with stress was related to the division of work at home and the difficulties in combining their private and public lives. These dilemmas and problems were intensified in a situation of diminishing resources in the welfare systems, which meant that the families – that is the women – had to take on more responsibilities.

In the beginning, the women were reluctant to discuss gender issues in the group. This was a dilemma for me as a researcher. Who should decide what it is important to discuss in a joint learning process – the researcher or the participants? I have chosen not to challenge the gender system directly, partly because of the vulnerability of the group and partly because I do not have the competence to guide such an empowerment process. Later on, the group took their own initiatives in understanding the gender relationship.

9.3.2 Organisational conditions – need of supporting structures.

In Action Research, the researcher often has a double role in both organising a change and a research process (Chapter 2). This is too heavy a burden, especially if you are a PhD student, which will be detrimental for both the practical and theoretical work.

My study was part of a programme organised by an R&D centre. In this centre there is a clear division of work between project leaders and researchers. This division of work is a way of dealing with this risk of the researcher being absorbed by day-to-day matters in a change project. To be an employee in such an R&D centre was an advantage. I could focus on the theoretical work. At the same time, the close cooperation and joint learning with the project workers was important in understanding and explaining the empowerment processes. The research was carried out in a sort of reciprocal collaboration both with insider and outsider teams (Herr and Anderson, 2005). My main responsibility in the project was to focus on the empowerment processes among the participants. I was not responsible for the development activities in the project, therefore I could be a participant observer of the activities I found interesting and important for my research. To be selective was the hardest part in my research process, because so many activities were interesting.

During the whole R&D process, I also had an affiliation with a university. This was important for me. It was important to establish a relationship with the research community and to regularly meet with other PhD students and senior researchers in different settings – seminars, conferences, daily meetings etc. This is also an important learning process for the universities, namely to deal with PhD students who are often working from "the outside".

In Interactive Research, the relationship with the participants is close but, out of necessity, of a temporary character. To arrange for a joint learning process includes a preparation for a withdrawal. This separation process is seldom described in the Action Research literature, although it is a more urgent problem in this research tradition compared to traditional academic research. It is a huge problem for a researcher, who has had a strong role in the change process, to withdraw and leave the participants to handle the things by themselves afterwards. It is easier for an Interactive Researcher to withdraw, because she/he has had a less important role in the change process. In my study, the separation phase is extended because of our joint effort in the dissemination process.

9.4 Some conclusions

I will try to summarize this chapter in terms of a few conclusions.

1. The involvement of the participants in the analysis can generate better theories

The active involvement of the participants in the theoretical work can lead to new insights, unexpected explanations, innovative perspectives, new concepts and theories – in short better theories.

My presentation here gives some evidence to support this conclusion. I have described how the participants reacted to the "over-rationalistic" ways of explaining empowerment in the existing theories. The theories were examined and seen as biased because of their exclusion of the physiological dimension of the disempowerment process.

The development of different element in a resource model of empowerment was important, but a rather traditional way of making an analysis. This model was useful as a first and necessary step in explaining the change process on an individual level. The resource model was a codification of the participants' own understanding of the empowerment process.

But critical research must go beyond a mere understanding among the participants. It must focus on hidden mechanisms and structures that are invisible, but could be grasped by a burdensome analytical work. The power perspective that I introduced and a relational framework were necessary ingredients in this theoretical work. As a researcher I had to challenge the participants' own interpretations, but I did so carefully, depending on the strong personal involvement in these matters and the risk for them of being exposed to people outside of their group. It is possible that I should have been more straightforward in this process.

I cannot present any astonishing findings as an outcome of my Interactive Research approach so far. I hope to be more outspoken about this in my thesis. But in general I will stress the advantages of an Interactive Research design based on my findings. It can give you access to hidden information, which is often concealed. It can involve the participants in a discussion of the findings and in creating new knowledge. In this way the validity of the research will be higher (see Chapter 6 and Chapter 8). The data will be less biased because of a genuine participation of the people involved. If you treat them as subjects in the research process, they will act as subjects and be co-producers in an open and critical examination of the findings.

How can a joint learning process be organised when different kinds of knowledge are involved? How can local, practical and uncritical knowledge be combined with a general, theoretical and critical knowledge? It cannot, if you stick to a static and dualistic conceptualisation formulated in this way. But if you, instead, use a process perspective on learning, the opposite poles can lead to a synthesis, which represents a deeper understanding.

The fundamental question is from what position you should start the joint learning process. In my study it was natural to start from the perspective of the participants that is to get an insight from inside and from below. Smith (1990) stresses the importance in understanding discriminated groups by placing them in the middle of the analysis and not in the margins. This perspective will give you a superior understanding of power structures.

The added value of using an Interactive Research design in my study is the close links that are established to the participants' everyday world, which create a deeper understanding and a better explanation of empowerment. I would not have gained the same kind of knowledge by using a traditional research method.

2. The need for supporting structures

Would I recommend a PhD student to use an Interactive Research design? Well, it depends on a lot of things. It depends on the research question, the interests of the participants, the time available, your own interest and capacity, but most of all it depends on whether or not you have a supportive R&D structure. We must learn from the mistakes made by Action Researchers in trying to be both change agents and researchers at the same time.

I think that it is necessary to have a supportive structure if you are going to be an Interactive Researcher. It is absolutely necessary to have such a supportive structure if you are a PhD student. The support must be organised both inside an academic context but also from a R&D centre with the project leaders. To be able to co-operate with the manager and the coordinator in the project was very important for me both from a practical point of view, but also as part of the joint learning process (see Chapter 15).

To summarise, Interactive Research is an interesting opportunity to produce innovative findings that are useful both for a practically and a theoretically oriented audience. I have learned a lot by using an Interactive Research approach, and I hope that my findings will be part of an ongoing debate about the varieties of research methods that are needed in a complicated an quickly changing society. In such a society, the citizens will no longer accept to be the objects of a research society of a traditional, academic and distant kind. The researchers have to be prepared to change themselves and develop new methods that are more inclusive and flexible.

References

Bhaskar, R (1978), *A Realist Theory of Science,* Hassocks: Harvester Press.

Bourdieu, P (1985), *Distinction: A social critique of judgement of Taste,* London: Routledge.

Cameron G. and Cadell, S. (1999) "Fostering empowerment participation in prevention programs for disadvantaged children and families: Lessons from ten demonstration sites". *Canadian Journal of Community Mental Health*, No. 18 (1), p. 105–121.

Davies, K. (1999) "Närhet och gränsdragning: att nå andra sorters kunskaper genom deltagande observation", in *Mer än kalla fakta. Kvalitativ forskning i praktiken*. Sjöberg, Katarina (ed), (Close and distant relations: to reach different sorts of knowledge through participating observation /*my translation*) Lund: Studentlitteratur.

Friedman, V. J. (2001) "Action Science. Creating Communities of Inquiry in Communities of Practice", in *Handbook of Action Research. Participative Inquiry & Practice*. Reason, P. and Bradbury, H. (eds.), London: Sage.

Goffman, E. (1959/1990) *The Presentation of Self in Everyday Life*, London: Penguin Books.

Gustafsson, R. (2004). "Tillit och respekt bortom Homo economicus och Homo sociologicus". (Trust and respect beyond the aspects of Homo economicus and Homo sociologicus /*my translation*.) *Sociologisk Forskning* No. 2 2004.

Gustavsen, B (2002) "Research and the Challenges of Working Life", in *Interaktiv forskning: för utveckling av teori och praktik* Svensson, L. et al. (eds.) (Vetenskaplig skriftserie från Arbetslivsinstitutet, Arbetsliv i omvandling 2002:7), Stockholm: Arbetslivsinstitutet.

Herr, K. and Anderson, G. L. (2005) *The Action Research Dissertation. A Guide for Students and Faculty*. Thousand Oaks: Sage.

Jonsson Ahl, H. and Florin Samuelsson, E. (2000) *Networking through empowerment and empowerment through networking*, (JIBS Research Reports No. 2000:1), Jönköping: Jönköping International Business School.

Eade, D. and Williams, S. (1995) *The Oxfam Handbook of Relief and Development*, Oxford: Oxfam.

Perneman, J-E (1997) *Utsatt möte: flyktingen, frivilligorganisationen och framtiden*, (Exclusiveness, the Refugee, NGO's and the future /*my translation*) Linköping: IPP; University of Linköping.

Rappaport, J. (1987) "Terms of empowerment/exemplars of prevention: Toward a theory for community psychology", *American Journal of Community Psychology*, No. 15(2), pp. 121–148.

Reason P. and Bradbury, H (eds.) (2001) *Handbook of Action Research. Participative Inquiry & Practice*, London: Sage.

Reynolds, T. (2002) "On relations between black female researcher and participants", in *Qualitative research in action*, May T. (ed.) London: Sage.

Rowlands, J. (1995) "Empowerment examined", *Development in Practice* No. 5 (2), Oxford: Oxfam.

Schön, D. (1983) *The Reflective Practitioner: How professionals think in Action*. London: Temple Smith.

Senge, P. and Scharmer, O. (2001) "Community Action Research: Learning as a Community of Practioniers, Consultants and Researchers" in *Handbook of Action Research. Participative Inquiry & Practice*, Reason, P. and Bradbury, H. (eds.) London: Sage.

Smith, Dorothy E. (1987) *The Everyday World As Problematic. A Feminist Sociology*. Boston: Northeastern University Press.

– (1990) *The Conceptual practices of power. A Feminist Sociology of Knowledge*. Boston: Northeastern University Press.

Van Maanen, J. (1988), *Tales of the Field: On Writing Ethnography*, Chicago: University of Chicago Press.

Williams, S. Seed J. and Mwau A. (1994) *Oxfam Gender Training Manual*, Oxford: Oxfam.

DITTE TOFTENG AND MIA HUSTED

10. The Common Third

The researchers, the participants and their common creation

10.1 Introduction

Our Action Research project "Imagination and diversity of work"[1] led to a methodological and practical search for a form of co-operation between researchers and participants that favoured our common engagement in the critical objectives of the project. The critical objective of this project was to develop new ways to overcome the social segregation, which arises due to developments in the labour market. The search implied turning away from a methodological focus on "close relations" or "intimacy" (Sennett: 1986) within the Action Research processes. Close relationships between researchers and participants might distract Action Research processes and lead researchers and participants into an area of trust, confidence and intimacy that can lead to extensive difficulties in relation to actions which aim to produce societal change. Marginalisation and segregation are areas, which are especially open to the development of intimate relations between marginalised persons, and professionals, where professionals increasingly look for the causes of segregation within the self of each marginalised person, just as the

---

[1] "Imagination and diversity of work" was an Action Research project investigating the dynamics between employment, marginalisation and social organisation. The project was conducted in the period 2001–2004 together with employees, people on the edge of working life and experts. The aim was to invent and qualify social sustainable workplaces, which counteract social exclusion. For further insight see (Husted and Tofteng: 2005).

methods of social help are linked to personal development (Mik-Meyer: 2004, Järvinen and Mik-Meyer: 2003). Thus, the practise of social and labour market politics is in the process of moving towards one of empathy or intimacy which emphasises the individual at the expense of an approach to segregation which sees segregation as an area of structural significance.

Our endeavour is to develop methods, which overcome or reduce the risk of emphasising intimate or therapeutic relations within Action Research processes. Here, we introduce the notion of a *common third*. This refers to the product of co-operation between the subject (the researcher) and the other (the participants). Metaphorically, it can be seen as an "area" or "space" which is created in Action Research and involves, methods, processes, actions and objects which together result in societal change, albeit on varying scales. The *common third* approach offers a contribution to the ongoing discussion concerning roles, ethics and relations in Action Research projects (Toulmin and Gustavsen: 1996, Heron and Reason: 2001).

The concept of *a common third* is in extensive dialogue with the theory of science propounded by Hans Skjervheim who points out that in order to overcome the doubling of reality (a researcher creates a research object and a research group for the purpose of research), the scientist has to acknowledge his or her own engagement, and enter a trinomial relation with the other, and the case (Skjervheim: 2001 (1957)). Within Action Research, van Beinum, Faucheux and van der Vlist have presented comparable reflections in connection with the ABX relationship (A represents the researcher, B represents the researched and X represents the case in which they are both engaged) as being one where *"the researcher and the researched are purposefully involved in a deliberate process of elaborating reality"* (van Beinum, Faucheux, van der Vlist: 1996, p. 197).

In forming a concept of *a common third* we are trying to elaborate on what Skjervheim calls *the case* and van Beinum et al. call *X* or *the elaboration of reality*. What changes occur to our understanding when we put our common concerns in a specific case up front?

In the following, we will investigate the methodological concept of *"a common third"* through a more detailed description of the processes that led to the creation of a leaflet[2], which was one of the activities in the project "Imagination and diversity of work". The story of the leaflet as a process of formation, and as a product, serves as a case to illustrate how *a common third* can be developed in Action Research projects. We open with a short description of the learning space, methodological approaches and orientations connected to the creation of the leaflet. This is then followed by an elaboration of the object related processes in Action Research. At the end of the chapter, we return to the significance of the leaflet which is discussed within the project "Imagination and diversity of work" as a whole.

10.2 The leaflet

We begin by introducing GRUM. GRUM became the name of a group of participants who live at the edge of labour market and took part in "Imagination and diversity of work". GRUM is short for Gruppen for Rummelighed Uden Marginalisering (Group for capaciousness without marginalisation). The letters in the anagram also correspond to the Danish word for "gruesome" or "cruel". The name GRUM was the group's choice. The formation of GRUM was initiated by the authors, we invited a broad group of people who were either unemployed, long-term sick, early retired, or employed on exceptional terms to participate in a project in which they would offer their experiences, criticisms and dreams concerning their working lives. The idea was to improve the feedback processes, which take place between working life and segregation, and, at the same time, to explore the possibilities for socially sustainable development in working life by drawing on experiences of segregation. It might be of some significance to emphasize that neither we as researchers, nor the members of GRUM considered us to be members of GRUM. As researchers, we had the role of collaborators with GRUM, however, with the peculiar twist that we initiated the formation of our partner. This division of roles became clear as the creation of the leaflet and the formation of experiences of living at the edge of labour market took shape.

---

2   The leaflet did not have a precise purpose in the beginning, but expressed an intention to communicate with other individuals in the same situation.

The preparation of the leaflet took place in the early stage of our cooperation with GRUM, and it was not among the activities we had planned. We had prepared a Future Creating Workshop[3] to be followed up by a Research Workshop, which would include experts and employees. These plans were carried out one year later, but the first attempt to hold the workshop failed because too few participants showed up. We decided to use the time scheduled for the Future Creating Workshop to explore whether the engagement in each others experiences and advice, which had dominated earlier meetings, could be developed into something useful for others. The idea of a leaflet had already been mentioned by one of the participants at an earlier meeting and was brought up again.

During that meeting, we prepared the room for a leaflet workshop. Blank wall charts were attached to the wall and we began by asking the participants which of their experiences of segregation were important enough to be included in a leaflet? All the experiences, comments or statements that were made were transformed into brief headlines or short statements, which we then wrote, on the wall charts. After a while, the wall charts were filled with comments, ideas and statements.

The workshop centred on five themes:

1. Enlighten colleagues – solidarity and humanity.
2. I am still useful in my view.
3. It takes a lot of work to get a flex-job.
4. It's good to be employed together with other part-time employees.
5. Probation at work before firing.

On the second day of the workshop, we went through all the themes in order to clarify and explore their meaning, so everyone had an idea of what the theme was all about. Some new headlines and comments were added, but the participants were generally satisfied with the themes as they were. The remainder of the day was spent talking about market segments, distributors, finances and recruitment. As researchers, we

---

3   For more detailed insight into the theoretical foundation and methodology of future creating workshops see Lise Drewes Nielsens article in Chapter 5.

tried to act as clerks and express the themes more eloquently before our next meeting.

Our next meeting took place about a month later and concerned discussing and improving the leaflet. We had made a draft for the leaflet relating to the five themes. The draft was sent out in good time together with the following questions: Is this what the leaflet should look like? What could the title be? What could the name of this group be? Is anything missing?

The participants did not comment on each passage in the leaflet. They reacted to what was lacking. For example, the leaflet did not include considerations of what to do when someone realizes that it is going to be difficult to keep a job on ordinary terms. This led to new comments and headlines about what you can do and whom you can turn to:

- Call the A-team[4] if work presents a problem.
- Go and talk to the people at Beta or the local authority.
- You can do a lot yourself – keep your own journal and write down whom you've been calling, whom you have talked to and what you have sent.
- Get a job description before starting – to be approved by the shop steward and by management.
- You have to be on your toes.
- You have to take part in defining how your job is designed.

During the next couple of months, different kinds of meetings took place. At some meetings, we went through the leaflet line by line. One of the researchers read out the leaflet whereupon the group commented passage by passage. In this way, the leaflet was slowly improved and the researchers' version was slowly transformed into the group's own version.

Other meetings were about testing the leaflet on others who could offer advice about how the problems should be presented. There was a visit from members of the Women Worker's Union who had had trouble keeping a job on ordinary terms. The leaflet was read out again

---

4   A-team and Beta are both local authority institutions with the task of securing or integrating people unable to work on ordinary terms by employment.

and commented on, and new suggestions concerning modifications and elaborations were made. Headlines were discussed and reformulated and new passages were inserted, which in turn demanded new headlines or new structures.

A consultant from the same union was also invited to comment on the leaflet. She pointed out that the leaflet was different and presented the human aspects of being in exposed job situations, and it therefore made a contribution to a field, which is mainly characterised by leaflets concerning rules and regulations. She was, however, puzzled that the unions were not mentioned in the section "where to go and how to seek help". This gave rise to a discussion about the experiences of help, or lack of help, from unions. Some of the consultant's comments were integrated into the leaflet and some were turned down. The discussion concerning the role of unions led to a new sentence in the section in question, namely "your local department and union can help – sometimes".

A couple of other outsiders discussed the leaflet. Two of the social workers from the A-team made comments and criticisms. One of their approved suggestions was to point out that additional work which colleagues take on for someone working on extraordinary terms is an organizational problem and not a problem caused by the individual's needs. Another contribution came from the wife of one of the participants. She worked as a journalist and went through the leaflet in terms of language and readability.

At one of the last meetings, we only worked with selected parts of the leaflet. GRUM had decided that the central pages of the leaflet were for colleagues and all the comments and ideas for the central pages were discussed and chosen. Another task was to choose and design a title and a front page.

Three ideas went further as the group drew suggestions for a front page:

- EXPOSED: The front page consisted of two drawings. A building that represented a place of work on the left hand side of the picture and a frame on the right hand side. Within the frame, a person on whom it is raining is sitting in a deckchair.
- AT THE END OF THE RAINBOW: The front page pictured a rain-

bow, which ends in the words: flex-job, early retirement, light job, securing a job. Below the words is a pot of gold.

- GAIN A FOOTHOLD OVER YOUR LIFE/ JOB SITUATION: In the centre of the front page there is a large foot surrounded by many small feet with words "is your back hurting?", "experiences of flex jobs", "too many systems".

GRUM picked the front page entitled "Gain a foothold over your job situation". Two participants drew the front page, which was approved by the others.

The work concerning the leaflet went on for about half a year. In this period, the work was borne along by the "trial readings" where external partners were brought in to comment on the draft. The trial readings were our suggestion. The idea of the trial readings was that the leaflet would be of a higher quality if it met all the relevant criticisms (like a small representation of the public sphere as a contribution to the process). GRUM approved the idea of trial readings and considered the relevance of each comment they received very carefully. Amongst the requests and comments were a number of suggestions about passages concerning how to get a flex-job and how the employers could establish re-entry or extraordinary job designs. GRUM declined. The leaflet was meant to be " from us who have been there" to "you who are about to go through it" and not an introduction to how to create jobs on special terms.

The leaflet was printed in October 2002 and was funded by the Danish Labour Market Authority (AMS). The leaflet was later reviewed by a Danish trade paper, which led to 1.500 leaflets being sent out on request. Those asking for the leaflet included private citizens, trade unions, social workers and unemployment funds. The leaflet is still used as educational material, and at client meetings by social workers working at either the council or the local rehabilitation agencies.

10.3 Learning space and alternatives to therapeutic practises

The creation of the leaflet took place in specific types of learning space where critiques and the social utopias of the participants were favoured and encouraged. During our co-operation with GRUM, we appealed and encouraged them to create a permanent leaning space able to hold and respond to free criticism, the recognition of subjectivity, respect and social imagination. To create a permanent learning space characterised by presence and exploration of these viabilities calls for a formation of co-operation and for an open horizon, where both researchers and participants take part in forming criticisms and ideas into new common actions able to open up possibilities for new developments on the labour market. At the same time, we were striving towards undertaking common actions not only tied to dialogic practises, but also to object related work. In everyday language, we call this attention to object related work, attention to *work itself*, meaning quite literally attention to what we do, why we are doing it, and how we are doing it. When doing this we denote work itself work as an activity consisting of linguistic, material, sensuous and imaginative processes.

The engagement with object related co-operations involves a certain methodological approach to the roles taken by both researchers and participants within the social framework of the Action Research project. The methods and roles of the researchers are designed to overcome the risk of empathic intimacy. Thereby, the methods and roles of the researchers also frame latitudes for the roles of the participants.

There is a certain kind of critique involved in this approach, which we also find in the work of Richard Sennett. Sennett presents a critical analysis of the social consequences of capitalism in "The fall of public man" where the tyrannies of intimacy play a decisive role for the development and improvement of society (Sennett: 1986). He outlines an ideology of intimacy, which involves a cultural belief that individual personality develops through experiences of closeness and warmth with others and a reigning myth that the evils of society are connected with impersonality, alienation and coldness. The critical consequences for society are that *"this ideology transmutes political categories into psychological categories"* (op. cit. p. 259), and that the measurement of social reality in psychological terms, excludes the civility of society, and thereby favours a narcissistic focus on the motives of the self.

Steinar Kvale suggests a similar critique in connection with qualitative research interviews, and directs our attention to the risk of reproducing a societal state of control and dominance during empathic interviews:

> The interview becomes an emphatic social technology for biographical reconstruction and reconfirmation of a fragile self. The emphatic access to authenticity in interview research thus recapitulates central cultural themes by placing the biographical narrating self in the centre of social research. (Kvale 2002, p. 5)

By placing the self in the centre of the research process, societal structures of power are left untouched, and so are the possibilities to direct the research process to experimental or developmental changes relating to societal life and organization.

Action oriented co-operation that takes place within themes highly affected by personal and emotional experiences is often at risk of being dominated by empathic insight into the participant's life. The themes within "Imagination and diversity of work" are such themes, where personal experiences of being declared incapable of managing one's own affairs, being socially excluded, or being substantially affected by threats of exclusion are predominant. However, when investigations into personal feelings determine Action Research processes, the project is at risk of ending up in a blind alley where understanding and closeness are considered necessary to produce empirical knowledge of certain experiences of social reality.

Some experiences can, however, be hard to understand – some choices or life courses can even seem incomprehensible. While the incomprehensible is waiting to be understood, it is denied social recognition in its own right. If giving up the intimate self forms a precondition for attention, it is more likely that the co-operation will confirm social inequalities than put them to the test or affect them. The work of Sennett suggests another approach that is concerned with autonomy and respect:

Rather than an equality of understanding, autonomy means accepting in others what one does not understand about them. In so doing, the fact of their autonomy is treated as equal to your own. The grant of autonomy dignifies the weak or the outsider; to make this grant to others in turn strengthens one's own character. (Sennett: 2004, p. 262).

According to Sennett, it is the granting of autonomy in decisions concerning one's own social reality that forms the notion of respect. The concept of respect presented by Sennett is interesting because it denotes a *social* aspect of autonomy as a practise we grant each other without the reservation that we have to be able to reflect our selves in the self of the other. Sennett, however, provides us with little clue as to how to operationalise this definition of respect. By introducing the notion of *a common third* we mark our contribution to methods handling "respect" in practise, as a particularly relevant method when cooperating with people who are socially underprivileged.

In our co-operation with GRUM, the method we used to facilitate autonomy was first and foremost put into practise by using the subjective experiences of the participants in GRUM as the central knowledge base from which the project could develop. At the same time, these experiences were used to strive towards a common or societal perspective concerning actions or initiatives. Also, the granting of autonomy was expressed by the capacity to participate with multiple motives and various degrees of intensity during our co-operation.

Approaching *a common third* calls for methods and roles to investigate personal experiences, to produce critiques and social utopias of common or societal significance. Role-plays, games and masks are predominant in our methods, as the role, mask or game allows us to investigate certain sufferings or dreams loosened from individual preferences or life context. Role-plays and games bring plasticity into the processes and open up the possibility for new products or utopian ideas to influence the objectives of the projects.

Our role as researchers was to establish methods and arenas where the critique and social utopias of the participants were being unfolded through different roles, masks or perspectives. As examples, we use "silent role plays", advocacies, actors and trial readings in the process.

These methods are comparable in their ability to put forward certain elements or perspectives for investigation and elaboration without being decisive for the product of the processes and without blaming sufferings, critique or individuals dreams. We are playing with roles, "voices" and perspectives to examine them for abilities to facilitate the creation of new forms containing both the critique and the utopian ideas of the participants. The processes are always oriented towards the creation of new forms, new products or new kinds of social organization. This is what we call "object related processes".

10.3.1 *Object related processes*

Our approach to social inequality and segregation was to pose a practical research question, namely "How can we imagine a workplace that does not produce social segregation?" Co-operation with GRUM was directed at different attempts to produce ideas related to this challenge. The creation of the leaflet was used to express experiences of segregation and ideas of how to maintain autonomy. Working with the theme of the leaflet, it was of methodological importance that neither of us was in a particularly exposed position or had something at stake. The creation of the leaflet was not about individual cases, causes of sickness or individual job chances. It was about the straining of subjective experiences of common concern when moving towards a life on the edge of labour market and about searching for joint initiatives and actions in which our common interests in the project could develop. Working with the leaflet formed a joint framework and constituted a common case where the participants could express their subjective experiences, criticisms and wishes, and we as researchers took the role of critical and curious opponents, designers of methods and occupational capacities in questions regarding the working environment and organisation of working life.

The leaflet was not in itself the common third but became a medium for creating *a common third*. You might say that we can understand the situation and the co-operation in terms of an area rather than in terms of relations. The processes were aimed at developing the leaflet and not about developing relationships. Relationships or even friendships are not in anyway "disliked" – any mutual sympathies or intimate relations that emerged during the project can surely be seen as an asset – but they do not form the solid ground for our co-operation. Or you could say that what characterises *a common third* is that the area is not about the subject or the other, but about something that goes beyond us and is yet rooted in the experiences, critique and dreams of our everyday lives. *A common third* is a notion of specific types of learning processes striving towards new practical actions or products of both subjective and societal significance. The leaflet was one of the concrete actions that succeeded in being a medium for practical experiments approaching *a common third*. *A common third*, however, stresses more extensive qualities within object related Action Research processes, than the creation of the leaflet indicates.

Action Research strives towards changing our social life and realities in order to resolve or affect social conflicts (Lewin: 1945). Working with Action Research, however, raises questions of what constitutes social life. The concept of *a common third* stresses object related constitutions of social life and attends to objects and moulding processes as significant elements in our comprehension of reality. Or to put it another way, the object related orientations in "Imagination and diversity of work" underline the significance of work and the social significance attached to the creation of objects.

Our methodological engagement with *a common third* is rooted in the concept of work as presented by Karl Marx. Marx understood the concept of work as a subject-object relation where subjective acquisition of reality runs through the shaping and comprehension of objects. To Marx, it was impossible to imagine a human being who possessed aesthetic sense, imagination, a critical faculty or sense of justice, without imagining objects through which these senses take form and develop (Marx: 1961, p. 67–102). Later, Adorno and Horkheimer elaborated on the relations between the organisation of society and objects as they examined enlightenment and the critical significance of objects, with the pessimistic view that *"factuality wins the day; cognition is restriction to its repetition; and thought becomes mere tautology"* (Adorno and Horkheimer: 1997, p. 27). Oscar Negt follows the materialistic conception, but argues for an emancipative perspective in relation to work and society. Emancipation should be achieved through residences for experiences of subjective and societal significance of products and work processes in everyday life (Negt: 1984). Or, to sum up the status of object related processes from Marx over Adorno and Horkheimer and back to Negt: Objects and object related processes are significant in order to comprehend <u>and</u> develop reality, but it is important that objects are regarded as workable and not as factuality if reality is to be developed by people and not decided by indispensable or unavoidable "objectives".

Richard Sennett presents another analysis of the societal significance of object related processes in work in his study of flexibility and inconstancy concerning the qualifications demanded by the labour market. Sennett points out that this inconstancy produces apprehension and anxiety: "*An apprehension is an anxiety about what might happen; apprehension is created in a climate emphasizing constant risk, and apprehension increases when past experiences seem no guide to the present*" (Sennett; 1999, p. 97). The past experiences of being good at one's work, knowing the machine, the technology and materials seem to be eclipsed by new demands of readjustment, interpersonal skills and personal development.

Creating the leaflet reflects object related processes in both the physical and mental senses. The work process stimulated both researchers and participants to relate to a common third in a subjective sense. The case and the object of our co-operation, brings together the local and contextual knowledge of the participants and the researchers' focus on commons and society. At the same time, learning processes rooted in the collective formation of experiences take place within the common third. Researchers and participants not only bring subjective experiences with them, collective experiences take form and gestalt as we are working with the leaflet as a medium. *A common third* develops as a collective learning process and as a common idea of products. In the case of the leaflet, the process led to a product. This is, however, far from always the case. *A common third* is our common effort to form new practises or actions – and sometimes we have to settle with common ideas or endeavours. For the time being, however, the process itself is *a common third,* as it has enabled us to discuss the matter in ways that both capture our subjectivity and go beyond us.

To introduce a notion of *a common third* within the co-operation with GRUM, it was necessary that both researchers and participants were able to "ration" their subjectivity to some degree. It was possible to introduce experiences by choice – or to choose between certain positions, arguments or ideas when relevant for the case. At the same time, it was perspectives of future actions and not of personal narratives that became the object of the co-operation.

10.4 The public realm and common perspectives

The word "common" is to be taken quite literally – the aim is to produce ideas of some common good related to general societal challenges. That is, however, also one of the biggest challenges in this type of Action Research project, namely to place the local knowledge in a common perspective, or to find common resonance in the participants' individual stories and experiences. How can a small-scale case such as the co-operation and the work on the leaflet be brought into a public sphere? And how can experimental work within the project meet "reality" without being overthrown? This challenge must be met during the co-operation.

The inner relation between the Action Research project and the project's ability to create dialogues with the public realm, interactions and diffusion is itself an important issue when it comes to Action Research. In the world of academia as well as among Action Researchers themselves, the critics of Action Research projects have been dominated by following arguments: Action Research is not good enough to diffuse into a broader societal context or into a broader theoretical framework (Toulmin and Gustavsen: 1996). How do we combine theory and practice without compromising either, and how do we ensure that new forms of practice can be developed without being overthrown by "the battle of schools" in an academic sense?

In this chapter, we have argued that turning towards the public sphere, and looking for common perspectives in small-scale co-operations are, in fact, ways to overcome the problems of combining theory and forms of practices. New forms of practice can, by the issues or themes they bring up or by practising a different social organization, underline new ways to approach societal questions and theoretical frameworks. The work within the co-operation represents a new form of social organization regarding questions of segregation and the labour market, which touch upon new perspectives of how to approach discussions of societal sustainability. It is important to notice that the work within the co-operation is not only a critical voice, it also contains ideas of how to maintain authority both inside and outside the labour market as well as new methodological ideas of how to encourage dialogues and exchanges of experiences, and ideas that cross the thin line between life as workers and life as marginalised. We will not go further into the results and processes of "imagination and diversity of work" as a whole, but settle for the significance of the leaflet.

10.4.1 *What happened afterwards*

Creating the leaflet facilitated the formation of GRUM while the leaflet itself became an important product for GRUM to use as an anchor for elaboration and dialogues. "Imagination and diversity of work" developed through a series of arenas in which utopian ideas suggested by GRUM to counteract segregation were elaborated in co-operation with utopian ideas suggested by a group of shop stewards to prevent marginalisation. The arenas were developed to include experts and stake holders with the tasks of improving and examining the realization of the ideas. The leaflet was taken through every arena and tested for its ability to open new discussions and new practises in matters of diversity and segregation. The aspiration was to use the experiences and ideas expressed in the leaflet as an object for dialogues with workplaces, social workers and within the people in the field of health care. GRUM became "a travelling GRUM" as a result of the processes within the arenas, and succeeded in making two public presentations of their critique and ideas based on the leaflet. Today, the leaflet keeps both the previous processes and dialogues as well as aspirations for future discussions in a public realm.

Current activities in the melting pot are the creation of a second leaflet and the invention of unusual jobs. Such experiments call for a public sphere to participate and to explore the experiment for common significance. The invention of extraordinary jobs is, just as the creation of the leaflet, a matter of public interest. Our harsh criterion of validation is that the results are valid when the processes and products of the Action Research project succeed in introducing a new kind of debate and/or experiment involving a broader public sphere. A gentle version of the same criterion is to examine whether the process and products have the potential for such debates and experiments and to examine and encourage the possibilities for realisation of these potentials.

In the Scandinavian Action Research tradition, as represented by Bjørn Gustavsen (Gustavsen, 1990: 2002), the keyword is dialogue. In this tradition, work is centred round different types of dialogue arenas, in which development and knowledge creation take place. One of the biggest strengths of this tradition is its sensitivity towards the organisations of new types of dialogues that involve multiple groups of actors. This is why our project has also been inspired by this tradition. Thus, it seems that a mechanism of selection is a part of the tradition, which can be addressed as a matter of representation. GRUM would hardly have been involved in the dialogue arenas, because of the simple fact that GRUM was not a group before the project started. In the tradition of dialogue, the point of departure is to involve existing "voices" and groups of actors within the organisation, not to create new groups or "voices" that do not already exist.

The involvement of GRUM as a new actor on the scene of "the diverse labour market" has been an important part of the co-operation.

In consonance with Lennart Svenssons' work using Interactive Research, the argument is that most of the actors involved in this kind of project look upon themselves as "people of action" rather than people of talk and analysis (Svensson: 2002). On this basis, they find it of much greater importance to "do" than to focus on discussions or analyse. The project is connected to the tradition of dialogue but at the same time, tries to denote actions as object related processes. Dialogues had an important role to play in the processes towards and within *a common third*. But they have been an integrated part, connected to the practical experiences within the co-operation. *A common third* contains more than dialogues and communicative praxis. It contains ideas, products or images of an alternative praxis that is anchored in experiences, senses, body and social context. The ideas, products or images are concrete in the sense that they represent an existing part of "real life". This means that hopefully the experiences and ideas of this project can be of inspiration to others and be a critical remark to the societal development.

Most important is the way in which the co-operation is based on "*a comprehensive experience context, which can be used by way of example, thereby serving as a productive source of inspiration in other context and situations"* (Nielsen, Nielsen and Olsén, 1996, p. 43).

The development of *a common third* through the leaflet contains object related learning processes in which the formation of GRUM as well as the leaflet itself served as productive sources of inspiration. It has shown to provide another input of knowledge and actions than traditional research on the field can offer. The leaflet has provided GRUM with an object around which to discuss labour market development and segregation in a public realm. Creating the leaflet was a process of formation of experiences, which produced knowledge and "voice" missing within the debates of marginalisation and labour market development. The preliminary discussions across the thin line between employment and marginalisation within the project have been promising. The future challenges are to create arenas of a broader societal significance in which we can explore preliminary discussions and ideas and examine the lack of connections between experiences of segregation outside labour market and the threats of marginalisation within.

References

Adorno, Theodor and Max Horkheimer (1997 (1944)): *Dialectic of Enlightenment.* London: Verso.

Van Beinum, Hans, Calude Fauxcheux and René van der Vlist (1996): "Reflections on the epigenetic significance of Action Research" in Toulmin and Gustavsen (ed.) *Beyond Theory.* Amsterdam: John Benjamin.

Gustavsen, Bjørn (1990): *Vägen till ett bättre arbetsliv.* Stockholm: Arbetslivcentrum.

– (2002): "Research and challenges of working life". In *Interaktiv forskning: för utveckling av teori og praktik,* Svensson, Lennart et al. (eds.) Stockholm: Arbetslivsinstitutet.

Heron, John and Peter Reason (2001): "The practice of co-operative inquiry: Research 'with' rather then 'on' people". In *Handbook of Action Research*, Peter Reason and Hillary Bradbury (eds.) London: Sage.

Husted, Mia and Ditte Tofteng (2005): *Respekt og realiteter – bevægelser mellem arbejde og udstødning.* Fredriksberg: Roskilde universitetscenter. http://hdl.handle.net/1800/1622

Järvinen, Margaretha and Nanna Mik-Meyer (2003): *At skabe en klient.* Copenhagen: Hans Reitzels forlag.

Kvale, Steinar (2002): *Dialogue as oppression and interview research.* Paper on www.psy.au.dk/ckm/newsletter/nb32

Lewin, Kurt (1946): *Resolving social conflicts.* New York: Harper & Row.

Marx, Karl (1961): *Selected writings in sociology and social philosophy.* London: Penguin Books.

Mik-Meyer, Nanna (2004): *Dømt til personlig udvikling.* Copenhagen: Hans Reitzels forlag.

Negt, Oskar (1984): *Lebendige arbeit, enteignete zeit.* Frankfurt: Campus Verlag.

Nielsen, Birger Steen, Kurt Aagaard Nielsen, Peter Olsén(1996): "From Silent to Talkative Participants. A Discussion of Technique as Social Construction". In *Economic and Industrial democracy* Vol. 17, No. 3. London: Sage.

Sennett, Richard (1986): *The fall of public man.* London: Faber and Faber.

– (1999): *The corrosion of character.* New York: W. W Norton.

– (2004): *Respect – the formation of character in an age of inequality.* London: Penguin Books.

Skjervheim, Hans (2001 (1957)): *Deltakar og tilskodar og andre essays.* Oslo: Aschehoug.

Svensson, Lennart (2002): "Bakgrund och utgångspunkter". In *Interaktiv forskning: för utveckling av teori och praktik,* Svensson, Lennart et al. (eds.) Stockholm: Arbetslivsinstitutet.

Sørensen, Aage B. (1992): "Aktionsforskning om og i arbejdslivet". In *Tidsskrift for samfunnsforskning,* year 33 issue, pp. 213–230.

Toulmin, Stephen and Bjørn Gustavsen (1996): *Beyond theory: changing organizations through participation.* Amsterdam: John Benjamin.

EVA AMUNDSDOTTER

11. Interactive Research for Gender Equality in Workplaces

Gender is something most of us just "do", as a spontaneous and familiar action. Gender is a "non-issue" in organisations with ambivalence between saying "gender is of no importance here", at the same time as efforts are being made in terms of gender equality. Patricia Maguire writes about the need to link together feminism and Action Research (Maguire, 2001). She believes that Action Research is expected to involve action and that this in its turn means that we need to examine social practices and structures. It has been and is a significant part of feminist research and also involves a critical perspective on power issues that she claims are on many occasions lacking in Action Research.

Action Research also uses the relational processes that are inherent in many feminist methods. A central issue is to critically examine how and what knowledge is produced and to try to interrupt silencing mechanisms in order to gain access to one's own voice. The task of Action Research grounded in feminism is consequently to interrupt and reveal mechanisms that create and maintain gendered power asymmetries (Maguire, 2000: 63). Maguire argues that Action Research which ignores feminist research is inadequate as an anticipated "emancipation project".

Interactive methods have been used in four networks in a research and development project. In their role as "change agents", 60 practitioners from 20 workplaces have worked for equal conditions for women and men in the different workplaces. Through interactive methods, and with a basis in gender studies, knowledge about the way in which gender is produced and about change processes has grown. Six years of research will be developed into a model for change, with the focus on gender in work organisations.

11.1 Presentation of the research project

"The sustainable company – focusing on gender equality" is a EU-funded project that started in 1999 and was aimed at interested workplaces in southern Sweden. They were offered the chance to participate (2–4 members) in networks for 18 months. It was conditional on the workplace management giving its support to a development and research project focusing on gender. The network participants were to put time into researching their work places, initiating a variety of activities and drafting an action plan for gender equality.

The first network consisted of five female-dominated workplaces. These were the ones who responded most quickly to the EU office's offer of participating in the project. The framework was development and change focusing on gender in working life, but what and how this was to be done was to be developed in interaction between practitioners and researchers/project managers. The participants conducted a survey of their respective workplaces during a research phase and subsequently proceeded into an implementation phase in which goals and activities were formulated. The participants, with the support of each other and the researchers/project managers in the network, drew up the action plan.

Minna Gillberg, PhD in Sociology of Law, and I devised the possible methods and models that could provide support for sustainable gender equality work. Together with the five work places, which were represented by 14 women and one man, various methods were tested and developed for the change process, expressed in a book, among other ways, by (Amundsdotter and Gillberg, 2001). Two years after the first network, three new groups were started. They were spread throughout Sweden and gender equality in the workplace was on their agenda.

In total, four networks with participants from a number of workplaces have been at the heart of the research and development project. Interactive methods have contributed to theory and methods that have been shared with others through dissemination conferences, in which the practitioners have played a leading role, as well as through publications. The following overview provides a picture of some of the methods and activities that have been used during the period when the project took place (November 1999–December 2005):

- Group meetings/network meetings
Between 12–20 meetings/network, varying from 1–2 days over a two-year period. The meetings consisted of exchange of experience, reflection, exercises (drama, evaluation exercises), leadership and change, gender theory, workplace reports, etc.
- Meetings of the smaller workplace groups
Method in two of the four networks: 2–4 meetings at each workplace co-ordinated by the researcher/project manager. All the workplace groups held meetings of their own.
- Dissemination conferences/workshops
Several dissemination conferences have been held involving practitioners and researchers/project managers. The practitioners took part as opening speakers and in workshops. In addition, on several occasions management and colleagues from the participating work places took part.
- Workplace survey from a gender perspective: each workplace group carried out its own research with a focus on the conditions in the organisations for women respective men. They documented and reported on it at the network meetings.
- Documentation in the form of two books, a report, an extended essay in gender studies, conference reports, interviews in newspapers, local news, etc.

11.2 The role of the researcher in a censored landscape

A parallel to gender as a "non-issue" can be drawn with the practitioners' research phase in the groups, when they were examining their own workplaces from a gender perspective. A common question, or uncertainty, which was posed, was: "How will we be able to see what we can't see?" The groups expressed a great uncertainty in their own ability to see what was related to gender. The question then becomes how Interactive Research can be conducted under these circumstances. There is great familiarity with the way in which gender is constituted and it makes the possibility of reflecting on a system, of which I myself, as an individual, am in various ways a part, more difficult. A number of methods for analysis and reflection have consequently been developed and actively used in the networks, for example, assessment exercises to enable awareness of the preconceptions one holds. In addition to this, a theoretical model of doing gender (Acker: 1999; Gunnarsson et al.: 2003) has been used to provide support for reflecting about doing gender in the different work places. However, it was their participation in the research, seeing that it was the practitioners themselves who examined their workplaces, which contributed insights and new patterns of thinking.

My role in the networks and out in the workplaces was primarily, as an expert in gender studies, to present gender theories and lead conversations and processes. In most cases, there have been two of us and I have been responsible for the gender expertise and the researcher role, while the other person has had a typical consultant's role. In the researcher role, I have particularly observed how gender is done in the groups and how change processes at different workplaces proceed. I have led analyses of their surveys and presented theory and understandings from a scientific field.

11.2.1 Development work in the form of a network

Research can represent a support for practitioners in networks for development work (Andersson et al. 2006). Some examples given are: the provision of support in highlighting the practitioners' experience-based knowledge, the development of a more profound understanding, the creation of critical distance to an individual's own experiences, development of analytical tools as a basis for reflection, guidance on how to act, and alternatives.

The examples correspond accurately with the researcher role I had in the networks. The starting point was learning together and the creation of subject relationships in which both parties participated in knowledge formation (see Chapter 6 about how interactive and feminist research can contribute to each other). The learning process, which has taken place, has been based on that intention where practitioners, researcher and consultant have influenced and learned from each other.

One of the networks continues to meet on its own initiative, with no funding and outside the EU project. The group is self-organising and is led by a practitioner and I take part in the role of a researcher. This group has been meeting for three years and represents an important source of learning as the fifteen members have both taken initiatives and attempted to make changes. The group provides ways into, and opportunities for, developing network theory, what members of a group can do for each other, when the members strongly emphasise the role of the network as the driving force in their ability to bring about development in their organisation.

11.2.2 *Native experience at the centre*

Should what I did in the networks be called participant observation? The concept is not particularly appropriate for what we did together. Instead of participant observation one might say participant experience (see Chapter 8). In non-participant observation from distance, factors such as language, norms, power relationships and motives are simply invisible. Use of personal experience must move from the periphery to the centre of the research process. The "what" and the "how" in this process constitute Interactive Research (see Chapter 8). In the networks our experiences have been the starting point for the joint processes that are supposed to contribute to a more profound knowledge, fresh insights and theories about change processes focusing on gender.

The traditional division between researcher and participant means that thinking and reflection are designated to a few individuals while others are responsible for the doing. This creates a lot of problems in validating knowledge and in communicating it (see Chapter 8). The view of a researcher and a practitioner as being complementary contributes to the division without challenging the view of how knowledge production comes about. In the joint learning processes we have had there was an ambition to combine theory and practice. Eikeland (Chapter 8) proposes the notion of master-apprentice and sometimes it is the researcher who is the master and sometimes it is the practitioners. Different roles emerge during the research process. I can conceive myself and the practitioners in both roles.

I am a woman and my experiences as a woman in working life, in the family, and of the gender order in society, were a part of our mutual learning processes. Just as the male consultant in two of the networks participated in processes on the basis that he is a man. Instead of setting ourselves aside, we contributed with ourselves and our experiences (see also Chapter 6). In this way, a confidence was built, as the increased validity.

11.3 Examples of the networks' processes
Theme 1: Doing gender – the individual, the group and the organisational level

The participants in the networks examined their workplaces from a gender perspective. The aim was to discover if and what in the work organisation was determined according to gender. The research phase was extended after having been tested in the first group as the participants felt that it was difficult to reveal the role gender was playing in the workplace.

The majority imagined that the conditions would not be as gender-marked as their own studies revealed: men received higher pay than women, they sat on more prestigious working groups, and they were given more expensive in-service training and better hotel rooms at conferences.

Several individuals were doubtful about doing the research; it took time and was demanding. In subsequent processes the practitioners were unanimous about the usefulness; the phase had involved them as co-researchers themselves. They became researchers in their own workplaces and several also involved colleagues in participating in a voyage of discovery of their own workplace. It also became a knowledge phase, as the studies and results from the others in the network produced new knowledge and insights. In one network, the results were so deeply discriminatory that strong feelings were aroused in the group. Surprise, anger, powerlessness were some of the emotions that were dealt with in a joint process.

11.3.1 *Women put the men in the group in a superior position*

The project's theoretical starting point was that gender is a social construction and created in interaction, in relation to others and oneself. Rules and preconceptions are maintained through actions that individuals take in relation to each other, which in their turn create conditions in an organisation. Gender is constituted at an individual, group and organisational level (Gunnarsson et al. 2003). It also means that gender was constituted in the networks and an example of this became clear through an exercise we carried out. In the exercise everyone had to choose two people from the group. When this had been done and the exercise concluded, it transpired that of 30 choices (15 people who made two choices each) men were selected 28 times out of a possible 30. There were four men and eleven women in the group. The four men were selected on average seven times each, while nine women were not once selected.

There was no particular reaction to this in the group; only when I summed up the number of votes was there a reaction. Above all, several reacted to the fact that they had not reacted. This was another incident that contributed to an increased awareness. Subsequently several individuals referred to this exercise as a wake-up call that helped the driving forces for acquiring knowledge and acting in other ways increase.

The incident gave me several theoretical insights: gender is produced in terms of relationships and is created and recreated in interactions between people. The second was that the interactions in which men come first, where male superiority is manifested in everyday life, is spontaneous and "natural". There is a familiarity with, or sometimes a denial of, how gender produces superiority and subordination, even among a group of people who are working for change. It is so obvious that it is hard to see.[1]

The experiences and ideas that emerged at the time, and subsequently, are one result of a learning process in which an interview, for example, could scarcely have produced the data that was produced through interaction. The practitioners provided each other with opportunities to

---

1   Male superiority needs to be developed and problemized, in the same way as female subordination, and modern men's studies is starting to address the theme.

understand the significations of gender that by being made visible could be worked on in everyday situations. Gender was not a "non-issue" as I wrote, but, on the contrary, visible and linked to the field of knowledge of gender theory.

The question needs to be set, if this visibility becomes synonymous with a change of experience and practical actions for the practitioners.

In this exercise I mirrored the group by making an observation. To return to Eikeland's idea about the changing roles between master and apprentice; in that moment the researcher role can be interpreted that I am the master and the practitioners are the apprentices.

11.3.2 Superiority and subordination

Power relationships in the gender order are often manifested through male superiority and female subordination at a structural level. We build and construct that which we ourselves perceive as female and male. People enter into invisible agreements that become a part of the construction, so-called gender contracts.

On the basis of some concepts from the field of gender studies, the women and men in the networks reflected on their own role in the construction of gender. The women reflected on the questions: When am I being subordinate? What do I gain by being subordinate? What is difficult about being subordinate? The men did the same, but with superiority as a theme.

The majority had not thought about the gender order in such concrete terms and long, lively conversations followed their own reflections. Several of the women stated that subordination is a habit. Furthermore, it can be convenient. Women told of how they choose to allow a man to take the initiative or various decisions because it is convenient.

Different examples of male superiority were given, also in other contexts such as the fact that a male change agent is treated with more respect than a female (see further on). Several men felt that male superiority involves privileges and it is therefore easy to feel a resistance to change. Their own resistance was therefore an obstacle to them in their role as agents.

Another research-project that addresses the agents own resistance to change, comes from a school, where a combination of feminist and

Action Research contributes to the issue of gender and change (Berge and Ve: 2000). Through interactive methods, different social practices among the agents could be understood and challenged.

The empirical data collected contributes to knowledge about how gender is constituted in interaction between people and how one's own self-image affects that interaction. Systems and structures are created when a sufficient number of people repeat an action (Elwin-Nowak and Thomsson: 2003). When the pattern is broken, a reaction is produced. Or in order to understand a social system, one has to change it.

Individual accounts of the habitual and convenient nature of subordination were collected in the network, but at a group level. It is comprised of both a habit – a pattern, which is repeated – and a convenience. I have conceptualised this as subordination as convenient.

The process gave insights into the group about the fact that both women and men need to change different practises in order to create long-term changes. What we did in the group ourselves was a step in that direction. Particularly for the women in the group, listening to each other's stories of subordination and the difficulty of breaking out of their own subordination created scope for action. The mechanisms became clear and there was a common experience of vulnerability by staying in subordination instead of action oneself. The stories of new patterns of action both in the workplace and in private relationships characterised relations in the groups. For example, several women became union representatives in their workplaces; one who became chairperson of her branch said that she would never have taken on a task such as this two years ago. In the first network, which consisted of five female-dominated workplaces, the concept was developed of what interaction between women can be like at a workplace and how female subordination is internalised and spread between women. For reasons of space this process is not described in the anthology.[2]

In this situation, I perceive the practitioners as the master and myself as the apprentice. I learn from their accounts and experiences of how the gender order is manifested in themselves. At first I was the master

---

2 An initial description is to be found in the paper ""Vi har ju inga karlar här...": om jämställdhetsbegreppets relevans för kvinnodominerade arbetsplatser' [""We Don't Have Any Men Here"...: The Relevance of the Concept of Gender Equality for Female-Dominated Workplaces'] (see references).

when I delivered the theory but then the roles changed. The concept of subordination as being habitual and convenient was generated through the process and becomes a part of fresh knowledge and theory about doing gender.

11.4 Theme 2: A learning process about resistance – a change of perspective

The practitioners met with resistance in various ways when they initiated actions in their workplaces. Some requested a "checklist" for ways to overcome resistance. It is a common situation, to try to find quick solutions, to "fix it" (a quick fix), instead of developing new abilities and possibilities for development (Senge and Scharmer: 2001). We started a learning process concerning resistance regularly at the network meetings: What actually is resistance? What creates resistance and what helps against resistance? On the basis of the questions we worked in several stages. During the process new perspectives on what resistance is were created – not something to be overcome at any price, but something to learn about, to understand more about and that resistance can contain opportunities.

Successes and difficulties with resistance were put on the table. We used the Forum Theatre method to look for different actions and strategies in relation to oppression or resistance. The audience takes the leading role in a play in which a group searches together for knowledge on an important issue. The ethics of Forum Theatre is to stop oppression. A subject, which formed the basis for a play, was the fear that as a person conspicuously involved in gender equality work being exposed to negative criticism by colleagues. Several plays were conducted on the theme, for example, a play where a person talks about gender equality at a staff meeting and is treated disrespectfully. By replacing the "exposed" individual and testing various actions in the situation, a dilemma was worked through and new perspectives on dealing with resistance were developed. In Forum Theatre, the point is to look for several alternative ways of acting in an oppressive situation, not to find *one* solution to a problem.

11.4.1 *Interactive methods on a feminist basis*

In one of the workplaces a group of men expressed very strong opposition to change. It was a closed group of men who played golf, had saunas and, above all, bet on horses in the form of a betting team. On several occasions the four practitioners from the workplace came to the network and spoke about, worked through and tried to find strategies for dealing with the opposition voiced by the group of men and the role it played at the school in setting norms (for masculinity, for how a man should behave at the workplace).

They had previously tried to get through to the members of the group by listening and communicating, but, in the opinion of the practitioners, with no result. The management did not act either, though both it and the gender equality group felt that the men were undermining the ongoing project. An important explanation for this might be that the management consisted in large part of women and that the gender order manifested itself in such a way that the men were allowed to undermine the on-going project.

The idea for their action arose after the learning process about resistance had commenced. Thinking about resistance, instead of receiving a checklist, was demanding, but it created new possibilities for action: "We got the idea after doing the laborious but practical work on resistance", said one of the practitioners: they formed a competing team – an open betting team based on equality, for everyone who wanted to join. A large number joined and furthermore they won SEK 19.000 on their second attempt. The role of the men's group was changed in the sense that it lost privileges of interpretation.

The action of the workplace group is an example of dealing with resistance, but it is also a contribution to formulating theory on how doing gender can take place in an organisation. It is an example of a workplace culture in which a subgroup, the group of men, maintains a power order and relationships of superiority and subordination. By means of a new action that which the practitioners carried out, a new order was created, in which the privileges of interpretation was changed. There are several researchers who attest to gender equality projects that management wanted to pursue, but where the workplace culture put obstacles in the way. The practitioners felt that what happened in the male group's workplace took place outside management structures and was not wanted from the management's perspective. I was at the workplace myself on several occasions and even met the management.

The action had several effects: the practitioners gained in confidence and colleagues came to them to discuss injustices or to put forward ideas for change. Furthermore, the management took action and told each of the men that they were not to undermine the change process. This is how this incident also contributed to a deeper understanding of the ways in which power and gender can interact with each other; the female management subordinated themselves to the men who were in reality subordinate to the women in the work organisation. However, when another subgroup took action, new opportunities for practices were created.

The work has been interactive – no checklists, instead a joint, critical learning process in the group about what resistance is. The work has had feminist starting points with a theory about gender order and change for equal conditions. This has been reinforced by the use of methods such as Forum Theatre with an anti-oppression ethic. I think that the combination of interactive methods with a feminist basis has produced results that have shown, among other things, that change is possible. Power relationships have changed the constitution of gender and superiority and subordination have been altered. It is not possible for me to come to a deterministic conclusion after our processes, something that, to some extent, has characterised gender theories (Acker, 1999). The project is contributing knowledge about change processes but also about how change can be observed in the actual making of gender in organisations. It also reinforces the conclusions that the researchers Berge and Ve drew from their Action Research project, where they speak about gender making as continuously ongoing actions in the organisation (Berge and Ve, 2000).

11.4.2 The gender of the change agent matters

The negative treatment, which was dealt with in the Forum Theatre as a fear, became a reality – for the women. One year after the networks started, 45 of the practitioners met. It was a very special occasion as there was a distance of up to 1.500 kilometres between the northern and southern networks. The aim of the meeting was to exchange experiences and create a dialogue about change processes. Some work took place in groups divided according to gender. The idea was to try to locate any gender specific events or experiences. Large differences emerged in the reporting of resistance in particular. The reports of the women's groups on the question of what resistance they had met all contained words such as: "Ridiculing, belittling, jealousy, domination techniques, aggression and personal attacks".[3] None of these words appear in the male groups' reports: "People listen more to male colleagues; the resistance we met is mainly our own resistance and convenience". The men spoke about their own resistance, the comfort of feeling privileged, while the theme of the women's experiences was that of vulnerability in the role as a participant in the project. However, resistance was commonly perceived as "lack of time, ignorance and the low priority of gender equality-work".

In other words, the gender of the change agent is significant. We can understand change processes in practice and it provides knowledge about change strategies.

11.4.3 *Personal change drives processes*

People learn best through and from each other, and participation in learning groups is crucial for efficiency and well-being. Cooperation, especially in helping each other through difficult change processes, always involves relationships (Senge and Scharmer, 2001). In the introduction to the get-together all 45 had the chance to speak briefly. The majority chose to tell each other about their "own journey" that this change process had meant for themselves. There seemed to be a strong desire to have the opportunity to talk about one's own change. Senge and Scharmer describe a similar experience when a group, which worked with sustainable development in their organisations, needed to speak about their personal journeys and challenges (Senge and Scharmer: 2001, p. 246).

There is a clear link between those who spoke about how they were

---

3 The words correspond with the theory of domination techniques articulated by the Norwegian Professor of Social Psychology Berit Ås.

personally affected and their ability to take initiatives at the workplace. It appears that a sliding scale could be drawn to link together the degree to which an individual was personally affected with their ability to act and initiative. A woman who had initially reacted strongly against participating stated two years later: "If it was possible to change me, it's possible to change anyone. I have really changed and it helps me when I think about the fact that now I am going to try to influence others. It has been a journey to understand that what I believed to be self-evident was not".

Her experience confirms Senge and Scharmer's comments about the fact that one's own change or journey becomes a driving force in the role as practitioner.

11.5 Theme 3 – Conditions and opportunities in a change process

The ambition of developing a model for change has been made concrete primarily through the network that is in its fourth year and continues to meet. Step by step we are producing concepts, trying to grasp mechanisms and explain the levels at which different incidents or mechanisms can be expected to end up. A current theme is the ability and opportunities the practitioners have in their role to take action. Several different industries and sectors are represented, which provides the opportunity to be able to see patterns as well as variations in different organisations.

This section briefly describes some of the processes we undertook to bring about conditions for change: one of them started with an individual reflection on the question: "What am I doing in the role of change agent when I neglect to act, even though I perceive or want something different?" From this individual reflection several dialogues commenced that subsequently became a joint analysis in the entire group. We discussed, and sometimes drew pictures of, what is culture and what is structure, what is interaction and what is self-image, etc.

On another occasion we went further and carried out a number of workplace processes. 3–4 practitioners from the same workplace sat and discussed with each other on the basis of the two questions: "What is it in the organisation that makes me take or want to take initiatives in the role of a person actively involved in gender equality issues? What is it in the organisation that prevents my ability or willingness to take the initiative?"

In different phases of the conversation the outer circle contributed comments, questions and observations. A short extract from one of these discussions:

- It is our group that makes me want to take the initiative. Without it I wouldn't be able to.
- A young woman was very nearly raped in the park last weekend. I spoke with her and tried to convey what I have learned about, for example, gender and violence. An incident such as this makes me want to take initiatives.
- There are four of us in the group, two women and two men. We two women are branded as rabid feminists. Powerful domination techniques are being used on us and I shut up. You end up in relative subordination so as not to be too disruptive.
- The payroll was a real disappointment. The unjustifiable wage differentials that we discovered and which were immediately corrected have now been recreated as there were only men at the top of the payroll.
- I am afraid to stand in front of the staff. I feel that I cannot reprimand or tell someone who is voicing opposition, because, after all, he is more educated than I am. When they sit there, with their arms crossed, looking on critically, I get stage fright. It is a hierarchy that makes me weak.
- The management really supported the work in the beginning, but now it feels as if they are slowly backing out. I believe it is the workplace culture that has created a pressure on the management to back down.

11.5.1 *Male norm to not lose control*

Several people in the circle around me found this familiar and all in all there is a lot of material collected in the networks about the lack of a mandate and clarity in the assignment of being a promoter of gender equality.

An additional fear was expressed, this time by several women: of losing control, of being too emotionally involved. "If I get too upset over an injustice at work, there is a great risk that I will lose control and become too emotional. Then I end up exposed to comments about the fact that, for example, I am not objective", said one of the women. The men did not recognise this at all, while all the women understood what she meant. It also led to a discussion about domination techniques and gender order, in which several people felt that the male norm in working life does not allow loss of control.

The workplace culture has been changed in many ways by the different initiatives that the practitioners have taken. At the same time all the networks have noted that the workplace culture is the most difficult to change. However, structures and power relationships are not easy to change either. Both variation and stability, which can contribute to a development of theory and methods of gender in organisations, can be observed (Kvande in Gunnarsson: 2003).

Through developing knowledge and methods about how gender is done in organisations and how change can happen, it is a challenge for the interactive gender research to link that knowledge with knowledge and theory about how the global power order from a gender perspective seems. What makes the male domination to consists, how do structural forces, strongly gender marked by men's power, function and so on. Through linking these fields together, strategies and experiences can be developed.

11.6 Summary

The interactive methods and the time put into developing mutual subject relationships provided support and access to experiences that I believe only emerge in situations of trust and confidence. The ambition to have subject-subject relationships, to try to have a discussion on equal terms, has long been present in gender research (Chapter 6, Maguire: 2001). Stories about workplace relationships subsequently emerged that produced a more profound knowledge of how gender is produced in organisations, relationally, symbolically and culturally. The first network, which consisted principally of women at female-dominated workplaces, provided important knowledge about how gender is constituted in same gender groups.

The learning process on the subject of resistance, a joint project, meant that resistance is not located outside us as individuals, but that reflection over our own resistance was an equally important part of the role of change agent, and the understanding of resistance. The process also revealed the different conditions the practitioners had in their workplaces depending on gender. Furthermore, one workplace group was inspired to take initiatives that involved changes to power relationships at the workplace, an action that also deepens the theoretical understanding of how a gender order can be altered.

It would not have been possible to achieve the knowledge that has been gained during these years through traditional academic research. The group processes in the networks contributed to new ideas and new patterns of practices, both for individuals and for workplace groups. This was dependent on the interactive processes that took place over a substantial period of time. Important theoretical contributions have been gained that I think would not have been possible without interactive methods. It was interactivity that created the actual core of the actions and insights and thereby new knowledge. The practitioners have, moreover, been co-researchers in their respective workplaces and participated in the analysis and dissemination of experiences. The basis of the processes has been that the practitioners have been active in their organisations in between our meetings and that we have subsequently worked through the actions, turned what might have been painful experiences into comprehensible ones and created mutual learning. The experiences, which have been developed and deepened concerning the action for change itself, provide a source of possible strategies to be derived from this research and development project.

The trust and the relationships, which grew over time, make the stories and experiences from the groups more valid. The group has created a collective process of discussion that would not have occurred or even emerged through, for example, individual interviews. Knowledge about the denial of the significance of gender in what conditions are like and how change can take place in working life has contributed to the groups assisting each other to challenge censor mechanisms. The group's development is the basis for the process and the knowledge gained has overtaken gender as a non-issue. Personal experience has moved from the periphery to the centre and the "what" and the "how" have been the Interactive Research (Chapter 8).

References

Aagaard Nielsen, K. and Svensson, L. (2005) "Action and Interactive Research: A Nordic Approach" (draft preliminary version of a first chapter).

Abrahamsson, Lena (2000) *Att återställa ordninge: könsmönster och förändringar i arbetsorganisationer* [*Restoring Order: Gender Patterns and Change in Work Organisations*], Umeå: Boréa Bokförlag.

Acker, Joan (1999) "Gender and organisation" in *Handbook of the Sociology of Gender*. Saltzman Chafetz, J (eds.), New York: Plenum Publishers

Adler, N., Shani, R. and Styhre, A. (2004) *Collaborative Research in Organisations: Foundations for Learning, Change, and Theoretical Development*, London: Sage.

Amundsdotter, E. and Gillberg, M. (2001) *Den jämställda arbetsplatsen: en metodbok* [*The Equal Workplace: A Method Book*], Stockholm: Bilda förlag.

Amundsdotter, E. (2002) "'Vi har ju inga karlar här ...': om jämställdhetsbegreppets relevans för kvinnodominerade arbetsplatser" ["'We Don't Have Any Men Here ...': The Relevance of the Concept of Gender Equality for Female-Dominated Workplaces"] Report No. 31, Stockholm: Centre for Gender Research, Stockholm University.

Andersson, M. et al. (2006) *The Art of Building a Partnership*, Stockholm: The National Institute of Working Life

Berge, Britt-Marie and Ve, Hildur (2000) *Action Research for Gender Equity*, Buckingham: Open University Press.

Gunnarsson, E., Andersson, S., Vänje Rosell, A., Lehto, A., Salminen-Karlsson, M. (eds.) (2003) *Where Have All the Structures Gone? Doing Gender in Organisations: Examples from Finland, Norway and Sweden*, Stockholm: Centre for Women's Studies.

Hirdman, Yvonne (1990) "'Genussystemet' ['The Gender System'"] in SOU 1990:44 *Maktutredningen* [*Commission of Inquiry into Power*].

Maguire, P. (2001) "Uneven Ground: Feminisms and Action Research", in *Handbook of Action Research: Participative Inquiry and Practice*, Reason, P. and Bradbury, H. (eds.), London: Sage.

May, T. (2003) (eds.) *Qualitative Research in Action*, London: Sage.

Reason, O. and Bradbury, H. (eds.) (2001) *Handbook of Action Research: Participative Inquiry and Practice*, London: Sage.

Senge, P. and Scharmer, O. (2001) "Community Action Research: Learning as a Community of Practitioners, Consultants and Researchers", in *Handbook of Action Research: Participative Inquiry and Practice,* Reason, O. and Bradbury, H. (eds.), London: Sage.

Skeggs, Beverely (1997) *Formations of Class and Gender. Becoming Respectable,* London: Sage.

CHRISTOPHER KJÆR

12. On-line Courses Supporting Local Project Work

Experiences Gained from Collaboration with a Global Organization

12.1 Introduction

The aim of this article is twofold. First, and from an overall perspective, the article will offer some experiences relating to methodology acquired when working with Action Research in a global organization. Secondly, and as a consequence of the former, the method used and the experiences gained will be evaluated on the basis of their contribution to the development of a theory for work-based blended learning, based on fundamental principles drawn from Illeris' didactic concept of *Project Work* (Illeris 2004). Central to such an approach to workplace learning[1] is the integration of formal and informal learning supported by web-based technology (Collis et al. 2004).[2] The development of a democratic theory for work-based blended learning is in itself inspired by the *Co-generative Action Research Model*, which endeavours to develop both theory and practice and the idea of *Communicative Actions in Arenas* in local and virtual on-line contexts (Greenwood and Levin 1998).

Characteristic for working with Action Research in a global organi-

---

[1] For a more overall, differentiated, and up-to-date perspective on workplace learning, see Illeris et al. (2004).

[2] There is an ongoing debate in the literature about the relationship between formal and informal learning, see Colley et al. (2002)

sation like the Danish company Danfoss is that, to a large extent, employees are globally distributed in a way that makes physical face-to-face interaction economically unfeasible.[3] This also means that, to a certain extent, interaction between researcher and enterprise collaborators is forced to take place through the use of Information and Communications Technology (ICT). Thus, the use of ICT plays a central role in the interaction between researcher and practitioners, and between practitioners.

To a large extent, the starting point for my approach to *Action Research* follows three ideas put forward by the Norwegian Action Researcher Øyvind Pålshaugen (2004), these regard the development of what he describes as *actionable*[4] *knowledge*. The first idea is that it is through interaction between theory and practice that knowledge turns out to be actionable. Secondly, the starting point for the development of a theory of work-based blended learning must be founded on the genuine use of knowledge and not just on theoretical arguments. Thirdly, that the knowledge creation to a large extent is based on theoretical reflections on practical experiences. In this chapter, the production of actionable knowledge is targeted at the development of theory based on these ideas. The consequence will be to emphasise two cases. The first case underscores my hard-earned but relevant experiences with an existing project in the company. A project I thought should be the empirical foundation of my doctoral thesis. The second case, which is the main case dealt with in this chapter, concerns the experiences I have gained when working together with the company on developing courses for sales technicians who were learning about new products at the Danfoss RA Web Academy.[5] This case will be discussed from the methodological

---

3 Danfoss has about 17.500 employees world wide, which means that Web-based learning and knowledge sharing are crucial for saving time and money when employees have to take courses on business related issues. The company is a leader within its core business concerning research, development and production, sales and service of mechanical, and electronic components for several industries (for further information about the company see http://www.danfoss.com).

4 The term "actionable knowledge" contrasts with that of "pure textual knowledge". This means that the context of investigation "has to be something more or other than other texts, the knowledge has to be retransformed into the kind of knowledge generally produced by Action Research" (Pålshaugen 2004, p. 113)

5 www.ra-webacademy.com

and theoretical perspective mentioned above. Consequently, the focus will be on the following issues:

- The influence of the rationales for production and development on Action Research.
- Case 1: The CO_2-network and its breakdown, lessons learned and new possibilities.
- Case 2: Designing virtual learning environments at the Danfoss Web Academy.
- Theoretical and methodical perspectives relating to case 2.
- Findings.
- Conclusion.

12.2 The rationales for production and development at the workplace

Being a newcomer to the field of Action Research, an important question to pose concerns which rationalities and forces I would face in the field, and how I would be able to deal with them.

12.2.1 *The production and development rationales*

It can be a big challenge to run an Action Research project in a large, global company. According to Ellström (2002), it is possible to operate with a distinction between a *production rationale* and a *development rationale*[6] both of which influence the potential for learning in the organization. Table 1 provides a schematic overview of the central differences (Ellström 2002, p. 340– 343):

---

6 Ellström's term *logic* I have translated as *rationale*.

Table 12.1 A Developmental and Production Rationale – some characteristics

DEVELOPMENT RATIONALE	PRODUCTION RATIONALE
emphasising: thoughts and reflection	emphasising: effective action of routine
alternative thinking, experiments and taking risks;	solutions to problems through adjustment of given rules/instructions
tolerance for differences, riskiness and mistakes;	simplicity and such like, stability and security
development orientated learning	learning aimed at controlling procedures and routine

In connection to this, the Action Researcher is typically a representative for the development rationale. But to have an impact on a large global organisation requires that the research (see below) and development rationale can be integrated with the production rationale in order to create a sustainable development project within the company (Svensson et al. 2002). This is a serious challenge for the Action Researcher who will often find himself in the tension between the two conflicting rationales.

The Action Researcher also has his own rationale to follow – *the research rationale* – which is affected by a personal view of how good research should be practised with regard to choice of methods, theories and continuity. This rationale will be described in detail later.

It is my experience that, to a high degree, the different rationales affect the design of the overall collaborative or co-generative learning environment that exists between the researcher and the practitioners. Furthermore, it is my opinion that the researcher who has knowledge of the rationales is in a better position to make appropriate decisions with regard to choice of methods. Moreover, it is difficult to navigate as an agent in the collaborative researcher-practitioner sphere, because the production rationale often has priority in relation to the development rationale.

12.3 Case 1: The CO_2-network and its breakdown, lesson learned and new possibilities

In this part, I will present my first experiences with Danfoss, which constitutes one of my research cases.

When I commenced my cooperation with Danfoss in connection with my PhD, the case dealt with the development of a virtual CO_2-network with the aim of collecting the latest research results concerning the substitution of traditional, not environmentally friendly, refrigerants with environmentally friendly CO_2, and informing the relevant employees about them. However, in order for co-operation to take place, it quickly became clear that it was necessary to adjust my research interests, so that these would be able to be a part of the practitioners` research question/ formulation of the problem. This was an extremely important experience, which I gained, in the kick-off phase of the Action Research project, an experience, which is, stressed elsewhere (Gustavsen et al. 2001, p. 33–34). Because of this, I had to change my personal interest in theoretical ways of presenting problems connected to web-based educational planning.

The practical co-operation between a manager, a refrigeration specialist from the company and myself may, in general, be described as a negotiation process in which all parties tried to establish a common ground. The introductory negotiation processes were extremely important and very decisive for the cooperation which was to take place between us, and, therefore, also for the development of my Ph.D. Together with my supervisor, I visited the company a couple of times in order to carry out the final negotiations. My experiences from these negotiations taught me that this was a relatively complicated process, since Danfoss is a large company, which is competing globally at the highest level for the market shares, and is doing so based on a financially administrated production rationale. As a PhD student, it is indeed a learning experience just to participate in such meetings and to be able to participate at the same level as managers and others from the company. This became apparent in connection with this first case after approximately four months, when Danfoss came to the conclusion that our common project should be closed down, since they could not live up to our agreement regarding the development of their own CO_2-network.

12.3.1 Lesson learned and new possibilities

In the following, I will summarize some overall reflections concerning action related to this first case. The kick-off phase of an Action Research project is very important, it can be characterized as a long process of negotiating meaning. This implies that a researcher must have a variety of competencies such as being able to make decisions, organise, manage, control, negotiate, design and evaluate processes and people. Decisions will typically be founded on a negotiation process where the researcher holds an empathic attitude to the practitioners' problems.

Another important element in the process of negotiating access for intervention in an organisation is that the researcher must enter a foreign field, and try to understand and implement long term strategies that support both the researcher's and the practitioner's objectives. A lot of investment in time and prestige is at stake during these introductory negotiations. The outcomes have direct consequences for future cooperation. In relation to this, Gustavsen et al. (2001, p. 231) stress one important point, which is also my experience:

> Research initially offers to locate the enterprise within a framework of generalized wisdom, with the argument that this wisdom will help the enterprise deal with its concrete problems. As the conversation unfolds, this, initial approach is subsequently reversed: instead of generalized wisdom being the framework into which the enterprise has to 'fit', the concrete situation of the enterprise starts moving into the foreground and generalized wisdom has to 'fit' this figure.

My point is that to some extent this also has to be the case for the researcher's use of method. This made me focus on a more humble methodological approach based to a greater extent on collaborative dialogues in virtual web-based and local communicative arenas. I simply had to balance my research rationale regarding theory and method with the company's production and development rationale, this proved to be a challenge.

Fortunately, as compensation for the closing down of the CO_2-network, the company suggested that I could join them in developing a completely new web-based course at the Danfoss Web Academy. This project will be described in the second case.

12.4 Case 2: Designing on-line courses for supporting local project work

We now turn to the main case dealt with in the chapter. The aim of my second project with the company was, in short, to support the development of a new course at the Danfoss RA Web Academy targeted at sales technicians who were learning about new products and solutions. I will start with a brief introduction to Danfoss RA Web Academy, which is part of the company's educational unit. Then, I will present a course design, which was the result of my collaboration with the company.

12.4.1 *The context of the Danfoss RA Web Academy*

Danfoss is a global Danish company that aims at being a global leader within its core businesses. Therefore, the company is continuously trying to strengthen the organization through the development of its employees' competencies. One way to realize such an ambition is via formal education in combination with work-based learning activities and informal knowledge sharing. With employees distributed globally, it is necessary for the company to make extensive use of ICTs in order to reach their targets. For this purpose, the company division Danfoss Refrigeration and Air Conditioning (RA) has developed a virtual platform: The RA Web Academy (www.ra-webacademy.com). From here, employees worldwide can sign up for different kinds of on-line courses combining asynchronous and synchronous activities on a virtual communication and learning platform with integrated audio and graphics.

12.4.2 *Course design*

Within this new context, I started to collaborate with a smaller steering committee, consisting of some managers and teachers, in order to build up a completely new course for sales technicians learning about new products for refrigeration systems. The course can be characterized as a virtual learning environment (Web Academy) created by combining synchronous on-line courses with student activity on an asynchronous platform and local project work. For me, the starting point with this work was the same as that of Dirckinck-Holmfeld (2002) who emphasises that web-based learning ought to be consciously based on theoretical assumptions concerning the pedagogy employed, e.g. in the shape of virtual project pedagogic and that the design of technology (ICT system) and virtual learning environment should support assumptions concerning the pedagogical theory employed. For this reason, the course design summarized in Case 2 (see below) is influenced to a large extent by an approach to work-based blended learning building on the fundamental principles taken from *Project Work* (Illeris 2004), and the design of *Virtual Learning Environments* (Dirckinck-Holmfeld 2002; 2004). The course included: a series of six synchronous on-line sessions (once a week) on the virtual learning and communications platform was combined with homework of parallel project work. The synchronous on-line courses and the asynchronous possibilities of the Web Academy were to provide the participants with both relevant information about products and feedback to the local project work. The project work was seen as the possibility for the participants to situate the course contents in a local and meaningful context. To support this in a suitable manner, the project work was structured into different steps, where each on-line session should support the participants' work with the project. The following quotation demonstrates the first step of the project work (homework) where, in a problem-oriented manner, the participant should try to place the course contents in a local and meaningful context (much in the same way as Gustavsen referred to above):

"Purpose: The homework assignments in this course all have the same aim: making a personalized presentation of the AKD[7] for compressor capacity control. During the course you will be making your own short presentation step-by-step to help you present the features of the AKD to your customers or colleagues in the way that suits your specific job tasks best. The purpose of the first homework assignment is to determine your personal objectives for making your own short presentation of AKD. Your objectives will depend on your typical work tasks and the way you are in contact with your customers. Some participants will use their presentations for making general sales arguments – others for providing more detailed technical information." (Course material – Danfoss)

---

7   AKD = product for controlling cooling systems

Two courses, each having eight participants were undertaken and completed in 2003/04.

12.4.3 *Theoretical perspectives relating to case 2*

In the following section, I will present some theoretical perspectives underlying the course design described above in Case 2, and my collaboration with the company. The first perspective deals with my approach to workplace learning, and the second perspective to the methodological design for collaboration with the company. These perspectives I will call *research rationales* and are strongly connected to the researcher's personal view of how Action Research should or can be practised with regard to the choice of theory, methods and continuity.

12.4.4 *Educational theory as the point of departure*

Where creating conditions for virtual education and learning at the workplace are concerned, it is my opinion that it would prove advantageous to take the starting point in educational theories. Especially when a company such as Danfoss wants staff that must increasingly possess competencies such as being able to collaborate virtually and be problem oriented. This type of work is becoming more important for, in particular, sales people who often have to co-operate with customers about the development of adjusted products/solutions (Victor and Boynton 1998). In relation to this, it is my claim that it is necessary to make explicit the assumptions concerning the theory behind the pedagogy used to support the best development of the company's employee's competencies. By using ideas for project work and learning in virtual environments, the didactic design was ideal for supporting both formal and informal learning (Collis et al. 2004).

12.4.5 *Mass customization and co-configuration – the collaboration between sales people and customers*

In Case 2, one of the pedagogic objectives was also to support the participants' integration of work and learning supported by the above-mentioned learning activities (on-line courses and project work). Because of this, the pedagogic design also had to support natural work processes characteristic for the company's sales technicians working in teams and together with customers. By using interviews, it became evident that, to a large extent, these work processes could be characterized as internal collaboration between employees and what Victor and Boynton (1998, p. 195) call mass customization and co-configuration. *Mass customization* "... requires designing a product (or solution) at least once for each customer." whereas *co-configuration* work has its focus on the continuous co-configuration between customer and producer. Active customer involvement is therefore important for the co-configuration process, because neither the producer nor customer alone possess enough knowledge to be able to produce a suitable solution. It is also a process where involvement in learning processes becomes necessary for both sales people and customers.

To support the natural work processes mentioned above, Illeris' *Project Work* was a considerable inspiration for the instructional design in Case 2.

12.4.6 Project work in Case 2

A characteristic of *Project Work* (Illeris 2004, p. 189) is that it is based on a series of fundamental didactic principles.[8]

Problem orientation – in educational programmes this is concerned with the content with which the participants work and learn from. Often the contents of educational programmes are determined by a curriculum, which specifies what must be learned. But this is typically not how the world is structured for the participants taking a web-based course in a company. Instead they structure their environment into *thematic areas* and *problem fields*. This means that a problem oriented approach to learning is necessary, because

"It is first and foremost when one works with finding out where the important problems lie, when one tries to formulate problems with precision and to develop patterns of understanding and proposals for solutions that the full learning challenge is established." (Illeris 2004, p. 177).

---

8 Because of the limited space the principle of *exemplarity* and *interdisciplinarity* will not be discussed, as they only had a minor impact on the didactic design in Case 2. (see Illeris 2004, p. 1989-90)

Regarding the didactic design in Case 2, the inspiration derived from this principle was to support the sales technicians' possibilities to situate the on-line course content in the thematic areas and problem fields as experienced by them. The project work with the sales presentation could be anchored in real workplace problems and situations concerning relevant issues like mass customization and co-configuration processes.

Participant direction – indicates that "... the participants themselves have the possibility for and are maintained as directing their learning to the highest possible degree within the given framework." (Ibid. p. 173). In relation to Case 2, the inspiration derived from this principle was to combine synchronous on-line courses with student activity on an asynchronous platform with local project work. The on-line course were to support the participant's development of a shared content repertoire and the local project work (homework) should give the participant possibilities for directing their own learning in relation to the thematic areas and problem fields experienced in co-configuration processes. Another important aspect regarding this principle is that it could support the integration of work and learning by giving participants possibilities to integrate on-the-job assignments carried out in the workplace as a part of a course, and thereby make the course as job-relevant as possible.

Group work – This indicates that project work normally should be carried out in groups to support among other things a "... wider range of input, perspectives and opinions and the larger working capacity of the group." (Ibid. p. 190)

Despite these possibilities, group work was, in the beginning, considered by the steering committee to be violating the individual participant's freedom and possibility to work alone. However, letting about four pairs of participants from different countries follow the course created a good informal local group work.

12.4.7 *The research rationale – seen from the idea of intervention*

In relation to running an Action Research project, the theoretical framework concerning pedagogy as described above is, implicitly, a part of the researcher's rationale. However, the researcher's methodological idea concerning intervention is just as important, as it is through this that the researcher, together with the organisation's representatives, must develop the present practice. A description is given in the following of the type of interventions; this is then followed by some reflections.

12.4.8 Local and virtual communicative arenas

Given my experiences from the first case, I paid more attention to the different rationales at stake and the necessity of trying to let my research rationale regarding method and theory fit the company's interest. Therefore, the best possible solution for fruitful cooperation was limited to the use of *communicative arenas* (Greenwood and Levin 1998 p. 117), which are relatively easy to cope with. The central idea was to create communicative arenas for learning processes, where the participants encounter each other. Regarding both Cases 1 and 2 these arenas were set up as a combination of several local and virtual web-based meetings carried out as virtual synchronous *iMeetings*[9] on the *Interwise* learning and communication platform. In this way, the use of ICT played a central role concerning interaction between the practitioners and myself. *iMeetings* were automatically recorded by the system and I recorded the local meetings. This possibility allowed later analyses of the collaborative learning and negotiating processes in the communicative arenas, and also helped me see the important points from the meetings. One important phase in the communicative arenas concerned the collaborative learning processes among the teachers, managers and myself, when we were discussing experiences from the courses. These experiences were discussed from two perspectives. Firstly from that of theoretical analyses based on data gathered through qualitative interviews and virtual classroom observations made by myself. In this way I represented the participants' perspectives. Secondly, they were discussed from the teacher and manager's perspectives.

12.4.9 Learning cycles

Following Engeström (1999, p. 383), the communicative learning arenas were part of overall learning cycles where going through a cycle ought

---

9   A web-based meeting room with integrated audio and graphics. For a detailed description of iMeetings on the Interwise communication platform, see www.interwise.com

help both the company and the researcher attain a higher level of knowledge etc. A learning cycle consisted of the following series of arenas:

1. Questioning and analysing existing practice → 2. Working out new solutions → 3. Implementing new solutions → 4. Reflection on the process → 5. Reflecting and evaluating the new practice → 6. Consolidating the new practice.

The intervention-like research rationale, which I discuss here, is a precondition for a certain continuity, which in fact means that the company agrees that at least two of the seminars were held for the staff. But unfortunately, the production rationale expressed through, among other things, internal staff rotations among managers and teachers postponed course three. In addition, the third course was developed on the basis of the first learning cycle. In this way, an upward learning spiral was created.

12.4.10 *Case 2: Lessons learned and new possibilities*

As in Case 1, I will summarize my reflections on the process of intervention by using basic distinctions of relations between researcher and practitioner made by Lennart Svensson's (2002, p. 10–15), and draw some parallels to the production and development rationales.

Svensson (ibid. p. 10– 15) emphasises four kinds of basic relations between researcher and practitioner. The relations are as follows: 1) Researching *on* – an expert opinion where the participants are regarded as objects. 2) To research *for* – another way of viewing the object *the researcher knows best and he/she is therefore prepared to assist and inform the practitioners on their roads to knowledge and development, but to a great degree the direction is already decided in advance* (Heron 2001, ibid. p. 11). 3) To research *on behalf of,* the researcher helps the practitioners accumulate knowledge themselves, but completely at the participants' wishes or on their premises. This means limited time for reflection and analysis, and for the development of theory. 4) To research *with* – a mutual knowledge construction. The direction and presentation of the research is created in dialogue and agreement with the participants and focuses on the asking of questions more than arriving with ready-made answers (cf. development orientated learning).

A close interaction between researcher and participant through the entire research process, i.e. " ... *by decision of participation in the problem formulation, by choice of methods, by collecting of data, in the analysis work, in the presentation of the result ...*" (ibid. p. 13).If this is as it was in the original then it has to remain like this

By using the method described, I had found a way to balance the company's production and development rationales by modelling my research rationale (theory and method) in a way that also suited the company. But as I see it, this struggle to obtain a balance has a strong connection to the relationship between the production and development rationales on the one hand and the researcher/practitioner relation on the other hand. The basic relations can also be characterised as different research rationales, and the four types of relations can be compared to the production and development rationales. One could say that the production rationale relates to the first three kinds of relations and that the development rationale relates to the relation *to make research with*. Svensson ranks the four kinds of relations in such a way that *to research with* is the best way to support *Interactive Research – for the development of theory and practice*. It is more realistic for me to have a combination of the four kinds of relations between researcher and practitioner depending on the present circumstances within the company. This also means that I am combining different elements from the four relations when developing theory, method and practice. One example concerns my use of theoretical input in the arenas about the above-described didactic principles taken from *Project Work*. Here the point made by Gustavsen quoted above became relevant because I had to fit generalized wisdom to the company's context which in itself was a challenge.

Summarizing my experiences, it is very important to pay attention to the way the company handles the balance between the production and development rationales, because it has a decisive influence on what kind of research relations you can have and develop with the company.

12.4.11 Case 2 – Findings and discussion

The findings presented below are based on observations made in the virtual classroom on the *Interwise* learning and communication platform, and qualitative interviews (Kvale 1997) with course participants.[10] Through what I characterize as an abductive process, the following figure concerning the course participants' learning emerged:

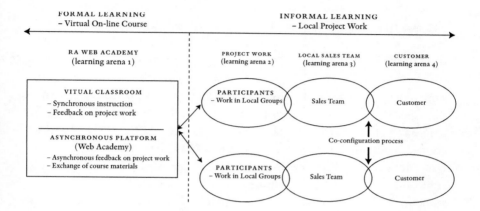

Figure 12.1.   Learning Arenas for Course Participants Combining formal and informal learning

As can be seen from the figure above, the participants' learning takes place in different virtual and local arenas. On the left side of the dotted line we have the formalized learning environment depicted as the RA Web Academy and including different virtual activities. A general perspective is that this learning environment covers what is normally characterized as formal learning with less participant direction, but with more emphasis on the teacher and curriculum. On the right side of the figure, the circles depict the course participants' work in local project groups, sales teams within the company, and the related co-configuration process between sales people and customers. The learning activities, which take place here, have a more informal learning structure, because they take place as part of the participants' (natural) on the job assignments. The participants' learning activities consist therefore of combinations of virtual web-based and local activities.

---

10   The course took place at the www.ra-webacademy.com

Looking at the illustration, it also indicates that learning has to be understood as a combination or interaction between formal and informal learning. Therefore it is of decisive significance that a focus is directed at the potential of the informal learning environment, and that it is properly integrated with the formal learning environment (see also Åberg and Svensson 2004; Bianco and Collis 2004). As mentioned above, letting pairs of participants from the same sales department take the course together only indirectly supported group work. But the interviews revealed that, to a large extent, these pairs were working together on their projects (homework). Surprisingly, it turned out that these pairs were also members of some kind of local informal sales team where the course contents and project work became important. A local arena supporting learning through processes of negotiation of meaning was established (Wenger 1998, p. 52). In this way, a virtual learning environment created by combining synchronous on-line courses with student activity on an asynchronous platform turned out to be a good support for local project work in different learning arenas.

The findings also represent an interesting point of departure for expanding the focus on learning processes in virtual environments to also include societal, global and democratic perspectives. This I found possible by using several key ideas drawn from the work of James Bohman (2004) Firstly, I interpreted what he refers to as transnational institutions to also include global organizations like Danfoss. By means of the didactic principles of problem-orientation and participant direction and the use of web-based technology, the company can support the creation of what Bohman calls "minipublics", as shown in the findings above. Minipublics would then correspond to the local sales teams and their embedded contexts. Secondly, the two didactic principles also support Bohman's idea of a "multiperspectival" and thereby democratic theory of globalization, because each local sales team (located worldwide) has its own point of departure regarding actionable knowledge and experimental collaborative problem-solving concerning homework and customer relationships. In short, my point is that a theory for work-based blended learning in global organizations must also be based on a democratic theory of globalization.

Summarizing, the main point is that it is difficult to design for learning to take place, but that a formalized work-based blended course design based on fundamental principles taken from *Project Work* can be a good support for local and more participant directed learning arenas. An aspect, which is now further, developed and implemented in a new work-based course design, so that the group work in different learning arenas is supported. In addition, it seems that most of the participants learning and competence development takes place outside the formalized learning arena and in the three different informal learning arenas.

12.4.12 Conclusion

As stated in the introduction, the aim of this article is twofold, by emphasizing some methodically gained experiences acquired through working with Action Research and by contributing to the development of a theory for work-based blended learning. This ambition where dealt with by drawing on Pålshaugen's three ideas regarding the creation of actionable knowledge. In this way, theory and method was put into action when working with the two cases. In addition, the present chapter presents some theoretical reflections about experiences gained through working with these cases. The following conclusion represents my temporary contribution regarding a first step towards a theory for work-based blended learning in global organizations.

Regarding the development of a theory for work-based blended learning in global organizations, I will emphasize what I consider most important. First of all, a virtual learning environment made by combining synchronous on-line courses with local project work seems to support the participants' learning and competence development. Of special interest is the combination of formal and informal learning environments where the didactic principle of problem orientation and participant direction supports an emergent creation of local learning arenas. In this way, the virtual learning environment with on-line courses, materials and project feedback become resources for learning by fully supporting the participant's perspective. A perspective that is closely related to e.g. co-configuration processes between sales technicians and customers. From a general perspective, it becomes important how the design of virtual learning environments support the interaction between teaching (on-line course) and learning (local arenas) in a way where they can become structured resources for each other. Moreover, it is suggested that the findings represent a good potential for integrating ideas from Bohman's Critical Theory of globalization and democracy, so that a theory on work-based blended learning in global organizations can be developed on democratic ideals.

For Danfoss, the consequence of these findings became a new course design where more attention was given to supporting learning and knowledge in local arenas.[11] In addition, findings were presented and discussed with others developing the course in the company.

Summarizing my methodological experiences regarding the development of theory and practice I will emphasize some aspects, which I find very important. Doing Action Research with a global company, method and theory have to fit the context of the company. So what you are able to do methodologically is controlled to a large extent by how the company balances between the production and development rationales. Therefore I find it very important to pay attention to this balance regarding one's possibilities for doing Action Research with a company. But in relation to this; being a researcher I also found it necessary to balance the two rationales in a way, which forced me to move between the different relations stressed by Svensson. In addition Greenwood and Levin's idea of communicative arenas proved to be suitable for on-line communication and learning in the steering committee. In the kick-off phase of an Action Research project, I experienced how important it is to let one's research rationale fade into the background and then, at a later stage, let it redefine itself in the problem-solving practice of the company in question. For an inexperienced researcher, it is a challenge to pursue academic objectives structured as abstract terms and then at the same time find them useful for the company.

References

Bianco, Manuela and Collis, Betty (2004): "Work-based blended learning in corporate settings: Exploring the role of the workplace learning partners". Presented at the Conference WORKPLACE LEARNING – From the Learners Perspective. Learning Lab Denmark. Copenhagen

---

11 This aspect is discussed in my PhD thesis.

25–27 November 2004. Sub-theme 3: Workplace-related eLearning.

Bohman, James (2004): "Towards a Critical Theory of Globalization: Democratic Practice and Multiperspectival Inquiry". In: *Concepts and Transformation 9:2*, (pp. 121–146).

Colley, Helen, Hodkinson, Phil, Malcolm, Janice (2003): *Informality and Formality in Learning*. London: Learning and Skills Research Centre.

Collis, Betty, Margaryan, Anoush and Kennedy (2004):"Blended Formal and Informal Learning Offers new Competence development opportunities", paper presented at the 11th Abu Dhaibi International Petroleum Exhibition and Conference held in ABU Dhabi, U.A.E., 10–13 October 2004.

Dirckinck-Holmfeld, Lone (2002): "Designing Virtual Learning Enviromonts based on Problem Oriented Project Pedagogy". In: Dirckinck-Holmfeld, Lone and Fibiger, Bo *Learning in Virtual Environments*. Fredriksberg: Samfundslitteratur.

Ellström, Per-Erik (2002): "Lärande: i spänningsfältet mellan produktionens och utvecklingens logik". In: *Utbildning, kompetens och arbete*. Abrahamsson, Kenneth, et al. (eds). Lund: Studentlitteratur.

Engeström, Yrjö (1999): "Innovative Learning in Work Teams: Analyzing Cycles of Knowledge Creation in Practice". In: *Perspectives on Aactivity Theory*. Engeström, Yrjö, Miettinen, Reijo and Punamäki, Raija-Leena (eds). Cambridge, MA: Cambridge University Press.

Greenwood, Davydd. J. and Levin, Morten (1998): *Introduction to Action Research: Social Research for Social Change*. London: Sage.

Gustavsen, Bjørn (2002): "Research and the Challenges of Working Life". In: *Interaktiv forskning: för utveckling av teori och praktik,* Svensson et al. (eds.) Stockholm: Arbetslivsinstitutet.

Gustavsen, Bjørn, Finne, Håkon & Oscarsson, Bo (2001): *The Role of Social Research in Innovation Policy*. Amsterdam: John Benjamins.

Illeris, Knud (2004): *Adult Education and Adult Learning*. Roskilde: Roskilde University Press.

– (ed.) (2004): Laering i arbejdslivet. (Learning Lab Denmark). Copenhagen: Roskilde Universitetsforlag.

Kvale, Steinar (1996): *InterViews: An Introduction to Qualitative Research Interviewing*. Thousand Oaks, CA: Sage.

Svensson, Lennart et al. (2004): "Arbejdspladsen: en arena for uddannelse for læring". In: *E-læring på arbejde,* Kanstrup, Anne Marie (ed.) (Learning Lab Denmark). Fredriksberg: Roskilde Universitetsforlag.

Svensson, Lennart, Brulin, Göran, Ellström, Per-Erik (2002): "Innovations- och lärprocesser i den nya ekonomin". In: *Interaktiv forskning: för utveckling av teori och praktik,* Svensson, Lennart et al. (eds.) Stockholm: Arbetslivsinstitutet.

Vygotsky, Lev S. (1978): *Mind in Society: The Development of Higher Psychological Processes.* Cambridge, MA: Harvard University Press.

Victor, Bart and Boynton, C. Andrew (1998): *Invented Here: Maximizing Your Organizatio's Internal Growth and Profitability.* Boston, MS: Harvard Business School Press.

Wenger, Etienne (1998): *Communities of Practice: Learning, Meaning, and Identity.* Cambridge: Cambridge University Press.

MARJA VEHVILÄINEN

13. Situated Agency in Interactive Research

Women's ICT Expertise and Regional Development

13.1 Introduction

This chapter reflects on the long journey of empirical research on agency and citizenship in a highly technically mediated society and its remote region, Finland and North Karelia. The research examined the practices of local inhabitants and their communities, the practices of local developers and organizations that were active in the development of the information society as well as national and regional information society policies. It took place in the latter half of the eighties, at a time when Finland, among other European countries, turned into an information society where citizens were to take responsibility for acquiring skills and access to information and communications technology (ICT). It further continued in the period when ICT was domesticated and the ICT hype was replaced by worries about the global economy in the early 2000's. Even though "expertise" was emphasized throughout both periods, still certain Digital Divides prevailed. The research focused on the agency and expertise of people, citizens, on the wrong side of the Digital Divides relating to gender and region. It made an alliance with the North Karelian developers who emphasized the local, situated and communal activity of inhabitants and supported people's everyday expertise in the nineties, as an alternative to the heroic technical expertise of well educated male engineers in big cities.

North Karelia is a vast region located on the eastern border of Finland. Like other Eastern and Northern regions in Finland, it has a high unemployment rate (up to 30 per cent in the eighties) and its population is declining. It has received structural funding for peripheral areas from the European Union since the mid-eighties. A number of these development projects focused specifically on citizenship and the information society at the local level, which was to be built up co-operatively by the inhabitants themselves. This was in contrast to the mainstream Finnish information society strategy (Sitra 1998) which aimed to make Finland a leading information society and which was based on the idea of liberal individualistic citizenship.

The North Karelian regional director Tarja Cronberg (1995–2001), familiar with the social shaping of technology and participatory approaches through her research background in Sweden and Denmark, wanted to develop a regional strategy based on people's situations locally. She proposed a study related to the development activities of the region to me, then about to receive a PhD on gender, ICT, expertise and participatory approach. I, as a member of a research group at the University of Tampere Work Research Centre, incorporated the North Karelian case into the Academy of Finland's research programme on Knowledge. I commuted to North Karelia regularly from 1998 to 2000 and occasionally until 2005, even though my job commitment changed in 2001.

I made pilot interviews in North Karelia in 1996, started the research project in 1998, and received further funding from the Ministry of Trade and Industry research program for two researchers, Sari Tuuva and Johanna Uotinen. We interviewed a wide selection of inhabitants (in a citizens' centre, a neighbourhood centre) and participants, coordinators and developers of various information society development projects (the regional citizens' net, women's ICT groups), attended meetings, and collected documents and media clips, even drawings by school children (Vehviläinen 2002; Uotinen et al. 2001). We also made theory based suggestions and discussed our research findings, had a dialogue, with the North Karelian actors.

In this chapter, I examine the practices of this dialogue, of Interactive Research by focusing on the relationship between theory and practice in the research process. I start by describing the theoretical and political understandings of my research approach and, secondly, describe the interaction between the research and the development work, paying attention to the theoretical understandings in both processes. Thirdly, I discuss the institutional setting and the competencies needed in the concrete Interactive Research process. At the end, I come back to the theoretical framework and reflect on its use in Interactive Research.

13.2 Theoretical framework and underlying politics

My research approach starts from the practices of people located in particular places and situations and examines the social and cultural orders that organise those practices, the dynamics of agency. This theoretical understanding is focused on the ways of seeing the social world and doing research (epistemology, methodology) rather than on the particular orders and definitions of practices (ontology). By starting from people's practices it lets the people themselves take part in the definitions of the social world.

I developed the main lines of the research approach in my doctoral thesis after I had worked together with a study circle of office workers designing ICT for their own work (Vehviläinen 1997). The study of the designing office workers related to the Nordic working life democracy research and British socio-technical participatory approaches, with a root in Kurt Lewin's classical studies, as well as the women's movement. This research approach gives space for the voices of the office workers themselves, for their definitions, expertise, and change. It connects these voices and agency to social and cultural relations. Voices are not expressions based on inner needs. They are constructed in a dialogue of the bodily and biographical, on the one hand, and the culturally, historically and socially shaped settings of people, on the other hand.

Citizens in the information society in the mid nineties faced a rather similar situation as the office workers did in my previous study. They were given the responsibility to gain skills in ICT. The question of people's voices, expertise and agency remained important, though now in the context of society and citizens.

The theoretical approach (described e.g. in Vehviläinen 2005b) is based on the institutional ethnography of Dorothy Smith (1990, 2005) and the theory of situated knowledge and agency advanced by Donna Haraway (1991). Dorothy Smith's institutional ethnography of textualities, social relations, and standpoints starts from the practices of actual people, their accounts and experiences, by giving voices to particular and situated groups, their ways of seeing and knowing, and then mapping out social relations that organize these practices. It enables two things, firstly, the study of the agency of gendered subjects and the various interpretations of these subjects, and, secondly, the search for persistence in practices and social relations embedded in them. Both the situated interpretations and definitions, which maintain a possibility for change, and dominating relations can be captured.

In Donna Haraway's cyborg subjectivity, a human is intertwined with an animal and with a machine. The animal in cyborg makes the subjectivity embodied, rooted and situated. The machine connects subjects to social and textual – and also material – relations and practices. The question of agency moves towards the social and textual construction of subjectivity, though in the manner of the "coyote as a witty agent" (Haraway 1991, p. 201), which respects the bodily and material in situated subjects. Voices of people are "knittings" where the bodily and situated "own" is interlaced with the social, textual and technical world. Women's and men's voices are voices of cyborgs, of technically mediated subjectivities.

People, women and men, have social (e.g. gender, global economy, regional) relations in their subjectivities, but they have a chance to undertake decoding too. They may create texts, i.e. ICT, that start from their situations in community centres, in neighbourhoods, and in work places. In order to have agency, they may watch the machine (e.g. the culturally male expertise in technology) in themselves and actively build bridges between the local and situated, and the global machine – from the starting point of the local. This process can be empowering, and it can be supported as well as studied in a research project.

These understandings of agency were further elaborated by the theory of feminist citizenship (Ruth Lister 1997). I examined the male expertise in technology through the understandings of feminist practices of mutual group support and symbolic mothers in Italian feminist collectives (Italian feminist thought 1991), which I first found through the work of Teresa de Lauretis (1987) and which are also discussed in feminist pedagogy. In terms of feminist politics, as described by Flis Henwood and her colleagues (2000), these resources equipped me for communal politics and the understanding of gender as doing and processes, distinct from the liberal equality politics and its emphasis on the choices of individual women. These were my guidelines when the research started.

13.2 Partners in Interactive Research: Co-operative production of knowledge

In my previous study with office workers in the mid eighties, it had been me, a researcher, who had acted as a resource person and a "developer" in the study circle. The study circle was run in the context of a large governmental bureau and within a program of work development conducted by the Centre of Vocational Education in Finland. The co-operation, although it had typical complications, was rather straightforward. The office workers and the bureau received ICT training, the Vocational Centre a report, and I myself received rich material that led me to the development of an appropriate research framework.

The situation was very different in the mid eighties. The European Union funding had launched a new sphere of development projects and a new, enlarging, group of developers. These projects, developers and the funding agents acted within the, often three year, frameworks that were defined by the regional, national, and the European Union authorities. Although people, citizens, and their concrete contexts were to be in an important role in the North Karelian development projects, as in my previous study, simultaneously, the research now faced a rather heterogeneous network of the development world. It was these networks that I traced through my pilot interviews after I received an invitation from the regional director in 1996. Although I had a dialogue with her on the level of the regional strategy, I wanted to, by following my theoretical approach, have interaction with concrete activities in the region, too.

A number of activities and development projects in the region emphasized people's everyday lives as a major starting point – parallel to the understanding of situated agency of my research. Social workers in particular had developed practices that supported people in articulating their own voices and developing activities of their own. They supported the residents by discussing, encouraging, and giving advice on their self-help and practical arrangements – but they never arranged things *for* people (see also Chapter 2). These practices backed up many of the activities that I came across, for example, women's ICT group NiceNet.[1]

In 1997, NiceNet gathered in a neighbourhood centre, which was supported by a (partially EU-funded) welfare network of residents and experts, including social workers, city planners and youth workers. The women themselves developed ICT skills from the starting point of their local everyday lives. They all pick berries from the huge North Karelian forests, and they had started their computer use by making labels for their jam jars. The group activist Tuula Ikonen (2001) had faced all male ICT groups in her neighbourhood centre, and she wanted to make space for women's uses of ICT: "There is a danger that women are displaced in information society development. They participate less than men in the construction of computer programs etc. During the eighties, the field has become even more male dominated." She called for establishing a local women's information technology group.

In 1998, Ikonen wanted to make the successful women's group a model to start new women's groups in the region and invited me to write drafts of the project plan and to articulate women's politics based on women's everyday practices. I agreed since ICT expertise has persistently remained male, and women's ICT group could thus "decode" the male dominated expertise of the machine, as Haraway suggests.

I accompanied Ikonen to planning meetings and we explained the gender bias in ICT expertise and the idea of women's own ICT based on women's everyday lives, which was to be discussed in women's groups with the support of women's teachers. Within North Karelian actor networks the project was then allocated to a big educational institution. Everyday practices were agreed as the starting point of learning, the contract was signed and six groups of 10–12 women gathered together in rural areas as well as in the regional capital for one and half years.

---

1 "NiceNet" has a double meaning in the Finnish context. It means a nice net, and it is a net of women.

The concrete project work, however, took the activity to an entirely new plane. The project manager from the educational institution, completely outside the previous process, saw that the project had to produce measurable results to the funding agency. Since the project took place in a big organization, it had to follow certain standards and bureaucratic procedures. Women's groups were taught by women teachers, as planned, but instead of giving room for the women participants' daily practices and group processes of feminist pedagogy and starting the ICT education from there, the teaching consisted of basic skills in ICT, and the women took standard exams for "ICT passports". ICT passports are routinely given in numerous educational organizations all over Finland, and they quite likely include central features of computer use. However, the approach, which used situated knowledge and everyday practices as its starting point became rather lost in the process, and the women's ICT groups' project moved from the understanding of communal and doing gender to the politics of liberal equality (Henwood et al. 2000). Paradoxically, the ICT passport, as a widely used product, would not have deserved development funding.

This suggests that people who had to make their living in the frequently changing short term project world had learned to refer competently to the current funding frameworks without really committing themselves to the project idea in terms of concrete practices. The understanding of situated knowledge and everyday practices could be acknowledged in the planning phase, but they were in a strong conflict with the very idea of building an effective development project. Everyday practices are fuzzy and cause unpredictable timetables. Some actors in North Karelia, social workers in particular, managed to overcome the contradiction, but the big educational organization could not support its project manager to do so.

This meant conflicts in the researcher-developer co-operation. I was invited to the steering group meetings of the project, and I continued to have a dialogue with the regional council, and gave feedback on this process. The women's ICT project manager, however, was not aware of the deep cultural gender bias in ICT expertise and thus did not see the point in women's everyday practices in learning ICT. My analysis only disturbed her, and that is why we decided to end the co-operation with this particular project. We nevertheless interviewed the participants and the teachers of the women's groups as planned. The North Karelian inhabitants who participated in the process were listened to on their own terms during the research.

The Interactive Research continued in a number of ways. The regional council – as well as developers from other projects and activities, especially those of the North Karelian citizens' net project and the citizens' café – wanted to have a dialogue with us researchers in meetings, seminars and via personal communication. The discussion dealt with experiences in concrete development, the role of regional authorities and the societal orders embedded in these. To articulate and acknowledge this co-operative nature of the knowledge process we published a book (Uotinen et al. 2001) on participation, social differences, and the locality with writers from three groups: North Karelian inhabitants, the developers of the local information society, and us as the researchers. Most of the time there was a clear consensus between research and development. Our mutual interaction gave us all a better understanding of the agency of citizens in the particular time and place.

The research project continued as a follow up study for several years, even though the North Karelian information society strategy changed dramatically from citizens' perspective to market oriented and technology driven development in the 2000s. The interactive phase, however, nearly stopped in 2001. Tarja Cronberg who had invited me to do the research moved to Denmark, and I myself had a job in Sweden for a couple of years. The data from the interactive period remained as a good basis for further follow-up materials: the researchers learnt to know the practices of their counterparts rather thoroughly.

13.3 Interaction in the research process: Institutional setting

Our research had independent academic funding from the beginning, and the North Karelian projects or authorities did not employ us researchers. This gave room to the development of a consistent and theoretically grounded study, even in situations where the local developers departed from the common agenda. Both our research and the development projects had a chance in gaining from the mutual interaction, but in a conflict situation none of the two had hierarchical power to make orders to the other one. I believe this was an effective way of doing Interactive Research: both research and development had a responsibility and possibility to proceed on their own terms.

The researchers of my group, their research methods and their rights for observations, were strongly challenged in the women's ICT group project. If they had been located hierarchically into the women's ICT group project, they would have given up. They were able to continue independent critical research only because they were paid by the research project (see also Chapter 11). Later I have seen a similar conflict in two other cases where the researcher was located within the development organization. The objectives of the development project dominated the research, and even the methods of the researcher, although they were the most common interview methods, were questioned by the developers, and the researcher ended up writing a separate report about the project, postponing the academic version to an "after project" period.

There are certainly many academically competent people running the development projects, but academic merits are not the criteria in the development work, and thus many developers have little competence in research and even less in theoretically elaborated research. It is not easy for them to understand the research process. When the current competition on project funding requires effective results, as emphasized in the managerial genre and practices, the research often looks useless for the short-term purposes of the project. Any research group in this situation needs an experienced researcher to talk to the development partners and to explain the aims and methods of the research by using the terms that are familiar to the developers.

Development projects need to prove that they are successful in order to get new contracts. They also often include an evaluation. A research project, which has critical views appears as a threat to the further economic situation of the developers. Perhaps no critical points can be incorporated into the project practices after the project has started – unless the criticism can be dealt in a broad framework, which relates to a long-term prospect in the development activity.

There was a further complexity in the research interaction. I was an outsider in North Karelia, lived in the capital of Finland working in a big university of social sciences, Tampere. In order to make the research as local as possible and to develop the research in the region, I recruited the researchers from North Karelia, and they became doctoral students supervised by a local professor, Seppo Knuuttila, from the University of Joensuu and me. The project, which was started by me, turned into a locally based research project at the University of Joensuu. It received funding both from the Academy of Finland and the Ministry of Trade and Industry, and one of the researchers published her doctoral thesis in 2005 and the other one will write her doctoral thesis in 2006. However, I myself did not get funding from the project after the first years, and I worked in many universities and had a number of different kinds of tasks. There remained, however, a commitment to supervise the doctoral students and to finish the project – which is not the best arrangement for anybody.

13.4 Competence for Interactive Research?

I have been involved in Interactive Research twice. The first time I was only beginning my doctoral studies and ran the longish office workers' study circle nearly alone – although Liisa Rantalaiho supervised me generously, as she supervised nearly a hundred doctoral students interested in Women's Studies from the eighties to the present decade. I was later able to write a doctoral thesis mainly because I had an opportunity to study in a Canadian sociology doctoral programme and to acquire the theoretical resources to sort out the material from the study circle. My studies at the University of Tampere had made me sensitive to qualitative methods and office workers' own voices, and the material lasted over my travels after theory. However, the current academic life would not tolerate this kind of slow and lonely process of building up a theory of one's own for Interactive Research.

I would no longer encourage a lonely doctoral student to do Interactive Research, not even under appropriate supervision, if this supervision is not institutionally connected to the project. One reason for this is the exceptionally demanding research setting (Kuula 1999) and the rich material, which benefit from previous research experience. The second reason is the researcher's relationship to the activity. The development world is complex, as we saw in the North Karelian study, and the research group should have competencies to meet the local, organizational, regional and maybe European networks which all may connect to the particular research case. The "real life" activities easily take over the research and researcher, and it is only a rather experienced researcher who can translate between the research language and the development language, and who can thus convince the development side of the importance of the research and take care of the independence of the research.

In the second case, I had become a senior researcher. I was invited to do the research by the director of the regional council, and I had an independent research funding. I did the research because I was (both politically and as a researcher) interested in the questions that could be examined through an Interactive Research – as had done in the first case as well. This second setting was, of course, most favourable for Interactive Research. The invitation gave me, although I was an outsider in the region, access to everywhere and whom ever I liked to talk to. Similarities in the large regional framework and my own research framework, situated knowledge, the social shaping of technology, communal local agency, made the research easier and let me even take part in concrete projects. However, even in this favourable situation, there were conflicts to be sorted out – and this often implied changes to the research plan.

The research plan in Interactive Research needs to be both flexible and grounded to a strong theoretical framework. The rearrangements in development activities often make the previous plan useless and even impossible. A strong theoretical framework enables the changes in concrete research tasks, while keeping the main course of the research steady. The researcher in Interactive Research needs competence to build the theoretical framework and to do quick (re)planning of concrete research tasks as well as have the competence to coordinate the relation between the framework and the evolving research tasks.

13.5 On the approach and methods in Interactive Research

Institutional ethnography is a good tool for Interactive Research. It aims to map the social relations (gender, for example) that organize concrete everyday practices, and the understanding of these relations is valuable to any development project. It starts from the same concrete practices as the project does. Then, in order to map the social relations, it examines various textualities that frame the practices.

People live and act locally and interpret, for example, ICT textuality in the context of their everyday life situations, but they do not make choices (e.g. of the use of technologies) independently from the rest of the social world. There are technologically and textually mediated social orders and relations present in their activity. Some of the relations are very local and are related to particular individuals and their subjectivities. Some of the relations are broad and global. In order to talk with the projects we needed to have material beyond the mere development projects. During the research process we examined (in addition to the interviews and following-up of the particular projects) regional, national and European information society strategies, media representations of ICT development and use, and most recently, even popular literature that captures and describes the phenomenon for large audiences.

This material was useful both in the dialogue with the development projects and even more so in academic writing. The North Karelian case by itself would not have been interesting outside the projects and their time. However, the framing textualities helped in articulating the long lasting social and cultural relations in the processes needed in academic publications. Furthermore, the many-faceted material was a starting point for the development of new conceptual tools and understandings. Haraway's situated knowledge and cyborg subjectivity took the form of gendered located politics and situated agency within the cases (Vehviläinen 2002). Liberal equality as broadly used in information society met an alternative, situated equality (Vehviläinen 2005).

In Dorothy Smith's institutional ethnography, the researcher explicates her or his relation to the examined social relations. She or he locates her- and himself to the researched relations and this means that the research process needs to be made transparent. On the one hand, this suits Interactive Research very well. Other partners need to understand how the researcher arrived at her or his analysis. There should not be any mysterious or secret knowledge that the researcher would possess. In the North Karelian case, my previous study with designing office workers and knowledge on feminist pedagogy significantly enabled the

Interactive Research with women's ICT groups – in addition to the invitation from the widely liked regional director. On the other hand, the locating of oneself is a particularly demanding task in Interactive Research. The researcher takes part in the articulation of the everyday practices that then are used as a research material. The researcher becomes very intertwined with the social relations, and it can be hard to examine this. Maybe the classic advice of having at least two researchers working together would be a good practical solution here, too.

Institutional ethnography research works in Interactive Research like in any academic research. The difference, however, lies in the issues to be discussed and published. Academic publications, for example, need to be embedded in academic literature and related to previous research. In an interactive dialogue with a development project, the researcher needs to be able to put the research into the context of the development work. She or he can bring in theoretical insight if they can be motivated from the perspective of the development activity.

Institutional ethnography is not a "grand theory". It is a theoretically grounded approach and methodology, which leaves room for the practices of actual groups of people and helps to explicate these practices. It works particularly well as a starting point for people outside the hegemonies and on the wrong sides of Divides – although is in no way limited to these.

Would I do Interactive Research again? Perhaps I would. However, I would need to have good reasons since Interactive Research is time consuming. If there were ways to study the phenomenon without an intensive research period, I would certainly do so and take care of my political commitments with the "social world" by other means, by giving talks in policy orientated seminars, by giving interviews to the media, for example. I would like to engage in Interactive Research in a good institutional setting with independent research funding. Furthermore, I believe I have not quite yet used the previous materials thoroughly. I need rather long intervals between the intensive interactive studies.

Acknowledgements: My warmest gratitude to Gabriele Griffin for clarifying comments.

References

Haraway, Donna (1991) *Simians, Cyborgs, and Women. The Reinventions of Nature*, London: Free Associations Books.

Henwood, Flis, Plumeridge, Sarah and Stepulevage, Linda (2000) "A Tale of Two Cultures? Gender and Inequality in Computer Education", pp. 111–128, in *Technology and In/equality: Questioning the Information Society*, Sally Wyatt et al. (eds.), London: Routledge.

Ikonen, Tuula (2001) "Muistikuvia Marjalasta maailmalle" (Memories from Marjala out to the world, in Finnish). In *Verkkojen kokijat paikallista tietoyhteiskuntaa tekemässä* Johanna Uotinen et al. (eds.), Joensuu: Suomen kansantietouden Tutkijain seura.

Kuula, Arja (1999) *Toimintatutkimus* (Action Research, in Finnish), Tampere: Vastapaino.

de Lauretis, Teresa (1987) "The Practice of Sexual Difference and Feminist Thought in Italy; An Introductory Essay", pp. 1–21, in *The Milan Women's Bookstore Collective: Sexual Difference; A Theory of Social-Symbolic Practice*, Bloomington and Indianapolis: Indiana University Press.

Libreria delle Donne di Milano (1991) "More Women than Men", pp. 110–122, in *Italian Feminist Thought: A Reader,* Paola Bono and Sandra Kemp (eds.) Oxford: Basil Blackwell.

Lister, Ruth (1997) *Citizenship; Feminist Perspectives*, London: Macmillan.

Sitra (1998) *Quality of Life, Knowledge and Competitiveness: Premises and Objectives for Strategic Development of the Finnish Information Society*. Helsinki: Finish National Fund for Research and Development, Sitra.

Smith, Dorothy E. (1990) *The Conceptual Practices of Power: A Feminist Sociology of Knowledge*. Toronto: University of Toronto Press.

Smith, Dorothy E. (2005). *Institutional Ethnography*, Lanham: Altamira-Press.

Uotinen, Johanna & Tuuva, Sari & Vehviläinen, Marja & Knuuttila, Seppo (toim.) (2001) *Verkkojen kokijat paikallista tietoyhteiskuntaa tekemässä,* (Local Information Society in the Making, in Finnish), Kultaneito IV, Joensuu: Suomen Kansantietouden Tutkijain Seura.

Vehviläinen, Marja (1997) *Gender, expertise and information technology*, PhD thesis, Tampere: University of Tampere.

– (2002) "Gendered Agency in Information Society: On located politics of technology", in *Women and Everyday Uses of the Internet: Agency and Identity*, Mia Consalvo and Susanna Paasonen (eds.) New York: Peter Lang Publishing.

– (2005) "The Construction of 'Equal Agency' in the Development of Technology", pp. 203–17, in *Everyday Innovators, Researching the Role of Users in Shaping ICTs*, Haddon, L. et al. (eds.), Dordrecht: Springer.

– (2005b) "The Numbers of Women in ICT and Cyborg Narratives: On the Approaches of Researching Gender in Information and Communication Technology", pp. 23–46, in *Lost and Found in Virtual Reality: Women and Information Technology*, Hannakaisa Isomäki & Anneli Pohjola (eds.) Rovanniemi: University of Lapland Press 2005.

RONNY SANNERUD

14. Methods for Developing the Construction Site as a Learning Space

14.1 Introduction

In this chapter I present my *experiences* based on using various Action Research methods for developing the construction site as a learning space. The project was established as a traditional socio-technical project using Thorsrud and Emery's principles (Thorsrud and Emery 1969). In the initial phase of the project, I was inspired by theories of situated or practice learning (Etienne Wenger 1998) as models for the interpretation of learning processes at construction sites. In the middle of the project, I saw the need for more creativity, and more dynamic participation processes. The Future Creating Workshop, which stemmed from a different Action Research tradition (see Chapter 5 by Lise Drewes Nielsen in this book), was introduced as a source of inspiration.

The Future Creating Workshop was introduced as a tool for providing a visionary direction for the experimental design. The project also involved biographical interviews so as to come closer to individualised backgrounds and perspectives of learning in relation to the construction work. These interviews are not discussed in this Chapter, though they contribute to a critical discussion of the theory of practice learning.

14.2 The project set up

The construction industry is a significant business sector in Norway. The construction industry is represented by The Federation of Norwegian

Construction Industries, which consists of fifteen trade associations. The project was carried out at a construction site owned by a major business entrepreneur in the Oslo area. It was organised in close co-operation with the Unions and The Federation of Norwegian Construction Industries. This project had a technical and vocational training profile. Its main choice was that of ascertaining how to develop the construction site into a place of learning.

The project's theoretical framework took Wenger's notion of "communities of practice" (1998) as its starting point. The four components – practice, community, identity and meaning – were used as the basic analytical concepts in the project. In addition, other concepts from a Critical Theory tradition such as "experience" and "subjectivity" became the focus of discussions.

The purpose of the project was to develop a didactical concept for learning at a construction site, based on participation and being operational and understandable for practitioners and connected to their daily work. The project's perspective was oriented toward the subject of construction and production.. It also had a political intention, which was to develop a concept that could create transparency in the building and production process, becoming, thus, an initiative leading to the democratisation of the work process.

The research questions were meant to be relevant for actions and planning at political levels; and it was important to come to an understanding of local conflicts in a project in which there seemed to be a consensus that learning skills and competencies are important for the enterprise as well as the industry as a whole. During the project's experimental phase, the research questions were directed toward the apprentices' learning processes, especially towards the dynamics of the didactical learning space at the construction site.

14.3 Research work: approach and organisation

The construction of buildings is organised such that both the workers and equipment are mobile. The research and development work spanned a period of three years, in contrast to the duration of the construction projects, which were usually completed during one year.

Therefore, the project had to be based at the enterprises' main office and involved the participation of people that were invited to be voluntary collaborators. These people constituted a group that could guarantee the continuity of the project independently of the construction contracts and their duration.

Having the organisation of production in mind, the project was divided into two phases in which the project leader, the carpenters' team leader, the union shop steward and the researcher constituted the core of the development work. The representatives from enterprise and industry – including the unions – became a "temporary reference group". This solution was chosen because the organisation of the construction activities did not allow the establishment and involvement of a larger and more stable group that could exist throughout the entire project. The research area can be described in terms of four levels or fields:

1) The first level is the construction site as an organisation with the apprentices, professional workers and a foreman all of whom who work within the construction site's community of practice

(The following fields have to be understood as the framework for the first and, in fact, the fourth became relatively peripheral.)

2) The second level is the enterprise as an organisation with its leadership and board of directors, shop stewards and association board who represent different standpoints and views, while still having common interests.
3) The third field consists of the industry organisations, the Workers' Association (LO) and the National Association of Construction Industry. These organisations were active during the project discussions and as partners.
4) The fourth field is the societal level, which consists of political decisions, publicity in the media, and situations and events happening nationally and internationally.

Before I discuss the design of the project and its approach, I will briefly present the research process. Figure 1 shows the schematic outline and how it has moved around in the various public sites.

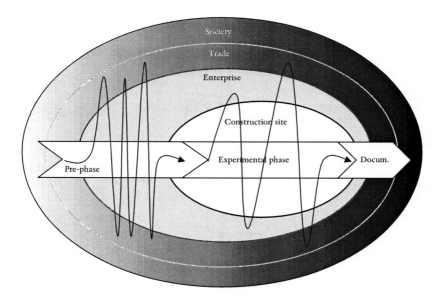

Figure 14.1: Phases and perspectives in the project.

14.3.1 Pre-understanding

The reasons for the project and its legitimacy rest on research reports and articles about the state of affairs in the construction business and site connected to the lack of quality, and a focus on health, the environment and safety.[1] The learning potential that exists in the organisation of the construction site and the work tasks is not utilised. In addition, a series of statements and newspaper articles dealing with the topic demanded action regarding education and training concerning the subject of construction. I refer here first of all to vocational training, and secondly to the further education of skilled construction workers and team leaders.

---

1   Reports and articles about the problems in the construction branch in Norway were published in various magazines and reports.

336

14.3.2 Pre-phase

The construction activity (enterprise, firm) is organised in a pre-determined way because production takes place where the building is, which requires the mobility of production equipment and personnel. The shop steward and the team leaders of the carpenters (and for training the carpenters) in the enterprise became key actors. The main union official was a watchdog concerned with agreements and principles in relation to the employees' rights and demands. The team leader for the wood workers who later became the project leader was a specialised professional and "pedagogue" in relation to the enterprise's challenges relating to questions about quality and training. The carpenters' team leader also had a wide range of contacts and co-operated with the professional milieu at various construction sites and organisations during the project.[2] The shop steward was the link between the construction workers, internally, and the Workers' Association, externally.

As a researcher, my contribution was based on my pedagogical competencies and experience gained from vocational training and I was, in addition, the facilitator of and source of inspiration in the project. In the pre-phase, the work was aimed at developing a learning concept within which a web application was a central part. The development of the web application consisted of structuring and designing the programme and it took place in the collaboration between the wood workers' representative and myself.

14.3.3 The experimental phase

This part of the project was set up as an experiment in which the concept of didactics would be tested and developed further. The experiment took place at a construction site, the workers which were apprentices and professionals. In this group, the latter functioned both as instructors and as a support base. It was during this phase that I proposed to use the "Future Creating Workshop". Before I present the methodological approach of the experimental phase, I will give a comprehensive

---

2 An example is "Byggforsk" which is a competence centre for the construction branch in Norway. Others are suppliers, upper secondary schools etc.

explanation of the research approach in regard to its values, practical approach and the insights gained during the project.

14.4 Research approach – values and methods

Some basic values such as democracy, transparency, equity, dialogue, freedom and teamwork were the topics of discussions during the research project. In the middle of the project process, I made an attempt to establish a deliberative (emancipatory) design or method: the Future Creating Workshop. The approach implied that the practitioners were considered to be the primary democratic agents in the project – and not only "partners to be listened to". The inspiration came from (Olsén, Steen Nielsen and Aagaard Nielsen, 2003). A consequence of this for the research work was that I had an attitude of "researching with" in contrast to "researching for" or "researching" (see Svensson and Nielsen Chapter 2 in this book). The development of new knowledge happens ideally through interaction, in a wide sense, between the practitioner and the researcher as equally important partners.

The research approach in the pre-phase of the project was inspired by socio-technical theory and the tradition at the Work Research Institute (Arbeidsforskningsinstitut – AFI) which is built on the basis of broad collaborative research that started in the sixties under the leadership of Einar Thorsrud and was connected to new ideas about the organisation of work and the release of human resources (for a more detailed description of the socio-technical tradition at AFI see Morten Levin's contribution in Chapter 7 of this book). The research project focused on the technical aspects of building construction, but it also had the purpose of developing the democratisation of the work organisation. Research and development was thus widely determined by the task of developing a concept of didactics aimed at learning on the construction site, and having roots in the existing and established ways of organising work. The development activities had their roots in the ideas that were developed in the pre-phase and were intended to be tested in an experimental phase. It became increasingly important for me to find methods to deal with the democratic aspect of the project's purpose.

Early in the project's execution phase, I participated in an Action

Research seminar and was inspired by the experiment "Industry and Happiness".[3] This project made use of the Future Creating Workshop to establish a utopian horizon through social imagination. As I understood it, the Danish Action Research project had a good method for strengthening the workers' everyday life experiences and hopes for the future; and it succeeded in utilising the utopian learning processes as a starting point for the democratisation of industrial production (Olsén, Steen Nielsen and Aagaard Nielsen 2003). On the basis of this inspiration, I became aware that my original approach to research had become too "instrumental", and had too few deliberative or emancipatory perspectives.

My reflections about the "AFI model" and "Industry and Happiness" forced me to make a critical revision of the approach to research due to a concern about an instrumentalist bias in my original design: The original project had a detailed plan of how to develop the concept of didactics for vocational training. I began to see a contradiction between a strong focus on the technical aspects of building construction and the subjective or social perspectives. The shop stewards had, of course, the role of ensuring the latter, but they were also able to participate in the technical aspects of learning and competence building.

14.5 Methodology used in the experimental phase

The *Future Creating Workshop* was used as one of various methods for preparing the experiment at the construction site seen as a community of practice. Of course, I also used other kinds of material in the design of the experiment. The early plans for implementing practice learning (based on a theoretical model (Wenger) and on talks (interviews) with key actors and biographical interviews with workers) continued, basically, to structure the design, but it became important to strengthen the democratic element of the design process.

---

3   "Industry and Happiness" is the name of a Danish Action Research project in the fishing industry. As in my projects, the Danish "Industry and Happiness" project aimed at developing democratic learning processes for qualifying workers in fish processing. In the discussion of Action Research methods that project has been known for the role of utopian processes in learning activities (see also Lise Drewes Nielsen's contribution in this book Chapter 5).

The Future Creating Workshop was chosen to develop a utopian horizon as an attempt to reorganise the collective mental picture of a construction site – to throw away the old and think a new. The Future Creating Workshop as proposed in Jungk and Müllert's model (Jungk and Müllert 1989) was made concrete and adjusted to the experimental phase, i.e. accommodated to the "reality" of the construction site, both in relation to the physical framework such as local conditions, the nature of construction tasks and staff, as well as the culture[4] among construction workers and in the construction industry generally.

The time allotted to a workshop is about five hours. The results transpiring from the Future Creating Workshop established a utopian horizon that is seen and interpreted in relation to the analyses of the other empirical material resulting from the experiment.

All activities were carried out at the construction site in small barracks usually meant for administration and/or as dining rooms. This setting became the framework that had to be taken into consideration in the entire methodological plan. The physical framework provided a constraint due to the lack of adequate space. In addition, there was a lot of noise coming from the construction site and the flow of traffic in and out of the barracks' area.

Although the Future Creating Workshop was not a form of work known to the construction workers, I regard it as successful in the sense that it brought about a moderate utopian horizon and the construction workers clearly enjoyed that way of working. After the workshop was over, it became clear that five hours was a short period for a Future Creating Workshop, but this was the framework we had previously decided upon. However, it ought to be mentioned that various participants expressed that five hours was a very long time to sit still, and they were not used to it. In spite of the given framework, the results obtained in the Future Creating Workshop were of such a quality that it justified including them in research work and the results were able to influence the design of the experiment.

---

4   After many years as a construction worker, I know the culture at construction sites quite well.

14.6 The experiment

The experimental phase was the period during which the construction workers participated in testing and developing the "unfinished" concept of didactics. As a researcher, I was active in giving guidance about how the concept ought to be practised and taking care of the open ends. The design was unfinished in the sense that the workers were meant to introduce their ideas from the Future Creating Workshop, when the experiment was operationalised.

Although most of the construction workers were informed about the project through written information, meetings and seminars carried out in various fora, they really had no specific knowledge about the use of the concept of didactics in vocational training. Prior to starting the project, the construction workers received some brief information about what the project dealt with and were invited to develop the "unfinished product". In this way, they became (voluntary) participants.

Thus, the first activity in the experimental phase was the Future Creating Workshop.

The themes for the workshop were: how the construction workers could imagine their ideal/optimal work place for learning and personal development, the good work place, and a good place to learn?

The research and developmental research question which lay behind the themes formulated for the Future Creating Workshop was the following:

> The construction site is not fully utilised as a place to learn. How can the construction site be developed to become a learning site?

In the initial phase of the project, there had been a presentation of the entire project and its aim of producing a product in the form of a didactic concept for the construction site. So it became important to integrate the construction workers in a way that they felt themselves independent of the instrumental aims formulated in the first phase of the project. The risk was that they would feel that their ideas had to be loyal to a didactic concept and so not feel free to propose more radical changes in the work organisation and in the established learning communities.

The empirical data shows that the Future Creating Workshop was a suitable approach. They expressed satisfaction with a work form that focussed on possibilities, although they were more used to thinking about limitations. Even though the Future Creating Workshop encouraged them to dream and imagine alternative forms of work organisation, they were still making suggestions with a quite limited utopian horizon.

To visualise what the construction workers regarded as challenges connected to the problem formulated as the theme for the workshop, I quote some of the statements made during the different phases. In the critical phase: *"In general, little time to learn"*, *"Unpredictability in parts of the production"*, *"Production workers do not have the necessary self confidence"*, *"Knowledge is power – Construction workers can learn up to a certain level"*. During the utopian phase they expressed positive ideas about the future. Typical statements were: *"To participate in the project development"*, *"To influence the production"*, *"Possibilities to be able to develop yourself as a professional worker through 'mutual visits' as apprentices"*. These quotations also express the need for influence on work and education as the wish to participate in the development in the site. As a result of the reality phase, a permanent workshop was established with a starting point in the ideas generated in the experimental phase.

This was not a project proposal/draft, but rather a thematic presentation of some ideas and issues for further elaboration. In this (part of the) work, the elements from the utopian phase were used as points of departure for the discussion of themes in the experiment. Here, I wish to refer to two main topics in the experiment:

- To use learning possibilities in construction processes in a more systematic way.
- To create interest for learning among company leaders and others in the industry.

The first topic was related to the workers' own concrete learning possibilities in the construction processes.

The second topic was related to the enterprise and to interest groups in relation to education and learning in the construction industry.

The Future Creating Workshop contributed to workers' feeling of ownership of the project. The construction workers' satisfaction with their own processes of learning was expressed through their statements about future perspectives. The Future Creating Workshop is a work process that gave a qualitatively good basis for analysis. There was also a feeling of safety among the participants because they were guided through the process and what they expressed was temporarily written on wall charts. The fact that the construction workers formulated realistic goals for the experimental phase seemed to contribute to greater engagement in the final evaluation. They discussed which goals were attained, why they were attained, which goals were not achieved and why this happened. Consequently, the evaluation was carried out consciously and was part of the participants' learning process.

14.7 What was the practical effect of the Future Creating Workshop?

The empirical contribution of the Future Creating Workshop was to provide the framework for the chosen construction site as a community of practice connected to the research question, i.e., how does a construction site function both in organisational terms and socially, and what does it mean for the apprentices' learning? Such questions can be examined in the light of the culture of the construction site and its established practice within which the formal hierarchy and the autonomous work groups/teams are known factors. The question was: What meaning does the organisation of the construction site – community of practice partnership and social quality – have for the apprentices' learning? The focus was aimed especially at the apprentices' learning. In addition, a comprehensive analysis of the collective learning at the construction site was also carried out.

The research approach contributed to the articulation of the construction workers' experiences at their work place. The empirical material collected in the Future Creating Workshop provided the basis for understanding other empirical results derived from the experiment, for example, the participants in the Future Creating Workshop were critical of certain aspects of the practice at the construction site, and were, thus, conscious of what it consisted of. However, the empirical material gathered on a day-to-day basis during the experiment showed that they practised the routines and rules that they criticised. These types of contrast and paradoxes were examined and discussed in relation to the theoretical sources of this research. In addition, the empirical material contributed to strengthening the links related to learning, reported in a series of studies carried out in the construction industry (Bjørnåvold 1992, 1993, Andersen 2001, Frøyland 2004).

14.8 The Project's results

In order to provide a short description of the project's empirical results, the project has been divided into a pre-phase and an experimental phase.

The empirical results from the pre-phase show how an Action Research project can be loaded with and reveal conflicts when the established practices and ways of thinking are challenged. This was especially the case at the level of the enterprise. It became clear from rhetoric and the documents circulating in the enterprise that several problems related to the positions of specific people and professional groups arose. The project appeared to be threatening because it could create transparency in relation to management dispositions and give the construction workers access to knowledge. It could, thus, disturb/upset the organisation's power relations. This problem was also expressed in the Future Creating Workshop, when the construction workers expressed that they could be educated up to a "certain" level. The processes also showed that the project was vulnerable, although it was well anchored in the enterprise's leadership and the shop steward. The project was stretched over a period during which, among other things, there was a replacement in the enterprise's leadership causing serious problems for carrying out the project. The conflict between the long-term thinking in the construction industry and in unions and the short-term view connected to the daily production demands of an enterprise also became very apparent.

The empirical contribution resulting from the experimental phase is especially related to the apprentices' learning within the framework of a construction site and to the dynamics in the community of practice. The construction workers were conscious that the established practice and the organisation of work were not satisfactory. Still, their mental picture of a construction site was so solid that they had difficulties in establishing a new practice, even though this practice had been pre-pared/arranged for the experiment. They tried, but went back to the "old way". A statement during the final evaluation connected to plan-ning and predictability in the building process confirms the problems associated with this attitude: *"Here we have had the opportunity, but we have in a certain way misused it ... or we have forgotten it"*. Although the lack of planning resulted in a series of conflicts, there was a consensus that there had been many good discussions about the professional aspects of construction.

The empirical data shows that it was a challenge for the community of practice to arrange comprehensive and interrelated activities that were perceived as being meaningful by the apprentices and as a point of departure for their learning. Within this picture, it became decisive that drawings and plans created a frame of reference for the change in practices.

Quality in the social community and the actors' competence (in a wide sense) becomes, thus, an essential factor for the apprentices' learn-ing. The establishment of an inclusive community/partnership seems to be a great challenge.

The challenges are, first of all, connected to the quality of the com-munity. However, it is also important to stimulate the ability and wish to organise a practice in which there is place for a collective prepara-tion/cultivation of experiences. Such elements are necessary to facilitate a societal dimension in a learning organisation.

Newly published reports about the construction industry state the need for both collective and individual learning at the work site. It is also stated that learning across the construction sites and projects are quite significant for the industry (Andersen 2004, Blomli et al. 2004, Frøyland et al. 2004).

14.9 The project's contribution to the theory of learning through practice

This project developed a concept for learning at the construction site as a result of empirical work. It was called the LAV-concept (LAV: Laering, Arbeid og Verdiskapning/English: Learning, Work and Value creation). The creation of the LAV-concept is a result of a dialogue with various actors at different "levels" in the construction industry.

Model for ICT-integrated work-place learning

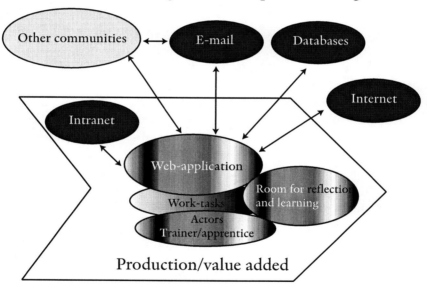

Figure 14.3   LAV-concept

The didactic concept "LAV" – learning – work – value creation is based on the following principles:

- Learning must be individually based (individual learning plan).
- Learning must be applicable/useful and of current interest – both for the vocation and in general.

- Learning must focus on the quality of processes, and products.
- Learning must have a societal perspective.
- It must focus on learning in day-to-day work.

The concept of value creation provides a wide definition within which learning is regarded as adding to the individual's competence, to the enterprise's and to society's.

Figure 3 provides a schematic presentation of the LAV-concept, which is characterised in terms of the following main components: 1) It is connected to value creation and production; 2) It creates interaction between work tasks – actors – and resources available through Internet; 3) It encourages reflection and learning; 4) It increases the possibility to maximise learning beyond the community of practice through a web application and the Internet.

The question then is how the didactic concept can be developed to advance learning possibilities in an industry that, in the best case, offers varied and meaningful work tasks and challenges, and in the worst case contributes to stress, troubles/difficulties and exclusion from active work (Frøyland et al. 2004). There will also be questions about whether this concept, when applied in a context of a new division of labour between the enterprises, will still contribute to learning and the development of competencies at the construction site? The project as a whole revealed that the potential for good solutions often become impossible because of too much stress and insufficient time to follow up on good ideas at the site level.

Etienne Wenger's concept of "communities of practice" now enters the discussion. The process of meaning negotiation can be regarded as both the choose part of Wenger's theory of social learning, as well as the problem within the theory. It appears that Wenger's concept of communities of practice is insufficiently contextualised to become a model for a new didactic concept. Although he refers to participation in various communities of practice, the concept does not ensure a solid elaboration and mediation of experiences. My empirical work shows that this is a problem.

My empirical material also shows that the apprentices' membership in the community was not worth mentioning. It appears that they did not identify themselves with the community, but experienced what it was like to have the status of an office boy. Consequently, they did not have the opportunity to show and use their competencies as much as they wished.

14.10 The project's contribution to the discussion of the researcher's role and combinations of various methods in Action Research

In the project, I have practised a variety of methods these included biographical interviews, the socio-technical facilitation of cooperation and conducting a Future Creating Workshop aimed at the development of a utopian horizon for the work organisation. Before I started the project, I did not realise the complexity of those different roles in the project when they have to be incorporated in one person. The problems of the different roles were linked to the tension between being a researcher who collects empirical material, and being an innovator "teaching" the participators and facilitating ideas. Another problem was that of elaborating statements and research questions together with the construction workers and other participants. Furthermore, I became very close, socially, to most of them, so I sometimes had problems with creating the distance necessary for maintaining a critical view of what was going on.

In spite of the difficulties, I have seen the importance of combining different methods. For example, I am sure that the introduction of the Future Creating Workshop was useful for gaining more and deeper knowledge about possibilities and conflicts in practice learning; but that on the other hand it did not result in practical constructive and consensual reform. So you have to face a kind of contradiction in choosing methods for Action Research, what is most important, a successful change arrived at in small steps, or the achievement of a deeper and more knowledge seeking strategy which includes enlightenment about conflicts in the creation of practice learning with a democratic orientation.

In my project, I also tried to use biographical interviews. The interviews made it possible for me to strengthen the individual dimensions in the development of practice learning, which was important in the construction of the LAV-concept. But I hardly succeeded in bringing the individual dimension into the collective discussion among workers/apprentices, and so I did not succeed in attaining the principle of "research with".

14.11 Conclusion

The Action Research approach seems to have revealed a sequence of relations that are not necessarily clear when using other approaches. There are various studies that have asked leaders of enterprises about their views regarding learning and the development of competencies. Almost without exception, they look at them as the most important things for an enterprise in order to be competitive, and to be an attractive workplace. This was also the opinion of leaders in the enterprise where this project was carried out. However, when the project's activities became concrete, a series of conflicts of interests and positioning arose in relation to the project's content and organisation. People in leadership positions, who had initiated the project, tried to leave the project later on.

This Action Research project is based on Kurt Lewin's triangle in which interested participants, learning/training and the researching reflections are the three main elements (Olsén, Steen Nielsen and Aagaard Nielsen 2003). During the execution of the project, the research approach was enriched by ideas borrowed from Critical Theory, which were brought together with the interactive approach of the socio-technical tradition. Values that provide democracy, openness, equity, and the view about the practitioner and researcher being equally valuable partners are fundamental for the whole research project. Although this is the ideal situation, there were of course several situations in which, for example, the "power free" dialogue did not happen at all, or in which structured Action Research methods were invisible.

The project contributed to illuminating several aspects related to learning through practice. It appears that construction site culture is part of construction workers' backbones, and that this can be an obstacle to the further development of the construction site as a place for learning. Another insight is that the lack of time for experimenting and learning can have the same implications. The practice used in the construction site is to a large degree involves both individual and collective learning. The focus is mostly on the technical/professional side leaving little space for the societal perspective. The construction site's community of practice leaves little room for a collective elaboration and mediation of experiences. The apprentices perceived their real participation and influence in the community as being quite limited.

Even in a project that was planned to investigate what was observable at the construction site and about the cultivation of experiences instead of the technical aspects, there were several impediments to establishing links between the construction site and daily life. These challenges became more visible when one of the apprentices was asked about the connections between work and daily life and he could not make this connection. This was an indication that work experiences and the daily life run on parallel tracks, and to a very limited degree confront and enrich each other (Salling Olesen 2000). That apprentice's entire communicative situation in the project was linked to the work place and his statements were therefore associated within this context. This is a confirmation of the problems described by Salling Olesen regarding how experiences of life experience from outside working life are only to a very small degree connected to experiences gained during the working life.

Within the previously mentioned LAV-concept, it is possible to discuss the problems presented in order to develop the construction site as a learning place further. It appears that the challenges will mainly be connected to the organisation of work that allows the workers to participate and have an influence on the whole process, from planning and execution through to the evaluation and quality assurance of the work performed. The "learning space" proposed by the LAV-concept challenges the collective cultivation of experiences within which the societal perspective must also occupy a space.

References

Andersen, Anders Siig & Larsen Kirsten (2001) *Det narrative livshistoriske interview: Introduktion til Fritz Schützes teoretiske og metodologiske arbejde.*

(Utvidet og revidert udgave af Småskrift No. 11 Livshistorieprojektet), Fredriksberg: Roskilde Universitetscenter.

Andersen, Bjørn (2004) *Restrukturering, medbesetmmelse og faglig innflytelese i entreprenørbransjen.* Veidekke og Selmer på 1990-tallet. Fafo.

Andersen, Lars (2001) *Slik oppnår du bedre økonomi og lavere sykefravær gjennom å fjerne stress, mas og misforståelser på din arbeidsplass. Tiltakshefte for bygge- og anleggsbedrifter.* Byggenæringens Landsforening: Hovedorganisasjonenes Fellestiltak.

Bjørnåvold, Jens (1992) "Komplementære eller konkurrerende lærings-modeller innenfor bygg og anlegg" in Mjelde, Liv og Tarrou, Anne Lise Høstmark *Arbeidsdeling i en Brytningstid*, Oslo: Ad Notam Gyldendal.

– (1993) *Bygg- og anleggsnæringen som læringsarena: Organisatoriske og normative forutsetninger for kompetanseutvikling.* NORUT Samfunnsforskning A/S.

Blomli, Mariann Jodis et al. (2004) Instilling fra arbeidsgruppe byggekostnader. http://www.odin.no/krd/norsk/dok/andre_dok/rapporter/016031-990070/dok-bn.html.

Buch, Anders (2002) *Social læringsteori.* Fredriksberg: Roskilde Universitetsforlag.

Frøyland, Kjetil et al. (2004) *Bygg og anlegg. Frafall og utstøting i bygge- og anleggsbransjen.* Arbeidsforskningsinstituttet.

Jungk, Robert and Müllert, Norbert R (1989) *Håndbog i fremtidsværksteder.* København: Politisk revy.

Olesen, Henning Salling in *Tekster om læring* Illeris, Knud (ed.) (2000). Fredriksberg: Roskilde Universitetsforlag.

Olsén, Peter, Nielsen Steen, Birger and Nielsen, Kurt Aagaard, (2003) *Demokrati og bæredygtighed: social fanatsi og samfundsmæssig rigdomsproduktion*, Fredriksberg: Roskilde Universitetsforlag.

Thorsrud, E. and Emery, F. (1969) *Mot en ny bedriftsorganisasjon.* (Samarbeidsprosjektet LO/NAF. Rapport 2) Oslo: Tanum.

Wenger Etienne (1998) *Communities of Practice: Learning, Meaning and Identity.* Cambridge, MA: Cambridge University Press.

Wenger Etienne (2001) Supporting communities of practice a survey of community-oriented technologies. http://www.ewenger.com/tech/ (2004).

JENS CHRISTIAN ELLE[1]

15. Other Futures are Possible

Cultural reorientations from a life world perspective

15.1 Introduction

The title "Other Futures are possible" could profitably be extended with "– and necessary". As I will show in this chapter, one will not have – if a certain methodological design and critical sensitivity is present – to dig deeply beyond the surface of reality to realize that the expressions of the people participating in Action Research contain an aspiration for, and a need to, transcend reality by means of radical reforms. Expressions that clearly surpasses the immediate agenda of the joint process.

In the first part of this chapter, I will outline my entry into the field of research and present the outcome of the first round of sessions with people working within public sector catering in Copenhagen. The research process was based on a widespread desire to involve different groups of professionals working in nursing homes in the development of ideas about how to implement and firmly anchor the continuing process of converting public sector catering to the use of organic foods.

The themes which unfolded at two *Future Creating Workshops* on the one hand contained elements pointing in the direction of pragmatic organisational redesigns, but on the other hand the profundity of the critique and visions clearly signalled that a real transformation in the direction of sustainability, increased health and democracy within pub-

---

1   Innovation and Sustainability/Department of Manufacturing Engineering and Management, Technical University of Denmark

lic sector catering should be created. This would be in contrast to the organisational set up characterizing the situation today. In order to gain a basic awareness of what is at stake, it has been necessary to examine the modernisation of public sector catering. This brief characterization also functions as a theoretical basis for the methical considerations concerning how to establish a process, which, in a meaningful and engaging manner, can bring us outside the ruling principles of reality, and give us an opportunity to develop scenarios for a saner modernisation of public sector catering.

Almost simultaneously with my recognition of the need for the development of alternative scenarios, it was clear that my initial ideas of "development from below" had to be improved. The design of my Action Research process was initially founded on a conception that development from below was synonymous with the gradual unfolding of ideas, theories and actions coming from an underprivileged group of participants. My actual findings show that the critical insights and social imaginations of the catering and nursery workers point in very intriguing directions. They also reveal how difficult it is for people to maintain a transcendent perspective when their feet, hands and heads buried in harsh everyday business., and, furthermore, how much it would demand from an Action Research perspective to facilitate such a process. With this in mind, I changed my focal point in the direction of scenario development using a much more divers group of actors having all kinds of positions within the structure surrounding public sector catering. I drew on the ideas of reflexive ecological modernisation (Hajer 1995) concerning how discourse coalitions could be merged and actively create specific story lines defining what has gone wrong and what to do. The concept is not unproblematic as I will show, but it provided substantial inspiration, and the discussion between *reflexive ecological modernisation* and *critical-utopian Action Research* has, among other things, resulted in the claim that it would be more appropriate to talk about "development from the life world"[2] rather than from "below" or "above".

---

2 The term *life world* refers in this chapter to the holistic cultural structure that contextualizes our social actions in everyday life, which also contains compensatory elements of what the social world could be.

15.2 The dish of the future (1)

In Denmark, during the last 15 years, a substantial effort has been directed towards the conversion of public sector catering to the use of organic products. A policy primarily based on environmental concerns. Product innovation, supply systems, and organic conversion strategies have improved significantly, but a range of obstacles to speeding up the process has been identified in a number of reports (e.g. Kristensen 2002). This was where I entered the scene.

My job was initially to investigate how the supply of organic food to large-scale kitchens could be strengthened, and the contours of an interesting Action Research project with participation of existing and potential actors along the supply chain were clear.

A search for collaborators began, and this journey brought me through a pair of unfruitful local initiatives and some interesting experiences, before I found my partner. The municipality of Copenhagen had decided to convert all the public kitchens to the extent that 75 % of the food would be organic. In order to gain the necessary experience, a number of pilot projects had been launched, including one involving eight nursing homes. During these first steps, I was intensely concerned about where to focus my efforts and I decided to take my point of departure in the institutions, and from there expand the dialogue to include the supplying agents and scientific bodies.

I suggested to the *Organic Conversion Secretary* and partners from the *Health Administration* of Copenhagen that the conversion of the eight nursing homes could be launched with a number of so-called *Future Creating Workshops*[3] including the participation of the residents and nursing home employees. Normally, these groups do not participate in the formulation and creation of development plans, and I was convinced that they possessed a diversity of ideas and resources that could be collectively merged into social innovations. These could subsequently be cultivated through the scheduled organic conversion courses[4] and

---

3 For a detailed description of the Future Creating Workshop see Chapter 4.

4 A key element in the concept of organic conversion is education of the staff. During these courses they learn about the organic principles, they analyse the prevailing production economy and they develop new organic menus.

thereby matured for concrete dialogues and experiments. The initiative was named *dish of the future*, I was to be the researcher in charge of the process. The next step was to invite the eight nursing homes to participate in the *dish of the future*. I knew it was difficult for the employees to find time to participate because of inadequate staffing, and I knew that most of the elderly were too weak to participate. Nevertheless, four of the eight nursing homes found the initiative so important that they sent a team of nurses, kitchen workers, managers and the elderly to two *Future Creating Workshops*.

The headline of the critique phase was *"What are we dissatisfied with in relation to the way we cook, serve and eat in our nursing home?* The many statements that were generated during the brainstorming session were object to a voting process and a subsequent thematisation resulting in a number of *critique themes* that with moderate violations can be summarized in the three following points:

1. Industrial cooking is charmless. The craft dimension has vanished in favour of dull mass production. The food is becoming boring and it is boring to cook. The ingredients are not fresh, and the food is being ill treated in the continuous process of chilling and reheating before it reaches its final destination, where it is often rejected because of its appearance and texture.
2. The dining rooms are impersonal and without atmosphere. The dining situation is characterised by chaos. Everything is done in a hurry and the level of noise is high. The staff does not have time for the individual's particular needs.
3. Rigidity in the process of planning. Everything is predetermined and individual ideas and suggestions from the staff seldom materialize into new ways of doing things. The knowledge concerning the elderly's different preferences in terms of food and eating do not reach the kitchens.

Subsequently, we went to the utopian phase, and the headline for the session was: *What would the cooking and eating look like if we could decide?* Rapidly a diversity of wishes was expressed that in outline looked like the ones that appeared in the *critique phase* but in reverse. With the same procedure, these statements were turned into a number of themes, which were the object of three hours of group work. In the end, the participants, which in general grouped around their own institution rather than thematically, presented their works. In extract:

1. The good food system: Local organic producers provide the catering supplier with high quality and low processed food, which, on a daily basis, is brought to the nursing home that has its own kitchen with a happy and highly skilled staff. In the kitchen, the food is made from scratch just before each meal. But the system also works the other way around. The elderly decide want they want to eat, and these wishes are executed in the kitchens. The whole system is realized by a huge amount of money streaming from the municipality, symbolised by (an utmost generous!) Uncle Scrooge.

2. The beautiful dining room. Two groups worked out prospectus for their dinning rooms and canteens. The rooms were bright, beautiful, homelike and saturated with good atmospheres. There were fresh flowers, tablecloths and candles on the tables. The rooms were multifunctional.

3. A nice meal: The staff, not wearing their uniforms, dines together with the elderly. The meal is characterised by peace, and presence, and a focus on the particular residents' individual needs. Everybody respects and lives up to the diet policy and the food ethic.

In spite of the fact that the participants were encouraged to ignore the prevailing principles of reality and express their inner dreams about the good meal in the good nursing home, it was striking how close their visions (with exceptions) related to the existing structural frames. But, at the same time, it was obvious how strongly the staff when discussing the scenarios about the future wanted to burst the organisational restrictions that in the present situation kept them from realising their own moral claims, professional ethics, and the desire for social recognition.

A *Future Creating Workshop* ends with a session where the participants are encouraged to engage in the further development of the particular visions (or elements from these). In this way, a number of enthusiastic groups left the workshop with their respective plans. In such situations, the need for some kind of follow up event cannot be underestimated, and later on in this chapter, I will return to how this process was continued.

In order to obtain a more in-depth understanding of public sector catering, which would be essential for an analysis of the workshops and for the further process of joint explorations of possibilities, I began to study the modernisation of public sector catering.

15.3 Public sector catering
– a one-dimensional modernisation

An elderly person living in a nursing home seldom complains. One day the most agile of the elderly turned up at the principal's office: "Have you tasted the soup today", she asked. "No", the principal replied, "I never join the meals". Something was obviously wrong, so she followed the resident down to the dining room and tasted the soup that was as salty as the Dead Sea. Before the soup had reached the plates, it had been sent out of the production kitchen to the local kitchen and then out to the respective wards where it was served by the staff. No-one had tasted the soup on the way. Who was the host for this meal? (*Økonomaen*, 2003)

Such episodes along with my immediate impression of smells, architecture and facial expressions from nursing home visits and the critical statements emerging from the *Future Creating Workshops* made me curios about the historical development of the food culture in public sector catering. The first thing that becomes clear is the fact that public meals have been of an inferior quality from the beginning (Hansen 1993). The history of public sector catering is not a mere history of decline, moving from the good meal to the dull meal. What is striking is why we, despite of an enormous increase in societal wealth, scientific knowledge about nutrition, health and human well-being and a true cornucopia of food are witness to severe malnutrition (Beck and Ovesen 2002), a considerable waste of food (Barton 2000), and widespread criticism of the public food culture in general.

If we take the workshop participants critique seriously, the problems with the food and the meals cannot be isolated to inattention and bad habits, but it has something to do with how the overall rationality expresses itself in the choice of technology and management systems. It became clear to me that the misery of public sector catering essentially had something to do with the lack of conditions for the rational and democratic organisation of the public institutions.

Public sector catering has, on the one hand, developed separately from the market economy; on the other hand, its *modus operandi* is tightly connected to a productivist[5] logic characterising society as such. Still fewer and larger units are engaged in the task of producing, distributing and serving food. Men (mostly women) are replaced by technology, demanding a narrow repertoire of skills. In terms of *working conditions,* some major achievements have incontrovertibly happened, but if we focus on the art of cooking, it is reasonable to claim that both within public sector catering and in society at large the work has been progressively fragmented, and stripped of its complexity, discretionary content and knowledge base (Braverman 1974).

Underneath we see a certain kind of rationality unfold. An instrumental rationality solidly chained to utilitaristic moral philosophy (Pedersen 2000). The modernisation of society in general is closely linked to a functional differentiation in the spatial organisation of the work as well as in the institutional surroundings. One dimension of this process combined with a positivist science is a reductionist view on the complex cohesion and interaction between the human, social and natural systems.

The public sector assumed a considerable size, and, in the eighties, came under attack from both left and right. From the so-called new right, a massive attack on the welfare state was launched accusing it of inefficient mechanisms of allocation, and of being morally reprehensible for both the givers and the receivers. New Public Management was the most prominent conceptual expression of this attack on the "social

---

5   Productivism is a term that primarily has been developed and used within rural sociology and food policy studies. For a comprehensive explanation see, for example, Lang and Heasman (2004). The term captures a certain mode of production that characterises modern societies since World War II. Some of the core terms defining productivism are intensification, concentration and specialization. It is a basic assumption among the proponents of post-productivism to oppose productivity to productivism, because the instrumental exploitation of human, social and natural capital that characterises productivism is impediment to long-term (sustainable) productivity.

democratic" public sector and became the dominant way of thinking and acting within the public sector focusing on: privatization, outsourcing, competition, management by contract, evaluation, standardisation etc. The market is, according to this ideology, the best way to create efficiency and development, and people are best motivated by economic incentives (Klausen and Ståhlberg, 1998, p. 12).

Despite the moral accusations against the public sector and the welfare state, the NPM strategies did not lead to the dismantling of the bureaucratic organisation of public sector catering, but rearranged the public sector in favour of private market forces and new forms of bureaucracy and management within the productivist paradigm. As Katrin Hjort emphasizes the public handling of tasks has moved in the direction of increased efficiency and intensification, thorough new forms of hierarchisation, specialisation and routinesation, a new form of modulisation and standardisation of the public services (Hjort, 2001, p. 53). Specified working descriptions cause an increased division of labour between the unskilled labours, which execute routine tasks, and skilled specialists who innovate, make plans and controls. (Hjort, 2001, p. 62)

The critique of the welfare state and the public sector has also been launched from the green and socialist positions in relation to both its economic sustainability and its consequences for human flourishing and social and environmental sustainability. The welfare state's long-time viability relies on economic growth, which has severe consequences for the human and natural environments. The social illnesses (life style related diseases, injury caused by jobs and environmental damages etc.) unfolding in the wake of productivist-economic growth will be self-defeating for the economy of the welfare state (Pierson, 1991, p. 193).

As Pierson remarks, it is reasonable to think that the welfare state will undergo considerable transformations due to social, economic, political and ecological pressures (Pierson, 1991, p. 195). This chapter is not the right place to unfold a discussion about what a reconstructed welfare society, organised around a new type of substantial rationality that provides the space for the unfolding of autonomy under consideration to the common good, could look like. Of course, it is crucial for transformative action to operate within a certain horizon defined by particular values and principles, but the essential challenge is to ask *how* the forming of the welfare state in general and public sector catering in particular can be repoliticized and democratised. The task of co-producing alternative scenarios for the modernisation of public sector (catering) is extremely important and has become the focal point of my research efforts. The question that arises next is how such scenarios can be created in a democratic and dynamic manner, which on the one hand go beyond the prevailing principles of reality and on the other hand seem meaningful and promising for the people involved.

15.4 Establishing a shared horizon

If we turn to the possibilities for social change or, more contextually expressed, the possibilities for a radical cultural transformation of public sector catering, it becomes absolutely necessary to search for, discuss and challenge the general conditions for processes of social change.

In the realm of environmental sociology, Maarten Hajer (1995) has formulated the concept of Reflexive Ecological Modernisation, which basically is about creating shared visions between normally differentiated communities of knowledge and praxis. Such a discourse coalition is shaped and centred on a specific story line explaining the reason for the whole wretched business, and how it can be countered by the development of new realities based on new reasons and rationalities. The challenge for the unfolding of an alternative process of modernisation must consequently be to form coherent proposals, which in a persuasive and exemplary manner comply with the needs of real social welfare.

> "The Challenge does not concern the goal but the process. The challenge seems to be to think of an organization of ecological modernisation as a process that allows for social change to take place democratically and in a way that stimulates the creation of a – at least partially – shared vision of the future" (Hajer, 1995: 280)

The interesting point in Hajer's argumentation in relation to ecological modernisation is his insistence that the prime challenge is not to solve the ecological crises, but to find patterns of modernisation that express how we as citizens want to develop our society, without to many negative side effects. Translated into the domain of public sector catering, the way to improve the nutritional state, the working conditions, and the resource use, is to discount the instrumental strategies that emanate from the techno-administrative apparatus in favour of cross-disciplinary proposals for another kind of modernisation without (that many) negative social and environmental side effects. A cross-disciplinarity that both relates to science itself but most of all between the domains of science and politics and other forms of knowledge and resources existing in civil society, in the sphere of the life world. It is not the point that the particular scientific and administrative disciplines have to dissolve in favour of multi-disciplinary entities. The point is that they have to connect in a more open and cooperative manner to the processes of modernisation. I will return to this discussion below.

According to Hajer, these discourse coalitions can be facilitated through new forms of so-called *reflexive institutional arrangements*, but only in a rudimentary way does he sketch out the contours of such arrangements. To the extent he actually tries to give his analytic theories a normative expression, it becomes quite clear that there are certain similarities to the dialogical oriented Action Research methodology that dominates the Nordic approach. For instance, Pålshaugens (1998) ideas about Action Research as a way to *reorganise discourses*.

But Hajer's approach is not unproblematic for various reasons. First of all, he only pays attention to the linguistic acknowledgements and expressions and does not seems to have an eye for the more aesthetic dimensions and those related to the senses of the lifeworld that for example come to life in Future Creating Workshops. Secondly, Hajer seems to neglect "the power of reality" when he suggests how shared horizons can be established through reflexive institutional arrangements. Collective processes of visualisation demand a certain *free space*, which I will touch upon below. Thirdly Hajer's approach is not committed to the creation of a pluralistic public sphere, and the creation of sketches based on the participants' desire for another lifeworld [Lebenszusammenhäng]. Instead, it is orientated to a relatively narrow group of professionals and their search for an intersection between their different discursive worlds in order to facilitate a smooth and consensus orientated ecological modernisation of society.

In *critical utopian action research*, I have found what I consider a prom-

ising and inspiring approach to how societal alternatives can be democratically formulated, qualified and tested in action.[6] In certain respects,
this approach has similarities to Maarten Hajer's "cultural politics"
approach to the modernisation of society. First of all, its commitment to
democratic social change, and secondly its renunciation of instrumental
and technocratic strategies. The disastrous side effects of the industrial-
ism must first of all be countered by the development of other types of
modernisation. If we only meet the health or environmental crises by
strengthening of the techno-scientific management the democracy will
forfeit.

First of all what characterizes *critical utopian action research* is its utopian orientation, which has its philosophical heritage in the works Ernst
Bloch and Robert Jungk (among others). By creating utopian images of
the desired future, the people involved in the process can simultaneously
be capable of seeing the restrictions, mechanisms of suppression, and the
irrational dimensions of the prevailing society and unfold societal solutions that transcend this society in the ways that the different domains
of life relate to each other. As Nielsen and Nielsen states in Chapter
4. "Only through the utopian categories can you understand human
democratic possibilities in any reality". In order to create the possibility
for a utopian orientation in the formulation of alternatives, it is necessary to put the prevailing principles of reality in brackets for a moment.
In other words, it is necessary to establish what is called a *free space*, and
the *Future Creating Workshop* is an example of such a *free space*.

The basic idea behind *critical utopian action research* is to establish
cooperation between the researcher(s) and the primary participants
around the development of democratic and sustainable alternatives. The
point of departure is a utopian oriented production of social alternatives based on the local actors" everyday experience, tacit knowledge,
and social imaginations about a better life world. The *Future Creating
Workshop* typically facilitates the first step. The concrete utopian ideas
that emerge from the workshop are, no matter how effectively the *free
space* unfolded, still fragile and need to be developed in order to gain the
necessary social robustness.

---

6 For a comprehensive and in-depth description of critical utopian action research, see
Chapter 3.

Another distinctive feature characterizing the *critical utopian action research* tradition is the critical dialogues with experts and specialist, which typically are conducted in so-called Research Workshops. The purpose of these dialogues is, first of all, to strengthen the participant's concrete utopian ideas. The invited experts are encouraged to connect to the overall ideas, and from this joint position enrich the ideas with their respective professional technical, social, legal, economic and/or ecological knowledge. These dialogues can also be seen as a way to mediate between the local, and the more common values, necessities and possibilities.

The role of the Action Researcher is both to guarantee a certain discourse ethic and to ensure that the rules of the game are kept so a democratic dialogue can unfold. But the Action Researcher is not a mere process agent, a neutral facilitator. The Action Researcher is engaged in the substance, and play in his or hers knowledge about social dynamics and contemporary societal reproduction.

15.4 The dish of the future (2)

When an Action Research process (and other kinds of social intervention) is launched, it is normally based on a certain model that is considered to be promising and rewarding – in this case the critical utopian action research and the ideas about reflexive ecological modernisation. But I also think that reality always behaves differently from that you initially hoped and expected, which underscores one of the main abilities of an Action Researcher – the ability to improvise and get the best out of the emerging crisis.

In my case, I ran into my first major crisis when I realised how impossible it was in reality to bring the processes initiated at the two *Future Creating Workshops* into the organic conversion course. This was due to an inflexible and strict course schedule that did not leave enough room for activities, which were not strictly concerned with the subsequent implementation and fulfilment of the political goals. Besides this, the course was designed so that the different professional groups were educated separately, which broke with the cross-disciplinary process I found so promising and urgent. It is worth reflecting on why things do not go the same way as initially imagined, and recognize where the methods were inadequate or where one's ability to make the necessary preparations failed. But, most important of all, do not let the wasted opportunities dominate the horizon. Crises are potentially pregnant with new possibilities.

On several occasions I presented my analysis of the *Future Creating Workshops* at the conversion courses, which caused a highly positive response in relation to both the content and the process. Particular among the course participants, the *dish of the future* was accentuated as an important event that was often referred to during the conversion course. I proposed the holding of a workshop in order to work through some of the central themes with a view of pollinating the future conversion courses with new insights and methods. The idea was, in accordance with the concept of the *Research Workshop*[7], to invite some of the surviving groups from the *Future Creating Workshop* to present their respective visions. In continuation of this presentation, a group of invited experts were asked, in an open and solidaric manner, to contribute with their professional insights and thereby strengthen the local drafts and the common dimensions that hopefully could be extracted from them.

I realized in my preliminary dialogues with these experts and professionals how much they, despite the relatively affirmative role they possessed within the system, nodded approvingly when I presented my cultural critique of public sector catering. I then understood what an enormous desire for a different approach lived a tacit existence, not only in the staff but also in the people working in the administrative systems and research institutions. When they got a chance to unfold their transcendent ideas they seemed to take it. Parallel with these talks, I engaged in three groups helping them to find a way to express the visions produced at the *Future Creating Workshops*. Except for one group that consisted of two very dynamic managers, it was difficult for me to encourage the nursing home employees to create coherent presentations that still contained some of the utopian energy that initially characterized their sketches. After encouraging talks, where I stressed the perspectives and opportunities they were momentarily inspired, but fell immediately back on everyday situations and incremental transformations within a very pragmatic horizon. These experiences made me

---

7   For a detailed description of the *research workshop* see Chapter 4.

decide that the right perspective for the further progress of my Action Research process was to create a new "we", consisting of a divers group of professionals.

The intention with the *Research Workshop* was twofold. On the one hand, it should provide the three groups and the conversion team with inspiration and a network. On the other hand, it should form the basis for a new "we" on the scent of a transcending project. In reality, the most promising perspective arising from this workshop was a strong emphasis of the how destructive the *new public management* concepts were for a trust and experience based (food) culture, and how much cross-disciplinary understanding and actions were needed. Unfortunately, there was no time for pointing to actual projects, which could constitute a new "we". So in order to continue the process, I took the initiative to establish an idea laboratory: *The good smelling nursing home.*

The purpose of the *idea laboratory* is to create concrete visions for a good smelling nursing home. Coherent sketches that show how a more substantial and ecological rationality can be unfolded in the construction of a nursing home with particular attention on the food and the meals. Ideas that could be thrown into the ongoing debates on how to tackle the crises of the welfare state, and hopefully form the point of departure for a social experiment. By establishing this idea laboratory, I expect to see an Action Research process that runs more continuously, a joint process of reflection, planning and action. The rest of the story is yet to come.

15.5. What did we learn from that?

The *Future Creating Workshop* is not just a method. Its design is immanently critical and in this case it formed a breeding ground for a powerful unfolding of critique and social imaginations, which in many ways shook my preliminary ideas of what was at stake in public sector catering, and made it difficult to maintain a perspective that gave priority to the development and implementation of an ecological rationality. Should a new food culture have a chance to evolve around a novel and rational (and un-rational) connection between human health, environmental balance and a sound economy, it would demand a fundamental rebellion against the ruling rationality saturating the management and development strategies embracing the public sector.

From numerous previous experiences with *Future Creating Workshops* I have been witness to how such *free spaces* potentially sets social imaginations and confined frustrations free. What has been striking in this process has been how easily these social imaginations and frustrations crop up when I, as a point of departure for talks with professionals and bureaucrats, in a naïve manner, am questioning the rationality behind public sector (catering) and encircles another paradigm. Everybody seems under such preconditions to express a far more radical critique of the status quo than their professional positions allowed them to state both formally and informally. For this reason, it is very difficult for a researcher and a transformation agent not to be attracted by the reservoir of frustrations and unreleased desires to transcend reality with coherent and meaningful alternatives that sprout in such situations. And it is very difficult not to identify the Action Researcher as an agent who's particular sphere of operation is about creating possibilities for a democratic and cooperative production a radical cultural reforms, rather than pragmatic reforms within organisational settings that are not contested.

It is inevitably a delicate and contested question as to what is to be considered as a process leading in the direction of sustainability, democratisation and happiness, and what is not. As far as my experiences and theoretical reflections tell me, radical social innovations pointing in the direction of the good society, must be based on a transdisciplinary approach that allowed the participants to create social innovation on the basis of their desires for another *life world* and subsequently systematically increase the robustness and exemplarity in an interactive relation with the surroundings. It demands the establishment of different forms of *free space*s and a certain productive tension between these spheres and everyday life in time and space. But it also requires that the researcher has a certain sensitivity towards relations and possible relations across the field and an ability to identify the intersection between the spheres of the various potential participants. In other words, an ability in an open, inquiring and inviting manner to create a preliminary story line that locates the diversity of professional and *lifeworld* rooted ethical claims and values within an alternative and meaningful horizon of development underpinned by a more substantial type of rationality.

My recent experiences have also made me more attentive towards how democratic development from below can be facilitated. It is inherent in the tradition of *critical-utopian Action Research* to privilege the underprivileged in the joint encirclement of a desired future and empower the participants and their projects in critical dialogues with friendly outsiders, helping the process to survive in the harsh reality, and exploit the cracks in ruling structures and rationalities in favour of a new societal coherence and reason. Transferred into my social field this approach encounters some harsh social realities, which make this strategy very demanding, especially for individual researchers with limited time. The elderly in nursing homes are generally too weak to participate, and the staff are so stretched in their working life that continuous participation is a good as impossible. The *Future Creating Workshops* showed a great awareness of the misers of modern public sector catering and underscores the diversity of social imaginations and resources that live in workers and potentially could be unleashed in processes of social transformation. In the wake of the continuous talks with experts, bureaucrats, researchers, unionists, managers, workers and the elderly it became quite clear that all the constituent elements of *the good public sector (catering)* exist as experiences and social imaginations just under the surface.

With this experience in mind, I do not think it is fruitful to think of development from below as something connected with a certain social hierarchy or class. Instead, I think we should acknowledge that we on one hand have a society which is increasingly culturally eroded, functionally differentiated and disciplined to a certain productivist and neo-liberal rationality, with a good portion of existential fear and insecurity as a result. But on the other hand the utopian ideas and social imaginations of alternative futures, of another and more transcendent life world, are ever more present across the societies different spheres. Development from a *life world* perspective is about creating space and time for the unfolding and merging of these social building blocs into robust social alternatives.

I find the notion of story lines shaping and shaped around discourse coalitions a way to tackle and overcome the functional differentiated and self-referential spheres of knowledge and practice, a very instructive and fruitful figure to have in mind when doing Action Research. But when it comes to how a shared horizon can practically be established democratically I doubt that Hajer's approach has much to offer. The utopian horizon that arose in the actual process is cross-disciplinary, but it is not consensus orientated. It is in clear conflict with the hegemonic system embracing the development of the public sector. But it is not without chances. Not only public sector catering, but also the public sector in general is saturated with crisis and the strategies of *new public management* and techno-rationalisation only seems to postpone and intensify this cultural crises. Coherent visions and sketches which are able to combine the need for social recognition, health, the beautiful, sustainability and democracy are not only possible but also necessary. My research has shown how a great number of people working within the system at different levels are rejecting the ruling rationalities in favour of something else and better. Who says that this doubt could not spread and open up the possibility for radical reforms and social experiments?

References

Barton, A. D. (et al.) (2000), "High food wastage and low nutritional intakes in hospital patients". *Clin Nutr* 19 (6) 445–449

Beck, A. M. & Ovesen, L. (2002) "Body mass index, weight loss and energy intake of old Danish nursing home residents and home-care clients". *Scand J Caring Sci.* pp: 16:86–90.

Braverman, Harry (1974) *Labour and monopoly capital: the degradation of work in the twentieth century*, New York: Monthly Review Press.

Danish Institute for Food and Veterinary Research (2004)

Christistensen, Gudrun (1998) *Diskursiv regulering af ernæringspraksis: en vidensarkæologisk og genealogisk analyse af rationaliseringstendenser i Statens Husholdningsråds pjecer om mad og ernæring 1936–1985*, PhD. Diss., KVL

Hajer, Maarten (1995) *The politics of environmental discourse: ecological modernization and the policy process*, Oxford: Clarendon Press.

Hansen, Else (1993) *Fra skånekost til menuvalg: økonomapersonalets og Økonomaforeningens historie fra 1960–1992*, København: Økonomaforeningen.

Hjort, Kartin (2001) *Moderniseringen af den offentlige sektor*, Fredriksberg: Roskilde Universitetsforlag.

Klausen, Kurt Klaudi & Krister Ståhlberg (eds.) (1998) *New Public Management i Norden*, Odense: Odense Universitetsforlag.

Kristensen, Niels Heine et al. (2002) *Anvendelse af økologiske fødevarer i kommuner og amter*, København: DTU & Fødevaredirektoratet.

Lang, Tim & Michael Heasman (2004) *Food Wars*, London: Earthscan.

Nielsen, Kurt Aagaard, Birger Steen Nielsen & Peter Olsén (1996) "From Silent to Talkative Participants. A discussion of Technique as Social Construction", in: *Economic and Industrial Democracy* Vol. 17 No. 3, London: Sage, Aug. (pp. 359–386)

– (2001) "Sustainability and Industrial Democracy", pp. 78–87, in: *Sustainability in Action,* J. Köhn, J. Gowdy, J. van der Straaten (eds.) Cheltenham: Edward Elgar.

Petersen, Jan (2000) *Hvad er rationalitet?*, København: Samfundslitteratur.

Pierson, Christopher (1991) *Beyond the Welfare State?*, Cambridge: Polity Press.

Pålshaugen, Øjvind (1998) "Development Coalitions in Working Life: the Enterprise Development 2000 Program", in: *Norway in Dialogues on work and innovation* Vol. 6, Amsterdam: John Benjamins.

Økonomaen (2003) The Danish Dietetic Association, Vol. 5.

EVA SCHWENCKE

16. Free Space in Action Research and in Project Oriented Traineeship

16.1 Introduction

In this article I present personal experiences gained from an Action Research project aimed at developing the culture of real life projects for 3rd year students at The Norwegian School of Information Technology (NITH) in Norway. The main conclusion of the experiment is that the students were encouraged to see new perspectives concerning their real life projects. They questioned their traditional student role and wanted to have more control over the project's initial phase: its establishment. They challenged the NITH's project culture, and wanted to provide an extended free space within project learning. The research also led to questioning the tutor's role as a representative of the institution. The experiment revealed that critical Action Research can relate itself to project learning in educational institutions.

The basis for my interest in Action Research is a background in practical work including teaching and learning. The most valuable experience I have gained is that learning and creativity take place in an environment where the content is perceived as meaningful, refreshing, and challenging, both for the curious student and for the inspired teacher.

The main project for NITH's third year students, the last of several learning project experiences, consists of an assignment; a real life project given by a private, public, or non-profit organisation not linked to the NITH. The students are meant to develop a functional product over a period of four months during which they spend three days a week in an organisation. This is considered the final practical exam for the

IT students. Through the reciprocal exchange of knowledge, the project creates an opportunity to forge useful links between the academic and the organisations' worlds. The students contribute to increasing the organisation's capacity, as well as to creative development within the organisation. Thus, the projects are contributing to academia's so-called third task, namely their participation in the development of businesses in the region (Brulin 1998). There are three parties in these real life projects, the students, the university colleges and, in the cases presented here, the enterprises. In this article I will focus on the students' role, and only touch on that of other parties portraying them from the students' perspective. Enterprises are usually quite satisfied with the projects and the majority make use of the products created by the students. To increase the quality and to have more inventive projects, however, a better dialogue between the students and their respective enterprises has to be developed. This concerns both the scope of the project and the development of the product. There is a need for a dialogue between equal parties, which should be characterized by reciprocity, confidence, respect and recognition. A dialogue based on asymmetry is always in danger of creating disrespect, mistrust, manipulation and rigid control. There are great differences in the ways that students handle this relation. In a traditional learning situation, the students often have difficulties feeling safe and as equals in the dialogue with the enterprise's representative. The traditional role of the student is often characterized by a) poor confidence in their own competencies, and therefore b) the expectation that the other party takes the initiative, asks the relevant questions, and prepares for the students' work, and c) lack of practice in using their own experiences and thinking alternatively.

Students often have important, special, competencies, which are unknown to the enterprise. However, at the beginning of a project, students do not always take the necessary initiatives to decide what competencies are needed. Many times they do not take initiatives to explore the meaning of the defined scopes and their contexts, including the specifications of demands, or they do not take initiatives to collaborate with the enterprise when making definitions. Even the cleverest students, the students with better marks, wait for the initiative to be taken by the enterprise or the tutor. With disrespect for their own competence, they end up carrying out orders made by others. The

traditional student role emerged through a long history of power relations between teacher and student, which were accepted as common
sense and were reflected by similar relations in society as a whole. The
relationship expresses a view of knowledge as a transmission from the
educated to the learner – with an accompanying lack of initiative.

Reflection has been an integrated part of project organized learning
at NITH from the beginning. For each project a "reflection note" has to
be written by the students. This has been a way of integrating reflection
into students' daily studies to strengthen learning. For this chapter, the
following definition of reflection was chosen: *"Reflection is more or less
conscious and more or less all inclusive judgments about the connections between
our acts and their consequences"* (Wahlhagen et al. 2002, p. 17[1]). The authors
make a distinction between *"how we are acting"* (reflection) and *"why we
are acting"* (critical reflection). But is this enough? Can Action Research
contribute to encouraging reflection? In this connection it is convenient
to use Argyris and Schön's (1983) work where they distinguish between
reflection making the changes of a single loop, and the reflection making the more basic changes of the double loop, the changes of structures
and prerequisites for actions.

Undertaking real life projects at NITH takes its inspiration from
Problem Based Project Pedagogy as formulated by Knud Illeris (1981),
and which is based on Oskar Negt's (1994) Critical Theory and John
Dewey's (2000) pragmatic philosophy. The pedagogy relating to project
work challenges the student's role in three ways: by making them
engage in real life experiences, by participatory undertakings and by the
relative free space at their disposal. The students gain different experiences from projects, and they do not benefit equally from making them.
So, in order to develop our knowledge of practicing real life projects, I
wanted to carry out an experiment introducing new perspectives drawn
from Action Research.

An Action Research project was chosen to make the students, through
their experiences, strengthen their subjectivity *before* they enter their
dialogues with the enterprises and the NITH:s tutor. In this way, they
were empowered and thereby able to reduce the asymmetry of the situation. A workshop where the representative from the enterprise, the

---

1 Translation mine.

NITH tutor and the students all participated in a Dialogue Conference was considered. However, it was necessary to give the students time and space, and an opportunity to find their own platform as a starting point for the dialogue with the other parties.

By strengthening the students' subjectivity and individuality, they will be able to experience the existing project culture at NITH, including constraints and attitudes, and possibly point to spaces that need improvement. This led to my research question for this Action Research project, namely: *"From asymmetry to symmetry in real life projects: What can be done to improve the project culture at NITH in order to facilitate the students in being real contributors to the enterprises?"* Project organized learning and Action Research have many commonalities. An important concept that emerged in my PhD work was that of free space (Nielsen 1996). Free space is a technique of counteracting the asymmetry, something more than empty time and room. The space is structured by a workshop organized in such a way that students create their own experiences in the free space. This will encourage processes, which will strengthen their subjectivity, ability, and the opportunity for more creative reflection. The free space in real life projects can contribute to strengthening the integrity and the creativity of the students and the integrity of the university college in relation to the business environment.

16.2 Free space's contribution to making change possible

The creative and initiating attitude that I often miss among the students can be seen as being rooted in ambiguousness, the choice is either to adapt to the dominating structures or not. Man can adapt to power, but not entirely. There is always a remainder, the transcendental ego, as in Hans Skjervheim's (1973) philosophy, that will not be disciplined or adapted. In the ability of man to reflect about his actions and himself, there is a possibility for change. This possibility "can be used or lie there unused". There are some possibilities of choice, which cannot be seen because they are unconscious. Man can choose to avoid making choices, letting others make choices for them, to let heritage and the environment, habitus, decide. That is also a choice, which Skjervheim emphasises. But do we have possibilities to choose, not just an apparent choice? Are we not all exercising power?[2]

16.2.1 Is power in each process?

Foucault's concept of the way power works in modern societies provides the hierarchical theories of power as being constrained from outside – power is gradually and increasingly socialized and internalized by the individual. Man himself carries anonymous power; power is in all processes. The discourses about right or wrong, rational and irrational, normal and abnormal are a part of our ordinary life, and they influence our perception of reality. The discourses decide the theme, and what and who is important, relevant and interesting. In measuring oneself in relation to the expressions of the apparently open public, it is most convenient to adapt to its norms.

What do the students do? Traditional hierarchies and the traditional complementary teacher/student roles have been reduced, to a certain extent, through the principles of "responsibility for one's own learning". At the same time, there have been changes in the structures of working life where Taylorism has, in some areas, become less dominant. The growing development of technology has focused on a need for the staff members' professional competence. Thus there is a tendency that projects offered by enterprises have changed character. From being dominated by performing technical problem solving, the projects offered have sometimes been more like a partnership involving dialogue and collaboration. Hence the content of power and the content of roles have changed. These tendencies open up the possibility for problematizing the students' real life projects and questioning how to improve the dialogue between the students and the enterprise from being one way to being mutual.

16.2.2 The free space of the Future Creating Workshop

To be able to develop alternative ideas and ways of thinking in everyday working life, critical Action Research has focused on facilitating partici-

---

2 These questions are posed in order to express the problem. As mentioned above, however, this will not be further developed in this chapter.

pation in a free space, an experienced based free space where "reality is set out of function" (Nielsen 1996), it is not only the discourse based free space. The ideas about free space are inspired by Robert Jungk and Critical Theory (Kurt Aagaard Nielsen and Birger Steen Nielsen in this book). The ambition with the idea of the social free space is that the participants strengthen their subjectivity, become more conscious about their ambiguities, their own ideas, alternatives and possibilities in the real world. This is not happening in a space of pure rationality, but in a space structured to make emotional experiences, and the critical reflections emerging from these experiences. The principles of the Future Creating Workshop are a way of structuring the social free space (see Lise Drewes Nielsen's Chapter in this book). This workshop is organized as a training area relating to the democratic learning processes with space for change and processes of renewal, to get to know possible activities to be used in real life. The Future Creating Workshop takes place in a room away from the work place with enough space for the physical movement of all the participants. It is performed in an atmosphere of democratic processes, accept and recognition. Learning processes are based on a space for social imagination, everyday life ways of thinking, and on having a joint objective. It is a general perspective of "being subjective" (Skjervheim 1976), this is not education for something instrumental.

The free space of the Future Creating Workshop is more physical than the free space based on what Habermas terms the language discourse (Gustavsen 2001). Experiences gained from the Future Creating Workshop can provide awareness about one's own wishes and requirements relatively independent of a predefined perception of reality and enhance distinguished alternatives through reflections.

Foucault's concept of power tries to close the image of a social free space. The technique used in Future Creating Workshops tries, however, to penetrate this concept of power and opens up for the possibility of subjectivity to distance oneself from the discipline.

16.3 The Action Research Project: "Better dialogue in real life projects" – the organizing and principles of the experiment.

The experiment *"Better dialogue in real life projects"* was undertaken during the autumn of 2003 and spring 2004 in relation to the Bachelor IT students' final year's project. The experiment must be understood in terms of the interface among three different fields, the culture of Information Technology, the culture of enterprise projects and the culture of learning projects. These three fields are influenced by the new information based and network based economy (Svensson 2002), and thus a twofold perspective exists, a development logic of hermeneutic and a productive logic of science. This twofold perspective is constituted by the interchange between, for instance, "reflection and processes" as opposed to "efficient action based on routine or rules", and between "alternative thinking" and "problem solving according to existing rules". The twofold perspective in these fields influences NITH, both its students and its teaching staff, and is experienced in the real life projects offered by enterprises. It leads to a certain amount of insecurity regarding norms of right or wrong, hence there is a high level of instrumentality and adaptive thinking, but also a level of open-mindedness, and curiosity concerning new work and modes of thinking.

NITH has a long tradition of having the students perform their bachelor real life projects in cooperation with private enterprises. The projects have been recommended due to the great amount of learning students engage in, and the enterprises' benefit and have therefore been prestigious for the NITH. However, the projects have been pulled between the influences of the development logic and the product logic. There is a discussion as to what extent the projects should be product oriented enterprise projects or, explicitly, also experience based learning projects. The culture of project work at NITH, which is expressed by the attitude and guidelines of performance, carries the two conflicting logics. It is a general perception that the project's method has great potential, its weakness being that students often seem to be led by short term instrumental demands from both the school and enterprise.

16.3.1 The organizing of the experiment "A better dialogue in real life projects"

The experiment included two project groups of five students each, and started at the beginning of the academic year in August 2003, and ended in June the following year. An important precondition was for the experiment to strengthen the work of the project.

The experiment incorporated three workshops:

- The Future Creating Workshop (workshop 1), at the start of first term
- The resource workshop (workshop 2), in the middle of first term
- The public and experience workshop (workshop 3), after examination in spring term

Between the workshops, meetings were arranged with each group with the intention of sustaining the groups' own long term principals for their work, their utopian ideas, to ensure that these were kept vivid and were not lost as the focus was on short-term activities. Two meetings were arranged between workshops 1 and 2, and four meetings between workshops 2 and 3. The principle of the free space was emphasised by the researcher (myself) who was neither as representative of NITH nor a group tutor. The researcher's detachment from the examination and the power to influence the assessments was important for the experiment.

16.3.2 Organizing of the Future Creating Workshop

The Future Creating Workshop was organized along Jungk's (1989) principles: the critical phase, the utopian phase, and the implementation/realisation phase. The scope of the workshop created an arena for students to establish their real life projects. The definition of the main theme was collaboratively elaborated: *"What do we want to work with in our project? How would we like the collaboration between the students, the enterprise representative and the NITH tutor to be carried out in our main project"*, and was directly connected to their own student project. The democratisation principle was implemented according to the workshop guidelines, and through organized training, the participants had collec-

378

tive experiences of democratic practice. In the critical phase, they had to use their own previous negative experiences with their earlier project work as the basis for their utopian ideas. Working with utopias through creative processes was the most important issue in the Future Creating Workshop. The intention was to be conscious of their inherent wishes and dreams. Through evolving a common document of realizable utopian sketches, the participants should also get to know each other's utopian ideas.

16.3.3 Students' utopian ideas: The ideal project – combination of professional and the personal wishes

The students have great expectations when undertaking their main project, which is done in the final term of their Bachelor's programme. Expectations about their project are influenced by the short-sighted requirements for good assessments, as well as an experience of the professional life in combination with everyday life. Similarly, this combination influenced the utopian documents: the dream of innovation, the product's usefulness to the public, the wish to be valued, the wish that the people surrounding them should be their partners in dialogue and supporters, the wish that the chosen enterprise meets the requests of a single mother: a town centre location, as well as regulated working hours. The utopian document functioned as a basis for developing criteria for choosing an enterprise and for normative guidelines for the project.

16.3.4 The students' results, the completed real life project

The two project groups, A and B, delivered their products to the enterprises and their written reports to the university college, received the highest grades. Group A delivered a prototype for a module for a large dental system. Group B delivered a "stand alone" application, a CRM system; a product completed for sale, and which was successfully launched on the marked a couple of weeks after the examination. Group B functioned as expected in the *"Better dialogue ..."*-experiment. On the basis of the students' initiative, the enterprise changed their system architecture during the project process. Group A had significant problems in the process of their project. Their product demanded a component, which was to be produced by another party in the enterprise. The component was not finished and the project group waited unquestioningly for a long time before recognizing the problem and reacting. They chose to develop a prototype product instead. In addition, they wrote their paper on why IT projects fail. As a learning project it turned out to be a success, but as a product oriented project it failed.

16.4 How did free space in the social experiment, "Better dialogue in real life projects" manifest itself?

I now go on to discuss my experiences gained from the social experiment, the organization, participants' expressions and actions, as well as my own reflections, based on the process' resumes and diary notes.

Did group A accept the asymmetric situation by immobilizing themselves? The student role confused them so that they did not take initiatives, trusting enterprise assurances and just waiting. Why should these students accept their asymmetric relationship? They all had the potential to see through the unequal situation and be able to change it earlier. Through participating in a *"Better dialogue ..."*-experiment, they had experience with democratic actions, were trained to use their previous experiences, and to use their utopian ideas as horizons and references for their activities. After being exposed to these experiences, the students did not, however, manage to change the relationship with their enterprise before it was too late for their assignment. This situation was too difficult for students to deal with, and it could not be expected that they could, they said. Hence the effects of a *"Better dialogue ..."*, experiment can be questioned. Did the training give the students the necessary consciousness of democratic processes, or was the training insufficiently systematic and for too short a time? Why did the experiment not live up to our expectations? These questions must be left open here, but they show that the research experiment did not produce clear short-term results. What could the potential be of experiencing structured free space in changing this situation? The students in group A could break the pattern of the powerless student role by being able to think in alternative ways and make their own strategy and plans by using their everyday perspective. By seeing themselves as equal partners in dialogue with the enterprise, the students could find ways of solving problems during the process. Experiences with structured free space can open this possibility. In a meeting in a *"Better dialogue ..."* experiment in February, the students in group A were confronted their utopian ideas and acknowledged the problem situation of their project. Their wishes to be equal partners and respected in the project process opened up the horizon. The free space revealed the problem, which was too difficult to express. They discovered each others' tacit feeling of uneasiness. The day after the meeting they started changing the situation by making relevant initiatives.

Why did the two groups have different results? Their real life projects had similar bases; apart from participating in a *"Better dialogue ..."*-experiment, they were all experienced students, almost the same age, had good assessments, ambitions, their engagement, same gender division (one woman and four men). They had different types of project and different enterprises chosen on well-founded criteria. Both assignments demanded high levels of IT knowledge, workload and self-reliance. Both were, in different ways, dependant on the surroundings, the first project was thought to be good enough for launching on the market. The other assignment demanded other parties in the enterprise make a component for their use. What distinguished the two projects? Two different fields distinguished the projects, firstly, the possibilities for the students to influence the project or business, and, secondly, the enterprise representative's acceptance. Group B, with their "stand alone" application, negotiated with their enterprise and proposed improvements to the system's architecture. Group A could have influenced their project in spite of their dependence on another party and in spite of the low degree of acceptance by their enterprise representative. They could have made a clarification of their own process of technology development at an early stage, as well as analysing and clearing alternative solutions and following up on schedules. Alternatives could have been the basis for negotiations about priorities and changes in the project process.

16.4.1 *The researcher's normative role and the free space.*
Were the democratic processes in the Future Creating Workshop

genuine, or were they hidden manipulation? How did the researcher's mindset influence the participants? By making use of a Future Creating Workshop, the researcher made a conscious normative choice of a research technique and method structured to encourage participants' way of working. The participants' experiences, perspectives and premises were the interesting issues. There were three ways of assuring democracy in this research experiment: a) the topic emerged from the collaboration between the researcher and the students, b) researcher assuring the democratic structure of Future Creating Workshop, c) the subsequent advocating of students' utopian ideas by researcher. a) The topic for the Future Creating Workshop was proposed by a researcher on the basis of knowledge about the students' reality and the researcher's own interests. The proposed topic was discussed and agreed on as being the common theme meaningful to everybody. All parties could, however, withdraw from the Future Creating Workshop if they did not feel they owned the topic and the process. b) The standard structures of the Future Creating Workshop were chosen to carry out a social experiment on the participants' premises. The essential task of the researcher as a workshop leader was to assure the creation and functioning of the workshop according to the established guidelines, and that the agreed theme guided the content of the workshop. It was important for the researcher to be the attentive and neutral workshop leader to ensure that the Future Creating Workshop accomplishing its intentions. c) The workshop leader's task was to remind the participants about their utopian ideas throughout the entire project process. Hence, the researcher's role was not neutral, but normative, to confront the participants with their expressed wishes to avoid them disappearing into the usual instrumental orientation of their study. Using the students' way to express their wishes through their utopian document, the researcher positioned herself normatively, avoiding, however, transforming their issues.

To sum up briefly, the researcher's effect is consciously used to develop democratic processes by a) establishing a common theme of Future Creating Workshops, b) engaging in structures of Future Creating Workshop on the participants' premises, c) following up of the participants' utopian ideas. In addition it is essential to underline the importance of researcher avoiding the role of a power embedded representative of the university college. Simultaneously, the achievement

was that the students gaining experiences of participating in democratic processes which have significance for being active partners in
democratic processes in the world of reality outside the Future Creating
Workshop.

16.4.2 *Inspirations for development of the tutor's role*

Inspirations for the development of the tutor's role emerged from the
Action Research social experiment. The experiment showed that the
empowerment processes could be set in motion through opening up
more evident free space. The students were supported in building their
self-confidence and they were encouraged to choose an assignment
that was meaningful to them, both short term and long term. They felt
that they could trust that the encouragement to make use of the free
space was real, not empty words. For instance, the February meeting
changed group A's attitude to the project showed that it was possible to
put processes in motion through the conscious use of free space. These
measures of free space should be possible for the tutor to apply in the
everyday life of the university. This would demand another understanding of the student and tutor roles. The project culture had to be further
developed by reducing the tutors' power representation and increasing
the legitimacy of the maintenance of free space for the students. The
tutors' focus should be to support the students in how they solve their
problems – not to put forward their own solutions of the problems. To
be able to achieve this, the tutors' culture and attitudes must be reflected
in the free space in the teachers' own working situation. The teachers'
organisation must be encouraging empowerment processes, so that they
know in what way they have power of influence in everyday life. In that
way, they can be proficient project tutors who sustain the free space and
the democratic processes for the students.

16.5 Conclusions

What experiences can be drawn from the Action Research social experiment? The research question was: *"From asymmetry to symmetry in real life
projects: What can be done to improve the project culture at NITH to facilitate*

the students in being real contributors to the enterprises?" The experiment encouraged the students to develop new perspectives on their real life projects and my own perception of the project culture. The students undoubtedly gained much in acknowledging the free space, especially in the initial phase of their project. The main conclusion so far raises the questions of how to facilitate free space for the students in their projects, and how to give them the opportunity to benefit from the existing possibilities presented by free space.

16.5.1 *Three important lessons can be drawn from this experiment*

Firstly, the students gained from developing their utopian ideas at the start of their project. It was important for them to control the initial phase to be able to choose the assignment, and have a feeling of power over the situation. They used the possible free space. On this issue, the students contributed proposals for structural changes, and improvements of project culture at NITH in accordance with the concept of the double loop (Schön 1983). They put forward the principle of students choosing the enterprise, and not the other way around, namely enterprises choosing student groups. Hence students can be the driving force in project development. Further, they want the information about the project premises and constraints to be given at an earlier time, not in October as now, but already at the end of their 2nd year, so students have more time to make preparations. They proposed that perspectives concerning free space should be a part of their curriculum in their 1st class. In addition, they suggested that the student groups should be expected to choose their enterprise early in the autumn and that the external breakfast meeting with enterprises offering opportunities, usually in October, could give the students further possibilities for choice.

The second interesting experience was that I, in my researcher's role, acknowledged a different free space relating to students than through my ordinary tutor's role. In my practice as a project tutor, I thought that I was always tutoring on the students' premises. Through my experience as a researcher without being the representative of the school, I used this independence for advocating the students' future wishes in quite another way than through the ordinary tutor's role. The students noticed this and related to it. What does this imply for the tutor's role at NITH in the future? How can the tutor's role facilitate the free space to a larger degree than today? Such discussions take place today among tutors and so the project has the learning culture at NITH.

Further, I pose the question of whether it was right to choose the Future Creating Workshop, a technique from the world of the humanities, in developing technology students' assumedly "narrow" questions. Is it relevant to bring the concept of free space and logic of everyday life into a world of technology regulated by the logic of the product? The two cultures correspond in their affectedness by human beings.

To be able to reflect about alternatives, however, it is sometimes necessary to withdraw from the real world, for instance a social experiment. Business leaders have been aware of this and had the opportunity of using social free space in their leader enhancement activities. Making working life and academia sustainable, we can encourage free spaces in daily life so that ordinary people have space for their everyday reflections. If the logic of everyday life is an alternative to the logic of the product, creativity and innovations can be put forward breaking patterns of power. Organizations' norms can be discussed, the possibility of thinking alternatively is opened, and the fact that solutions are not predefined, can be discovered. This requires a constant consciousness to question alternatively transcending constraints simultaneously relating to reality.

16.5.2 Implementation

The final challenge in the Action Research project is how the results are implemented at NITH. The diffusion process is a constantly returning theme within Action Research, as further elaborated in Chapter 2 of this book. The most important thing in that sense, to my opinion, is that the existence of the social experiment and students' engagement has confronted the atmosphere of consensus and revealed some central questions, made some values evident, and initiated discussions in the organization. It has become more legitimate to discuss experience-based learning, students' free space and democratic participation among teachers and tutors. It has also become meaningful to discuss dialectic processes between structures in the project culture and learning processes. It is crucial, however, that both teachers and leaders are involved in the further development of the common goal and scope: better student learning culture – enhancing further request for and thus sustainability of the NITH. These are future processes.

Has the Action Research experiment contributed to developing the project pedagogy? Many similarities between the project pedagogy and critical Action Research have emerged. The main perspective of student's empowerment is in the foundation of project pedagogy, even if it has changed much since the seventies (Ulriksen 1997). However, the importance of this Action Research experiment has primarily been the contribution of a more distinct free space perspective with a utopian horizon through the Future Creating Workshop. Secondly, my own experience of the tutor's role as the representative of power has been more evident. Further progress at the university college will, however, reveal if new cultural perspectives can be opened. So far, these experiences have brought new angels to the space of pedagogy of real life projects to be challenged by developing categories for PhD work in the future.

References

Brulin, G, (1998) *Den tredje uppgiften: högskola och omgivning i samverkan*, Stockholm: SNS Förlag

Dewey, J. (2000) "Barnet og læreplanen", pp. 120–134, in *Tekster om læring*, Illeris, K., (ed.), Fredriksberg: Roskilde Universitetsforlag.

Gustavsen, B. (2001). "Research and the Challenges of Working Life". In *Interaktiv forskning för utveckling av teori och praktik*, Svensson, L. et al. (eds.) 2002 Stockholm: Arbetslivsinstitutet.

Illeris, K. (1981), *Modkvalificeringens pædagogik: problemorientering, deltagerstyring og eksemplarisk indlæring* København: Unge pædagoger.

Jungk, R. and Müllert, N. R. (1989): *Håndbog i Fremtidsværksteder*, Copenhagen: Forlaget Politisk Revy.

Negt, O. (1994) "Hvad skal en arbejder vide for at finde sig til rette i verden i dag?", in B. S. Nielsen et al., *Arbejde og subjektivitet* (Skriftserie for Erhvervs og voksenuddannelsesgruppen 26/94), pp. 43–62. Fredriksberg: Roskilde Universitetcenter.

Nielsen, K. Aa. (1996). *Arbejdets sociale orientering*. Copenhagen: Forlaget Sociologi.

Schön, D. (1983). *The reflective practitioner*. New York: Basic Books.

Skjervheim, H. (1976): *Deltakar og Tilskadar og andre essays*. Oslo: Tanum-Norli

Svensson, L. et al. (eds.) (2002): *Interaktiv forskning för utveckling av teori och praktik*. Stockholm: Arbetslivsinstitutet.

Ulriksen, L. (1997) *Prosjektpædagogikk – hvorfor det?* Unipæd-prosjektet, Erhvervs- og voksenuddannelsesgruppen, Fredriksberg: Roskilde Universitetscenter

Wahlgren, B. et al. (2004). *Refleksion og læring. Kompetanceudvikling i arbejdslivet*. Copenhagen: Samfundslitteratur.

KURT AAGAARD NIELSEN

AND LENNART SVENSSON

17. How to Learn Action Research

We have presented eight chapters written by PhD students or by those who have recently completed their PhD. The chapters are substantial in the meaning that they present results and experiences from ongoing or finished Action Research projects.

The authors were asked to reflect on how and what they have learnt about Action Research during their PhD projects, what they learned from Action Research history or theory, and what they learned by experience – from the difficulties they encountered, happy incidents and solutions, personal education etc.

In the following pages we will draw parallels and make analyses relating to each chapter. We end by providing some advice for teaching and learning Action Research, and thoughts concerning future challenges.

First we draw attention to what we found was most surprising: none of the authors regret or complain about the obligatory involvement of their universities[1] in their doctoral projects. Most of the eight authors are aware that the involvement of their universities causes problems and difficulties such as keeping to a planned timetable, spending so much time managing practical relations, and do coordinative work, so that one hardly has time left for the necessary reading and reflecting state of the art in the research field. This we know from dialogues with the authors at a PhD-course in 2004.

---

1 Four of the authors began with their Action Research projects being hosted by a University; the other four invented projects which were created outside universities and the involvement of University was in the form of cooperation.

On the contrary, all the chapters signal a *positive* internalisation of theoretical and methodological concepts and ideals as part of the reflection on activities in the field. Here we observe a cultural change; for many years Action Researchers were excluded or excluded themselves from the traditional academic context. Action research was identified, and identified itself, as being in opposition to both mainstream and critical academic discourses. Often books or reports written by Action Researchers started with a critique of traditional academic research as being unproductive or even useless because of its abstractness or its objectifying empirical approach. The critique involved a kind of polarity in relation to universities. The substance of the critique is still there; but at the same time young Action Researchers do include themselves in researchers' societies – and not only in an Action Researchers' society. They learn from their involvement in the universities.

You can explain this as a purely cultural change expressing the fact that Action Researchers have become more relaxed in the landscape of researchers' professional positions. We presume this is not the only explanation. The change of attitude might just as well be in that of the university population. As mentioned in Chapter 2 the move towards the Mode II paradigm of knowledge is administratively and practically undeniable for the some of the universities' population, and so the more relaxed attitude may also express the fact that Action Researchers have become a bit more welcome in the universities/amongst academics. We do not claim that we are moving towards a new harmony based on the Mode II paradigm, but the positions are unclear and today you find Action Researchers arguing against the pragmatism found in the Mode II paradigm (see Svensson and Aagaard in Chapter 2; Nielsen and Nielsen in Chapter 4) and you can find those who are not Action Researchers arguing from within a Mode II paradigm.[2]

---

2   In Gibbons' and Nowotny's examples of the coming Mode II paradigm there is no obligation to employ an Action Research methodology. What you find is a trans-disciplinary obligation and not necessarily a reorientation of the division of labour between creators of knowledge and the creators of change processes.

17.1 Learning Action Research from historical trends and experience

In chapters 1 and 2 Action Research history was said to be moving *from an experimental design towards a learning design*. The trend is related to the surfacing of the Mode II research paradigm. The experimental design should develop new forms of organisation and democratic participative structures, and as a generalisation the experiments should open up the possibility for politically supported reforms in working life, community development etc. In the learning design, you give up that ambition and, as in the Mode II paradigm, the meaning and truth proclaimed in the projects are local or contextual. All the doctoral projects presented above follow this trend to a certain degree. None of them hold the idea that you can easily generalise knowledge and, so to say, through enlightenment come to reforms in large scale.

The problem of generalisation, however, is seen as important in all the chapters. The two chapters written by Norwegians use a design, which seems very close to the classical socio-technical model. Ronny Sannerud initiated his Action Research project in cooperation with partners in the construction industry with the shared idea of setting up an experiment with new participative arenas for professional learning as practice-based learning. In a narrow sense you can say that the project came to nothing because the model ceased to be implemented after the project was completed. Sannerud uses the experiment as a platform for reflection among planners to improve the interchange between learning at schools and workplace learning. So the ambition was to achieve some kind of new, general, knowledge about practical learning. You cannot call it an attempt to arrive at a more general theory, but you can, in the sense of learning from case studies (Flyvbjerg 1998), call it an attempt to illuminate knowledge, which can be used in the political processes of planning.

Eva Schwencke is also very explicit in calling her Action Research project an experiment. She defines the possibilities of generalisations from the experiment as a question of : 1) implementation through a new dialogue about the experiment in a larger arena – a local public sphere; 2) a development of the concept of project learning in IT – education. She hesitates to make generalisations but struggles with the problem of bringing the experimental, local, learning to two different kinds of public: the local public sphere of the educational institution where the experiment is being undertaken, and a professional public.

Ditte Tofteng and Mia Husted's, and Jens Christian Elle's chapters use the concept of experiment positively. The projects behind the chapters are, however, not organised as experiments, but as learning arenas, which aim to installation of social experiments. Both projects turn the discussion about the experiment on its head: they spend much effort in preparing a "bottom up" social experiment which also means that they actively involve experts, professionals, politicians etc. in the planning of a (future) social experiment. One can interpret their projects as an effort to reach a long term goal: public learning based on bottom up social experiments. So, from the beginning, they aimed at transcending the local perspective and practical horizon. If they succeed in their projects, they attack the problem of structural conservatism inherent in the Mode II paradigm and in the form of Action Research, which follows a learning design.

The projects positively dealing with an experimental design in Action Research follow the idea of experiments as being a tool for creating *free space* (see also Chapters 3 and 4). This entails establishing arenas, which neutralise the power of reality. The experiment is in that sense a tool allowing social change and reforms, which might seem un-realistic. Robert Jungk (1975) writes thus about the arguments for social experiments:

"The greatest advantage of using social experiments (in social or political reforms) is the reduction of fear. The fear about risks connected to untried reforms has to be taken seriously. A social experiment – also illuminated by researchers – cannot totally take away the fear, but it can be reduced substantially" (*our translation*; Jungk 1975).[3]

So at least in that tradition of recent Action Research, the notion of "experiment" is still going strong and is seen as a critical tool which, can be used to avoid conservatism in the learning design.

---

3   R. Jungk wrote this in a postscript to the German edition of Meadows et al. *Limits to growth: Die Grenzen des Wachtums* (1975).

In the chapters contributed by the Finnish and the two Swedish authors, the trend towards learning design is confirmed. But in all the chapters, the authors try to turn the "local learning" towards more general concepts such as Ann-Christine Larsson's discussion of the implications for a theory of empowerment.

We can conclude that the doctoral students have been critical when adopting the Mode II arguments; they have evidently turned their project design in a direction of "learning design" but without forgetting the need for reflection about general societal structures.

Another trend to be observed was the movement *from a consensus paradigm, to a conflict paradigm and back again* to consensus-oriented Action Research. Only Sannerud started the project with an assumption that normatively aimed at a consensus based regime of collaboration between partners (in this case in the construction industry). Most other chapters make no such assumptions. Instead, they let the dialogues reveal whether consensus or conflict illumination should be the result of the research project. On the one hand, Eva Amundsdotter's Interactive Research project on gender starts with the assumption that male domination is a part of the culture of working life. On the other hand, she searches for a general change in gender culture at the working place. The dialogues in the project partly end up by making dominance transparent, and partly overcoming the dominance by means of institutionalised reflection on inequality in working life. The researcher, herself a gendered individual, helps maintain the twofold perspective.

In their project, Mia Husted and Ditte Tofteng strive to establish solidarity and a respectful dialogue among people excluded from ordinary labour market and between excluded people and included people. The excluded people (present in the cooperating group) experience suppression and lack of recognition. They end up creating respectful dialogues and shared activities with groups of people included in the labour market; but they have not yet been able to open a respectful dialogue between themselves and the Social Authorities. The project illuminates this relation in order to make it an objective for public discussion. Their project is an example of the need (sometimes) to start with the issues which are excluded from main stream discourse. The consensus orientation found in dialogue projects often makes such strategies impossible. Researchers' theoretical assumptions about people being structurally excluded from dialogues can facilitate new challenges.

The doctoral projects illustrate that the return to consensus can be practised as a return to an open ended dialogue allowing a perspective illuminating conflicts in the public sphere as well as allowing the creation of consensus-oriented dialogues for practical or institutional reforms. To decide when, and how, the Action Researchers facilitate conflict illumination and when, and how, he/she facilitates consensus-oriented dialogues is, of course, a part of the collaboration. However, each step in the facilitation process challenges theoretical assumptions made by the researcher and calls for a combination of critical social science theory and practical experience.

A third trend to be observed in mainstream Action Research we term the move *from employee-based values to broader values*. None of the doctoral projects have defined basic values in terms of strengthening workers' influence or as labour power, and none of the projects are institutionally connected to one part in a collaborative regime alone. In that sense, the trend towards broader values is confirmed. Projects are established to develop or civilise actual institutional practice: Eva Amundsdotter does not promote women's values or interests, but awareness about gender-relations as a quality in working life as such, Jens Christian Elle does not promote old people's interests in care and healthy food or nurse's interest in meaningful work, but ecological and socially sustainable living. Eva Schwencke does not promote student's interest in their own education, but her project promotes values of a democratic balance between the humanistic and technological orientations present in their education.

As the doctoral projects do not reflect on their institutional dependences (finance and leading researchers' control) to any great extent, we cannot reflect on how the values and orientations get modified by power in pragmatic negotiations. The problem of dependency on the institutional set up among researchers and collaborators is there; and we find that researchers today have a professional task to establish ethical rules and some kind of freedom in methods to let the broad values and orientations come up and become essential elements in dialogues. It may be in insisting of a so called *free space* as in Eva Schwencke's project, or in the insistence on an independent research path in any developmental Action Research project as in Marja Vehviläinen's project.

In Marja's project, the research supervisor from the university had a democratic function as an independent (interactive) partner in contrast to the more instrumental approach based on the values by the practical collaborators.

The broader values of Action Research only get the critical or democratic impact when the institutional frames of the research can successfully demand a methodological freedom and independence. As Ann-Christine Larsson's project also indicates, we face the necessity of not being a lonely researcher involved in Action Research, and engaging in both developmental work and critical reflection. As an individual Action Researcher, it is difficult to manage the need of relative freedom in the interpretations of values involved in the projects.

The fourth trend we observed can be formulated thus: *from grand theory or visions to pragmatic Action Research* – orientation towards realistic goals in the local context. This trend we interpreted as both a theoretical and a political trend. The chapters based on the PhD projects reflect both aspects.

Christopher Kjaer articulates an interesting reflection of the dilemma between having pragmatic considerations in the design of Action Research and considerations pertaining to the general theory of learning. On the one hand, his pragmatic considerations lead him to adjust his methods and the researcher' role to the necessities defined by the production logic. On the other hand, he argues that the experiences gained from the project should be generalised or interpreted in relation to a general theory of virtual learning; a theory with implications for the structure of education in a global world. He attempts to make the Action Research process useful for the further development of a general theory of distance learning. Kjaer's chapter is the most ambitious of the PhD projects in terms of turning experiences gained in the research towards the development of a general theory or of a theoretical field. As we also see in most of the other projects, Kjaer spends so much energy engaging the pragmatic dialogue based learning that the mediation to theoretical development is hardly completed. (We have the impression that Kjaer admits the limitations himself).

In the PhD projects defining themselves as being within the tradition of Critical Theory, the ambition to reflect the dilemma between grand visions and pragmatic results takes place as an attempt to give priority to developing utopian ideas within the core group of collaborators. Jens Christian Elle explicitly prioritises utopian ideas of the *good smelling nursing home* as a step towards a vision of a sustainable societal development. Eva Schwencke gives priority and space to students articulating utopian ideas about their education. To do so, is seen as a contribution to generating new visions and utopian alternatives to challenge a world which is becoming increasingly "network like" and without ideas about alternatives to the market economy. The attempts are however vulnerable; often new utopian horizons generated in Action Research projects collapse before moving into public debates. In Jens Christian Elle's project, he successfully reorganised his research plan in a way that the utopian horizons could be developed in dialogues involving intellectuals and critical professionals; but this also meant the postponing of pragmatic practical activities involving the workers and the old people in the nursing home.

Particularly in the Action Research projects inspired by Critical Theory, we find an active reflection and experimentation concerning how to mediate between big visions and pragmatic practical change processes (see for example Nielsen, Olsén and Aagaard Nielsen 1996). The problems of mediation between visions and pragmatic practice are not only related to new subjective orientations and dilemmas, but also to new political conditions. We live in an era without expressions of big reform projects in political institutions and organisations. We will not conclude whether this is an irreversible new condition for political change in a global world or whether it is a temporary expression of neo-liberal domination. Action research and Interactive Research is a scientific approach to investigate that question.

The fifth trend we observed in Chapter 2 was formulated thus: *from use of single methods to broad variations.* In Action Research's childhood, the methods used were the round table group work and the search conference. The PhD projects presented in this book represent a much broader scope of processes such as dialogue conference, future creating workshops, research workshops, dialogue circles, observations, interviews, public festivals etc. Today's Action Researcher combines different methods – often followed by a reflection about the qualities of the methods in relation to the general Action Research approach. Ann-Christine Larsson and Marja Vehviläinen open up the possibility for a use of methods drawn from academic psychology, sociology, economy, anthropology etc – connected to their conscious division of labour between a research person and a developmental person in the same project. In this process, Action Research or Interactive Research is able to open up the possibility for a useful dialogue about methods and techniques in the academic disciplines; this is a dialogue, which until now has exclusively taken place in anthropology.

17.3 Conclusion

In general, our analysis shows that Action Researchers learn from the Action Research history. The dilemmas expressed in the trend-formulations are dilemmas, which the doctoral students try to qualify. Everybody experiences the dilemmas and the lack of an open-minded researchers' community to help taking decisions related to dilemmas. To learn Action Research or Interactive Research means to join such (pluralistic) communities. Perhaps the Nordic countries are, relatively speaking, the part of the world with best possibilities for such communities. But even here we have only just started to build the necessary open-minded networks. PhD-courses can be useful tools in the creation of the networks and communities. The courses can open a space for an ongoing discussion; also about some of the issues, which had peripheral reflections by the authors writing on PhD projects. We will mention three main problems with this attempt:

1. The question of how to go further in integrating gender perspectives into Action Research. As gender is a part of the researchers' *habitus*, gender has to be at stake in all kinds of Action Research projects. The issue must, in the future, be developed in relation to interpretations and experiments with the researcher's role in specific Action Research projects.
2. The question of how to go further in terms of reflections about economic and institutional dependencies in Action Research. An ongoing development of ethical questions and questions of tools or methods claiming "free space" is one way. Another one is to open the door to experiments with a division of labour between

researchers and facilitators in change processes and learning dialogues.

3. How do Action Researchers or inter-active researchers develop their knowledge in a more theoretical way? There must be a continuous discussion of how our knowledge can challenge and be challenged by the academic community. With our subtitle of this book – beyond practice and theory – we are suggesting an upheaval of the dichotomy between theory and practice. Situated or local knowledge should challenge theories of social structure and institutions; and academic theories of social structure and institutions should challenge and irritate pragmatic practical solutions. Today's Action Research has not come very far in the search for a vivid relation between theory and practice To move on with this problem involves much better dialogues between traditional academics and Action Researchers. Such dialogues can take place in journals, books and at conferences. We find no serious arguments left for a strong polarisation.

References

Flyvbjerg; Bent (1998): *Rationality and power. Democracy in Practice.* Chicago: University of Chicago Press.

Jungk, Robert (1975): A postscript to German edition of Meadows et al.: Limits to Growth. In German language: *Die Grenzen des Wachtums* (1975).

Nielsen, Birger Steen; Olsén, Peter; Aagaard Nielsen, Kurt (1996): "From silent to talkative participants: a discussion of technique as Social Construction". In *Economic and Industrial democracy.* Vol. 17.

Index

* The concept is introduced on pages set in *italics*

A

Action knowledge 28, 55
Application 20, 21, 146, 165, 211, 230,
    337, 347, 379, 381
Apprentices 202, 203, 208, 222, 223,
    224, 225, 226, 228, 284, 334,
    335, 337, 342, 343, 344, 345, 347,
    349, 350

B

Blended learning 9, 297, 298, 304, 312,
    313, 314

C

Case study 242, 245, 246
Change agents 49, 256, 277
Change processes ix, xi, 9, 29, 31, 36,
    49, 66, 170, 277, 280, 281, 288,
    289, 390, 396, 398
Citizens' perspective 324
Co-action 39
Co-generative Action Research 297
Collaboration 6, 50, 56, 92, 100, 101,
    102, 105, 106, 146, 147, 148,
    149, 150, 151, 180, 188, 189,
    190, 211, 217, 219, 221, 253,
    303, 305, 306, 337, 375, 378, 382,
    393, 394
*Collaborative inquiry *38–39*, 49
*Common Third *259–275*, vii, 9,
Communities of Practice 257, 316, 351

Complementarity 217, 224
Conflict 5, 17, 26, 30, 31, 33, 50, 109,
    148, 151, 171, 227, 323, 324, 325,
    344, 369, 393, 394
Conflict paradigm 17, 393
Consensus 5, 26, 28, 30, 31, 32, 33, 34,
    35, 55, 94, 105, 108, 109, 148,
    151, 155, 156, 324, 334, 345, 362,
    369, 385, 393, 394
Consensus paradigm 26, 30, 31, 32, 393
Counter Public Sphere 8
Critical mass 28, 37
*Critical theory *77–85*, xi, 6, 7, 63, 66,
    68, 70, 72, 73, 106, 110, 151,
    233, 314, 315, 334, 349, 373, 376,
    395, 396
Critique 6, 64, 65, 66, 77, 80, 84, 85,
    94, 105, 107, 112, 199, 211, 213,
    215, 216, 217, 226, 227, 228,
    230, 245, 256, 266, 267, 268,
    269, 270, 273, 353, 356, 358,
    360, 365, 366, 367, 390

D

Danish Action Research network 155
Democratic dialogue 89, 93, 94, 96,
    150, 166, 167, 177, 251, 364
Democratic knowledge 84, 85, 155
Developmental Work Research 159,
    163, 165, 166, 167
Development rationale 299, 300, 302,
    310

*Dialogue Conference *95–100*, 6, 89, 110, 112, 174, 374
Didactical concept 334
Dilemmas 10, 17, 18, 25, 35, 50, 117, 118, 252, 396, 397
Discourse coalition 10, 361
Discriminated groups 255
Doing gender 280, 286, 287, 323

E

Empathy 137, 260
Employee-based values 26, 31, 34, 394
Empowerment 242, 248, 249, 258
Epistemology 2, 7, 73, 74, 76, 81, 85, 111, 138, 153, 200, 319
Ethical aspects 51
Everyday practices 123, 206, 322, 323, 328, 329
Experiment 11, 28, 69, 70, 74, 78, 83, 94, 102, 104, 105, 172, 174, 196, 199, 200, 213, 215, 273, 337, 339, 340, 341, 342, 343, 344, 345, 366, 371, 373, 377, 378, 379, 380, 381, 382, 383, 384, 385, 386, 391, 392
Experimental design 36, 37, 74, 333, 391, 392
Experimental development research 167

F

Fact-finding 47, 48, 53
Feminism 119, 140, 199, 277
Feminist methodology 131
Feminist Politics 321
*Feminist research *129–138*, 7, 40, 117, 118, 119, 121, 122, 123, 124, 127, 277, 280
Financial domination 18
Formal learning 311, 312
*Free Space *371–378*, 11, 12, 81, 217, 362, 363, 380, 381, 383, 384, 385, 386, 392, 394, 397

*Future (Creating) Workshop *100–107*, x, 11, 83, 262, 333, 337, 338, 339, 340, 341, 342, 343, 344, 348, 355, 357, 363, 365, 366, 375, 376, 378, 379, 381, 382, 383, 385, 386
Future Scenario Workshop 107

G

*Gender *118–141*, ix, 5, 7, 9, 10, 18, 31, 34, 35, 117, 199, 252, 253, 277, 278, 279, 280, 281, 282, 283, 284, 285, 286, 287, 288, 289, 291, 292, 293, 317, 318, 320, 321, 322, 323, 327, 381, 393, 394, 397
Gender Contract 130, 139
Gender Differences 142
Gender equality 140, 141
Gender relations xi, 253
Grand theory 5, 26, 36, 329, 395

H

Habitus 205, 206, 208, 209, 225, 229, 230, 374, 397
Health xii, 30, 31, 32, 33, 34, 35, 48, 60, 140, 141, 158, 159, 164, 168, 176, 179, 180, 181, 185, 187, 243, 273, 336, 353, 358, 363, 366, 369
Help-seeking client 6, 46, 50
Hermeneutic 3, 67, 68, 70, 71, 74, 75, 203, 377
High Science 21
Historical Perspective 143, 181

I

Idea laboratory 10, 366
Idealized design 54
Immanent Critique 211, 215, 216, 217, 226, 227, 228
Informal learning 10, 297, 305, 311, 312, 313

Information and computer technologies (ICT) 21, 39, 126, 166, 298, 304, 308, 317, 318, 319, 320, 321, 322, 323, 325, 328, 329
Institutional ethnography 320, 327, 328, 329
Interactive method 9
Interdisciplinary 154, 187, 189
Intimacy 137, 156, 259, 260, 266

J

*Joint learning 249–256, 4, 6, 14, 23, 38, 39, 40, 241, 242, 244, 245, 281

K

Kontextaufhebung 230

L

Labour market 9, 15, 30, 32, 33, 96, 102, 131, 159, 161, 242, 243, 244, 249, 259, 260, 261, 266, 269, 271, 272, 273, 274, 275, 393
*Learning design 391–393, 5, 26
Learning Lab Denmark x, 145, 154, 314, 315, 316
Learning network 166
Learning Space vii, 261, 266, 333, 334, 350
LOM programme 96, 100

M

Marginalisation xii, 133, 259, 261, 273, 275
Mediation 35, 80, 81, 97, 347, 350, 395, 396
Mobility xi, 337
*Mode I 19–21, 5, 17, 24
*Mode II 18–25, 5, 7, 17, 29, 32, 35, 39, 40, 56, 57, 65, 66, 84, 112, 119, 129, 132, 143, 155, 390, 391, 392, 393

Multi-disciplinary perspective 19

N

*Network 278–282, 13, 21, 29, 41, 59, 96, 99, 101, 145, 155, 157, 161, 166, 167, 285, 286, 287, 290, 292, 299, 301, 302, 321, 322, 366, 377, 396
New Production of Knowledge 1, 4, 12, 18, 19, 22, 24, 143
New social practice 198
Nordic countries v, vi, 1, 5, 7, 13, 19, 23, 24, 25, 26, 27, 29, 30, 31, 32, 35, 37, 40, 89, 102, 127, 129, 133, 143, 144, 168, 397
Nursing home 10, 355, 356, 357, 358, 365, 366, 369, 396

O

Ontology 68, 70, 72, 319
Organic conversion 355, 364

P

Paradigms 30, 170, 193, 194, 196, 202, 215, 226, 228
Participant experience 207, 229, 281
Participation ix, x, 6, 14, 22, 28, 36, 38, 39, 52, 53, 56, 57, 69, 71, 73, 75, 81, 87, 93, 96, 97, 98, 148, 158, 166, 173, 174, 178, 203, 216, 219, 220, 223, 227, 251, 255, 256, 276, 280, 289, 310, 324, 333, 334, 335, 347, 350, 355, 368, 372, 375, 385
Participative research 58
Partnership 6, 32, 35, 39, 55, 246, 343, 345, 375
Peer-evaluations 21
PhD-course 249, 389, 397
Planned change 47, 219
Pluralistic approach 2, 17
Pragmatic 5, 19, 26, 29, 35, 36, 53, 63, 66, 67, 72, 75, 76, 77, 84, 85,

144, 198, 202, 226, 353, 365, 367, 373, 394, 395, 396
Problem-based learning 182
Problem-based research 19
Production rationale 299, 300, 301, 309, 310
Professional rules 20
Programme-based development 160
*Project work *303–305*, xii, 9, 217, 232, 307, 312, 313, 323, 373, 377, 379
Psychoanalysis 206, 207
Public sector x, 7, 10, 22, 32, 33, 144, 150, 162, 180, 186, 243, 353, 354, 355, 358, 359, 360, 361, 362, 365, 366, 367, 368, 369
Public sphere 8, 36, 80, 227, 229, 232, 265, 272, 273, 362, 391, 392, 394

Q

Qualitative methods 37
Qualitative scenarios 107
Quality network in the municipal sector 166

R

R&D institutes 13, 15, 17, 19, 20, 24, 29, 32
R&D programmes 26
Reflexivity 24, 76, 133, 134, 135, 194
Regional research institutes 164, 168, 181, 184, 185, 185–186, 187, 189, 190
Regional universities 20, 24, 32
Relevance ix, 14, 153, 193, 265
Researcher qualifications 52
*Researcher role *48–57*
Research financiers 32, 129, 186, 187, 394
Resistance 9, 48, 152, 284, 286, 287, 288, 289, 293

Rhetoric 39, 227, 229, 232, 344

S

Scenarios 94, 104, 107, 108, 354, 357, 361
Scientific community 5, 15, 20, 34, 54, 64, 151, 152
*Search Conference *89–96*, 6, 7, 110, 113, 174
Social experiment 28, 83, 102, 104, 366, 380, 382, 383, 385, 392
Social imagination 39, 68, 79, 80, 81, 82, 83, 84, 266, 339, 376
Social management 47
*Socio-technical experiments *91–92*, 30, 96
Socio-technical school 26, 36, 38
Study-group Action Research 149
System approach 28, 29

T

Tavistock Institute 26, 49, 74, 90, 170, 175, 216
Third task 23, 24, 160, 372
Triple Helix 22, 28, 42

U

Usefulness 7, 8, 10, 15, 17, 24, 26, 110, 111, 112, 129, 165, 202, 241, 242, 244, 282, 379
Utopia 103, 104, 108
Utopian horizon 37, 39, 78, 339, 340, 342, 348, 369, 386

V

*Validity *117–129*, 6, 7, 8, 69, 112, 147, 193, 194, 197, 198, 199, 200, 202, 203, 204, 206, 210, 211, 212, 215, 225, 226, 231, 232, 255, 282
Virtual learning environments 299, 313

W

Work-based learning xii, 303
Work conference 166, 167
Work organisations ix, 9, 91, 216, 221,
    226, 228, 278